Animals in the Military

Animals in the Military

FROM HANNIBAL'S ELEPHANTS TO THE DOLPHINS OF THE U.S. NAVY

John M. Kistler

ABC-CLIO

Santa Barbara, California • Denver, Colorado • Oxford, England

Library of Congress Cataloging-in-Publication Data

Kistler, John M., 1967–
    Animals in the military : from Hannibal's elephants to the dolphins
of the U.S. Navy / John Kistler.
        p. cm.
    Includes index.
    ISBN 978-1-59884-346-0 (hardback) —
    ISBN 978-1-59884-347-7 (ebook)
    1. Animals—War use—History.   I. Title.
    UH87.K568   2011
    355.8—dc22   2011004925

ISBN: 978-1-59884-346-0
EISBN: 978-1-59884-347-7

15   14   13   12   11   1   2   3   4   5

This book is also available on the World Wide Web as an eBook.
Visit www.abc-clio.com for details.

ABC-CLIO, LLC
130 Cremona Drive, P.O. Box 1911
Santa Barbara, California 93116-1911

This book is printed on acid-free paper ∞
Manufactured in the United States of America

Dedicated to all the animals of history that have benefited our lives on Earth, and the men and women who cared for them.

Contents

Acknowledgments

Many thanks to Dale Wagner for proofreading this work. Also thanks to Brian Brooks for trips to military libraries and archives.

Introduction

Human civilizations wax and wane, like the Moon in its periodic phases, through ceaseless phases of peace and war.

Most societies frown upon one man killing another, yet glorify the organized annihilation of "the enemy." Wars change many rules of conduct, whether by choice or by accident. Society wants men and women to live calmly with each other during times of peace, but if war arises, its citizens must fashion weapons and rain death upon foes. The pursuit of victory not only permits the enlistment of volunteers but may force unwilling parties to join the fray. Young men are conscripted via "the draft" during large conflicts. For the last 4,000 years, governments have also drafted nonhuman creatures into the grisly arts of war. Biologically speaking, humans are defined as animals; but in common speech, and in this book, we refer to nonhuman creatures as animals.

In modern First World nations like the United States of America, we do not think of animals in war. New technologies have almost eliminated the usefulness of beasts in battle. Yet this is unfamiliar ground in the history of the world's conflicts. Into the 1930s, generals were still debating whether trucks and tanks would supplant mules and cavalry horses. Before the 20th century, no army could forgo the use of vast numbers of animals in its ranks.

This book, *Animals in the Military*, describes the work of nonhuman creatures in human warfare. Although the author seeks to be thorough and comprehensive, covering all types of animals and their roles in armies, the work cannot be exhaustive, portraying every battle. *Animals in the Military* will provide a foundation for understanding the martial uses of each creature.

A handful of other books have approached this subject, but most have been limited to either a specific species or a specific war. By being specific, these works can be more thorough, but in doing so they may lack broader context and historical perspective. Ideally, one might think, the subject should be covered chronologically. However, the flow of history becomes confusing to the reader while jumping between multiple species on every page. The best compromise is to break down the book into the larger sections of "Animals in Combat," "Animals in Support," and "Animals in Incidental and Experimental Roles." Within those three conceptual groupings that show the type of roles shared by the animals, each species will have its own chapter, within which the history will be revealed in a chronological manner.

A few chapters will be lengthy because certain animals have long and intricate histories in warfare, with much information recorded about their deeds. Other chapters will be short. Though camels have long been used for war, few of their ancient exploits were written down. Some records may exist only in languages unfamiliar to the author and thus cannot be illustrative here.

Animals in the Military does not limit the analysis to species that actually engaged in combat. In fact, very few animal species were trained to bloody enemy soldiers. The first section of this book, "Animals in Combat," includes animal warriors, transporters, and messengers. Elephants and dogs actually fought in combat. Horses carried soldiers into battle. Pigeons acted as relay messengers for troops in combat zones. Insects became the intentional spreaders of disease by some armies against their foes, in a more insidious sort of combat. These five types of animals joined the battlefield in significant and dangerous ways.

Section two studies animals in support. These are beasts that did important work for the army as a whole, but usually away from combat operations. Mules, donkeys, and oxen worked as "beasts of burden" in transportation and supply of the troops. Camels carried troops to the close vicinity of battle but remained behind the lines while their riders fought. Numerous species traveled among groups of soldiers as mascots; basically, morale workers or pets for the psychological help of the army. More recently, a few creatures have become "lost ordnance" seekers and mine hunters, protecting troops from hidden dangers.

Section three looks at the incidental and experimental uses of animals in warfare. In short, some creatures have been tried briefly as martial devices, or fell into the role by accident, just being at the wrong place at the wrong time. Critics may say that these are not "real" uses of animals in war, but the author believes that any significant attempt to use creatures for warfare (successful or not) is worth a glance.

No doubt there will be errors, hopefully minor, found in these pages. The author is not an expert in all of the animals or battles described in this book. As a trained librarian and researcher, the author gleans information from many resources. These sources will be cited and provide a helpful bibliography for further study by the reader. If *Animals in the Military* goes into future editions, corrections would be welcomed.

Students and pleasure readers alike should find points of interest throughout *Animals in the Military*. While organized in a manner useful for research, the subject matter provides numerous tales of heroism and peril, not to mention surprise and humor. Dozens of photographs and artworks illustrate the hard-to-describe appearance of creatures and events that we have difficulty imagining. The history of our world has been shaped by wars, and our wars have been shaped by animals.

In November 2004, Princess Anne dedicated an Animals in War Memorial in Hyde Park, London. The memorial includes sculptures of horses, mules, and many other animals. The inscription reads "They had no choice" (Koenig, 297).

Animals in Combat

1

Dogs

Ancient Dogs

Canines helped humans to fight in conflicts long before organized warfare began. Some archaeologists suggest that the domestication of dogs began 15,000 years ago. Certainly the relationship between humankind and canines predates the training of horses by thousands of years. Dog skeletons have been found along with human remains in tombs dated to as early as 10,000 BC. (Rogers, 24)

The process of domestication may have begun when wolves scavenged for scraps near human camps, eventually leading to the human adoption of pups. The relationship is symbiotic: rewarding to both human and animal. "The dog found a pack that fulfilled its emotional and physical needs, with a wise and powerful pack leader who could offer it more effective care and protection than an alpha wolf could." Some scholars propose that the dog/human relationship enabled humans to become dominant in the world as we used the abilities of dogs to help our societies grow and prosper. (Rogers, 1, 17; Grandin, 305)

Dogs have senses and abilities that surpass those of humans. Although humans have better daytime (color) vision, dogs see more clearly in dim and dark conditions. The membrane around the retina in a dog's eye, the tapetum, reflects light into the retina twice, giving the animal two chances to catch an image rather than just one. Dog noses hold more than 20 times as many smell receptors as human noses, and the part of the brain that interprets smells is 4 times as large in dogs compared to humans. Dogs can hear, smell, and see better (at night) than people can. The earliest humans adopted canines into their tribes probably as nighttime sentinels. Hunting cooperation led to a radical improvement in the ability of human clans to obtain meat. One modern confirmation of this impressive claim: in one Bushman community of seven hunters, the one man with trained hunting dogs brought in 75 percent of the meat for the tribe. (Haran, 78; Mott; Rogers, 24)

One writer discounts the majority of ancient references to dogs used in warfare, claiming that the original sources are often mistranslated, misunderstood, or exaggerated. Such detailed criticism of ancient sources is beyond the scope of this work; most sources are not so skeptical. (Karunanithy, *Dogs of War*)

The first evidence of canine warriors appears around 4000 BC, from Egyptian pictures of soldiers with leashed dogs attacking their enemies. A mastiff-type dog guarding a royal throne appears in a seal from Ur dating from about 3000 BC: this huge style of canine became the standard war dog and was later called the Molossian breed in the Greek era. (Dempewolff, 60; Wendt, 56)

Egyptians used dogs in military operations in the Libyan desert as early as 2000–1600 BC and later at garrisons in Palestine. (Karunanithy, 69; Murray, 91)

The Hittites of Anatolia (Turkey) painted pictures of their war dogs on the walls of temples and exported the dogs to many foreign lands. The ancient Assyrians used a rather complicated name for the mastiff-type breed: tablets refer to them as the "chained-up mouth-opening dog." (Wendt, 56; Rogers, 30)

Polyaenus wrote that King Alyattes II of Lydia unleashed his war dogs against the Cimmerians in a battle around 605 BC. The dogs "fell upon the barbarians, as they would on a herd of wild beasts; tore many of them, so as to disable them and put them from action and put others to flight." (Karunanithy, 70)

In the sixth century BC, Ionian (Greek) art showed dogs participating in battle amid chariots, cavalry, and infantry. When the Persians invaded Greece under Xerxes, they brought a large number of massive dogs from India, so fierce that they had supposedly been sired by tigers. Among the Greek defenders, a dog followed his Athenian soldier to camp and fought with his master in the Battle of Marathon (490 BC), even earning a place on the mural celebrating the Greek victory. Aelian wrote that when the Ionian Greeks used dogs, "the dogs, which were fearsome, aggressive and ferocious to encounter; rushed forward and disturbed the enemy formation." (Rogers, 35; Karunanithy, 74–75)

During the Peloponnesian Wars of Greece (431–404 BC), the city of Corinth kept 50 guard dogs near the seashore. One dark night while the human guards lay in a stupor from drinking, enemy Greeks landed to attack. The dogs viciously charged at the invaders, but 49 were killed. The sole survivor, a dog named Sorter, escaped and fled to town, rousing the sleeping soldiers. When Corinth survived the invasion, he alone received honors for saving the city. His collar was engraved "Sorter, Defender and Savior of Corinth," and a monument was engraved with his name and those of the 49 canines that died protecting the city. In ancient times, owners sought guard dogs "of ample bulk with a loud and sonorous bark in order that it may terrify the malefactor." (Lubow, 26; Karunanithy, 18)

Alexander the Great (356–323 BC), an innovator of warfare, tested many weapons on and off of the battlefield. Having recently captured 15 Persian war elephants at Gaugamela, he may have tested two animals in one combat. According to the historian Pliny:

> When Alexander the Great was on his way to India, the king of Albania had presented him with one dog of unusually large size… [Alexander] ordered an elephant to be brought in, and no other show ever gave him more delight: for the dog's hair bristled all over his body and it first gave a vast thunderous bark, then kept leaping up and rearing against the creature's limbs on this side and that, in scientific combat, attacking and retiring at the most necessary points, until the elephant turning round and round in an unceasing whirl was brought to the ground with an earth-shaking crash. (Pliny, 105–7)

The only dog belonging to Alexander that we know by name was called Peritas, though Peritas may or may not have been the animal donated by the king of Albania. Peritas was called a Pugnacis, perhaps a bulldog, known to the later Romans as a Molossian dog. (Lockwood, Samuel, 83)

The "Molosser" dog breed seems to have started in Tibet as a hunting and guard dog, a huge mastiff style of animal. When the Persians were defeated by the Greeks at Marathon, many captured Persian dogs were kept as trophies. Later cross-breeding led to the bulldog and other breeds. One story claims that Peritas saved Alexander at Gaugamela from a Persian war elephant by biting the pachyderm's lower lip, giving Alexander time to escape, but sacrificing himself in the process. However, few historians believe that elephants fought at Gaugamela: most sources wrote that the pachyderms were captured in the supply train after the battle. Conceivably, Peritas could have performed this heroic service at a later battle in India, or the Pliny "dog versus elephant" story could have been spiced up a bit and become a combat legend. Just as Alexander's horse Bucephalus would have cities named in his honor, so Peritas had one city named after him, with a monument in its central square. (Wikipedia, "Molosser"; Stall, 166; Ruthven, 199)

Contemporary with Alexander, but westward of Greece in Epirus (modern Albania), Aeneas Tacitus wrote that a common use of dogs was as messengers. Tacitus says that the sender would sew a letter into the collar and send the dog and message to another person. There is no mention of this as a military practice at the time, though armies might have done so. (Karunanithy, 164)

One of Alexander's distant relatives who became famous for his use of elephants, Pyrrhus of Epirus, had a significant encounter with a soldier's dog. According to Plutarch, Pyrrhus found a dog waiting loyally by the body of a murdered man, its master. He had been there three days. After burying the man, Pyrrhus kept the dog. A few days later, while Pyrrhus was reviewing his troops, the dog "saw its master's murderers filing past" and rushed at them. The king had the men questioned, and they confessed to the murder. (Rogers, 39)

A few centuries later, the Romans classified sporting dog types into three classes. Pugnaces were fighting dogs used in combat or the arena games, usually obtained from Asia. Sagaces, often raised in Greece, were known as the smart animals kept as pets. Celeres were swift dogs used for hunting, brought from Northern Europe. Greek and Roman soldiers equipped large dogs with spiked collars and trained them to attack enemy troops. (Lockwood, Samuel, 82–83; Rogers, 37; Brophy, Miles, and Cochrane, 323)

Roman historians did not frequently mention the brave animals used in their legions, like elephants, horses, and dogs, preferring to give all the credit to their human soldiers. Some accounts claim that canines belonging to the British tribes defeated the Roman dogs decisively in the century before and after Christ. In 101 BC at the Battle of Vercellae in north Italy, the Romans under Gaius Marius found themselves attacked by "hordes" of dogs led by "blond haired women of Wagenburg." The poet Grattius Faliscus in the time of Caesar Augustus wrote that "if you are not bent on looks and deceptive graces (this is the one defect of the British whelps)," you would prefer vicious British dogs to the Molossian type. Romans then took to breeding British mastiffs. Polybius, sometimes known to exaggerate, credits a Roman general with fitting dogs with blankets and pots of Greek fire so they could run among enemy cavalry and sear the bellies of the horses. (Karunanithy, 10; Rogers, 43; Wendt, 81)

In 121 BC the Celtic Gaul king of the Allobrogres was followed by many dogs, "for the barbarians of this region use dogs also as bodyguards," wrote Appian. Celts made simple coats of armor for their war dogs, with steel blades welded on to injure Belgian and Gallic tribesmen. Attila the Hun deployed canine sentries to warn against approaching enemies. Roman dogs frequently wore chain-mail cuirasses for protection. The column of Marcus Aurelius (AD 121–180) shows Roman dogs wearing chain-mail and spiked collars. (Karunanithy, 7; Dempewolff, 60; Richardson, 23)

Only brief mention is made of war dogs between the end of the Roman Empire and the Renaissance. One story of Saint Patrick landing in Ireland in AD 433 describes a large Irish wolfhound named Luath. A local noble thought the strange monks landing on the beach were invaders and sent Luath to attack them. Luath wore a heavy metal collar with sharpened spikes and hardened leather body armor. According to the story, as Luath drew near, Patrick knelt down to pray, and Luath, rather than attacking, licked him. (Coren, 23)

During the Middle Ages, armored dogs protected caravans from bandits. Irish stories about cattle raids, circa AD 1000–1100, include a dangerous wolf-dog that jumped into a chariot to tear the head off an enemy before killing the chariot horses. (Brophy et al., 323; Karunanithy, 14–15)

An invasion of Poland around AD 1250 by a coalition of Russians, Tartars, and Lithuanians purportedly included a large number of trained attack dogs. A Scandinavian historian wrote that the fighters of Finland had a novel method of countering Russian cavalry. "No less support is given to these Finns by their huge, snapping dogs, since the Russians fear and flee these as much as the Persian horses do camels. These dogs attack the nostrils of the horses, as they have been trained to do, by leaping up and biting them. Hence in their terror the horses suddenly rear up on their hind legs and throw their riders to die there and then or to be taken prisoner." (Karunanithy, 94–95)

Some medieval knights kept attack dogs, but their roles in combat are rarely recorded. In 1333 before a battle, a Scottish champion and an English champion faced off in single combat. The Scot, named Turnbull, took a large black mastiff with him, but the English knight, Robert Benhale, cut the dog in half and then killed the Scotsman. (Turnbull, 24)

Spanish and New World War Dogs

The Spaniards began using dogs at least by the 1260s, as King Jaume I of Aragon-Catalonia supplied guard dogs to garrisons of regional castles. (Karunanithy, 185)

When Christopher Columbus returned to the New World in 1493, Don Juan Rodriguez de Fonseca, in charge of supplying the expedition, included 20 mastiffs and greyhounds as weapons. The Spanish destroyed the Guanches of the Canary Islands by use of war dogs. Later the dogs fought the Moors. The mastiffs, which could weigh as much as 250 pounds and stand three feet high at the shoulder, were brute attackers, while the greyhounds were speedy and made lightning-quick strikes, often trying to disembowel their opponent. In May 1494 the Jamaican natives did not look friendly, so Columbus ordered an attack. One war dog caused absolute terror, so Columbus in his journal wrote that one dog was worth 10 soldiers against Indians. During the Haiti campaign, opposed by a huge native force, all 20 dogs fought at the Battle of Vega Real in March 1495. Alonso de Ojeda, who had fought with them against the Moors, commanded the dogs. He released the dogs shouting, "Tomalos!" (basically, "Sic 'em!"). An observer said that in one hour, each dog had torn apart at least a hundred natives. The island was taken largely by terror of the dogs. Later conquistadores including Ponce de Leon, Balboa, Velasquez, Cortes, De Soto, Toledo, Coronado, and Pizarro all used war dogs. (Coren, 72–75)

Some Spaniards started a cruel practice called "la monteria infernal" ("the hellish hunting") or "dogging," setting the dogs on the chiefs or other important people in tribes. When their leaders were torn to shreds, the tribes often surrendered. To increase the ferocity of attacks, some conquistadores fed the dogs on the flesh of natives. One Portuguese fellow "had the quarters of Indians hanging on a porch to feed his dogs with." The dog Amigo helped in the conquest of Mexico. Bruto, belonging to Hernando de Soto, assisted in the conquest of Florida. When Bruto died, the Spaniards kept it secret, because the natives feared him so much. (Karunanithy, 46, 101; Sinclair, 147; Coren, 76)

A dog named Mohama gained a soldier's share of the booty for fighting courageously at Granada. Perhaps recognizing the Spanish love for war dogs, in 1518, King Henry VIII of England sent 400 war mastiffs "garnished with good yron collers" (spiked collars) to the Holy Roman Emperor Charles V of Spain. Apparently one of Charles's foes heard of this acquisition and started collecting war dogs of his own. At the siege of Valencia,

Statue depiction of ancient dog armor. (Mary Evans Picture Library.)

the iron-clad mastiffs sent the newly trained French dogs fleeing with their tails between their legs. (Thomas, 153; Jager, 16; Dempewolff, 61)

The Spanish sent war dogs to their New World campaigns to help conquer much of South and Central America. Just as the invaders' horses terrified the natives, so did the dogs, because the likes of these creatures had never been seen. The Aztec king, Montezuma, was told that the Spanish dogs were huge, "spotted like ocelots, with ears doubled over, great hanging jowls, blazing yellow eyes, gaunt stomachs, and flanks with ribs showing." They "went about panting, tongues hanging out. Their barks astounded the Mexicans since, though they had their little dogs, they did not bark; they merely yowled." A mastiff belonging to Francisco de Lugo barked most of the night, causing the local people to ask if the beast was a lion. They were told that the dogs would kill anyone who annoyed the Spaniards. The dogs often preceded the horsemen in column, panting with "foam dripping from their mouths." (Thomas, 180, 234, 267)

A German explorer accompanied the Spaniards to Colombia and saw a brigade of mastiffs used to scout out ambushes by the Chibchas Indians. These animals wore quilted armor to protect them from arrows, and they learned to kill the natives by tearing out their throats. The Indians were terrified of these dogs. (Dempewolff, 61)

An account in 1553 says Pizarro's dogs were "so fierce that in two bites with their cruel teeth they laid open their victims to the entrails." (Karunanithy, 108)

The Spanish were not the only nation using war dogs during the 16th century. In 1598, English troops landed in Ireland with 3,000 war dogs, though their deployment is not known. (ibid., 109)

During the English Civil Wars (1642–1651), a leading loyalist to the crown, Prince Rupert, had a favorite dog, named Boye. Boye looked like a white poodle, though he was larger than a normal poodle. Because Rupert allowed the dog to follow him into battle, next to his horse, the enemy began to call Boye a devil dog, empowered by demons to bring victory to the king's forces. An opponent Roundhead, Sir Thomas Fairfax, told his officers, "it has occurred to certain of us that only with the death of that hound from Hell can our victory be assured." Spies tried to kill Boye, but the dog's witchcraft purportedly foiled the attempts. More likely, Boye survived long because Rupert protected him, even allowing the dog to sleep

Becerrillo, the Spanish Attack Dog

Becerrillo, or "Little Calf," with reddish hair and black eyes, became the most famous of the Spanish conquistador army animals. A contemporary account says that "he attacked his foes with fury and rage and defended his friends with great valor." Becerrillo bore battle scars all over his body and killed scores of enemy warriors. When chief Guarionex led a surprise night attack, Becerrillo killed 33 natives during the battle. However, one time in Puerto Rico, a dog handler tried to get Becerrillo to attack an old woman just for fun. The woman fell to her knees and begged the dog for mercy, and Becerrillo sniffed her and walked away. When Ponce de Leon arrived and heard the story, he ordered that the Spaniards stop all petty attacks on the people and said, "I will not permit the compassion and forgiveness of a dog to outshine that of a true Christian." Becerrillo did not meet a peaceful end, however. Pursuing a party of Carib warriors in a stream in 1514, he was hit by a volley of arrows. He died when he reached the far bank. (Thomas, 153; Coren, 77; Stall, 53–55)

One of Becerrillo's descendants, named Leoncillo (Little Lion), accompanied Balboa when the explorers found the Pacific Ocean. Leoncillo did not instantly kill; he was more flexible. When ordered to catch a native he would grab the man's arm in his mouth. If the man came along quietly, they walked slowly to Balboa. If there was any resistance, the dog ripped him apart. (Karunanithy, 183; Coren, 76)

in his arms every night. On July 2, 1644, Oliver Cromwell's forces attacked Prince Rupert's at the Battle of Marston Moor, killing 4,000 men—and Boye. Boye's body lay pierced by many bullet and stab wounds. Prince Rupert wept publicly, and the parliamentarians pushed on with renewed vigor to destroy the king's forces. (Cooper, 172–73; Gardiner, 141; Coren, 46–49)

During the French and Indian War (1754–1763), dogs were sometimes used unofficially by soldiers to track enemies in the forests, but the British military of the era did not like the idea of having "barking" dogs give away their positions. Although the brilliant Benjamin Franklin proposed using dogs to protect the American army against ambushes during the Revolutionary War (1775–1783), his idea was ignored. Aside from George Washington's gallantry in returning a British general's captured dog in 1777, canines played no role in the conflict. (Karunanithy, 201–2; Sanderson, 17; Murray, 91; Stall, 72–73)

Dogs in the 19th Century

One author says that "the most famous war dog in history" was a crossbred Poodle named Moustache and fought with the French in the Napoleonic Wars (1803–1815). Moustache stood as sentry to protect his camp from ambushes, especially at night. One evening while camped in Italy, the Austrians prepared a sneak attack, but Moustache barked loudly and awoke the French. He also identified spies by their smell, since false uniforms could not mask foreigners' smells to the alert canine. Moustache most distinguished himself at the Battle of Austerlitz. Austrians had killed the flag-bearer and one enemy had swiped the unit's standard, but Moustache tore out the man's throat and carried the flag back to his company. For this heroism, Field Marshal Lannes, Duke of Montebello, decorated the dog. On March 11, 1811, a Spanish cannonball killed Moustache, who served with the French Army for nearly a dozen years. (Richardson, 45–47; Dempewolff, 61–63)

Napoleon hated dogs but once commented about a memorable incident with a dog, while reciting his memoirs: he and some others were walking the field on the moonlit night following the Battle of Bassano in Italy when a dog leaped out from under a corpse. "He came running toward us and then, almost immediately ran back to his dead master, howling piteously. He licked the soldier's unfeeling face, then ran back to us—repeating this several times…it's a fact that nothing I saw on any other battlefield ever produced a like impression on me. This man, I said to myself, has friends, perhaps…and here he lies, abandoned by all except his dog.…I had watched the execution of maneuvers that were bound to cost the lives of many among us, and my eyes had remained dry. And suddenly I was shaken, turned inside out, by a dog howling in pain!" (Coren, 194)

Sir Henry Morton Stanley, the explorer, mentions that Africans near Lake Victoria kept fierce dogs for war. This may be the Wakedi people of

Uganda, who supposedly had dogs as large as young lions used against their enemies the Waganda. (Karunanithy, 91)

The first time that the U.S. government used dogs in a military capacity was when it deployed tracker bloodhounds in the Second Seminole War (1835–1842). The army bought 33 bloodhounds from Cuba and hired several handlers. The plan was for the dogs to locate the rebellious Native Americans in the tough terrain of the Florida swamps. When the northern pacifists, Quakers, and abolitionists heard that dogs would be used to track humans, they called it "cruel and barbaric." The loud public outrage affected the army, so that the dogs were ordered to be constantly muzzled and kept on leashes, unable to harm anyone; thus in reality the dogs were hardly even used. (Hamer, 134; Prucha, 294–95; Karunanithy, 138–39)

Native Americans of the plains had been using dogs to pull cargo long before the United States pushed westward from the Mississippi River. The dogs pulled primitive vehicles called "travois," which were sort of like sleds, with a platform or net slung between two trailing poles. The Spanish who observed travois dogs wrote that each dog could pull 50 to 75 pounds for up to 12 miles in a day. Some tribes used hundreds of travois dogs and hundreds of sentry dogs. When the Indians began breeding horses, the dogs were less useful in pulling loads. In the 1850s at the Klamath River in southern Oregon, settlers shot several Indian dogs. In retaliation, the Indians shot one of the offenders' horses, and thus began the Klamath War. (Baur, 20–23, 27, 188)

The American Civil War (1861–1865) included many dogs, though most acted in an unofficial capacity. A brown and white bull terrier named Jack was a fire-department mascot who joined the firemen when they volunteered for the 102nd Pennsylvania Infantry. The men said that he recognized and obeyed all the bugle calls and participated at the battles of Spotsylvania and the siege of Petersburg. During combat, Jack would hunt for his injured human friends and then lead help to the fallen men. Outside of combat, Jack specialized in locating clean water for the thirsty soldiers, and he grabbed chickens for them when they were hungry. He was twice captured by the Confederates: one time he was simply released, but the other time the Union traded a prisoner to get Jack back. The troops gave him a silver collar, but sadly, this may have been Jack's doom. Soon he vanished and was never seen again. (Stall, 170–71; Palagruto, 15)

Another northern mascot was Sallie of the 11th Pennsylvania Infantry. At the Battle of Gettysburg in the summer of 1863, Sallie became lost in the confusion. She found some of her soldiers lying dead on the field and remained with their bodies for days. Finally a Massachusetts regiment found Sallie, fed her, and sent her back to her remaining troops. In February 1865, a few months before the end of the war, Sallie took a bullet in the head at the Battle of Hatcher's Run, in Virginia. After her death, a statue of Sallie was put into the base of the monument to the 11th Pennsylvania Infantry at the Gettysburg battlefield. (Seguin, 24–25)

A Confederate spy named "Mrs. M." obtained detailed information on Union troops for General Beauregard by going across the border into the North. Travelers heading south were always searched at the border. To smuggle secret documents past the sentries, she created a thick fur garment to wrap around her dog, hiding the papers beneath it. When she reached General Beauregard's tent, she used a knife to cut the dog's garment free to give him the reports. (ibid., 50–51)

The best known canines among the Confederates were infamous, gaining evil reputations along with the nasty places where they worked and lived. The prisons used to detain captured Union soldiers used guard dogs to maintain order.

Capt. Henry Wirz of the Andersonville Prison in Georgia kept 13 hounds, purportedly to maul escaping soldiers. Spot, a Cuban bloodhound, weighed 159 pounds and stood three feet tall. At Libby Prison in Richmond, Virginia, the Union captives feared an even larger animal named Hero. Sources say that Hero was a Russian bloodhound weighing 198 pounds and standing three feet two inches tall and over seven feet long. Though some accounts have Hero terrifying Union prisoners, other sources say that Hero was gentle and never tracked or harmed prisoners. After the war, Hero's owner wanted to make lots of money by selling him as a dog-fighting champion, thus he claimed that Hero fought bears and intimidated the Union soldiers as a massive, fearsome monster. (Lemish, 8; Seguin, 110–11; Palagruto, 42–43)

Dogs in World War I

Before the 20th century, dogs were only a small, unorganized part of human warfare. A few canines participated in combat or as auxiliaries, but for the most part the dog was simply a battlefield pet, or mascot, brought along by an admiring owner. In the 1898 Spanish-American War, Capt. M. F. Steele of the 6th Cavalry used his dog Don through the Cuban jungle to help detect ambushes, but Don had no special training or part in the army itself. Though Steele recommended that the army begin using dogs for anti-ambush work in jungle terrain for future actions, his ideas were ignored. (Sanderson, 17; Hammerstrom, 9–10)

During the Spanish-Moroccan wars, the Riffs of North Africa tied human clothing on dogs and ran the animals back and forth along the front lines to draw Spanish rifle fire and thus reveal enemy positions. (Brophy et al., 324)

The idea of using dogs as relief workers began to grow in the late 19th century, perhaps from true tales of dogs swimming out to save drowning men or carrying medical supplies to lost hikers in the Alps. The Russians used ambulance dogs during the Russo-Japanese War (1904–1905), for instance. In World War I (1914–1918), the Red Cross and organizations like it trained and mobilized a remarkable force of relief dogs that would save thousands of lives.

The Germans called such animals "Sanitary Dogs." Germany had the earliest start in regard to using dogs for war. They began experimenting with war dogs in the 1870s, as local clubs were asked to breed and train them for military use. By the beginning of World War I, the Germans had 6,000 to 7,000 trained animals. Gray or black dogs were preferred for frontline work since they were less conspicuous targets. During the war, Germany used 30,000 dogs for messenger and ambulance work. A Sanitary Dog carried a saddlebag with water and medicines and would walk around to find a wounded man, then stand still for the man to take supplies from the pouch. If the man was too injured to medicate himself, the dog went to find help. (Lemish, 12–13; Jager, 21; Cooper, 73; Going, 1)

It was no simple matter to find an effective method by which the rescue dogs could alert medics that a victim had been found. Barking was discouraged because it might draw enemy fire down upon the wounded man or the dog itself. An early system was for the dogs to pick up a small piece of equipment from the wounded soldier, like a canteen, and take it back to the medics. One French dog named Captain found 30 wounded men in one day, bringing their hats and helmets back to the medics as a signal for help. When the animal could find no easy item to pick up, he or she was trained

German medical dogs, World War I. (Courtesy National Archives.)

to tear off a piece of clothing, such as a sleeve or collar. In time, it became apparent that having the rescue dog rip clothing off of wounded men was not preferred, since it might further injure broken limbs or open wounds. The Germans came up with a good solution. They invented a leather sausage to hang from the Sanitary Dog's collar. When the canine found a wounded man, rather than having to grab an item, he could run back to the medics and hold the sausage in his teeth. The Allies took the same idea but used a stick called a Brinsell which became the standard for Red Cross casualty dogs. (Dempewolff, 116; Lemish, 12–13, Sanderson, 71–72)

Rescue dogs learned to hunt for wounded men in trenches, in foxholes, behind trees, in mud, and in barbed wire. Wounded men would often crawl deep into holes to protect themselves from further harm, yet this hid them from medics. The dogs scented on fresh blood and sometimes smelled for breath to find unconscious men who could not move or cry out. The animals had to be trained to distinguish between the dead and the living so they wouldn't waste time on corpses. Red Cross dogs also carried water bottles and small medical supplies so that lightly wounded men could patch themselves up well enough to return to the rear for help. (Sanderson, 46, 71–72; Rogers, 80)

Aufgespürt

Rescue dogs carried medical supplies to wounded men in World War I.
(Mary Evans Picture Library.)

The effectiveness of casualty dogs is beyond dispute. One French dog named Prusco looked like a white wolf. He dragged wounded men into protective craters or trenches if combat was ongoing, before seeking the medics. Prusco located over 100 wounded men after a single battle. A team of nine rescue dogs found 252 hidden casualties after the battle at Rheims in just one night. The record, as far as we know, is held by a Belgian shepherd named Topsy. She is said to have found nearly 2,000 men trapped in barbed wire during her service. The French began their rescue dog program in 1906, but Marshal Joseph Joffre hated dogs and canceled the training work in 1914. Fortunately, a new leader reinstated the casualty dog program in 1915. The lives saved by canines in their role as rescuers can hardly even be estimated. (Dempewolff, 115; Lemish, 14–15)

The Red Cross and other groups used large dogs, weighing 80 pounds or more, to pull ambulance carts. At times, lightly wounded men could climb onto the two-wheeled gurney themselves, or medics could put a wounded man on the gurney, and the animals would pull him to an aid

German medical dog team, World War I. (Mary Evans Picture Library.)

station. "They could go where motorized ambulances could not; they presented a smaller target than horses and could work without a man to direct them." The British used large dogs like Canadian huskies to pull stretchers and wounded soldiers in combat against the Bolshevik army near Murmansk and Archangel. (Rogers, 80; Lemish, 15; Dean, 8)

Dogs proved themselves in another military capacity: as messengers. Early 20th-century electronics, such as telegraphs and telephones, did not work well in the damp trenches. Pigeons provided much of the long-distance communication, as they could fly up and over enemy troops and wing their way back to headquarters. In fact, some dogs carried a canister on each side, to deliver fresh pigeons to the troops. For short-range messages, human runners sprinted in some missions, but under heavy fire, dogs were the answer. A dog, carrying a message in his collar, could run four or five times as fast as a man and presented a smaller target to enemy snipers. The best messenger dogs were believed to be the Airedales, collies, sheepdogs, and retrievers, with Airedales predominating. Faster animals like greyhounds did not prove useful: they were too "jumpy." A colorful flag on the dog's message tube alerted friendly troops to the fact that the dog was carrying a message, so they knew to leave the animal alone to accomplish its mission. It was a court-martial offense to stop a working dog, not because the men would harm the dog but because being friendly and calling the animal would slow it and distract it from running the message to headquarters. (Rogers, 81; Dempewolff, 96; Gardiner, 94)

April 14, 1918, Ancerviller, France. A dispatch dog, presumably German, was shot trying to cross barbed wire, became entangled, and died. (Courtesy National Archives.)

There were two types of messenger dogs: those for one-way work, and those for round-trips. "Estafettes" made the one-way trip, while "liaison dogs" trained with two men so they could run from one in the regiment to another at headquarters and then back. Liaison dogs never became common, because they required twice as much training and two handlers rather than one. They could run five miles in speedy fashion, through difficult terrain, and even in bad conditions like fog or smoke or darkness, which hampers pigeons. Pigeons do not work at night, while dogs prefer the night, with excellent vision in darkness. (Lemish, 18; Richardson, 74–75; Dempewolff, 95)

The first famous messenger dog of World War I, Bobbie, was an Alsatian working for the French Zouave regiment against the Germans at

Flanders. The Zouaves suffered under heavy attack, so they sent Bobbie to ask for supplies and reinforcements. Bobbie was shot, tumbled over, and lay still for a few moments, but got up. Snipers hit the dog again. Bobbie crawled most of the way and died just short of the destination, but allies saw him, retrieved the message, and sent help. For this bravery in action, Bobbie received a burial with honors. While casualty dogs wearing a Red Cross symbol were technically protected from being targeted by the enemy, messenger dogs were prime targets. At Verdun, the famous mongrel named Satan wore a gas mask and carried a pigeon on each side but reached the French on only three legs. An Irish terrier named Paddy traveled nine miles through pockets of poison gas and was partially blinded, but later recovered. Some dogs concealed their wounds well. After one messenger dog keeled over unexpectedly, a postmortem found that the canine had a bullet in its lungs and shrapnel through its spine, and these objects apparently had been inside the animal for many weeks. (Dempewolff, 95–96; Rogers, 81; Lemish, 18; Cooper, 78–79)

Many small dogs were kept by soldiers in the trenches not for any official task, but for friendship, or for the simple duty of keeping down the population of mice and rats. Young Adolf Hitler, fighting with the 16th Bavarian Reserve Regiment on the western front, owned a dog named Foxl

---

Russian Spy Dogs

World War I Russian spies provide a somewhat humorous story regarding messenger dogs, particularly untrained animals. To get secret messages past the enemy's security checkpoints, agents would roll up documents and place them into a small aluminum tube. Then they would find a stray dog, feed it a little so it would follow them, then and stick the tube in the dog's rectum. Sentries carefully searched the spies at the checkpoint and allowed them to pass when no contraband was found. The dog would follow, and the spies would retrieve the tube later when the dog defecated. This subterfuge worked well until one day the stray dog decided to defecate next to the sentry post, and the aluminum tube shot out with the dung, and the spy was caught. (Dempewolff, 63–64)

---

and kept it with him in the trenches, calling Foxl his best friend in the war. The British assigned sentry dogs to some trenches, trained not to bark but to growl if intruders were sensed to be approaching. Airedales excelled at this type of work. (Barber, 124; Gardiner, 162; Jager, 59)

Great Britain seemed unwilling to enter the "war dog" business. Early in the war, some citizens became worried that pets would consume scarce meat supplies and demanded that the government exterminate dogs and cats. After two years of war, the military belatedly asked citizens to donate animals for the war effort. In the early days of training, the canine recruits faced hand-grenade explosions: those who could not overcome their fear of the noise were sent home or shot. The British founder of the war dog program, Lt. Col. Edwin Richardson, had some interesting ideas about physical attributes of dogs that, to his mind, signaled fitness or unfitness for training. He said that the dog's tail hinted at its wartime abilities: a curled or bent tail meant the animal was frivolous and unsuited to war. The Royal Society for the Prevention of Cruelty to Animals raised money to build kennels for sick and wounded dogs; these were kept at the horse veterinary hospitals in France. (Cooper, 56, 74–76, 81–83, 169)

The French and Belgians used many dogs for hauling loads. Cart-pulling, long the duty of horses, mules, and oxen, might seem too much for dogs. Yet just as larger dogs pulled small ambulance carts, so they could pull small machine guns. In 1915, the Vosges Mountains of France proved to be a killer of horses and mules as they struggled to pull artillery pieces and ammunition up the slopes, especially Pian di Neve at 6,108 feet. The French imported 400 huskies from Alaska and Canada. The canines worked out great because they could eat the dead horses on the way up and down (each dog eating 1.5 pounds per day). Dog teams transported tons of ammunition, provisions, and firewood to the 4,000 soldiers fighting there over two years. Some 8,000 dogs were brought in for this work. (Brophy et al., 324; Dempewolff, 109–10; Dean, 4–5)

The United States entered the war late and so did not utilize dogs much on the battlefield. For sentries the U.S. Army had to borrow French dogs, but because the animals understood only French spoken commands, it caused difficulties for the American troops. The most famous dog with the U.S. Expeditionary Force, Stubby, a brown and white pit bull terrier, came with Cpl. Robert Conroy to France. He was not trained, yet he

Dogs pulling carts in World War I. (Courtesy National Archives.)

learned to warn the men of incoming artillery shells, as he could hear the shells five seconds before the soldiers could. Stubby learned to find help for wounded men. Once he caught a German spy in his trench, latching on to the man's butt until his capture. For this Stubby was awarded

French Red Cross ambulance drawn by dogs, World War I. (Courtesy John Kistler.)

the rank of sergeant by the commander of the 102nd Infantry Division. Stubby fell wounded twice, once from a German poison gas attack, and later by grenade shrapnel. As his fame grew, French women made him a fancy blanket and medals began to adorn it. He met President Woodrow Wilson and later led veterans' parades back home. His photo was taken with General Pershing when he received the Humane Society medal; he sat for a painting by Charles Ayer Whipple; and when he died, his body was mounted in the Smithsonian. (Stall, 150–51; Lemish, 25–26; Dempewolff, 65–71)

More famous than Stubby was the soon-to-be movie star Rin Tin Tin. He was a German shepherd pup found starving in a German trench kennel by U.S. Army corporal Lee Duncan in 1918. Rin Tin Tin did not fight in World War I but often portrayed a war dog in the movies, and Duncan himself helped to train war dogs for the U.S. Army in World War II. (Ruthven, 220; Stall, 115–17)

German Army dogs and handlers wearing gas masks. (*Wonders of Animal Life*, J. A. Hammerton, ed., vol. 4. London: Waverley Book Co., n.d., circa 1930, p. 1461.)

One U.S. Army training guide for dogs in World War I lists "carrying timed explosives into the enemy's trench prior to a charge" as an aspect of infantry dog work, but there is no description of the training or implementation of such a task. The author of the training guide noted that there were not enough dogs to waste them on suicide missions... yet. (Jager, 67, 79)

The casualty estimates for dogs in World War I vary widely, between 7,000 and 16,000. Those numbers represent the killed-in-action animals, not including the postwar executions of "unneeded" war dogs. France alone is estimated to have killed 15,000 canines at war's end. (Sanderson, 6; Lemish, 29)

The Hartsdale Canine Cemetery in Hartsdale, New York, is a memorial for dogs that served in World War I. (Lemish, 12, photo)

Dogs in World War II: European Theater

Many nations purged their ranks of animals, including dogs, horses, mules, and pigeons, after World War I, thinking they would no longer have a role in warfare. Electronics and internal combustion engines promised a mechanized future. The Swiss, on the other hand, founded a war dog school in the Rhone Valley in 1924. Officers had to take a four-week training course and yearly refreshers, learning to use messenger dogs. The Polish Army trained soldier dogs at Rembertow, near Warsaw, starting in 1937. The Polish tried many breeds but preferred the German Alsatian police dog. Germany continued to train dogs for war at a hurried pace. (Going, 174–75; "Animals in the Polish Army")

Early in World War II, the British government told their citizens that food rationing meant they should kill their pet dogs. More than 200,000 dogs died in gas chambers, in this food savings plan. Soon, Nazi Germany boasted of an army of 70,000 trained dogs and said it sent some 25,000 dogs to Japan. The German Army had built a dog training school in Frankfurt in 1934 and it claimed to have trained 200,000 dogs as sentries, scouts, and messengers during 1939–1940. Upon learning this the British quickly rescinded order to kill dogs and instead asked citizens to donate dogs. On the home front, trained and untrained dogs became experts at search and rescue efforts in the rubble of collapsed buildings during the German blitz. A dog named Irma located 192 people, 21 of them still alive under the

Nazi Dogs on Parade

Though the Nazis had the early advantage in war dogs, a minor problem cropped up one day when an army parade marched past the Fuhrer. German dogs were trained by voice command and by hand signals. The animals learned that raising the arm with a palm flat and upward meant "stay." Of course, when the soldiers raised the famous Nazi salute and said, "Heil Hitler," the dogs all stopped and the handlers stumbled over them, causing chaos in the parade formation. The training centers were immediately ordered to discontinue the "stay" hand signal. (Dempewolff, 86)

wreckage. Such animals came to be known as Blitz Dogs. (Dempewolff, 73–75; Going, 2; Gardiner, 138; Cooper, 163)

In November 1940 at Dunkirk, as the routed British forces abandoned continental Europe, it is said that French tramp dogs dived into the water to rescue hundreds of drowning soldiers as they desperately tried to reach the boats. (Dempewolff, 111)

In a pinch, any breed of dog might be adopted into a military role, but of 30 breeds tried, 7 stood out as the most useful. German shepherds, Belgian sheepdogs, Doberman pinschers, collies, Siberian huskies, malamutes, and Eskimo dogs became the preferred canines. Belgium continued to use huge Matin mastiffs to pull supply carts and machine guns. (Hamer, 69; Dempewolff, 105)

Mine-sniffing became one of the significant new roles for canines in the military. Some dogs are able to scent traces of explosives buried even four feet under the surface. One surprising aspect of mine-sniffing dogs is the vastly different verdicts rendered by various sources on their work. Some authors and military experts decry the mine-sniffing dogs as ineffective, while others laud their work as outstanding. To some degree, the differing opinions are based on the good or bad experiences had by some soldiers with the animals, and the definition of "success." The military has often defined successful mine-clearing efforts as 95–99 percent accurate, meaning the animal or system could miss only a tiny percentage of mines.

It is hard to imagine any animal or system with such a high success rate in wartime conditions. If an animal or system did successfully locate a high percentage of buried explosives, it hardly seems fair to label the venture a failure. Nevertheless, this stigma of "unreliability" kept many nations from deploying mine-sniffing dogs during World War II. (Arts, 12; Sanderson, 74)

A British dog named Ricky, a Welsh sheepdog, was expert at finding mines along railways. British mine dogs would sit down near the site of any detected explosives until the trainer brought in a mine-clearing crew. The Soviets used a dog named Zucha to search airfields and hundreds of miles of railroad tracks for mines. They claim that Zucha located 200 mines (or 2,000; sources vary) in just 18 days. The Americans did not train dogs for mine-clearing roles, yet occasionally a keen canine saved his troops anyway. A German shepherd named Peefke led some American troops through the Italian Alps. Once on an empty trail, he alerted as if there were enemies, but none were seen. With careful inspection his handler found that a trip wire had been pulled across the trail, attached to three mines that might have destroyed the whole unit. A few months later, Peefke was hit by an enemy hand grenade and killed in action. (Cooper, 90–91; Sanderson, 61–62, 74; Roberts, 24)

The Soviets also deployed dogs in a more controversial role during the war. Desperate to slow the Nazi advance into Russia, dogs were caged without food for a few days, then given small amounts of food to be found only under a tank, with its engine running. Thus the animals came to associate rumbling tanks with a place to find food. The dogs were fitted with a cradle-type saddle on their backs, filled with 20–25 pounds of high explosive and a rod detonator projecting upward. When German tanks were near, the suicide dogs were freed, and ran straight for the panzers, exploding when the steel rod touched the underside of the tank. Lieutenant Konkoff of the Soviet Army stopped a Nazi advance in the Izyum sector with such dogs destroying nine heavy tanks and two armored cars. The dogs were used again at Kalinin, where an observer said the panzers rushed about wildly, zigzagging and turning in flight to avoid the dogs, but a few tanks fell victim to the mobile mines. With this, the advancing Germans began to shoot all dogs on sight, fearing they might be turned into suicide dogs. In propaganda, the Soviets claimed the dogs could easily separate themselves from the harness and not be killed, and that one dog had blown up six panzers, but this seems unlikely. The anti-tank dogs, called *panzerabwehrhunde* or *hundeminen* ("dog-mines") by the Nazis, did succeed in damaging or destroying at least 30 panzers, yet this is far short of the 300 claimed by Soviet newspapers. The Soviets did eventually stop using the dogs as mobile mines, probably because the animals would often run toward Soviet tanks, which produced a more familiar engine sound, and thus posed a danger to their own army. (Sanderson, 74; Dempewolff, 59; Cooper, 95; Malaparte, *Kaputt*, 219–23; Wikipedia, "Anti-Tank Dog")

The United States used more sentry dogs in its own territory than it deployed overseas. It needed to guard its long Atlantic coast, and soldiers alone were not enough. In June 1942 there were multiple reports of German saboteurs arriving by dinghies released from U-boats, caught with money and explosives to target American facilities. When Cmdr. McClennand Barclay of the U.S. Naval Reserve sent a letter to the *New York Times* suggesting that the U.S. Coast Guard use dog patrols on the beaches, the Coast Guard responded quickly. Within a month, a horse stable at Elkins Park was converted into a kennel and dog training school. Each dog with its human handler would patrol the beaches for two periods of four hours each day, with fewer hours during cold weather. They wore canvas boots to protect their paws from shells and stones and glass, and some wore donated blankets. It is not clear whether the patrols captured many infiltrators, but the animals did sometimes discover bad news: the bodies of people from vessels sunk by U-boats along the coast. Dipsy Doodle found 22 bodies from a tanker torpedoed off the New Jersey coast. Three thousand patrol dogs worked during the 1943 peak, but as the U-boat threat diminished, the sentry dog program was scaled back. (Going, 131–36)

Guard dogs worked at many bases and depots to safeguard supplies against saboteurs, though they receive little credit since their duties were not so "heroic." A British boxer named Simmi proved very effective against thefts, reportedly bringing 86 intruders to justice in Palestine. (Cooper, 87)

Sentry dogs near the battlefield could discover well-hidden enemies by their scent and then point out the enemy location to allies. The common term for this role of canines is "scout dog," since their work is more offensive than defensive. In Tunisia near Ousseltia, the Germans sent sentry dogs with sniper teams. The white dogs, used because they were harder for the enemy to spot against the sand than dark-colored dogs, would point at enemy soldiers like a bird dog might point at a game bird. The snipers were thus able to spot opponents more easily and at greater distances. These canine sentries were also trained to duck and hide when the enemy pointed guns at them. The Soviet dog Barss was a specially trained sniper-locator and is credited with spotting hundreds of German snipers, but he was shot one day by a Nazi marksman. Americans later used this spotting tactic against Japanese snipers in the Solomon Islands. (Dempewolff, 117–19)

Two German shepherds that landed with American troops near Casablanca on November 8, 1942, show the variety of reactions that dogs can have to combat situations. Mena and Pal traveled in the landing craft with soldiers, and their craft was heavily struck by enemy fire. Mena suffered "shell shock" and henceforth could not do her patrolling duty, but she did meet the famous war dog Chips and bore nine puppies, four of which returned to Front Royal, Virginia, for training as war dogs. Pal was injured by the shelling but survived and worked in patrols and as a night guard dog. Guard dogs in North Africa spent more time protecting supply depots and rear-duty soldiers from thieves and bandits than in combat. (Going, 39–41)

Chips, the first U.S. war dog sent overseas during World War II, a husky–collie–German shepherd mix, was too aggressive for his human family: he bit the garbageman and was donated to the U.S. Army. He trained well and became a sentry dog for the 3rd Infantry Division. The long Atlantic voyage made Chips seasick. His unit worked under General Patton in Tunisia against Rommel and the Italians in 1942. January 14–24, 1943, Chips guarded the house where President Franklin Delano Roosevelt and Prime Minister Winston Churchill lived during their conference at Casablanca. (Stall, 165; Ruthven, 54; Harmer, 66–67; Going, 30–31)

In July 1943, Chips and his handler, Pvt. John R. Rowell, landed in Sicily. The Americans were pinned down by machine guns in a "pillbox" fortification on Blue Beach, camouflaged as a peasant's hut. Rowell unleashed Chips and ordered him to attack. Chips charged, and was hit by several bullets, yet knocked one machine gun over, burning his hair on the hot barrel, then grabbed the gunner by the throat and ripped out his jugular.

The other two Italians fled and were shot by American troops. Despite his wounds, Chips caught 10 Italian infiltrators in a night raid, 10 days later. The army awarded Chips the Purple Heart and the Silver Star on November 19, 1943, for his efforts, but someone complained that awarding medals to animals denigrated the awards, so the medals were rescinded as "contrary to Army policy." So Chips's company gave him some medals of their own. Chips accompanied the troops all the way into Germany. Gen. Dwight D. Eisenhower posed for a photo with Chips, but forgot that sentry dogs should be petted only by their handlers, and got his hand bit when he tried to pat Chips's head. As the war drew to a close, Chips was discharged and sent home to his owner. (Ruthven, 54; Harmer, 66–67; Stall, 165; Sanderson, 54; Going, 33–34)

Though most dogs worked on the ground, some accompanied their human handlers to sea in ships and into the sky aboard aircraft. Dogs can detect a far greater range of sounds than humans, and thus the animals could hear an aircraft before the sailors noticed it. The *New York Times* reported that "Commanders of British warships on North Sea convoy duty have discovered that dog mascots, mostly mongrels, seem to detect aircraft long before their engine vibrations reach men's ears. The skipper of one ship insists he has instructed his men to watch the dogs 'point' and keep their guns tentatively trained in the direction of the point." The ships had to be cautious to dog alerts because the animals could not distinguish between Allied and enemy aircraft. The largest dog to serve at sea in World War II was the Saint Bernard named Bamse, the mascot of a Norwegian minesweeper serving near Scotland. Bamse saved at least one sailor who fell overboard, swimming the man to shore. When the battle-stations alarms sounded, Bamse ran to a forward gun turret and had a tin helmet put over his head. Bamse died of unknown causes in late 1944 but posthumously earned the Gold Medal from the People's Dispensary for Sick Animals. There are two identical statues of Bamse, one in Montrose, Scotland, where he died during the war, and one in Honningsvag, Norway. On November 3, 1944, an Alsatian named Rifleman Khan saved his handler, Lance Cpl. Muldoon of the 6th Cameronians, during a night assault on the Dutch island of Walcheren, near Antwerp. An enemy artillery shell broke their boat in half. Muldoon was drowning, but Khan grabbed his tunic in his teeth and pulled the man to dry land.

Khan earned the Dickin Medal for valor. (Going, 158; Stall, 158–60; Gardiner, 118)

The Dickin Medal, donated by the People's Dispensary for Sick Animals, is engraved "for Gallantry, we also serve." It ribbons are green, brown, and pale blue, to symbolize valor on the seas, on land, and in the sky. (Cooper, 88)

Perhaps the strangest idea for war dogs in World War II came from a mysterious man named Victor, who wanted to train dogs to pilot anti-submarine torpedoes. Since the plot was similar to B. F. Skinner's experiments to have pigeons guide missiles into enemy warships, Victor went to Skinner and ended up abandoning the dog-torpedoes to work on the pigeon-missiles. (Peduta, 27)

Dogs participated in the air war both as passengers and as jumpers. A black and white British mongrel named Rob, with an eye-patch, served with the SAS in North Africa and Italy as a para-dog. He made more than 20 successful parachute jumps and seemed to love the experience. The British called such animals "Parapups." On August 14, 1944, paratroopers were warned by their dog and handler of a coming German vehicle and were able to ambush and destroy it. (Cooper, 89; Kramer, 7; Lemish, 116–17)

Most flying dogs rode as mascots rather than jumpers. A Soviet dog named Dootik flew with Squadron Leader A. I. Nefedov. When their bomber was shot down behind German lines, Dootik made a long journey back to the Soviet side and found help to rescue his bomber crew. American B-17 Flying Fortress crews often carried a mascot dog. Skipper, a Scottish terrier mascot, lived in a raft for some days with his crew when their B-17 was shot down. Happily they were all rescued. Stuka, another "Scotty," named after a German dive-bomber, accompanied the crew of the bomber *Memphis Belle* on 25 missions over Germany. Skippy wore a specially fitted mask during flights over North Africa. When he died, the airmen buried him in an empty bomb shell and attached it under the wing of an aircraft for a final flight tribute. (Roberts, 22; Harmer, 44–45; Gardiner, 153; Kramer, 77)

No German dogs returned home. The last survivor was run over by a tank in the last days of war. (Dean, 91)

Dogs in World War II: Pacific Theater

Japan received a "gift" of about 25,000 trained war dogs from Nazi Germany: most were German shepherds, with a few Dobermans. These animals were used in China and the Malay Peninsula as scouts, messengers, and guards, though a few carried medical supplies or pulled a cart with a 50-pound suicide bomb. Gen. Ishii Shiro used many dogs to guard his secret Manchurian biological warfare prisons, where the dogs were loosed on escapees or disobedient captives. Little is known about Japanese war dogs because records were not kept about the animals. (Dempewolff, 123–25; Going, 3; Harris, 37)

In 1935, a U.S. Marine Corps book called "Small Wars Operations" included a paragraph suggesting that dogs could be used to find hidden enemies and spot ambushes. This idea may have come from a marine who trained dogs to lead patrols in Haiti in the 1930s. The advice was completely ignored, until December 7, 1941. After the Pearl Harbor attack, the army in Hawaii immediately appealed to residents asking for dogs to be donated: more than 5,000 were brought forward. These animals were quickly trained and sent to outposts all over the Hawaiian Islands to defend against possible invasion. General Emmons at Hickam Field in Hawaii had a specially trained guard dog standing at his door, and no one could enter without the general personally ordering the dog back. Brig. Gen. William R. White said that these dogs discovered many Japanese soldiers camouflaged in the jungle. Each branch of the U.S. military started its own war dog training program. In general, sentry dogs required 8 weeks of training, while scouts and messenger dogs needed 13 weeks of instruction. (Going, 27, 43–43, 54–55; Dempewolff, 92)

Army standards usually required a donated dog to be male, stand 23–28 inches tall at the shoulder, weigh 55–83 pounds, have an age between 14 months and 3.5 years, and be healthy, though there were exceptions. Arthur Roland wrote "The K-9 Corps Song" as part of the dog-collection campaign. "From the kennels of the country, from the homes and firesides too; we have joined the canine army, our nation's work to do.... So bare our fangs in man's behalf and the cause he is fighting for; we are glad to serve as members of Uncle Sam's trappy, scrappy K-9 Corps."

Scout dogs were taught not to growl or bark because enemies would be alerted to the animals' location. The handler learned to interpret the dog's body language, such as pointing and ear movements, so that the handler's training was as intense as the dog's. Certain breeds of canine posed problems as scouts and had to be used in other roles. Dalmatians, for instance, were easy for enemies to spot, and army attempts to dye their coats a khaki color never worked well. Natural pointing breeds, like Irish setters and bird dogs, kept pointing at birds rather than Japanese during tests in New Guinea and fell out of use. (Sanderson, 38, 44, 87; Dempewolff, 72)

The jungle terrain of many Pacific islands encouraged the use of dogs as sentries, messengers, and ambush-detectors. The canines' superior sense of smell and hearing enabled them to notice clues that humans could not find. Six men and eight dogs worked with the Australians in New Guinea to stop the Japanese advance. The War Department (now the Department of Defense) officially credits these dogs and handlers with leading patrols that killed 180 Japanese and captured 20 more during 53 days of patrols on New Britain. Because the climate damaged electronic equipment, many dogs served as messengers. Sandy, a shepherd, ran through tall grass, swam across a river, jumped over a barbed-wire fence, and found her trainer to call in artillery support. In late 1942, 14 sentry dogs protected Henderson Field against Japanese attacks. One dog named Hey, a German shepherd–chow mix, located a Japanese sniper and located an enemy mortar-fire spotter who had been attacking the airbase. (Dempewolff, 91; Going, 44–53)

Though the U.S. Marine Corps started its dog training program last, in late 1942, the program became the largest and best recorded effort in World War II. Numerous effective Japanese ambushes of marines at Guadalcanal brought the corps to desire its own sentry dogs. The War Dog Training Company started at Camp Lejeune, North Carolina, with the Doberman Pinscher Club of America voluntarily doing the recruiting. Though German shepherds and Dobermans had relatively equal numbers in the marine camps, the "Devil Dog" nickname came to be more associated with the Dobermans, perhaps more feared by the enemy. The first six animals were "inducted" on January 26, 1943. (Going, 54–59; Lemish, 59–60)

The marines trained dogs only for scout and messenger roles. The dogs were given one meal a day: horse meat and biscuits. The fastest animals, good at running through difficult terrain, became messengers,

U.S. Marine Corps dog wounded in the battle for Guam. (Courtesy National Archives.)

also carrying packs with maps, ammunition, and medical supplies when needed. A few dogs were timed at covering one mile in four minutes through dense vegetation. Carl Spitz, owner of the Hollywood Dog Training School, helped to train the marine Dobermans. Obstacle courses included barbed wire, machine-guns firing blanks, trenches filled with water, and model ship-decks for swinging dogs down as if to landing craft. This thorough training helped Spitz to recognize and remove dogs that lacked the courage or stamina to handle the battlefield conditions before being deployed. Between 25 and 30 percent of canines were rejected for physical or emotional reasons during the training process. (Going, 60–61, 73; Putney, 17, 25)

The dogs trained in North Carolina then traveled by train to California, then by ship to the Pacific islands, a two-to-three-week voyage. The animals each had a crate on the deck, with shading shelters stretched over the crates, but the dogs trained on deck for most of the daylight hours. A fake stump was set up for a "potty spot." Chaplains aboard ships noted how quiet the animals were during Sunday sermons—this was because they had been trained not to bark. The first battle test for the "Devil Dogs" came at Bougainville. (Going, 75–76)

The original plan was to lower each dog in its crate to the Higgins landing craft, but practice showed it was much faster to use a simple rope sling to swing the animal (not the crate) to the boat. It took one minute to send down each dog to the landing craft in this manner. Though warships had pounded the beaches, Japanese pillboxes were dug in behind the tree line, firing mortar shells at the invaders. The dogs were split up into three Higgins boats: one of the boats nearly capsized from an artillery near-miss. This campaign would take three grueling months, including torrential rains that created mud deep enough to sink bulldozers to their roofs. (ibid., 77–78)

Twenty-one Dobermans and three German shepherds landed at Bougainville on November 1, 1943. Each handler carried five days of rations for the dog. When these ran out, two cans of C rations could be substituted. One of the Dobermans, a black and brown scout dog named Andy, weighed 75 pounds and could jump eight feet straight up. Immediately upon landing, Andy led a company of marines up a trail to scout Japanese forces and delay enemy reinforcements. Andy worked off-leash about 25 yards ahead of the handler. He alerted four times to danger, and the marines captured or killed all the Japanese snipers and patrols spotted, without any casualties of their own. This initial success was a big morale boost for the troops and handlers. Marines would sometimes compete in digging the largest foxholes, with room for handler and dog, knowing that the Japanese could not sneak up on them during a little nap. Six weeks later, however, Andy was hit by a truck and killed, and the marines wept. (ibid., 79–89)

Caesar, a messenger dog, slept in a foxhole beside his trainer on day two of the Bougainville invasion. He woke his trainer just moments before a hand grenade landed in their hole. The handler threw it back, killing the eight Japanese infiltrators nearby. One of the Japanese shot and wounded Caesar, who was saluted by the marines as he was carried on a stretcher to a medic. (ibid., 95–96)

Not all of the marine leaders believed strongly in the canine program, however; sometimes this lack of faith led to disaster. In one such incident, a scout dog named Rolo alerted several times, but the patrol leader refused to believe there was any danger, and he ordered the handler and dog to continue straight ahead. The Japanese ambush centered all of their fire on the dog, yelling "Doggie Doggie!" and killing Rolo, as the first dog casualty of the marines. The Japanese had learned that the war dogs were high-value targets and made killing dogs a priority in all combat in the islands. Not all dog losses were fatalities, however. By the seventh day of the campaign, two dogs were deaf from shelling and two others shell-shocked and panicky, thus out of action. The marines discovered that bitches were more likely to become panicked by combat, and in future training only males were used for combat roles. Two dogs and two handlers died during the Bougainville campaign. (Going, 56, 80, 99–102, 124–25; Putney, 182)

The U.S. War Department became interested in the Soviet suicide anti-tank dog program and started a trial program at Fort Belvoir in 1943. Rather than targeting enemy armor, the animals were trained as "bunker busters" to enter Japanese tunnels and fortifications with timed explosives. The animals, called "Demolition Wolves," were to sneak into an enemy bunker and wait. The Bunker Dog Project canines wore 20-pound explosive backpacks with an attached 300-foot electrical wire, so the bomb could be detonated remotely. Two key problems kept the marines from implementing the plan. No one could be certain that the dog would always go to the target and not return to "friendlies" and accidentally blow up allies. The main reason, perhaps, was that no one would donate their dogs to the military once it was learned they might be used as suicide bombers. (Arts, 11–12; Wikipedia, "Anti-Tank Dog"; Lemish, 89–91)

Another short-lived experiment for the marines was training dogs as mine detectors. Though the animals found 96 percent of the mines in training, officers did not really like the idea. Furthermore, the training program and methodology proved to be ill-planned. Some of the training sought to make the dogs afraid of metal devices, thus afraid of mines and alert to them, but instead the dogs became afraid of all metal objects, including their own food bowls. Unable to overcome the fear once instilled, only six mine dogs were ever sent to combat. (Putney, 40–42)

A shipment of 108 dogs on the Liberty Ship *Benjamin Ide Wheeler*, from Louisiana to India and then Australia in 1944, showed some dangers of sea travel. Heavy typhoon weather made the dogs sick. Then brutal heat turned the deck into a stove top, actually blistering the dogs' feet. Handlers made little boots for the animals, but this didn't work well. Two dogs died of heatstroke during the journey. (Lemish, 103)

Some dogs not sent to the Pacific island combat zones traveled instead to the China-Burma-India theater as scouts and messengers. A German shepherd named Wotan who was not considered "aggressive enough" alerted soldiers to many enemy snipers and ambushes in Burma. He also proved his courage by fiercely attacking a Japanese infiltrator. One dog named Judy learned to help mules cross rivers by swimming beside them and directing their heads toward the nearest bank. Scout dogs in Burma also located seven American soldiers who had been captured by the Japanese. The men had been buried alive with only their heads sticking above the ground. The enemy had urinated on them after beating and kicking them, leaving them to die, but the dogs brought help. All seven men survived, though one lost an eye, another was deafened, and they all had emotional scars. The British employed some scout dogs to track Japanese who were hiding in caves, but little information is available about these efforts. (Harmer, 56–57; Essin, 183–84; Lemish, 108; Murray, 59)

The island-hopping strategy of the U.S. troops saw dogs becoming a regular part of operations, but more dogs were used in the invasion of Guam in the summer of 1944 than any other World War II battle. Their efforts proved to be highly successful. One unit made over 850 patrols without the loss of a single soldier. The 1st Marine Brigade, with 20 dogs, 26 handlers, and the veterinarian Lt. William Putney, did 450 patrols. The dogs alerted 130 times, finding and killing 203 enemies. During nighttime security, the canines alerted 40 times with 66 enemies killed, said General Noble in his report. One night, 25 Japanese penetrated marine lines and began bayoneting wounded soldiers at the division hospital on the beach, even killing doctors, but Putney freed the dogs and they were able to kill the marauders. During the marine advance from Mount Tenjo to Agana, a marine war dog led at every point of a marine division, for the first time in history. Ten dogs were killed by Japanese rifle fire during the initial days of landings, then 15 more were killed in mop-up operations. With a dog in front, the handler was also in the front, thus making "Marine Dog Handler" one of the most dangerous jobs in World War II. Fifteen handlers would die in combat during the war, receiving 5 Silver Stars, 7 Bronze Stars, and 40 Purple Hearts. (Lemish, 126–27; Putney, x, 180)

When a dog died, the military sent the donating family a letter saying something like this: "It is with much regret that we inform you of the death of your dog [name] whom you so generously donated through Dogs for Defense for use by the armed forces. A war dog certificate is forwarded herewith. A mere certificate of death is, indeed, poor compensation for your patriotic sacrifice, and the Army is not unaware of it. We, too, are sorry to lose so prominent an animal and assure you that your generosity is sincerely appreciated." Sometimes a handler would include a personalized letter with more details, but not all families learned the exact fate of their former pets. (Going, 28)

The marine corps actually created a promotion system with a non-official rank for the dogs, based on length of active service, going up one rank each year. The animals went from corporal to sergeant to platoon sergeant to gunnery sergeant and, finally, master sergeant. This rank system meant that, in a sense, the dogs sometimes outranked their own handlers. Each animal handler carried the official "papers," a small passport-style book, often with a black-and-white photograph. In this book were kept the name, age, size statistics, training schedule, deployment dates, and other significant events, written down by the handler. The marines kept all of these books, and they may be viewed on appointment at the National Archives in the Washington, DC, area. (Lemish, 60; Going, 59)

Because dog names were often repeated or common among multiple animals, we sometimes cannot know whether the same dog performed heroic deeds on different islands or whether these were different dogs. Prince, for instance, was the name of several Devil Dogs. The Prince handled by Cpl. Virgil Burgess was a Doberman messenger on Iwo Jima and carried bandages to many wounded men. A Doberman named Prince, but perhaps not the same animal, joined the 5th Platoon in August 1944, joined the 3rd Platoon after the war, and then served in 1946 as a guard for the president of the United States with the marines. Another Prince, a German shepherd, worked in the islands with Cpl. Edward M. Lucas. Lucas sent a letter to Prince's owners: "Prince and I are a complete army of our own and are doing a swell job hunting Japs. Prince has the honor of being the only dog assigned to military intelligence on this island. He is giving me the best protection, assistance and friendship a man can expect, and I am giving him the best care in the world." (Harmer, 27–28; U.S. Marine Corps, 18; Going, 29)

September 1944 was the bloodiest time for the U.S. marines in the Pacific, who fought on Morotai and desperately for the Peleliu Islands. On Morotai, a collie named Buster saved 17 men of F Company of the 155th Infantry by getting a message out for reinforcements. Conditions on Peleliu were far worse. Coral on the beaches cut the feet of many war dogs, and the incessant artillery shelling put four dogs out of commission from shell shock. A Doberman named Hans completely snapped, attacking his own handler, who had to shoot the animal. (Lemish, 126, 130–31)

Although the proportion of trained dogs that failed in this manner was small, some officers said the dogs could never be retrained to return to civilian home life and ordered that after the war, all the dogs should be immediately euthanized. Some were "put down" this way, but Lt. William Putney heard about this and refused to sign any death certificates until the marine corps had at least attempted to retrain the animals. This plan was accepted, and the corps ordered retraining, of about 8 to 12 weeks, for all returning war dogs. The retraining process included socializing the animals to multiple handlers and giving them more and more freedom. The retraining was incredibly successful. Of the 559 marine corps dogs who came back to the United States after World War II, 540 showed no signs of danger and returned to their original owners. Of the 19 animals destroyed, only 4 were killed for being dangerous or panicky; 15 had serious ailments developed in the islands. In recent years, Lieutenant Putney led the drive to build a monument to war dogs, now set up on the island of Guam. (Putney, 207–9, 216, 224; Hamer, 85; Lemish, 144–45)

20th-Century Military Sled Dogs

Sled dogs have an interesting history of their own in the military operations of the 20th century. Because armies have rarely operated in extremely cold climates, there is no long history of military sled dogs. Ironically, it was the increase of new technologies that spurred the need for sled dog teams.

For instance, communications by telegraph or telephone to bases in inhospitable places required the laying of wire and bringing of supplies. Later, when it became common for aircraft to traverse the tundra, sled dogs had to be trained to rescue downed pilots because other means of recovery were ineffective in the frozen landscape.

Lt. Billy Mitchell was the first U.S. military officer to purchase sled dogs, in Alaska circa 1901. In prior years, distant bases made seasonal contracts with locals to bring supplies by sled dog, but Mitchell wanted Fort Egbert to be more self-sufficient. He purchased 200 sled dogs. He was in charge of laying telegraph lines in frozen regions of Alaska. Buying and using sled dogs was a learning experience, and Mitchell discovered that some fierce dogs had to be castrated and have their incisors filed down to keep a semblance of order among the animals. (Dean, 2)

The British dabbled briefly with reindeer and dog sleighs in northern Russia near Murmansk as they tried to help the czarists against the rising revolutionaries in 1918, but the war was over before the British could engage. (Sutton and Walker, 115–18)

Nazi Germany had the initial advantage in Europe for its tens of thousands of trained war dogs at the beginning of World War II. However, their training programs produced sentries and scouts and medical dogs: no sled-pullers. The Germans were very upset when they found Soviet snipers whizzing by on sleds pulled by "polar dogs" (probably the Samoyed breed). These white dogs would pull Soviet marksmen clad in white masks and cloaks up to German positions on a low sled for sniping. The snipers would pick off several enemies, then when the Germans could start to return fire, the dogs would pull the snipers back to safety. (Dempewolff, 108; Going, 169)

The Soviets trained as many as 50,000 dogs in World War II, mostly white dogs for winter operations. The Soviets used huskies to pull low-wheeled or sled gurneys with wounded men to the hospital. In the Gzhatsk sector, in deep snow where horses and mules could not pass, these special platforms pulled by dogs carried 1,239 wounded men to safety in five weeks. The dogs would pull ammunition and small medical supplies on the gurney toward the front line, then a wounded man could be placed on the cart for a return to a hospital. It is said that the dogs delivered 327 tons of ammo in this manner. One Alsatian, named Bob, found and brought back to safety 16 wounded Soviet soldiers who had crawled into craters and ditches. (Dempewolff, 109; Going, 3, 169)

The Nazis began training sled dogs in 1943 for the 6th SS Mountain Division, fighting in Finland against Soviets. Sixteen animals were assigned to pull sleds with ammunition to the troops and to bring back wounded men. One of the soldiers kept a diary and wrote that his dog team brought out 354 wounded soldiers, both German and Soviet. None of the dogs survived, but they were buried with military honors. (Dean, 86–88)

The U.S. Army started a base for the training of sled dogs in the Rocky Mountains near the Continental Divide, at Camp Rimini, Montana, in 1939. The region was known for heavy snows and cold weather, but even here, summer visited. When the snows had all melted, the snow dogs trained by more creative means. Old Austin car body chassis were pulled along as if they were sleds. Teams were technically eight dogs each plus one spare, but the spare was always hitched up as a team member anyway, so the teams numbered nine dogs each in reality. The dogs learned basic commands such as heel, sit, down, cover, stay, come, crawl, drop, and jump, for the first two weeks. Sled dogs tend to be strong animals, and they can work as pack dogs when sleds are not needed or available. A malamute or husky can carry 35 to 65 pounds on its back and travel 100 miles in 24 hours. (Dean, 15–16, 27; Going, 18–19; Dempewolff, 105–6)

In 1943 much of the impetus for training the sled dogs was a planned invasion of Norway. Some published photographs at Camp Rimini in 1943 show snow dogs pulling sleds with .30-caliber machine guns and show some animals wearing gas masks. This led to incorrect newspaper reports that sled dogs would be moving gunnery platforms, but in reality it was just a publicity stunt, and heavy machine guns were not planned for use in that manner. Once the invasion of Norway was called off, the sled dog teams moved entirely to training for search and rescue operations in arctic regions. (Dean, 17, 27)

In April 1943, tests for parachute-dropping sled dogs began. The first tests worked with a simple drop from a tall tree, then progressed to actual aircraft drops. With much practice, a special parachute was designed and named the Rimini dog parachute. It was very successful, and the Canadians wanted to try it but dropped their plans when animal rights groups

Digestive Problems of Sled Dogs

The United States' well-known Dogs for Defense program, in which civilians donated their animals to the army, did not help the sled dog program because few Americans owned sled dog breeds such as malamutes or huskies. Most of the animals had to be purchased from Canada. This led to some rather unique health problems among the dogs, since many Canadian dogs had eaten frozen freshwater fish containing parasites. "It was not a pretty sight driving a dog team down the road with tapeworms several feet long hanging out behind the dogs," said one soldier. (The Camp Rimini veterinarian developed a surgical procedure to get rid of the worms.) One day a dog was seen hacking, when it coughed up an Indian's moosehide jacket with beadwork. The dog was fine after vomiting up the jacket, but among the soldiers, the standing joke was "I wonder when he's going to cough up the Indian." (Dean, 34)

protested the idea. Nevertheless, some dogs seemed to enjoy the jumping and got their "wings" pin after five jumps. They usually jumped as a pair, with two dogs in each harness, strapped together. Since a rescue attempt might be hundreds of miles from the nearest base, the sled dogs, the sled, and the human rescue team sometimes had to parachute in, if no suitable landing strip could be found nearby. Air Transport Command established units of malamutes, huskies, Eskimos, and other dogs at bases in Greenland, Presque Isle, Maine, and Alaska. The North Atlantic Wing alone had 300 sled and pack dogs with two-way radio sets. Sled dogs were the preferred teams, but in some terrain only pack dogs without sleds could reach remote locales. These animals were usually large dogs like Newfoundlands or Saint Bernards. The larger canines could also pull a pulka, a two-poled stretcher type of sled. (Dean, 30, 71–79; Going, 15)

One formation of two B-17 bombers with five P-38 fighters ran out of fuel and landed on a glacier in Greenland. Dogsled teams reached the planes, rescued all 25 airmen, and saved some important equipment. In another case, a British bomber crashed in Greenland on a sheet of thin ice. The nearest humans were 500 miles away. Dog teams were flown in as close as possible, rescued the men, and removed key components of the plane, before the plane fell through the ice and sank. (Sanderson, 68)

The snow-fought Battle of the Bulge in the winter of 1944–1945 brought 209 sled dogs from Greenland and other arctic stations to fight against the Axis invasion. However, by the time the dogs arrived at the front, the snow had melted, so they were sent back to their bases. (Sanderson, 71; Dean, 91)

The U.S. military sled dogs saved about 450 men and millions of dollars of equipment during World War II. Improvements in motorized sleds and aircraft, however, led to the quick demise of the dogsledding military units. In June 1946 all of this work was discontinued, with the equipment and dogs sold as surplus materials. (Dean, 42, 67)

The only national military sled dog unit remaining in operation is the Danish Sledge Patrol Sirius. They do surveillance in remote areas of Greenland, on patrols taking months at a time. (Dean, 98–105)

War Dogs after World War II

After World War II, most canine programs were dismantled in spite of recommendations that the successful systems be continued. The southern Korean peninsula remained under U.S. control, and many buildings in Seoul were protected by canine units. When the Korean War began in 1950, some of these sentry dogs took on combat duty. The 26th Scout Dog Platoon training in Fort Riley, Kansas, sent one squad immediately; the rest of the unit shipped off to Korea 10 months later and became the mainstay canine units for the conflict. The training center then moved from Kansas to Fort Carson, Colorado, where the sled dogs had been training since World War II. The 26th received a citation in 1953 for its valued participation in hundreds of scouting expeditions and for saving "countless casualties" by warning of nearby enemies. One German shepherd scout dog named York led 148 combat patrols over two years and won the Distinguished Service Award. At least one unit, Tactical War Dog Platoon, 7th Regiment, 1st Cavalry Division, was trained on site in Korea after local acquisition. Five platoons of canines and handlers went from the United States to Korea, but at war's end the program was scrapped. The Air Force, on the other hand, used sentry dogs on a generally continuous basis after World War II. Dogs deployed to bases in Asia usually spent three weeks training at Showa Air Station in Japan, acclimating to the humid climate. (Olive-Drab; Hammerstrom, 27–28; "Post World War II")

A few dogs rocketed into space during the new "space race." Sputnik II, launched by the Soviet Union in 1957, carried the stray dog Laika (dubbed "Mutnik" by American newspapers) into orbit, where the animal suffocated. Technically, some space dogs were part of military programs, but only in the sense of experimental projects. A few planners proposed that dogs be used to carry nuclear weapons (on suicide runs) and hoped that others could carry Geiger counters on their backs to test for radiation during nuclear war. When the U.S. Air Force expanded its sentry dog program to protect Minuteman missile silos and airbases in 1956, the army reinstated its dog training program. During the Vietnam War (circa 1965–1975), dogs became a very popular commodity in the armed forces, though many stories are yet untold because of numerous "confidential" documents regarding the program. (Stall, 15; Lemish, 162–63, 217; Murray, 16, 20, 38)

In the early stages of the Vietnam War, the United States tried to simply "prop up" the South Vietnamese government with aid and advisers. The United States provided canine sentries to protect key South Vietnamese facilities as early as 1961, but locals had no veterinary care and did not continue to train the animals: they quickly died. Ninety percent of war dog deaths in the early years of the war were due to malnutrition, as the South Vietnamese Army of the Republic of Vietnam (ARVN) could not justify feeding dogs nutritional foods when the people themselves were hungry. The diet recommended for an army dog was more expensive than a full day's wages for the average ARVN soldier. Many ARVN soldiers were Buddhists, who said they feared that by working with dogs they might be reincarnated as dogs. The large German shepherd dogs used as sentries could weigh up to 80 pounds and were intimidating to ARVN soldiers. Some ARVN soldiers held the superstition that black dogs were evil and thus would refuse to work with black Labrador retrievers, for instance. The whole country of Vietnam was said to have only 20 veterinarians, and none of them worked with dogs. Of 327 trained war dogs donated by the United States in 1964, only 130 were alive in 1966. Reportedly, some of the dogs were eaten, since canines are regularly food items in Asia. A major raid by the Vietcong (VC) at Bien Hoa Air Base, destroying six B-52 bombers and damaging 20 others, renewed ARVN efforts to use canine sentries, and the program became known as Project Top Dog 145. Within two weeks of the raid, 40 handlers and 40 dogs arrived to work as sentries at key installations. The program was so successful that the Air Force Air Training Command at Lackland Air Force Base in Texas took up the training of sentry dogs in 1964, with the navy following in early 1967. (Lemish, 169–73, 234; Murray, 8, 16, 21, 25; Hamer, 89–90, 134; Denega, 39)

The air force paid, on average, $150 for each sentry dog, then sent it for training. Dogs were carefully checked before purchase, but even so, over half the dogs failed basic training. About half of these lacked the physical abilities to perform satisfactorily, while the rest proved to be gun-shy or "under-aggressive." The army trained military police at Fort Gordon, Georgia, to become sentry dog handlers. After initial training, they went to Okinawa for courses at the Sentry Dog School. There the soldier and dog were teamed up and would remain together for the duration of the man's tour of duty in Vietnam. Then the handler would return to the United States, while the dog was reassigned to a new handler. (Murray, 22–24)

The Vietcong continued to attack airfields frequently. On December 5, 1966, at Tan Son Nhut air base, handler Airman Second Class Robert Thorneberg patrolled with dog Nemo. The dog alerted and was shot in the head, but charged the enemy when Thorneberg lost consciousness after suffering multiple bullet wounds. Nemo killed two infiltrators; two others escaped. Later, Thorneberg was rescued, and Nemo guarded his fallen handler. Nemo lost an eye and returned to Lackland Air Force Base, where he became a canine recruiter. (Sanderson, 82–83; Lemish, 177; Gardiner, 119)

Sentry dogs were important, but scouting and trap-detection became the key roles of canines during the Vietnam War. Just as the U.S. marines used scout dogs to spot enemy snipers and foxholes in World War II, so the animals would use their keen sense of smell and hearing to locate ambushes and mines in the jungles of Asia. The British had success with tracker dogs against the Japanese in World War II, then trained Labrador retrievers as trackers, using them in Kenya, Cyprus, Malaysia, and Borneo. Great Britain set up the Jungle Warfare School in Jahore Bahrue,

Malaysia, and the U.S. Army started sending officers there to learn the system. (Murray, 59–60)

In the mid to late 1960s, consultants in the United States were hired to train mine-hunting dogs and tunnel-scouting dogs, with an estimated $10,000 price tag for each trained animal. Though effective, they suffered a 25 percent casualty rate in Vietnam. Dangers for the dogs included heat and humidity, but more often, lack of rest. In one 1965 shipment of 50 dogs, 2 died of heatstroke the very first day. Some commanders valued the animals so much that the handlers and dogs worked till they dropped. Experience showed that a dog should not have to walk more than four miles before actively working, yet commanders would sometimes insert the dog and handler some 20 miles from the area to be searched, thus exhausting the animal and reducing its effectiveness. Still, when the initial testing period for the army was completed, a survey showed that 85 percent of patrol leaders believed the dogs enhanced security. Only 12 percent said the dogs were no help, and 3 percent claimed the dogs actually hindered the military's work. By 1966, a marine lieutenant reported that "well over two thousand Marine lives have been saved since the insertion of the 1st Scout Dog Platoon into Vietnam." After a few years, the army decided it no longer needed to hire consultants to train the dogs and used an internal training program, but some believe the quality of training suffered greatly as a result, particularly among the mine and tunnel dogs. The army tracker dog training began at Fort Gordon, Georgia, and began sending teams to Vietnam in 1968. (Lemish, 187, 201–5; Murray, 30, 88; Lubow, 196–99)

The highly stressful jungle warfare environment meant that not all of the dangers came from enemy engagements. Recreational drug use by friendly troops could present problems, as guards could become "so freaked out on drugs they would shoot at anything that moved," including the dogs. Some handlers intentionally injured their dogs by smashing their paws so they would not have to go on patrols. The leadership was forced to order these handlers to walk point without the dog, and this put an end to injuring their own animals. Military regulations or simple stubbornness meant that many dogs would die on the battlefield. Some commanders and pilots refused to allow wounded dogs on helicopters, claiming that only muzzled and crated animals could be brought on an aircraft, despite clear orders to the contrary. In one case, a dog named Trouble and his handler were supporting a patrol, when the handler was wounded. The man was carried away in a medevac helicopter, but Trouble was left behind. Three weeks later the emaciated animal arrived at home base and slept in his handler's cot, awaiting his return. No one is sure how Trouble found his way back. (Murray, 28; Lemish, 224–27; Gardiner, 134)

The technical superiority of the American military could not cope with the crude booby traps and mines set by North Vietnamese forces. Electronics could not detect many of the devices laid by the enemy, nor could they locate the many tunnels and "spider holes" where Vietcong forces hid. In the summer of 1967 the U.S. Army Limited Warfare Laboratory decided to see if dogs could be effective mine and trap detectors, to be called M-dogs. The lab contracted with Dr. Robert Lubow and Dr. Eugene Bernard to study the feasibility of the proposal. At a training site in Shotwell, North Carolina, dogs and handlers learned to detect ordnance buried underground, hanging in the air, or located up to 10 feet perpendicular to their path. The dogs learned to "sit" only when they sensed a mine or trap or tunnel, so the handler had no ambiguous signals as to why a dog sat down. The animals were taught inaudible signals, by whistle or by hand motions, so the enemy would not be alerted to their presence. (Murray, 78–81)

The six-month testing period proved successful, with 90 percent detection of "hostile artifacts" along the march path. Most of the targets the dogs did not detect were very old, or the scents had been washed away by heavy rains. The dogs alerted to 76 trip wires with explosives, 21 tunnels and punji pits, and 6 enemy personnel in the trials. M-dog teams began deploying to Asia to find real ordnance. They found even nonmetallic mines that electronics would not have detected, including a 40-pound C-4 explosive with a pressure-type detonator. *Infantry* magazine reported that dog teams should be integrated into all engineer battalions in Vietnam. In December 1969, the commander of the 38th Infantry Platoon scout dogs wrote that the animals had located five booby traps, five weapons caches, two mines, and 29 tunnels and spider holes. A month later, four M-dog teams helped troops to inspect the vicinity of Long Thanh Airfield, where they found 10 tunnels near the base. (Murray, 82–87)

In general, Labrador retrievers were the preferred tracking dogs (to follow a single scent), while German shepherds took the lead in general scouting and alerts on multiple targets and dangers. The German shepherd breed can hear frequencies as high as 35,000 hertz and can close their inner ears to block out general background noises. Handlers liked their perky ears because the shepherds point their heads and ears at possible targets to hear better, helping to alert the handler. Floppy-eared dog breeds cannot point their ears well. A major problem arose with the acquisition of German shepherds, however, when the German Shepherd Club stopped selling dogs to the army. There was a rumor, perhaps true, that the second shipment of dogs sent to Vietnam had no one to meet them at the airstrip. Anxious to unload the cargo, the plane crew gave them to a Special Forces sergeant who did not know what to do with them, so he sold them to the locals for food. Though never admitted, this sort of failure in organization and logistics created problems for the army. Bloodhounds were tried in the tracking role, but they could not control their noisy, howling natures, so the army accepted the Labrador retriever instead. The British used all colors of the Lab breed including yellow and black, but in Vietnam it was feared that the yellow animals would be more easily seen by the enemy and shot, so mostly black Labs were deployed. (Lemish, 219; Murray, 11, 41, 98; Hamer, 134–35)

Scout dogs were trained to be versatile, to meet many of the needs of soldiers in the field. According to the 1969 lesson plan for scout dogs used at Camp Ray, Bien Hoa, "The mission of a scout dog is to support tactical units by detecting and giving early silent warning of any foreign presence outside the main body by: 1. Warning against ambushes. 2. Warning against snipers. 3. Detecting enemy hideouts or stay behind groups. 4. Detecting enemy caches of food, ammunition, and weapons. 5. Detecting mines and booby traps. 6. Warning of enemy approach to ambush patrols and listening posts." Most often, the scout dog and handler "walked point," which meant they moved silently ahead of a unit to provide warnings to the trailing men about ambushes, traps, or enemy units. The 2nd Marine Scout Dog Platoon received credit for 500 enemy killed and discovering numerous NVA bases and other camps between July 1968 and October 1969. With the great success of both army and marine scout dog teams, the armed forces brought in 26 scout dog platoons by 1969. (Murray, 11, 29, 47, 55)

With success came greater dangers, as well. The Vietcong put high bounties on dog handlers, ranking "it number two right behind helicopters, as a target for destruction," wrote Vietnam historian Col. W. H. Clark. To collect the bounty, a Vietcong soldier must present one of the dog's tattooed ears to his superiors as proof of the kill. Aside from simply saving personnel and equipment, the dogs had a major psychological effect on the enemy. (Haran, 141; Murray, 27, 36; Hammerstrom, 38)

While scout dogs were a protection and close-range enemy detector for allied patrols, tracking dog teams became the more offensive weapon for seeking out and destroying the enemy. These teams included one dog, the handler, and a visual tracker. They trained at Fort Gordon, Georgia, in a three-part program. For five weeks the tracker learned to follow visual tracks in the field. For three to nine months (depending on the level of the dog's prior experience) the handler and dog worked together to identify tracks. At the end, the two men and the dog spent three weeks working together. Normally the Labrador retriever was two years old at the beginning of its training, and it was hoped the animal could work up to six more years after training. Although not specifically trained to detect traps, the retrievers often did. Retrievers had a good disposition and easily adjusted when a new handler or visual tracker joined the team. (Murray, 67–68)

Though the British tracking teams were trained to be "hunter-killers," the U.S. Army decided that its tracking units were not to engage the enemy, only to locate enemies and call in aircraft, artillery, or reinforcements to destroy the foe. In the field, it was also determined that three more men should be part of the team: a noncommissioned officer, and two cover men for security. Teams often followed and recovered captured Americans or lost patrols. After an engagement they often followed the enemy trail back into the jungle. The age of the track was the critical factor in following a scent: ideally the team could begin investigating within two or three hours of the last contact. After a day, the smells or visual clues would be diminished or washed away in the rain. (Murray, 69–72)

A 1969 article in *101st Airborne* magazine cites two specific instances of tracker team success in Vietnam. One tracker team with the 1st Battalion, 327th Airborne Infantry, maintained contact with an elusive NVA army so that U.S. forces captured two Soviet 85-millimeter cannons. In another incident, a visual tracker, a handler, and a dog captured 10 Vietcong hiding among villagers in a rice paddy. The handler, Thomas Kimbrough, had taught the dog, Tarka, to alert at booby traps. "On quite a

Boatswain's Mate Third Class Robert E. Dutcher and his sentry dog are silhouetted against the sky at dusk during a patrol on Son Tran mountain in Da Nang, Vietnam, while a flare descends in the background. (Courtesy National Archives.)

few occasions, Tarka has refused to go further, in spite of my persistence. I have found trip wires, mines, and punji pits in our path, which he would not let me walk into." Nevertheless, only 11 platoons of combat tracker teams operated in Vietnam for the United States between 1966 and 1971. (Murray, 72–75)

Australia also employed tracker dogs in Vietnam from 1967 to the end of the war. On patrol the handler would carry his own gear plus five cans of dog food, five packets of hard biscuits, a brush, a comb, and insect repellent. The team was usually brought to an area by helicopter and winched to the ground. Interestingly, the Australians named all 11 of their dogs after Roman emperors. (Haran, ix, 69)

At least 1,100 dogs served in Vietnam in the field, with about 5,000 more in other locations, says a U.S. military source. Another source writes that 4,000 dogs worked in Vietnam, saving 10,000 soldiers. With the rotating handlers, over 9,000 men worked with the dogs on 84,000 missions, claiming 4,000 enemy killed and finding thousands of weapons caches and bunkers. (Murray, 8–9; Hamer, 140; Lemish, 239)

Unlike the happy endings of World War II and Korea, when the military dogs returned home, both the Australian and the U.S. armed forces decided to leave them all behind. The military leadership first claimed that the dogs were too aggressive to be "untrained" and sent into civilian life, in spite of the fact that this untraining had been successful after both World War II and Korea. When the outraged public spurred Congress to order the military to bring the dogs home, the leadership agreed to return all

German shepherd Silver and U.S. Navy SEAL doing reconnaissance in Vietnam, 1968. (Courtesy National Archives.)

"healthy" dogs. They then proceeded to find something unhealthy about the vast majority of animals, so that only 120 canines returned. The rest were given to the South Vietnamese Army and left to unknown fates. Unconfirmed reports claim that some marines euthanized their dogs rather than leave them to be eaten by Vietnamese or starve to death. Australia claimed it would violate quarantine laws to bring its war dogs home and so left them behind also. As Burnam wrote, "Dogs that served in WWII and Korea were repatriated with their devoted handlers. It was not to be so for the valiant animals that fought in Vietnam. For their service, their heroism, their bravery under fire, they were disposed of, killed, buried, and all but forgotten." (Murray, 26; Lemish, 234; Hamer, x, 147, 205; Burnam, 256)

Military Dogs after Vietnam

Armies in several countries have continued to train dogs for war and for peacetime martial tasks in modern times. Sentry dogs, for instance, support the security of installations even when war is not imminent. The United States, Switzerland, and Sweden in particular have maintained working dog programs, along with the armies of Great Britain, Australia, Malaysia, and Thailand. (Murray, 101)

In some cases, the end of war meant the death of dogs. When the Berlin Wall fell in 1989, marking the end of the Cold War, East German officials ordered the deaths of 10,000 German attack dogs that had patrolled the wall zone, as they were considered to be "too vicious" for reintegration into society. (Kohut and Sweet, 86)

During the Falklands War (1982) between the United Kingdom and Argentina, the British trained dogs to detect mines. Though early training seemed to be successful, the canines were ineffective at finding explosives buried under a few inches of water, and so the dogs were not deployed. Dogs are currently trained for the British Army at the Melton Mowbray RAVC center. This installation has trained more than 10,000 canines, at a rate of about 300 per year, to serve in various stations around the world. (Cooper, 92–93)

According to unconfirmed reports, the Israelis used suicide dogs in Lebanon in 1989. Purportedly the dogs wore explosive packs and followed enemies into caves or bunkers, and an Israeli soldier remotely detonated the bomb. Israel has denied these allegations. Also in 1989, the United States deployed a few patrol dogs to Panama during Operation Just Cause to oust Manuel Noriega. (Lemish, 248–49)

In Operation Desert Storm (1990–1991) the United States sent 80 dog teams to Kuwait for security and to locate enemy explosives. Frequent sandstorms in the region caused eye problems for the canines, requiring eye ointments and other remedies. For the first time, the breed Belgian Malinois worked for the army, trained in sniffing for bombs. The Belgian Malinois actually looks very much like the German shepherd, and most people cannot tell them apart. The breed was chosen because it suffered far less hip dysplasia, which frequently hobbles the German shepherd. A few times each year, military personnel travel to Europe to select healthy animals for about $3,100 each. Carlo, one such animal, detected 167 caches of explosives and traps of cluster bombs in two months. Sgt. Christopher Batta, his handler, received the Bronze Star in 1991 but gave it to Carlo. (Lemish, 248; Mott; Hammerstrom, 54ff.; Gardiner, 8)

After September 11, 2001, terrorist attacks on the United States, the war dog training center at Lackland Air Force Base, 341st Training Squadron, doubled its number of animals in training to about 350 in just one year. Between 2001 and 2010 the number of war dogs has increased from 1,300 to 2,800. The dogs train for 100 days, five days a week, with rubber balls and toys as their reward for good work. Explaining the value of war dogs, Gen. David Petraeus, in a 2008 *Air Force* magazine article, wrote, "The capability they bring cannot be replicated by man or machine" and "their yield outperforms any asset we have in our inventory." (Mott; Maloney)

Recent technological advances have brought better protection for war dogs. A company called K9 Storm in Winnipeg, Manitoba, Canada, makes custom-fitted armor for dogs. The bulletproof vest has a wireless camera, speakers, and a microphone built in so the handler can see and issue commands through a remote audio system, workable to 300 yards. The company says that a working dog costs up to $50,000 to purchase and train, so a $20,000 vest is a good investment. One police dog took two .45 slugs from a suspect at close range without injury when wearing the vest. Thus the war dogs of the future may have a higher survivability rate in combat than in years past. (Blum)

Mascot Liberty Hound aboard the USS *Pluck* in 1971.
(Courtesy National Archives.)

U.S. marines have been using bomb-sniffing dogs, usually black Labradors, in the Afghanistan war (2001–present). According to Cpl. Andrew Guzman, a handler, the canines are 98 percent accurate in detecting explosives. Another source puts the effectiveness of bomb-detecting dogs at 80 percent, still much higher than the 50 percent rate of other means. In one incident in 2009, marines who were trapped by the Taliban in a compound were instructed to wait for dogs to clear the area of mines. They did not wait, and IEDs (improvised explosive devices) killed two soldiers. A Lab named Brooks with tan fur has been deployed three times and found at least 14 bombs. A British Army Labrador named Treo found multiple IEDs and saved soldiers from casualties in 2008. Treo received the Dickin Medal. Most of the dogs operating in the Middle East are Labrador retrievers, said to be easier to train than German shepherds. One civilian contractor in southern Afghanistan planned to have 300 canines on-site by summer 2010. Only two of the war dogs in Afghanistan had been killed in the five-year mission there, as of fall 2010. In March 2011, British Lance Cpl. Liam Tasker was shot by insurgents while searching for IEDs with his springer spaniel, Theo. This team had located 14 explosives and weapons caches in just five months, a "record" for a team, and so were on a short extension of their deployment. A few hours after the handler died, Theo also died, of a seizure. War dogs can usually work for five to six years, but the rough terrain of Afghanistan is said to be very hard on the animals' joints. (Gutierrez; Ackerman; "Black Lab"; "UK Army"; Talmadge)

After the public-relations debacle of leaving all the dogs behind in Vietnam, military dogs that lived beyond their working years were euthanized. In 2000, the U.S. Congress passed a law to permit handlers to detrain and adopt the dogs they worked with when the animal's military years were ended. In subsequent years, the adoption program has expanded so that owners can include police officers and other well-trained persons. Nearly half of the animals are now "retired" to good homes rather than put down. (Putney, 224; Mott)

The Pentagon continues to refuse to create medals for awarding to dogs, saying that medals are solely for people. The U.S. War Dogs Association, a nonprofit organization, has produced a two-inch medal, the United States Military Working Dog Service Award, for deserving dogs nationwide. About 30 canines have received the award thus far. (Maloney)

The May 1, 2011 (May 2 Pakistani local time), U.S. Navy SEALs raid that killed terrorist leader Osama bin Laden included a trained dog, but no information about its breed or the role it played has been released thus far.

There are various statues in memory of a few war dogs on battlefields of the United States, but the first memorial for dogs was set up at Hartsdale Pet Cemetery in New York in 1918 for heroes of World War I. World War II dogs have been similarly honored at sites in Lincoln, Nebraska; the University of Tennessee; and the island of Guam. (Hamer, 149; Lemish, 252)

2

Elephants

Ancient Elephants

Of all the creatures used by military forces throughout history, only elephants have been regularly trained to mangle enemies in personal combat. From time to time dogs sprang upon the enemy, but pachyderms have crushed foes for thousands of years. The reader will find a more exhaustive presentation of their gargantuan rumblings in the author's book *War Elephants*, published in 2005. Most of the information found in this chapter can be found in greater detail, with extensive footnotes, in that work.

The word "elephant" may come from the Greek word for "mountain," *lophos*, emphasizing its bulk (Grant, 132).

Our distant ancestors killed mammoths, mastodons, and elephants for food. Peoples of the Indus Valley from 2600 to 1900 BC killed pachyderms with poisoned spears and arrowheads. Modern people who have eaten elephant flesh seem to be split in opinion as to its flavor: some call it delicious, others despise it. Certainly a downed elephant made for large meals for the hunters able to kill one.

We do not know with certainty which nation first taught elephants to fight in human wars. The first rumors of pachyderm warriors appear in three parts of Asia between 2000 and 1100 BC: Syria, India, and China. Ivory hunting in Mesopotamia soon annihilated the Middle Eastern elephants, leaving only Southeast Asia as the hub of elephant warfare. African elephants shared brief roles in warfare in the regions of Sudan, Ethiopia, Egypt, and Algeria in the centuries before Christ. (Spinage, 265; Hutchinson, 110; Barnett, Early, 1; Rennie, 214)

How did elephants first become workers for humanity? Probably, an elephant calf became separated from its herd and wandered into a human village. The people cared for the animal and discovered that a young elephant could be trained to do useful tasks. Unexpected benefits to the community included safety, as snakes, crocodiles, and even tigers will avoid areas with elephants. The simplest and most useful job an elephant could perform for people would be transportation. Pachyderms are famously sure-footed in all terrain, and they easily pass through deep jungle and forest without fear of predators. Thus, people could ride in safety to various destinations, carrying extra cargo. In fact, the most common use of elephants by military forces throughout history has been in a support role: carrying supplies. (Scigliano, 117)

The elephant's massive frame does not actually make it an efficient pack animal. Pound for pound, in fact, the donkey totes far more than a pachyderm. Since donkeys and horses eat less, cost less, and require less training, why would elephants ever be used?

Though the elephant carries less in a size-to-weight-bearing ratio, it still carries significantly more in a single load. Loads carried on horses, mules, or camels must be split in two to hang over both sides of the animal. If the cargo capacity of a donkey is 150 pounds, that is 75 pounds balanced on each side of the animal's back. The pachyderm parcel can be a single 750- or 1,000-pound piece. The British discovered that eight elephants could carry a disassembled Bofors anti-aircraft gun through the jungle, for later assembly, to use against Japanese planes in the Burma region in World War II. (Cooper, 152)

The elephant is a rather tall mammal, at least double the height of a horse or donkey. Thus its loads are carried well off the ground: especially useful when traveling in moist terrain where rivers and streams must be crossed. Dry gunpowder, food, and clothing are highly desirable to any army. Finally, the elephant has a life span of perhaps 60 years. If the animal is captured and trained at age 20, it has the potential of serving for 30 or 40 years. The average pace of elephants, three miles per hour, compares with that of horses and mules. (Harfield, 26)

Capturing an elephant can be a challenge. For a quarry weighing from two to five tons, a simple rope around the neck and feet will not suffice. Ropes will work when handled from atop trained elephants, called "koonkies." Generally females, these elephants can move quietly into a herd of wild pachyderms with a rider or two on their backs, who loop lassos over the heads of the desired animals. Two koonkies will come alongside, and the target elephant can be bound securely between them and led away for training. Surprisingly, the captured animals never attack, even though afraid of the men and ropes. There are two drawbacks to the koonkie method of capture. Only one or two elephants can be caught this way before the crying captives cause the rest of the herd to flee. Also, unless you have a few trained elephants already to act as anchors, this will not work.

A common but dangerous way to catch an elephant is to dig a pit and cover it with branches, then panic a herd into running through the area, hoping an animal falls in. Of course, a youngster or an old pachyderm might fall in, neither of which is good for working. Further, the animal may be injured in the fall. If a desirable animal is caught, the men restrain the elephant, then dig a ramp into the pit so the elephant can climb out and training can begin.

The best method for capturing "good" elephants, and one that has been practiced for thousands of years, is to trap the entire herd, then let the undesirable members leave. The huge trap is called a *keddah* or *kraal* (from which we get the word "corral"). People build enclosures near heavily used elephant paths and grazing pastures, then construct a wide funnel passageway leading to the narrow trap gate. Using firecrackers or drums, people drive the herd into the funnel, force the animals into the enclosure, and close the gate. If available, a few koonkies or calm trained female elephants will already be in the kraal to help calm the new captives and separate out the animals to be freed. The people choose which pachyderms to keep, and one by one those are tied to the walls of the enclosure.

Elephants have never been domesticated in the modern sense of the word. We do not breed elephants for desirable qualities as we do dogs and cats; in fact, we have problems getting pachyderms to breed at all. Trained working elephants live in the forests and come "to work" with their trainers (called "mahouts") for a few hours each day. Practically speaking, trained elephants act much like human employees; they trade hours of labor for special fruits, thorough baths, and attention from their human friend the mahout. Very few elephants are raised in captivity. Most are captured as adults and then trained to work, and they seem to accept this relationship willingly.

The oldest known story of elephants in combat is shrouded in myth, but it contains many plausible elements and thus may be based on historical truth. An Assyrian queen named Sammu-ramat from about 800 BC may be the real figure behind the beautiful Queen Semiramis. Purportedly she had been a prostitute who married the Assyrian king of Babylon, then had her husband executed and took over the nation. Her generals wanted to invade India to plunder its wealth, and she agreed. However, her spies warned that the enemy king Stabrobates was already capturing elephants from the forests, anticipating an attack. (Fraser, 28–29)

This report from the spies reveals exactly the sort of misunderstanding one would expect from agents with no familiarity with war elephants. To the eyes of the spies, the Indians were going into the forest and capturing wild elephants for the army. In fact, these had to be tamed elephants, since they could not be caught and trained in the short time before an expected attack. Unlike horses, few elephants ever lived in stables. One elephant eats 300–400 pounds of food each day: enough for 20 horses. The mahout leaves the elephant to its instinctual foraging in the forest from evening to morning and simply teaches the animal to come into camp for treats and work in the early part of the day. Thus, food costs are low, and both elephant and army are happy, at least during peacetime. The spies from Babylon were just seeing the trained elephants being collected from the forest where they had been left to eat in time of peace.

The Assyrians had no elephants for their army; the pachyderms of the Middle East had been exterminated by ivory-hunters long before. It was already known that horses were frightened of elephants, not to mention foot soldiers. The queen therefore undertook a three-year project of preparing devices to counteract the Indian elephants. Supposedly, her army collected 300,000 black ox-hides to create gigantic figures shaped like elephants, to fit atop thousands of camels. These fake elephants would hopefully frighten the enemy cavalry and pachyderms long enough for her superior infantry to win the battle. Though the king of India was quite surprised by the elephant-looking camel-puppets, the real elephants were not terrified. Diodorus wrote:

> The army of Semiramis withstood the onslaught of these monsters for only a short time; for these animals are of incredible ferocity, and relying on their inherent physical strength they easily slaughtered everyone who opposed them. A prodigious killing then took place, and death took many forms, as some fell beneath their feet and others were torn apart by their tusks, while yet others were tossed about by their trunks. Multitudes of corpses soon lay about in heaps. (Murphy, 25–26)

Queen Semiramis was wounded with an arrow and a javelin, and she did not last long as ruler after the defeat. (Bottero, 146)

The Middle Eastern empires did not give up on their desire to gain the wealth of India. King Cyrus of Persia, who had conquered Babylon, was killed in battle against Queen Tomyris. Her army included elephants, which terrified the Persian cavalry. Cyrus's horse reared up, throwing him off, and he was killed. Some decades later, another Persian king had elephant problems. In 520 BC, King Darius loaded camels with bushels of flammables and planned to light them up and send the flaming camels at the enemy elephants. No record tells us whether the ploy worked, but he lost the battle. (Rawlinson, v.3, 387; Higham, 153)

During the Shang dynasty of China, war elephants were kept and trained before 1000 BC, but little information describes their use. The rapidly expanding population and need for farmland left little jungle for pachyderms, and so elephants became rare in China after 300 BC. In Europe, elephants had long been extinct. The fossilized bones of mammoths and mastodons confused the Greeks. The skulls of elephants and their ancestors have a giant central sinus cavity front and center and no obvious eye-sockets on the sides. The Greeks may have interpreted these bones as proof of the mythical Cyclops. (Mayor, *First*, 55–56)

India would long remain the central hub for capturing and using war elephants. Early Buddhist texts wrote that King Bimbisara of Magadha (558–491 BC) owned elephants that bore metal spikes on their tusks and wore leather armor. Plate armor rarely protected elephants, because the animals easily overheat. Cloth armor was lightweight but not very effective.

Leather armor could be wetted and fitted atop the elephant, then it would harden to the desired shape. (Basham, 3)

At first, only the rider, the mahout, rode on the war elephant's neck. He used a hook in one hand, called an *ankhus*, to guide the elephant when voice and foot commands were not enough. In his other hand he could carry a long spear or a javelin to hurl at foes. By the sixth century BC, armies discovered that three men could ride on the elephant's back, throwing javelins or shooting arrows. Sitting astride the elephant provided no protection for these riders, so soon the "howdah," a tower for the animal's back, was invented. Held in place by a cinch strap around the elephant's stomach, the small wooden tower with side shields protected two or three archers or javelin-hurlers. In some armies, 10 percent of the pachyderms worked as signal platforms, with a leader and flagman beating drums and waving flags with orders for the troops. (MacMunn, 29; Paradine-Palmer, 116)

Few detailed records exist for elephant warfare in the ancient Eastern world, but the Western world would soon see the pachyderms for themselves.

Elephants Meet the West

The Persian Empire invaded Greece repeatedly. King Philip II of Macedon spent years uniting the Greeks and building an army to invade Persia. His sudden assassination enabled his ambitious young son Alexander to take the reins of Bucephalus to attack the east.

Alexander won two major victories, captured Egypt, and then pushed his heavy cavalry and infantry toward Babylon. King Darius III, desperate to find some means of stopping the Greeks, called for allies in India to send help. They sent 15 elephants. The Zoroastrian scriptures called elephants "creatures of Ahriman," meaning demons, but the Persian generals hoped the devils might frighten Alexander's cavalry. When the Macedonians arrived at Gaugamela, all the elephants stood in the front Persian line, to keep the invading horsemen from charging at the king in the center.

The Persian plan was sound, but Alexander unexpectedly refused to attack upon arrival. Why? The only difference between this Persian battle line and prior deployments was the elephants in the center. Alexander, as a boy, had studied under Aristotle. Aristotle wrote briefly about elephants, just hearsay from visitors in the Far East. "Elephants fight fiercely with one another, and stab one another with their tusks...Indians employ these animals for war purposes, irrespective of sex....An elephant, by pushing with big tusks, can batter down a wall." The Greeks decided to reconsider their normal attack on the center because they did not know how their heavy cavalry might react. (Aristotle)

The Persian troops stood in formation all night long, fearing a night attack. The chariot horses were not accustomed to elephants, and the darkness started them into a panic. Rather than have complete disorder in the ranks, the Persians sent the elephants to the rear to wait with the baggage. When Alexander attacked in the morning, his initial deployment avoided the center, but after seeing that the elephants were gone, he punched his heavy cavalry through the center. When the great king of Persia fled, the huge Persian army disintegrated. The Greeks captured the 15 elephants with the plunder.

Depiction of King Porus of India on his elephant Ajax battling against Alexander the Great. (Mary Evans Picture Library.)

Alexander kept the elephants for his own army, probably so the Greek army could learn about the animals and how they could be used in warfare. In 327 BC, the Macedonians started their invasion of India. Alexander collected more than 100 elephants from small fiefdoms in Afghanistan and Pakistan but halted at the Hydaspes River. King Porus of India, with 200 war elephants and a large army, prevented the Greeks from crossing. Unable to ford the river in the face of superior numbers, Alexander arranged for a sneaky night crossing some 20 miles upriver, during a thunderstorm. Only infantry and cavalry accompanied Alexander; he had no way to get his own elephants across.

Alexander's allies told him how to fight against elephants: using axes and archers. Archers, they said, should launch arrows at the elephants' eyes and at their riders. Infantry should chop at the elephants' trunks and hamstrings. Because his horses refused to approach the elephants of King Porus, the foot soldiers had to face the 200 beasts with their axes. Curtius wrote:

> The elephants, applying to good use their prodigious size and strength, killed some of the enemy by trampling them under their feet, and crushing their armour and their bones, while upon others they inflicted a terrible death, for they first lifted them aloft with their trunks, which they had twined around their bodies, and then dashed them down with great violence to the ground. Many others they deprived in a moment of life by goring them through and through with their tusks. (Pant, 93)

After a gruesome fight, with elephants suffering hacked trunks and slashed leg tendons, the Macedonians gained the advantage. Arrian wrote, "The elephants were now crowded into a narrow space...most of the drivers of the elephants had been shot down, some of the elephants had been wounded...maddened by suffering, attacked friends and foes alike and in all sorts of ways kept pushing, trampling, and destroying." King Porus fought from the back of his elephant, named Ajax. Said Plutarch of this elephant, "during the whole battle, [he] gave many singular proofs of sagacity and of particular care for the king, whom as long as he was strong and in a condition to fight, he defended with great courage, repelling those who set upon him; and as soon as he perceived him overpowered with his numerous wounds and the multitude of darts that were thrown at him, to prevent his falling off, he softly knelt down and began to draw out the darts with his proboscis." (Arrian, 53–54; Plutarch, 490)

Both Ajax and King Porus survived their wounds. Porus swore allegiance to Alexander and remained king of northern India. Alexander had gold rings struck for the elephant's tusks saying "Alexander, the son of Zeus, dedicates Ajax to the Sun." However, another Indian king to the south, with thousands of war elephants, threatened to attack the invaders. Alexander's army mutinied and refused to go further, demanding to go home. (Scullard, 71)

Alexander the Great lost his temper. He wept and shouted and tried all manner of persuasion to change the minds of his troops. He may have angered the tired soldiers further by even denigrating their fear of elephants. According to Curtius, Alexander said that he would never use elephants because they are more dangerous to their own side than to their enemies. Historians have seized upon this statement as proof that "the best generals" viewed elephants as poor weapons. However, the Curtius quote is doubtful at best, according to experts like H. H. Scullard. Perhaps Alexander did say something like this during his harangues of the mutineers, but, obviously, in collecting elephants, he intended to use them. He already possessed as many as 130 pachyderms before arriving in India, then he took 70 more from Porus and marched back to Babylon with at least 200. They served as guards around the royal palace. Alexander then appointed a new position in the Macedonian army: the leader of elephants, called an elephantarch. This is one of the last things Alexander did before his death. (Rennie, 212)

Greek Elephants

The elephants of India lost the Battle of the Hydaspes to the Greeks of Alexander the Great, but they won the war. The prospect of facing 4,000 war elephants in their next battle, after barely overcoming the 200 pachyderms of King Porus, led the Macedonians to mutiny. Alexander and the army returned to Babylon, where he installed a new leader, called an elephantarch, to train 200 elephants for the army.

Alexander died on June 13, 323 BC, leaving his young empire in chaos. He left behind no proclaimed heir. His bevy of ambitious generals immediately argued over who should be in charge, and thus began the long civil war known as the War of the Successors. Many of these commanders had fought against the elephants at Hydaspes, and so elephants became the central focus of the new arms race, as every army wanted them. Because the War of the Successors was a complex affair with numerous participants and constantly rotating alliances, the reader may want to look elsewhere for a more detailed history. Here, only the elephants' roles will be considered.

Perdiccas controlled the elephants and the capital, Babylon, at first. When some infantry soldiers demanded that Alexander's mentally disabled brother be installed as king, Perdiccas surrounded the soldiers with elephants and had dozens of them trampled to death on the spot. He was confident that he could consolidate power, and he hoped that the final victory would come by personally burying Alexander the Great at home in Macedon. The long tradition had been that the new ruler buried the old ruler before claiming headship. Perdiccas's opponents knew this, and they plotted to stop him. When Perdiccas sent the body west, General Ptolemy, who claimed Egypt, sent an army and stole the corpse. Ptolemy quickly hid the body in Egypt. (Scullard, 78; Tarn, "Greece," 467)

Perdiccas needed the corpse, so he took an army, with 40 elephants, to Egypt to retrieve it. Ptolemy first met the invaders at Fort Camel (Castellum Camelorum) in May 321 BC. The elephants attacked the palisades, ripping the sharpened stakes from the ground to clear a path to the walls of the fortress. Ptolemy showed his men how to use long spears to stab the mahouts and poke out the elephants' eyes. The lead elephants thus wounded, the animals turned and fled, trampling their own men and forcing a retreat. Perdiccas tried to bypass the fort by crossing the Nile River. He used horses and elephants as a breakwater to slow the current, but hundreds of crocodiles showed up and ate at least a thousand of the Greeks, with thousands more drowning and floating away. These two defeats led Perdiccas's soldiers to murder him in his tent and return to Babylon, leaving more than 35 elephants to Ptolemy. (Diodorus, *Diodorus*, 108–9; Kincaid, 16)

Antipater, the leader in Macedonia, rushed to Babylon to restore order and put down the murderers of Perdiccas. He took 70 elephants back to Greece and ordered Antigonus the One-Eyed to squash the rest of Perdiccas's allies. Alexander had trusted Antigonus and left him to conquer and control Anatolia so that Persia could not cut communications with Greece. (Billows, 27–29)

Antigonus had to fight against two of Perdiccas's allies. Eumenes, who had been Alexander's secretary, and Alcetas, Perdiccas's brother, each had an army in Anatolia. Using trickery, Antigonus terrified Eumenes' army, which fled, though Eumenes himself escaped. The One-Eyed then made the swiftest march ever recorded involving elephants. His army moved 300 miles in just one week, averaging 45 miles per day. Five of the 70 pachyderms died on the journey. Alcetas's army was still sleeping when Antigonus arrived and sent 65 elephants rumbling down the hillside. The army immediately surrendered, and Alcetas killed himself. (Scullard, 78)

The escaped Eumenes had not given up, however. He was able to hire many of the mutinous infantry who had killed Perdiccas, but best of all, he convinced a Greek to do treachery. Eudamos, the Greek envoy in northern India, murdered King Porus and stole 125 elephants. When Antigonus found Eumenes' army he was shocked to find that the enemy had an advantage in elephants.

The 317 BC Battle of Paraetacene is important as the first recorded combat between two armies with elephants. Both foes put the pachyderms on the wings of the army to keep cavalry from flanking them. The battle was indecisive and both sides withdrew. A few months later, as Eumenes' army divided into six groups for winter forage, Antigonus marched across the desert to surprise the enemy. His men lit fires on one cold night, so Eumenes' scouts saw the lights and tried to mobilize.

As Eumenes' army groups tried to reform, his elephants were closest to the enemy. Antigonus sent cavalry to kill or capture the elephants, and Diodorus wrote about this skirmish:

> Those who were in charge of the elephants resisted at first and held firm even though they were receiving wounds from all directions and were not able to injure the enemy in return in any way. Then when they were becoming exhausted, the troops sent by Eumenes appeared and rescued them from danger.

Though the cavalry arrived in the nick of time, some of the mahouts and their elephants had been injured, or at least traumatized, by this raid. When Eumenes and Antigonus again lined up for battle, Eumenes set "the weaker" elephants on one side. Presumably the stressed or riderless pachyderms could not be considered as reliable at the Battle of Gabiene. (Diodorus, "Armies," 337–41)

Both sides put towers on some of their elephants: this is the first mention we have in Western history of howdahs being used in battle. Eumenes had a large numeric advantage in elephants on his left wing, so he ordered them to charge the few pachyderms of Antigonus. Eumenes' lead elephant got into a wrestling match with the opposing pachyderm. In such conflicts, the struggle continues until one elephant turns to flee: then the opponent sticks his tusks in the enemy animal's sides. Eumenes' beast was gored and fell down dead, leading the rest of his companions to flee. Meanwhile, in the confusion of the dusty plain, Antigonus's forces captured Eumenes' camp, including all their wives, children, and loot. The infantry all surrendered to Antigonus. Eumenes and the traitorous Eudamos were strangled.

Now Antigonus owned all of the empire from India to Turkey, lacking only Egypt and Greece. Will Durant cleverly wrote that "Antigonus I (Cyclops) dreamed of uniting all of Alexander's empire under his one eye." (Durant, 558)

Elephant Countermeasures

As the Greek generals tried to gain personal control over Alexander the Great's empire, they tried to get elephants, but not all of them were successful. Thus, anti-elephant devices and tactics had to be designed.

The Greek governor, Antipater, had taken 70 Indian elephants to Macedonia. His son Cassander wanted to take over when Antipater died, but another general, named Polyperchon, took command and the elephants. Civil war broke out in Greece, with some cities loyal to Cassander and others to Polyperchon.

Polyperchon led an attack on Megalopolis with his army and 65 elephants. The townspeople dug a moat and used catapults, but the enemy was able to undermine a section of wall, which collapsed one evening. There was not enough time to fix the wall, so the people turned to Damis, a veteran from Alexander's army. Surprisingly, he ordered the townsfolk to clear away the rubble from the street to make a clear path for the enemy to march in. He assumed rightly that Polyperchon would send in the elephants first.

Damis, who had been in Asia with Alexander and knew by experience the nature and the use of these animals, got the better of him
[Polyperchon] completely. Indeed, by putting his native wit against
the brute force of the elephants, Damis rendered their physical
strength useless. He studded many great frames with sharp nails and
buried them in shallow trenches, concealing the projecting points;
over them he left a way into the city...the Indian mahouts did their
part in urging them to rush into the city all together; but the animals,
as they charged violently, encountered the spike-studded frames.
Wounded in their feet by the spikes, their own weight causing the
points to penetrate, they could neither go forward any farther nor
turn back, because it hurt them to move. At the same time some of
the mahouts were killed by the missiles of all kinds that poured upon
them from the flanks...The elephants, suffering great pain because
of the cloud of missiles and the nature of the wounds caused by the
spikes, wheeled about through their friends and trod down many of
them. Finally the elephant that was the most valiant collapsed; of the
rest, some became completely useless, and others brought death to
many of their own side. (Gaebel, 212–13)

This is the oldest recorded use of caltrops, ground traps, against elephants. The elephants rushed back over their own troops, and Polyperchon
had to retreat from Megalopolis.

Alexander the Great's mother, Olympias, helped Polyperchon and
took over the care of his 60 elephants. Cassander attacked and trapped her
in the city of Pydna, putting it under siege. The people were starving, even
resorting to cannibalism, and though they tried feeding sawdust to the elephants, they all "pined away for want of food." Olympias was executed.
(Rennie, 213)

In the eastern empire, Antigonus set his son Demetrius in charge of the
defense of Gaza in southern Palestine, to keep King Ptolemy bottled up in
Egypt. Cassander of Greece, Ptolemy of Egypt, and Lysimachus of Thrace
allied themselves against Antigonus. In the summer of 312 BC, Ptolemy
left Egypt to attack Gaza.

Demetrius had 43 elephants; Ptolemy probably owned some but did
not bring them on the march through the arid terrain. Instead, Ptolemy

tried out a newly designed form of caltrops. The problem of laying ground traps is twofold: you must ensure that your own troops do not step on them, and afterward you must dig them up or leave them forever. Ptolemy solved this problem by connecting tetrahedral-type spike devices between ropes or chains. Egyptian soldiers could lay them out in front of enemy cavalry or elephants easily, then later pick up the whole chain again. When Demetrius sent his elephants charging at the Egyptians, they stepped on these linked caltrops. Their horrible screams caused the uninjured elephants to turn and run in panic. Demetrius's whole army fled, and Ptolemy captured the elephants. (ibid., 214)

Ptolemy sent an ally, Seleucus, back to Babylon, where he had been a popular leader. This would open another front from which to undermine Antigonus the One-Eyed and his designs to conquer the Greek world.

Seleucus took Babylon and then went toward northern India to reclaim it as Greek territory and capture elephants for his army. The new king of India, Chandragupta, defeated the Greeks badly. However, they signed a truce. Seleucus gave one of his daughters to marry Chandragupta and surrendered Pakistan, Afghanistan, and all claims on India, in exchange for 500 war elephants with mahouts and staff. (Rawlinson, *Sixth*, 61)

The allies against Antigonus now planned a multipronged attack. Cassander and Lysimachus would invade through Anatolia in the west, Ptolemy from the south, and Seleucus from the east, to defeat the One-Eyed and his son.

Antigonus had a slight advantage in infantry and cavalry, but he did not know that Seleucus was bringing 480 elephants (20 died in the hard march from Pakistan). Ptolemy was deceived by spies, and, thinking the war was already lost, he retreated to Egypt. At Ipsus, Seleucus put 100 elephants in the front line center against Antigonus's 75 elephants but kept 380 pachyderms in the rear. Demetrius commanded the cavalry and charged ahead. He drove away Seleucus's cavalry, then turned to hit the flank and rear of the infantry, but discovered why the 380 elephants remained in the rear. Seleucus moved them in a line out behind Demetrius's cavalry. The horses refused to approach, and so Antigonus's infantry was surrounded, with no hope of support. Antigonus fell in a hail of javelins, while his son could do nothing but escape with his horsemen. This battle at Ipsus in 301 BC is considered to be "the greatest achievement of war elephants in Hellenistic military history." (Tarn, "Heritage," 504; Gaebel, 226)

Elephants in Egypt and Italy

Ptolemy had fought with Alexander the Great and had personally seen the terror of war elephants. When the Greek civil wars began, he took his loyal army to Egypt and created a dynasty that would last for hundreds of years. There was no easy route to India, however, for collecting elephants and their mahouts for his army. Ptolemy did get more than 30 pachyderms from the abortive Perdiccas invasion, but he knew these animals would not live more than 20 or 30 more years.

Almost all of the elephants taken by Alexander from India were males and so could not breed. Seleucus, who received 500 Asian elephants from Chandragupta, must have gotten some females in the group, since he attempted to start a breeding program at Apamea in Syria. Cavalry horse stables were established near the elephant stables, probably to acclimate the animals to one another. After defeating Antigonus, the three other allies feared Seleucus would be the great power, so they allied against Seleucus. Ptolemy saw the importance of elephants for future warfare and so his Egyptians needed a consistent supply of elephants and of men to train them.

First, Ptolemy decreed that African elephants should not be killed, because they were wanted for the army. This law was intended for Egyptian-controlled Ethiopia and Sudan, because Egypt itself had killed all of its elephants for their ivory some 2,000 years before.

Ptolemy II Philadelphus undertook the collection of African elephants. These animals were not the gigantic African savanna elephants (*Loxodonta africana*) most familiar to modern television viewers, but the African forest elephant species (*Loxodonta cyclotis*). The forest pachyderms are a bit smaller than Asian elephants and much smaller than the savanna elephants.

The Ethiopians known as Kushites had a long history of training war elephants, said Arrian, but few records exist about Kushite warfare. The giant temple complex at Musawwaret es Sufra includes a relief showing an elephant dragging a line of prisoners behind. The Ptolemies sought for Kushites to ride elephants and help in their capture. Ptolemy II sent scouts to locate the best sites for catching elephants, and he established ports along the coast of the Red Sea for transporting the animals back to Egypt. The main ports at Ptolemais Theron and Berenice Troglodytica included specially built docks and ramps to accommodate the hefty behemoths climbing on and off of boats. Hundreds of soldiers went on one-year expeditions to catch elephants. They used the Indian method of driving a herd of pachyderms into a gorge or corral and then keeping the desirable animals for training and shipment north. (Welsby, 43–44)

It would be some time before African elephants and Asian elephants would fight against each other in battle.

When Lysimachus of Thrace died, King Seleucus of Syria thought to march into Thrace and then Greece, to claim them. One of Ptolemy's banished sons, named Keraunos, snuck up on Seleucus, stabbed him in the back, and declared himself king. The Syrian army, lacking any other leader, accepted this change of command. Keraunos took control of western Anatolia, Thrace, and Greece.

Perhaps having difficulty providing food for the dozens of elephants in his army, Keraunos gave all but one pachyderm to Pyrrhus of Epirus, who was mounting an expedition into Italy. Months later, however, in 279 BC, the Gauls invaded. Keraunos rode in front of his army on his elephant. The Gauls wounded the elephant, seized Keraunos, cut off his head, and carried it on a pike in triumph.

Perhaps the Gauls were not afraid of the single elephant in this battle, but the very next year, they were less confident. The son of Seleucus, named Antiochus, had big problems, with Keraunos stealing his western army and with Ptolemy coming from Egypt with raids. His main elephant and cavalry base at Apamea declared its independence, so Antiochus had to ask India for more elephants. They sent 20. Ptolemy paid the Gauls to invade Syria to wipe out Antiochus. The Gauls outnumbered the Syrians badly, but one officer gave Antiochus some good advice. The historian Lucian wrote:

The King had sixteen elephants, and Theodotas instructed him to set these in the fore-part of the battle. For when the elephants moved out, the Galatian horses became mad with fear and swerved backwards. The scythed chariots tore their own ranks. The Macedonians and Greeks followed up with an immense slaughter. Only a few of the Galatians escaped into the hills... but the eyes of Antiochus were full of bitter tears. "Shame, my men," he broke out, "is all that we have got this day. Our deliverance we owe to these sixteen brutes. But for them, where should we have been?" And the King commanded that the trophy should bear nothing but the figure of an elephant. (Bevan, 143)

The original trophy seems to have been replicated as a collectible. In 1881, archaeologists found a five-inch-tall terra cotta sculpture of an Asian elephant, with rider and tower, trampling a Galatian soldier.

With multiple small kingdoms in Greece and Macedonia vying for power, one young man wanted to travel afar for adventures. Pyrrhus, young king of Epirus (modern Albania), received messages from Greek cities in Italy begging for help. These commercial ports were being threatened by a growing power they called "the wolves of Italy," from the city of Rome. Pyrrhus, who was a cousin of Alexander the Great, and friend of Demetrius son of Antigonus the One-Eyed, decided to fight these Romans. He "borrowed" ships and soldiers and 50 elephants from Greek kings for this adventure in 280 BC. (Kincaid, 64)

Pyrrhus's fleet ran into a storm near the eastern coast of Italy, and many ships were lost. This may explain why he had only 20 elephants for the first battle against the Romans at Heraclea. The Roman infantry was holding well against the Greek phalanx formation, but when Pyrrhus charged the 20 elephants, the Italians panicked. Archers in the howdah towers killed many, and the pachyderms themselves trampled and gored the Roman infantry. Dio wrote that the carnage stopped only when one elephant received a deep wound, and its screams caused the other elephants to turn and run. The Romans had never seen an elephant before and did not even know what to call them. The first name given to them by the Italians was "Lucanian Oxen," Lucania being the region where the animals were first seen.

The Romans, while frightened, did not surrender. They prepared a new army and designed some interesting elephant countermeasures.

According to Dionysius of Halicarnassus, the Romans produced 300 special wagons:

> These waggons had upright beams on which were mounted movable transverse poles that could be swung round as quick as thought in any direction one might wish, and on the ends of the poles there were either tridents or sword-like blades or scythes all of iron; or again they had cranes that hurled down heavy grappling irons. Many of the poles had attached to them and projecting in front of the waggons fire-bearing grapnels wrapped in tow that had been liberally daubed with pitch, which men standing on the waggons were to set afire as soon as they came near the elephants and then rain blows with them upon the trunks and faces of the beasts. (Dionysius, 389–91)

The Italians deployed these wagons on the wings, where the elephants had attacked in their first battle. Seeing the contraptions, Pyrrhus quickly deployed the elephants to the center and had skirmishers rush out to destroy the wagons. Again the Romans fled from the elephants, for the most part. However, one brave legionnaire cut off the trunk of one pachyderm, and a few others were killed. Pyrrhus famously said, "Another victory like this and I shall be ruined!"

Rome considered surrendering, but Carthage, a naval power from North Africa, promised to help Rome if they kept up the fight. Carthage was taking over Sicily and feared that Pyrrhus would come help the Greek cities in Sicily.

The Romans continued to seek ways to oppose the elephants, and at Maleventum they finally succeeded. There are three different versions of what happened, but all three stories include the same key ingredient: fire. Flaming javelins and arrows, or flaming torches, may have been the device that frightened away the pachyderms. The most famous and clever possibility included another animal, the common pig. One author wrote that the Romans doused pigs in grease and pitch, lit them up like living torches, and tossed them before the elephants. The elephants hated the pigs' squealing shrieks, and they turned to flee. The same tactic had worked for the Greek city of Megara some 15 years earlier; perhaps the Romans had heard the tale.

Pyrrhus had run out of money, and the kings of Greece refused to send him any more men or elephants, so the king of Epirus sailed home, swearing to get revenge on the ungracious Greek rulers.

Pyrrhus was now a famous adventurer. He was able to persuade an enemy army to defect to him, and thus he gained a new supply of 24 elephants. He arrived at Sparta one evening in 272 BC, but he decided to wait for morning to attack. During the night, the women and children of the city built palisades and dug a trench, while the few men of the city slept and prepared for battle. In the morning, Pyrrhus could not get through the defenses, so the army traveled to the city of Argos.

Pyrrhus had allies in the city, who opened the gates of Argos in the middle of the night. Foolishly, Pyrrhus ordered the elephants into the city first. They made so much noise that people woke up and sounded the alarms. Pyrrhus ordered a retreat, but the rush of his army coming in stopped anyone from getting out.

"To add to the confusion, the largest of Pyrrhus' elephants had fallen athwart one of the gates. Another elephant, whose name Nikon has survived, missed its mahout, who had been mortally wounded and had fallen off the beast's back. It dashed through the retreating force until it had found its master's dead body. Lifting it with his trunk, it put the body across its tusks, and wild with grief and rage, it charged in all directions, trampling down everyone whom it met." (Kincaid, 101)

In the confusion, an angry mother threw a heavy roof tile down on the enemy. Pyrrhus was struck on the head, and he fell off his horse, stunned. A soldier of Argos hacked off his head, and the battle was lost.

One of the lesser known legacies of the famous Pyrrhus was a memoir he published about the battles he fought in Italy. One copy of this book would eventually find its way to a future leader named Hannibal.

Elephants of Carthage

Carthage, the famous city in modern Tunisia, first met with elephants when Pyrrhus invaded Italy and had a short excursion into Sicily. The Carthaginian army realized that North Africa flourished with elephants and had heard that Egypt was catching and training the beasts, so they started up their own elephant program. They captured pachyderms from Morocco, Algeria, and all around the Atlas Mountains. Carthage built stables right into the city walls capable of housing 300 animals. They hired "Indians" to ride the animals, but the word "Indian" itself had become synonymous with "elephant rider," so these may have been

Egyptians, Kushites, Indians, or even blacks who learned the trade. (Scullard, 149)

After Pyrrhus left Italy, the Romans decided to take Sicily away from Carthage and the Greek cities. Carthage tried to use elephants against the Romans at Agrigentum in 262 BC but failed miserably. In 256 BC Rome sent legions under General Regulus to North Africa to destroy Carthage itself, to win the long war in Sicily. After repeated losses to Rome, Carthage hired a Greek named Xanthippus, from Sparta. Xanthippus had worked with elephants before and may have read Pyrrhus's book. Xanthippus used the big elephants to rumble ahead of his army. What little cavalry the Romans had, fled when the horses could not face the pachyderms. The elephants crashed through Regulus's tight infantry formation, and the Carthaginian cavalry surrounded the legions. Few survived to escape back to their ships. One writer claimed that Regulus was captured and later mangled to death by an angry elephant. (Diodorus, v.11, 109)

In Sicily, after the disaster with Regulus, Romans fled at the sight of elephants. A clever Roman commander named Metellus, though, hatched a plan. Using javelin-throwers to harass the Carthaginian elephants and anger the mahouts, he baited the elephants to charge ahead and become trapped at a ditch. Archers and slingers pelted the animals with missiles until the pachyderms turned and fled, crushing their own army columns. Metellus then burst out of the nearby city with his legion and inflicted a major defeat on the enemy. The Romans captured more than 100 elephants. Metellus then designed a gigantic raft made of jugs, and in this way he ferried elephants across the Strait of Messina for his triumphal parade in Rome. After parading the animals through Rome, the Romans had no idea what to do with them, so they were killed with javelins in the Circus. (Scullard, 152)

Hamilcar Barca, general of Carthage over Sicily, held out for seven years against superior Roman troops. In 241 BC, the wealthy rulers of Carthage decided that the war against Rome was too expensive, and they made peace. The African troops, made up mostly of mercenaries, returned to Africa for payment and left Sicily to the Italians. This ended the First Punic War but did not bring peace to North Africa. The rich rulers of Carthage claimed that because their troops did not "win" the war, they would be paid only a small percentage of the promised wages. The mercenaries went on a rampage and joined with Libya in a war against Carthage.

The so-called Truceless War was a horror, with no mercy shown to prisoners. The mercenaries would hack off an enemy's limb and leave him to bleed to death. Hamilcar was ordered to destroy the army he had trained himself. Using 100 war elephants, he defeated the larger mercenary force and received the thanks of Carthage. Rome, during the Mercenary War, broke all of its promises, stole Carthaginian islands and possessions, and threatened invasion when Carthage protested. Hamilcar Barca hated Rome, and he wanted to find a way to destroy it.

Carthage owned parts of Hispania, modern-day Spain. Hamilcar took a small army and some elephants to Hispania to start building a larger army, with which to conquer Italy. His family included sons Hannibal, Hasdrubal, and Mago, who swore hatred of Rome. These three boys would grow up to be called the Lion's Brood by their enemies. Hamilcar gradually expanded Carthaginian influence in Spain and grew his army. The Barca boys lived with the army and learned military tactics. Surrounded by mercenaries and conscripts from many lands, they learned the languages and skills of each ethnicity. When Hamilcar was ambushed by an Iberian tribe, Hannibal's uncle controlled the army for several years. The three young Barca boys grew up with war elephants. Hannibal took over the army of Hispania in 221 BC.

For two years, Hannibal pacified the tribes of Hispania to ensure that their base would be secure when they marched toward Italy. Hasdrubal would stay behind to guard Hispania in case the Romans tried to flank them with an invasion by sea. Hannibal took a large army with 37 elephants on a 1,500-mile march starting from southern Spain in May 218 BC. The army averaged 19 miles per day, and they had no difficulties until they reached the Rhone River in late August.

Hostile Gallic tribes across the river refused bribes to allow the army to pass peacefully. While the Africans built giant rafts to carry the elephants across, Hannibal sent the cavalry northward to cross and flank attack the tribes. Even with the hostiles cleared away, the river was a problem for the elephants. They did not like the rafts. As Roman historian Polybius recounts:

As soon as they were standing on the last rafts, the ropes holding these were cut, the boats took up the strain of the tow-ropes, and the rafts with the elephants standing on them were rapidly pulled away from the causeway. At this the animals panicked and at first turned round and began to move about in all directions, but as they were by then surrounded on all sides by the stream, their fear eventually compelled them to stay quiet... but some became so terror-stricken that they leaped into the river when they were half-way across. The drivers of these were all drowned, but the elephants were saved, because through the power and length of their trunks they were able to keep these above the surface and breathe through them. (Polybius, 219)

Elephants are excellent swimmers, but these animals had lived for decades in arid Spain and had not practiced swimming, thus they feared the river. Though all 37 pachyderms reached the far side as planned, their

Hannibal Crosses the Rhone. Hannibal's elephants did cross the Rhone River on rafts but did not wear towers at the time. (Engraving by Henri-Paul Motte, n.d., circa 1880s.)

experienced mahouts were all dead. This would be a costly disaster for Hannibal, who lost the skilled elephant riders. Now several days behind schedule, the Carthaginians had to rush to the Alps. If they began the crossing too late, snow would make the trails impassable.

The army started up the western side of the Alps in mid-October. The barbarian guides were treacherous and led the army along narrow trails and into dead ends, while mountain tribes dropped stones and showered them with arrows. Not many soldiers died, but whole lines of pack animals panicked and fell over the cliffs to their deaths, taking food supplies with them. As the army climbed above the tree line, the food ran out. A huge boulder across the narrow path blocked the path for three days before engineers could crack it and push it aside. Ice and snow caused the route to become slippery, while lack of food caused the elephants and men to lose weight and lose strength. By the time the Carthaginian force stumbled out of the Alps into northern Italy, Hannibal had lost two-thirds of his army in the cold mountains.

All 37 elephants survived the Alps crossing, but they were weak. The Romans quickly dispatched an army to hit the Carthaginians before they could regain strength. Hannibal used ambushes and superior cavalry to destroy the legions, but 36 elephants died at the Battle of the Trebbia. The last remaining beast, named Surus, became Hannibal's steed, and remained so for the next 15 years. From various bits of information derived from Roman historians and poets, it seems that Surus was an Asian elephant, with only one tusk, and he often wore a red blanket with a red shield on Hannibal's howdah seat. (Scullard, 175)

Hannibal roamed up and down Italy for more than a decade, crushing any army that the Romans sent out, yet he could not capture Rome, lacking siege equipment and the manpower needed. Rome sent legions under Scipio, a young commander, to take Hispania away from Hasdrubal Barca. Using brilliant formation tactics, Scipio defeated each Carthaginian army to face him. Hasdrubal was barely able to slip away, and he marched with his army across Europe to cross the Alps and reinforce Hannibal.

Hasdrubal crossed the Alps without difficulty, but the Romans intercepted a messenger and knew where to expect the new Carthaginian army. Two consular armies were waiting. Hasdrubal had 10 elephants, but the Romans pelted the animals with arrows and javelins. Six died; four fled and were later captured. The Romans tossed Hasdrubal's head into Hannibal's camp the next day. (Polybius, 425)

The following year, Mago Barca raised an army, and seven elephants, but once again the Romans intercepted them in northern Italy and destroyed the force. Scipio, having conquered Hispania, landed his legions in North Africa to attack Carthage. Hannibal and a small part of his army got into ships and sailed home to Africa to protect the capital.

Carthage sent an army to oppose Scipio before Hannibal returned. Pretending to make peace, the Romans spied the African camp and made a sneak attack at night, setting fire to the barracks and stables. One hundred elephants were burned to death chained in their stalls, along with numerous horses. (Herbert, 125)

Hannibal arrived to find a battered army of conscripts and 80 newly captured elephants. With Scipio marching toward Carthage, he could not spend time training his rabble, though he did have a core of veterans from the war in Italy. The Romans bribed some of the Numidian cavalry to join the legions, and for the first time, Hannibal was at a cavalry disadvantage.

Perhaps hoping that the elephants might cause disorder in the Roman infantry, Hannibal sent all 80 animals charging straight ahead in the front line at the Battle of Zama. These Romans were veterans, and Scipio knew how to deal with elephants: he had faced them repeatedly in Hispania.

Scipio deployed his army in lines rather than the normal checkerboard formation, leaving nice paths for the elephants to run through. He gave trumpets to thousands of the legionnaires, so that when the elephants charged, his men all blew their horns. The tremendous racket terrified the animals. Some of them ran right down the open lanes to the rear, and other pachyderms turned back and damaged their own African allied infantry. Eleven elephants died; the rest were later captured. (Polybius, 475)

Hannibal was defeated. Carthage signed a peace treaty, vowing never again to train elephants and ending the Second Punic War. Hannibal had to flee to Eastern Europe when Roman assassins came looking for him. For a few years, Hannibal worked as a mercenary general, until the Romans found him, and he took poison.

But Rome feared Carthage too much to let it continue. Without provocation, Rome invaded and laid siege to the city. The starving people called on the gods to bring back their dead war elephants to save them. In 146 BC, Rome took 50,000 slaves, killed the rest, and destroyed the city utterly.

Roman Elephants

A basalt monument found on the coast of Eritrea tells how the Egyptian navy under Ptolemy III Euergetes captured elephants from Sudan and Ethiopia for war, thus continuing the work of his father and grandfather. For hundreds of years, the Syrians and Egyptians periodically fought, usually in Palestine. In 246 BC the Egyptians captured many Syrian elephants in a great victory. (Scullard, 134, 138)

According to Jewish belief, Ptolemy IV Philopater became angry at the Jews and ordered the Alexandrian Jews to be trampled by "a horde of elephants," but the beasts refused. (Encyclopedia Judaica, 1348)

The only battle of history where Asian elephants fought against African pachyderms was at Raphia in 217 BC. The Syrians fielded over 100 animals, while Egypt deployed 73. Polybius wrote that "most of Ptolemy's elephants were afraid to join battle, as is the habit of African elephants; for unable to stand the smell and the trumpeting of the Indian elephants, and terrified, I suppose, also by their great size and strength, they immediately run away from them before they get near them." The African elephants in use by Carthage and Egypt were the small forest species, not the gigantic savanna animals, which has led modern skeptics to doubt the ancient historians who called Asian pachyderms larger and stronger. (Scullard, 139–40)

The battle of Raphia was a draw. The Syrians' elephant victory did not help the loss of their infantry. However, Ptolemy was angry at the elephant defeat and actually sacrificed some of the surviving animals to the sun god and canceled the war elephant capture programs in the south. Henceforth, all nations would come to believe that African war elephants were inferior to Asian elephants, so the two species did not meet again on a battlefield.

The Syrians continued to buy or trade for elephants from India for use in war. The Battle of Pania in 200 BC was fought in two different parts of the field. In the main charge, elephants defeated the Egyptians quickly. In the secondary battle, the Egyptians caused the Syrian soldiers to flee, but a line of elephants slowed the enemy pursuit, and the northerners regrouped and counterattacked. The success at Pania returned Judea to Syrian control. (Bar-Kochva, 154)

At about this time, Scipio Africanus defeated Hannibal at Carthage. Rome then turned its anger against Greece, which had allied with Carthage. The Romans invaded Greece and took elephants in their legions. The oft-repeated "truth" that Rome despised elephants as useless in combat is utterly false. Romans, in fact, used pachyderms frequently; they just did not brag about it, preferring to credit their famous infantry, not animals. The military historian Hans Delbruck grudgingly admits the Roman fondness for elephants. (Delbruck, 562)

In 199 BC the legions arrived at Lyncestis, but the Greeks would not leave their fortress. Consul Flaminius asked King Massinissa of Numidia to send more elephants. At Cynoscephalae two years later, when the Greek phalanx infantry attacked the legions and pushed them back, Flaminius sent elephants against the Greeks' left flank, breaking their formations completely. (Scullard, 179)

Hannibal escaped to the east and joined up with Antiochus III of Syria, who had defeated Egypt at Pania with his elephants. When Antiochus invaded eastern Greece in 192 BC with Hannibal hired as advisor, Rome panicked. The Roman army again asked Numidia for elephants and received 15. The Italians pushed the easterners back, but the Asian elephants of Antiochus hampered the pursuit. In the Battle of Magnesia, Antiochus possessed three times as many elephants as the Romans, so the Romans kept theirs in reserve.

The Seleucids, rulers descended from Seleucus of Syria, including Antiochus, deployed elephants in groups of 8, called "ile" (squadron), or 16, called "elephantarchia" (herd). When the Romans gained the advantage, the Syrian phalanx infantry formed into defensive squares with elephants in the center. Roman archers then pelted the pachyderms with arrows and javelins, so the animals rampaged and broke through their own formations, leading to the defeat of the 50,000 Syrian troops. Only 15 Asian elephants "escaped alive on that day of slaughter." (Kincaid, 179; Rennie, 229)

For peace, Rome demanded that Antiochus no longer keep war elephants.

Rome, always paranoid about the loyalty of conquered nations, began to doubt Greece again in 171 BC. Preparing to strike the Greeks the Romans obtained 22 elephants from Numidia and found 12 of the elephants from the Battle of Magnesia—old veterans, as well. Immediately the Roman army began suffering shortages of food. An elephant eats about 10 times as much as a cavalry horse, a few hundred pounds of fodder per day, and Greece was not a good place for grazing. (Roth, 61–64)

The Roman elephants defeated the Greek cavalry under King Perseus at Phalanna. We know this because Perseus immediately started an unusual program. "In order to make sure that the beasts should prove a source of terror to the horses, he constructed images of elephants and smeared them with some kind of ointment to give them a dreadful odour. They were terrible both to see and to hear, since they were skilfully arranged to emit a roar resembling thunder; and he would repeatedly lead the horses up to these figures until they gained courage." Perseus also trained a brigade of special "elephant-fighters" with spiked helmets and spiked shields to try to keep the pachyderms at bay. (Dio, v.2, 307)

In June 168 BC the Romans and Greeks fought at Pydna. Again, the Greek phalanxes pushed back the legions, but the elephants flanked the heavy infantry again to end the Third Macedonian War.

The Roman legions also used African elephants frequently to pacify the tribes of Hispania, which they had taken from Carthage during the war with Hannibal. As usual, the effectiveness of Roman troops depended greatly on the leadership ability of their generals. Consul Q. Fulvius Nobilor sent the Roman army and elephants up to the walls of a fortified city, where a Spaniard dropped a heavy stone on an elephant's head. The wounded beast shrieked and fled, causing the whole elephant corps to trample the Romans in retreat. A decade later, one selfish Roman commander, angry at being replaced, took away all the elephant and cavalry food, letting them starve.

The supplier of Rome's elephants, the North African province of Numidia, became hostile to Rome and stopped sending pachyderms. For years, the Numidians used guerrilla tactics to keep the legions at bay. In 108 BC, the Numidians hid 44 elephants in a thick forest near the Muthul River, intending to ambush the Romans. Instead, the elephants were spotted, and they were unable to maneuver in the thick brush. The Romans killed 40 pachyderms and sent the remainder back to Rome for parades.

Polyaenus wrote that Julius Caesar took one elephant to Britain to terrify the tribesmen, with great success, but many historians deny the story because Caesar did not mention the incident in his own commentary. After the invasion of Britain Caesar did immediately mint a coin with an elephant trampling a dragon: the dragon was the symbol of Britain. Julius would get much more experience with elephants in future years, when allies of Pompey in North Africa opposed him. To help his men learn how to oppose the African elephants in battle, Caesar brought a few circus elephants from Rome. "[Caesar] had ordered elephants to be brought across from Italy to enable our troops not only to become familiar with them, but also to get to know both the appearance and capabilities of the beast, what part of its body was readily vulnerable to a missile and, when an elephant was accoutered and armoured, what part of its body was still left uncovered and unprotected, so that their missiles should be aimed at the spot.... the cavalry hurled dummy javelins at them; and the docility of the beasts had brought the horses to feel at home with them." (Caesar, 259)

At the battle of Thapsus in 46 BC, Caesar's men successfully drove away most of the 64 enemy elephants using arrows and sling-stones. One pachyderm did crash into the Roman camp, but a veteran soldier hacked the animal's trunk with his *gladius* (sword), causing the beast to retreat. Caesar later captured all of the animals and used them to terrify a rebellious nearby town. (ibid., 281)

It seems that Julius Caesar took all of these elephants to Rome, in the hope of starting a breeding herd. He was preparing for a campaign against the Parthians in the east, who relied almost entirely upon cavalry. Soon, however, Caesar was murdered.

After Julius Caesar, the Romans found much less use for elephants. The long Pax Romana, peaceful decades during the reign of Caesar Augustus, reduced the need for war elephants. Simultaneously, the wealth of Italy brought a huge increase in the importation of ivory. The forest elephants of Africa, once respected as martial colleagues, quickly became targets for destruction. In less than a century, the North African elephants were driven nearly to extinction by the Roman lust for ivory trinkets.

Elephants in the Middle East

The Seleucids, after the defeat at the Battle of Magnesia, continued to train and use war elephants, in part because Rome did not seem interested in the Middle East. Antiochus IV Epiphanes ("God Manifest") invaded Egypt, but a Roman legate threatened that Rome would attack Syria if Egypt was not abandoned immediately. Subdued, but angry, Epiphanes marched home. Judea staged a revolt, and the angry Seleucids stormed Jerusalem, installed an idol of Zeus in the Jewish Temple, and left an army to stamp out Judaism. (Dio, 361)

A family of zealous Jews started a guerrilla war of resistance against the Syrians, known as the Wars of the Maccabees (167–160 BC). Five brothers—John, Simon, Judas, Eleazar, and Jonathan—gathered warriors to oppose the troops of Epiphanes. By December 164 BC, Judas Maccabeus had retaken Jerusalem and started the tradition of Hanukkah by purifying the temple. The Seleucids counterattacked with an army including 32 war elephants and 32 soldiers guarding each elephant. Eleazar saw that the elephants were causing panic among his Jewish troops, so he charged alone under an elephant and stabbed it deeply from beneath. The animal died and fell atop Eleazar, killing him. Losing courage, the Maccabean army retreated. As the enemy advanced, the Syrians were ambushed in narrow valleys where the elephants could not effectively maneuver, and the Seleucids were defeated. The state of Judea became independent and remained so for 100 years. (Sekunda, 9–11, 28)

The Seleucids had more difficulty acquiring elephants in these years, so they worked hard to improve the armor of their pachyderms. They designed armored leggings to prevent hamstring attacks and they designed scale armor with the plates facing upward, to reduce dangers from spearmen. The Syrians put armor over the leather cinch that kept the howdah on the elephant's back, to stop enemies from hacking the strap to bring down the tower. They produced an ornate elephant helmet with a fan-shaped metal shield for the mahout to hide behind. (ibid., 72)

The Seleucids were finally driven out of power by the Parthians in 130 BC, when 20 Asian elephants caught Antiochus VII by surprise in winter camp and completely destroyed the Syrian army.

The Parthians of Persia used elephants in coordination with their cavalry armies. Occasionally Roman legions would try to destroy the swift Persians, but they rarely succeeded. In AD 115, Emperor Trajan captured the Parthian capital of Ctesiphon on the Tigris River. The *carroballista*, a rapid-firing catapult that fired large darts, had great success against the Parthian elephants. (Gaebel, 229)

Though the Romans were victorious, a new enemy rose from the ashes of Parthia, called the Sassanids, who collected hundreds of elephants for battle. Emperor Severus lost the battle against 700 armored pachyderms, but called it a victory because the Romans captured 18 elephants. Because of Persian pressure in the east, and weakness in Rome itself, Emperor Valerian divided the empire into eastern and western sectors. The Romans also hired more mercenary cavalrymen to face the growing numbers of horse-borne enemies. The Sassanids invaded Mesopotamia, captured Valerian, removed his skin, stuffed it with straw, and hung it as a trophy in a temple. (Montgomery, 124)

The Persians rode south as far as Ethiopia, using heavily armored horses called *cataphracts*, where they were surprised to meet a strong army of Kushites. "The main point of resistance, some way back, was a line of armoured elephants carrying on their backs towers manned by bowmen... many of the cataphracts succeeded in getting through this first line of defence and bore down on the elephants; but they were met by such a cloud of arrows aimed at their eyes that most of them were soon immobilized, and the survivors, having tried in vain to break through the solid barrier presented by the bodies of the elephants, retired in disorder." This battle is the last we hear of Kushite war elephants. (Rattenbury, 114)

The Sassanids came to believe that Christians were Roman spies. Shapur II sent 300 elephants to destroy the city of Susa, whose population was mostly Christian. Shapur also laid siege to the city of Nisibis. Christians believe that Saint James, a local bishop, prayed for pests to annoy the besiegers. Gnats and mosquitoes threw the elephants and horses into confusion, wrote Theodoret. Twelve years later, Shapur II returned with a new strategy. Diverting a nearby river, he created a lake around Nisibis, which weakened the wall and caused a huge section to collapse. Wishing to take advantage of the fallen wall before the city-dwellers could make repairs, the king ordered the troops to immediately charge ahead into the water and mud. "The horses became quickly entangled in the ooze and mud which the waters had left behind them as they subsided; the elephants were even less able to overcome these difficulties, and as soon as they received a wound sank down, never to rise again, in the swamp." (Rawlinson, *Seventh*, 163–64)

Emperor Julian left Constantinople, the capital of the eastern Roman empire, at modern Istanbul, to strike Shapur II's base at Ctesiphon. The march took too long, and the Romans were running out of supplies, so they headed home. The Sassanids pursued and harassed the rear of the Roman column. On June 26, 363, the Persians launched a surprise attack. Javelin-throwers on the backs of Sassanid elephants sent the Romans into confusion, and Julian was hit by a javelin and killed. (Rawlinson, *Seventh,* 226–28)

The year 571, called "The Year of the Elephant," is the start of the story of Muhammad and the Islamic religion. The Christian king Abraha of Yemen intended to destroy Mecca, and he took war elephants along for the battle. According to some histories, as the army approached Mecca, the lead elephant stopped, knelt down, and refused to go any farther. The rest of the elephants would not budge while the leader had halted, so the army stopped. Then a plague, or miracle, struck the army of Abraha, who were forced to retreat. The Koran says that God had dealt with the army of the elephant. (Sykes, 509)

Civil wars had weakened the Sassanid Empire. Muhammad's following grew quickly, and soon the Arab expansion threatened Persia itself. In 634, the Arab cavalry fled before the Sassanid pachyderms. Abu Obeidah dismounted his horse and ran ahead to attack the main elephant, to inspire his troops to regroup, but the beast grabbed him in fury and crushed him underfoot. His army fled. (Rawlinson, *Seventh,* 216–217)

Two years later, a three-day battle at Cadesia saw the Muslims better prepared for anti-elephant warfare. Archers distracted the animals while Muslim footmen ran to cut the straps that held the howdahs. The strategy worked, but the Persian infantry drove back the attackers. On day two, the Muslims tried charging with horses and camels "dressed up to resemble elephants." The Persian horses did shy away and flee, but the victory was not complete. On the final day, the Arab infantry attacked the elephants' eyes. When they drove a spear into the lead elephant's eye, and a second animal lost an eye to a missile, the whole pachyderm force turned in retreat. The Arabs were victorious. (Sykes, 495)

Elephants of Asia

The Ceylon Chronicle (of Sri Lanka) includes many stories about war elephants. One poetic tale from about 150 BC tells of King Dutugamunu and his elephant Kandula trying to capture an enemy city.

> The city had three moats, and was guarded by a high wall. Its gate was covered with iron hard for foes to shatter. The elephant knelt on

his knees and, battering with his tusks stone and mortar and brick, he attacked the iron gate. The Tamils from the watch-tower threw missiles of every kind, balls of red-hot iron and [vessels of] molten pitch. Down fell the smoking pitch upon Kandula's back. In anguish of pain he fled and plunged into a pool of water. "This is no drinking bout!" cried Gothaimbara. "Go, batter the iron gate! Batter down the gate!" In his pride the best of tuskers took heart and trumpeted loud. He reared up out of the water and stood on the bank defiant. The elephant-doctor washed away the pitch, and put on balm. The King mounted the elephant and rubbed his brow with his hand. "Dear Kandula, I'll make you the lord of all Ceylon!" he said, and

Asian commanders could see the battlefield better on elephant-back. (Photograph taken by the author in Thailand.) (Courtesy John Kistler.)

the beast was cheered and fed with the best of fodder. He was covered with a cloth, and he was armoured well with armour for his back of seven-fold buffalo hide. On the armour was placed a skin soaked in oil. Then, trumpeting like thunder, he came on, fearless of danger. He pierced the door with his tusks. With his feet he trampled the threshold. And the gate and the lintel crashed loudly to the earth. (Basham, 459–60)

At least 2,000 years ago, the Gajashastra, a compendium of veterinary science of the elephant, accurately identified treatments for pachyderm wounds and maladies. Elephants were highly prized and received the best possible medical care in India. (Bandopadhyay, 9–10)

According to legend, in AD 40 the Trung sisters of Vietnam freed their people from the Chinese, riding elephants into battle. The Champan army (of Vietnam) used war elephants against invading Chinese in AD 605. (Scigliano, 120)

Scholars and historians often call the vast numbers of war elephants claimed by Asian armies "exaggerations." This is partially a misunderstanding of the term "war elephants." When an Asian source states that the army owned 60,000 war elephants, but only 5,000 animals fought in the battle, it is not a contradiction. Only a small percentage of pachyderms in an army can actually fight: a majority are simple baggage carriers and pack animals.

Sultan Mahmud and his descendants the Ghaznavids ruled much of Asia from the 10th through 12th centuries. The Muslim Ghaznavids tried many new tactics with elephants, including a battering ram for bashing city walls or gates, using five animals: presumably four carrying the ram between them, with the fifth swinging the ram. Mahmud fought one battle in the winter of 1007–1008 in deep snow. "[T]he execution wrought in their ranks by the Sultan's elephants completed their demoralisation. One of the elephants, lifting Ilah Khan's standard-bearer in his trunk, hurled him into the air and then catching him on his steel-clad tusks, cut the wretch in two, while others threw down riders from their horses and trampled them to death." Tusk swords became a common weapon on the battlefield. The elephant's tusks would be shortened, then iron or steel swords fitted to the ends. (Bosworth, 118; Nazim, 35, 151)

During one invasion, saboteurs made a daring night raid on Mahmud's elephant camp. They gave powerful drugs to many elephants, and the animals went berserk, destroying the camp. Some brave mahouts were able to gain control of the crazed pachyderms and lead them away. Before normal battles, mahouts frequently provided alcohol or drugs to inflame the pachyderms to violence or courage. By creating rituals, like the beating of drums and drinking of wine before battle, the animals became accustomed to the excitement and more apt to fight. (Ranking, 277; Bosworth, 116)

64 Kubla Khan on four elephants

Marco Polo's exaggerated tale of the magnificent howdah of Kublai Khan of the Mongols. (*Historical Researches,* by John Ranking. London: Longman, Rees, Orme, Brown, and Green, 1826, Plate 64.)

The Mongols invaded Muslim territories in the early 13th century. Genghis Khan did not have much interest in elephants, but Kublai Khan kept up to 5,000 for carrying his lavish caravan and baggage. In Burma in 1277, the Mongol cavalry would not approach the enemy elephants, so the men dismounted at a distance and showered the animals with arrows until they fled the field. In 1298 the Mongols failed to take India, largely because of 2,700 enemy elephants. (Ranking, 84)

A Burmese general named Si Lunfa attacked southwestern China in 1388 with an intriguing and inexpensive piece of equipment to protect the elephants' sides. Bamboo tubes hung down at the animal's side at the horizontal, with spear-points dotting the bamboo, thus creating a sort of spiked collar to keep enemy troops from trying to climb up to harm the riders. The clever armor did not actually help the battle, however. The Chinese used crossbows to panic the pachyderms. According to one source, soldiers trained to walk on stilts so they could attack men on elephant-back. (Elvin, 15; Hamid, 48)

Timur, also known as Tamerlane, invaded India in 1398. The Sultan of Delhi had only 120 war elephants because long civil wars had drained his power. New technologies had increased the number of weapons available for use on elephant-back, however. Gunpowder, called Chinese snow, brought small rockets and hand-grenade hurlers to howdahs. Timur's men were terrified of the elephants, almost to the edge of mutiny, forcing him to take action. He built palisades of sharp stakes to ensure that the elephants would not charge their camp. He tied buffaloes from the baggage train with dried brambles on their heads, ready to be lit, to frighten the elephants if they charged. Tamerlane also had his blacksmiths produce hundreds of spiked tetrahedral caltrops to throw in front of the pachyderms before battle. (Ranking, 133–34)

In fact, none of these precautions were necessary. Tamerlane won the battle without much difficulty. Purportedly he wanted to see the captured elephants weep for losing the battle, so he had snuff rubbed into their eyes to make their eyes water.

Tamerlane kept the elephants with his army and marched to the Middle East. Damascus was so terrified of the elephants that the city surrendered when the first pachyderms appeared at the gate.

Execution by Elephants. (Engraving by Butler.) (*An Illustrated History of the Holy Bible,* by John Kitto. Norwich, CT: Henry Bill, 1868, p. 441.)

Elephants of Thailand

For 50 years, about AD 1540 through 1590, Thailand and Burma fought each other, often using elephants. Queen Suriyothai and her daughter rode with King Manacharapad against Burmese invaders, gaining a short-lived victory. When Thailand was liberated from Burma, the saying arose, "Thailand won its freedom on the backs of elephants." (Scigliano, 120)

The Mughal or Mogul dynasty ruled India through the 16th and 17th centuries. Akbar, one of their greatest rulers, adored elephants. He had special aptitude for riding the most violent pachyderms, enjoying the thrill of personal combat and sport. His armorers developed a special armor called lamellar, made of small overlapping plates laced together over cloth, thus providing a flexible, lightweight, and effective protection. During an attack on a Hindu fortress in 1568, an elephant named Jangia killed 30 enemies before a foe hacked off its trunk. Jangia continued to fight, killing 15 more foes before dying of its wounds. (Leong, 58–64)

Although mentioned in documents as early as the sixth century AD, trunk weapons appear most frequently during the life of Akbar and his successors. A trunk weapon is carried by the elephant in its trunk, as opposed to swords simply mounted on its tusks. The most common trunk weapon was the chain mace. A heavy piece of metal slung back and forth by the elephant could effectively smash man or horse without presenting much danger to the animal itself. Some accounts tell of trunk swords and scythes up to three feet long.

The Mughals treated their war elephants with the greatest respect and love. The king's favorites received the royal treatment, having their own tents, their own cooks, and even a personalized silken cord with which the king could measure the animals' girths to see if they were maintaining their weight.

In spite of the special care provided to Asian war elephants by their keepers, the development of more accurate and larger cannons and guns would doom the huge animals.

Colonial and Modern War Elephants

After Rome fell in the fourth century AD, Europe forgot about elephants. The only pachyderm to appear in Europe for hundreds of years was a gift from the Muslim Caliph Harun, sent to Charlemagne (also called Charles the Great). Charlemagne sent a Jewish ambassador to visit the caliph and asked if he might send an elephant. One beast, named Abul Abbas, sailed west to Italy. Abul Abbas marched to Germany in a grand caravan of gifts from the east, much to the delight of astonished peasants along the path. Charles the Great had a home built for the elephant in Augsburg, where the animal loved to swim in the Rhine River. In 804, the Danes invaded Belgium, and Charles took Abul Abbas on campaign with the army, but he did not fight. The elephant died several years later, perhaps of pneumonia, and some believe that a famous set of chess pieces left by Charlemagne was carved from his tusks. (Hodges, Richard)

More than 400 years later, Emperor Frederick II, Holy Roman emperor (1194–1250), fought in the Crusades and returned to Europe with an elephant. After winning a battle near opponents in Milan, Italy, Frederick rode in a chariot pulled by the pachyderm.

In 1621 the Turks known as the Zaporozhian Cossacks invaded the Ukraine and Poland with a huge army, including four elephants. This was the last invasion of Europe by elephants. In the future it was Europe that would be invading the elephants' lands in Asia and Africa.

European powers such as Great Britain and Portugal would ask small nations for exclusive trading rights, and if refused, brought in armies to conquer the countries. Even with tiny militias, the Europeans could defeat huge enemy armies because they had superior weapons and better tactics.

The Elephant rescuing a Soldier.

The Elephant Rescuing a Soldier. (*The Intelligence of Animals with Illustrative Anecdotes,* from the French of Ernest Menault. New York: Charles Scribner & Co., 1870.)

Plus, Asians and Africans relied too heavily on their leaders. The British might just shoot the enemy king or general off of his elephant and watch his whole army flee.

Once in power, the colonial conquerors learned to use elephants for themselves, though never in a frontline position. Elephants became the bearers of artillery pieces for the army in India until 1895. During the Abyssinian War (Ethiopia) of 1868, 44 elephants pulled cannons over hundreds of miles of mountainous desert. British artillery batteries during the war with Burma included nine elephants and 290 bullocks. During the Nepal War of 1814–1815, the British army under General Ochterlony had all of its supplies carried by elephants and human porters. (Holder, 255; Sutton and Walker, 38)

During the siege of Paris in 1870, part of the Franco-Prussian War, the Germans used circus elephants to pull heavy artillery pieces across difficult terrain. A pachyderm from the Hamburg Zoo may have moved heavy equipment for the Germans in World War I. Other elephants, from the

Elephants pulling British cannons in India, 1892. (Courtesy Library of Congress.)

Hagenbeck Circus and Animal Show in Berlin, pulled coal carts around the city. (Koenig, 184)

World War II saw the surprising and effective return of elephants to the battlefield. In 1942, a swift Japanese invasion swept across Burma because the Japanese stole mahouts and their elephants from logging companies working in the teak forests. The Japanese army units were able to traverse otherwise impassable jungles to reach deep into enemy territory. The British gathered as many logging elephants and mahouts as they could, but to use for engineering tasks of clearing roads and building bridges.

The Japanese elephants suffered badly, because most commanders feared they would run away, so they were kept chained in camp. Thus kept from grazing, the animals starved. British Royal Air Force pilots were also ordered to strafe and bomb Japanese elephant columns. Of an estimated 6,000 elephants used by the Japanese, only 1,652 were recovered after the war. The best-selling book *Elephant Bill* by Lt. Col. John H. Williams tells the story of elephant laborers in World War II. Williams used his elephant Bandoola (and 53 other elephants) to evacuate sick women and children from Burma as the Japanese advanced. (Cooper, 154; Ruthven, 16)

Allied elephants built log bridges using local materials and helped the British and Americans clear paths to enable attacks on the Japanese. The British discovered that eight elephants could carry a disassembled Bofors anti-aircraft gun on their backs. Unfortunately, General Wingate forced one mahout to badly overload a female elephant to cross a river. She sank and drowned under the heavy equipment. (Cooper, 152)

The U.S. Air Transport Command used elephants at airstrips from which planes carried supplies and heavy drums of fuel to China. General Turner trained elephants to move the fuel drums into the airplanes and also to tow disabled planes from the runways.

The U.S. military only faced elephants during one war: Vietnam. The North Vietnamese used elephants to carry cargo through the jungles, thus avoiding the heavily bombed Ho Chi Minh Trail. The 559th Transportation Group was one unit using elephants to carry goods through Laos. To stop the flow of munitions and supplies to enemy forces, the U.S. Air Force ordered its pilots to strafe and bomb elephants. When a pilot from Helicopter Squadron 265 asked how he was to recognize "friendly" elephants from enemy elephants, he was told to look for mud on their legs and stomachs,

Elephant battery along the Khyber Pass, circa 1895. (Courtesy the
Library of Congress.)

Peshawar Mountain Train. Elephants being loaded with cannons for
transport in India. (*Illustrated London News*, Jan. 31, 1857, p. 87.)

indicating the animals had been on trails. In general, though, the pilots just shot any elephant sighted in "unfriendly" regions of the country. (Beckett, 104; Prados, 44, 221)

In one incident, made famous by the 1995 Disney movie *Operation Dumbo Drop*, the military planned to deliver trained elephants to a friendly village. One plan was to push elephants, wearing giant parachutes, out the back of a C-130E cargo plane. The air force insisted that the animals be heavily drugged, lest they panic and smash the planes from the inside. This plan was abandoned, and instead, four drugged pachyderms were carried away by helicopters in a giant net. Unfortunately, the media attention alerted the Vietcong to the plan. When the helicopters dropped off the elephants near the village, they machine-gunned the elephants. Three died, and one escaped into the jungle. (Morris, Jim, 62)

The only region on Earth that still uses war elephants is Burma, or Myanmar. Myanmar has been ruled by a military junta for almost 20 years. The Karen and Mon peoples of southern Burma have been waging a guerrilla insurgency against Myanmar, using 20 to 30 elephants as porters for ammunition and weapons.

The long history of man and elephant fighting together is nearly ended.

3

Horses

Chariot Horses

On the American continent, horses ran free until about 9,000 years ago, when they suddenly vanished. Humans might have eaten horses at the time, but since sloths and mastodons became extinct around the same time, the widespread destruction of mammal species remains a mystery. For this reason, the history of equines in the military is largely a subject of Europe, Asia, and Africa. (Edwards, 23)

The domestication of dogs long preceded that of other species including oxen, sheep, and horses: the relationship was simpler. The human/dog bond is more of companionship in a side-by-side manner, and mistakes in the relationship are rarely fatal. By exploiting the superior senses of hearing and smell in canines, mankind greatly increased its capacity for hunting, expanding the potential of civilizations for fast growth. Humans' comparatively poor senses no longer hindered their ability to find food, with the help of dogs. Now they needed speed. "Highly intelligent, yet as a biped agonizingly slow, man would learn to harness the horse's speed and strength through domestication of Equus Caballus...a partnership of the world's brainiest biped and the world's fastest quadruped." (Kelekna, 20)

Bedouin tradition holds that the archangel Gabriel assisted God in creating the horse and that Noah's great-great-grandson Baz was the first to attempt domestication of wild horses in Yemen and thereafter the Arabian horse. Scholars cannot rule out the involvement of a man named Baz, but

Depiction of an ancient horse-drawn wagon, an early chariot.
(Mary Evans Picture Library.)

Yemen is not the generally accepted region for the beginnings of horse training. (Edwards, 30–33)

Horses would become the primary transportation system for humans. No one is certain when the first horses were tamed and selectively bred, though the domestication of horses certainly started between 4500 and 3000 BC on the Eurasian steppes that stretch from Eastern Europe to China. The Botai culture in the Kazakh region shows evidence of organized horse rearing. (Kelekna, 1, 22, 29, 35; Gaebel, 32; Edwards, 29)

Men did not choose horses as weapons, per se, since equines are not fighters. In fact, equines tend to be panicky at signs of danger.

Another curious emotional feature in the horse is the liability of all the other mental faculties of the animal to become abandoned to that of terror. For I think I am right in saying that the horse is the only animal which, under the influence of fear, loses the possession of every other sense in one mad and mastering desire to run. With its entire mental life thus overwhelmed by the flood of a single emotion, the horse not only loses, as other animals lose, "presence of mind," or a due balance among the distinctively intellectual faculties, but even

the avenues of special sense become stopped, so that the wholly de-
mented animal may run headlong and at terrific speed against a stone
wall. (Romanes, 329)

This propensity of the horse to panic requires human riders to train the
animals thoroughly. The rider must exude confidence. Horses can sense
fear in other horses, and in their riders, probably through the changing
smell of sweat. Though humans can rally themselves to greater courage in
the face of fear, once horses become frightened, it is very difficult to calm
them. (DiMarco, 77)

Charles Darwin rode horses and made careful observations in regard
to their fear and anger.

Horses when savage draw their ears closely back, protrude their heads,
and partially uncover their incisor teeth, ready for biting…When
pleased, as when some coveted food is brought to them in the stable,
they raise and draw in their heads, prick their ears, and looking intently
toward their friend, often whinny. Impatience is expressed by pawing
the ground. The actions of a horse when much startled are highly ex-
pressive. One day my horse was much frightened at a drilling machine,
covered by a tarpaulin, and lying on an open field. He raised his head
so high, that his neck became almost perpendicular; and this he did
from habit, for the machine lay on a slope below, and could not have
been seen with more distinctness through the raising of the head…His
eyes and ears were directed intently forwards; and I could feel through
the saddle the palpitations of his heart. With red dilated nostrils he
snorted violently, and whirling round, would have dashed off at full
speed, had I not prevented him. The distention of the nostrils is not for
the sake of scenting the source of danger, for when a horse smells carefully at any object and is not alarmed, he does not dilate his nostrils.
Owing to the presence of a valve in the throat, a horse when panting
does not breathe through his open mouth, but through his nostrils; and
these consequently have become endowed with great powers of expansion. This expansion of the nostrils, as well as the snorting, and the palpitations of the heart, are actions which have become firmly associated
during a long series of generations with the emotion of terror; for terror has habitually led the horse to the most violent exertion in dashing
away at full speed from the cause of danger. (Darwin, 128–29)

Horse Fights

Horses can fight, but they rarely do. In a herd, one stallion rules the mares and foals. If another male approaches his herd, there will be a vicious fight. If one horse goes down during the combat, the standing animal tries to break the opponent's legs, kicking for damage, sometimes even killing the challenger. Stallions do rear up to kick, but generally mares will kick only with their hind legs, or they will spray urine against their attackers. (Kelekna, 17–18, 39)

Horses were not much ridden in the first 2,000 years of domestication. Ancient equines were considerably smaller than the modern horse. As humans intentionally bred stronger beasts to each other, this artificial selection created progressively larger animals. What did horses do before carrying riders? Pull carts.

The marvelous invention of the wheel did not come until about 3500 BC. Before wheels became common, horses pulled people and cargo on sledges, sleds with runners, not only for use in snow. For more information about ancient carts, see chapter 7. Oxen, donkeys, and teams of horses pulled sledges and heavy wagons. Over the centuries, improvements in wheels and the use of lighter-weight materials lightened the carts. (Hyams, 19)

Carts for use in battle were called chariots. The earliest chariots were heavy four-wheeled wagons, used as early as 2600 BC in China. Horses, at this time, were becoming more common in the grasslands of the steppes but rarely appeared in the more arid Mesopotamia. In 2100 BC there is a written record about domestic horses, yet 300 years later, the famous Code of Hammurabi offers no laws about horses. With carts being so heavy, while horses remained small and uncommon, oxen and donkeys were more commonly used. (Hamid, 3; Hodges, Henry, 104; Hyams, 18)

Perhaps the oldest literary reference to chariot horses comes from the Bible book of Job, chapter 39, verses 19–25. "Do you give the horse his strength or clothe his neck with a flowing mane. Do you make him leap like a locust, striking terror with his proud snorting? He paws fiercely, rejoicing in his strength, and charges into the fray. He laughs at fear, afraid of nothing; he does not shy away from the sword. The quiver rattles against his side, along with the flashing spear and lance. In frenzied excitement he eats up the ground; he cannot stand still when the trumpet sounds. At the blast of the trumpet he snorts, 'Aha!' He catches the scent of battle from afar, the shout of commanders and the battle cry." (NIV translation)

Technological improvements allowed chariots to shrink, while horses grew larger. One way to lighten the vehicles was to trade solid wooden wheels for spoked wheels. In Anatolia (Turkey) circa 1900 BC the chariot carried two soldiers: a driver and an ax-bearing warrior, pulled by two horses, with the reins running through nose rings. Once the army vehicle weighed less than 100 pounds, it was light enough for horses to pull, and the military recognized that horses were far swifter than oxen and donkeys. The old ox-drawn battle wagon carried men to battle at a speed of less than 2 miles per hour. The new horse-drawn chariots could fly at 20 miles per hour, a tenfold increase in speed. (Kelekna, 52, 65; Smith, 8)

Almost overnight, horses went from novelty animal to the queen of the battlefield. By 1770 BC, a horse was worth 7 bulls, or 10 donkeys, or 30 slaves. Within a hundred years, every army sought to build chariots and train horses to pull them. The Hyksos conquered Egypt with chariots in the 17th century BC, and when the Egyptians drove out the invaders, Egypt developed a chariot arm in their own forces. They even mummified some of their favorite horses. (Kelekna, 95, 104–5; Steiner, 18; Cooper, 21; Williams, 40)

The Hittites became the major power in ancient Anatolia, Syria, and parts of Palestine. They used large chariots carrying three men: a driver, shield-bearer, and archer, all armored including the horses. These heavy vehicles were not very fast, but they did frighten infantry. Much of what we know about ancient chariot warfare is thanks to the Hittites. (Cotterell, 82–83; Kelekna, 96)

In about 1360 BC, a Mitannian named Kikkuli wrote a manual to help the Hittites learn how to train horses to pull their heavy vehicles. The training program lasted seven months, though some animals "washed out" quickly if they could not handle the workload. They trained together as two-horse teams, and if one horse died or failed from the program, it could take weeks to acclimate the new pair to each other. They trained day and night. At midnight, the beasts were harnessed to a chariot for a one-mile gallop. After, they were bathed in warm water, rubbed dry, and fed.

At dawn they ran again. Each day the gallops increased in length until the team could travel six miles. They were fed and rested proportionately, depending on the length of the run. This is one of the most thorough animal training programs known from ancient times. The Hittite chariot corps was elite. By 1300 BC, chariot designs improved further, increasing speed, though the Hittites preferred heavier vehicles that could carry the three men. (Cotterell, 74–75, 82–83; Kelekna, 99; Hodges, Henry, 163)

Two world powers matched their charioteers and armies on the field of battle in 1274 BC at Kadesh. Egypt organized its chariot corps into squads of 10, and platoons of 50 vehicles, seeking a ratio of approximately one chariot for every 10 infantrymen. Egyptian vehicles carried only two men, a driver and archer. Each chariot corps hired quartermaster staffs to recruit and train horses, and hired craftsmen to build and repair the chariots. The young Pharaoh Rameses II led the Egyptians north through Palestine to force the Hittites out. Rameses wore golden armor "like Ba'al in his hour" and rode alone in a chariot with his pair of horses named "Victory." Muwatalli II the Hittite king held his infantry back, expecting that his 3,500 chariots would sow disorder among the invaders before a major attack. Initially this worked, but the Egyptians used 2,000 lighter chariots and speedy light infantry to kill the charioteers and drive Hittite cavalry off the field. Imagining the battle at Kadesh, Smith wrote, "We can almost see the clouds of dust and hear the rumbling wheels and the sounds of wounded men and horses, the latter emitting when mortally stricken a scream very much like that of a woman in agony before falling with lips drawn back in ghastly parody of a grin." Though the battle is historically viewed as a draw, both sides called Kadesh a victory. Both sides lost large numbers of chariots, and Rameses beheaded many commanders who fled in their chariots. (Cotterell, 68–69, 12–13; Smith, 11–12; Sinclair, 13; Gabriel and Boose, 5, 48, 73, 82)

The Greeks lagged in chariot warfare because the Greek terrain was not conducive to raising horses. The rocky, mountainous country did not provide enough grassland for horse grazing. Though chariotry was never a prominent part of their military, chariot racing remained the national sport of Greece for 1,500 years. Being near the Hittites, however, the Greek city-states had to develop a chariot-service for defense. Since chariots performed best on flat ground, the Greeks quickly converted to horseback cavalry when the equines were large enough to handle riders. (Kelekna, 176; Edwards, 80; Hyams, 17; Everson, 2)

The Bible generally condemns chariots because such vehicles seemed to reduce the Jewish people's trust in God. Joshua's army feared the Canaanite and Hittite chariots but took Palestine nonetheless. Later, the Israelites were constantly reminded by the prophets not "to multiply horses." At the time, kings measured their strength by the number of warhorses and chariots owned. Rather than capture enemy horses, Jews were ordered to hamstring the animals. Not all kings obeyed the laws of Moses. King David, though hamstringing most of the chariot horses captured, kept a hundred vehicles and their mounts (II Samuel 8:4). King Solomon collected lots of horses. Solomon owned as many as 40,000 chariot horses, though the Bible records 1,400 chariots and 12,000 charioteers in I Kings 10:26. (Toperoff, 123; Cooper, 21; Edwards, 33; Herzog and Gichon, 58–60, 117–18)

In China, chariots were in use by 1300 BC under the reign of Wu Ting. Wu negotiated a deal with the Huns to acquire their excellent horses. Together, the Chinese and Mongols established a stud farm capable of raising 300,000 horses. One innovation by Chinese charioteers was a long lance, 16 to 20 feet long, called a *mao*. Soldiers in the chariot used the lance defensively to cover their army when in retreat. Some Chinese records refer to four-horse chariots, but this is likely a two-horse chariot with one spare horse tied on each side as backup animals. Like the Hittites, the Chinese preferred a three-man crew, with a driver, archer, and mao handler. A few "flagship" chariots carried a leader who gave signals to the Chinese troops with flags and drums. They beautified chariots with lovely decor: tiger-skin coverings, fish-skin arrow quivers, pennants, and bells. At the Battle of Chengpu in 632 BC, some chariots bore foot-long bronze blades along the sides to cut down enemy foot soldiers. (Creel, 146–52; Gabriel and Boose, 177, 187; Hamid, 4; Cotterell, 195, 211)

Assyria conquered the Hittites along with Arabia, Iran, Iraq, Turkey, Syria, and Israel, and Assyrians liked the Hittite idea of large chariots. As their chariots became heavier, to carry four men, more horses were required to pull them. They designed yokes for three and even four horses. One reason the Assyrians sought to control such a vast empire was that the geographical core of their territory had no grasslands and could not support large numbers of horses. Conquest was required in order to keep a large army fed. A highly trained horse was worth 35 slaves or 500 sheep to the Assyrian army. The Assyrian vehicles carried a driver, a guard, and two archers. Their chariots used larger wheels, to give the archers a higher firing platform. The Israelite king Ahab joined a coalition of nations in 854 BC at the Battle of Karkar, contributing his force of 800 chariots, trying to stop the Assyrian expansion. Though the allies deployed 3,940 chariots, they failed to stop the invaders from Ninevah. At Karkar, the Assyrians used only 1,200 chariots but added 12,000 cavalrymen, the latest innovation in warfare. Supplying vast numbers of horses required a new military science: logistics. The Assyrian *musarkisus* (horse recruitment officers) could obtain and process 3,000 horses per month for the army. Large numbers of horses also required the army to form engineer brigades, to build strong bridges for the animals to cross. (Smith, 13–14; Cotterell, 240; Kelekna, 106; Herzog and Gichon, 163; Gabriel and Boose, 5, 8, 94, 98, 102–3)

By the 10th century BC, selective breeding had created equines large enough to bear a human's weight on their backs, rather than just pull carts. Simply carrying a human did not make a horse into a military tool. Chariots were mobile artillery platforms, carrying archers or javelin-hurlers, with the exception of the Chinese, who used extra-long spears. What weapon could a warrior on horseback carry? A sword is not long enough to reach many enemies. Before the invention of the stirrup, a spear-charge on horseback could dislodge the spearman from his own animal.

The new and improved weapon that enabled horsemen to become lethal weapons was the recurved composite bow. Short, light bows allowed a horseman to fire as many as 12 arrows per minute from the saddle. The new bows used sinew with four times as much tensile strength as plain wood: thus it drew the same weight (energy expended by the archer to pull the bow tight) and provided more energy for longer-range firing. The Assyrians, though still using big chariots, quickly seized upon the new weaponry. Just 100 years after the battle with Ahab, Assyrians had almost completely supplanted the chariot with the simple cavalryman. (Kelekna, 3, 63, 77)

Chariots did return briefly from about 400 to 150 BC. A clever new Persian addition to the chariot was the attaching of six-foot long scythe blades on the ends of the axles. The rapidly spinning blades could cut the legs off of infantrymen. The old archery model of chariotry had lost its fear factor to enemy ground troops, but flailing knives on a speedy platform brought a renewed terror to the chariot. They helped to win the battle of Cunaxa in 400 BC, but their return was short-lived. Horses had become better at carrying soldiers than pulling them behind. The chariot became more of an ornamental joyride, with Roman generals celebrating their triumphs by riding in four-horse chariots. (Everson, 202–3; Gabriel and Boose, 231; Smith, 25)

The First Cavalrymen

In the second millennium BC, when horses were much smaller, a man could not easily ride on one. A small horse can bear a man's weight only if he sits on the haunches, over the animal's back legs. The Medes and Persians of ancient Iran first succeeded in breeding larger horses to carry soldiers. An infantryman and a cavalryman are quite different, in simple mass. "To each man's stature is added the height and weight of his mount. He is six-legged, he stands twenty-four hands high, he weighs a thousand pounds. He is merged mass and movement." The Persians developed many new accoutrements to improve horsemanship. The Persians, or their neighbors the Scythians, probably invented the saddle with cinch: a major step up from the simple blanket. Though good horsemen could ride without a saddle, the new padded device added some comfort, enabling riders and horses to cross longer distances. The Persians upgraded horse-control systems, such as bridles and reins. (Hildinger, 15; Kelekna, 3; Downey, 56; Quammen, 37; Steiner, 37)

Along with the increased horse size, advanced bow technology created the new military superweapon: the cavalryman. "Horse and bow together delivered to the steppe warrior the devastating combination of speed and maneuverability couple with the ability to kill from afar, allowing the mounted steppe nomad to engage in wide-ranging military tactics that were to confound pedestrian and chariot armies alike." (Kelekna, 77)

The Assyrians first capitalized on the new weapon. Early on, mounted warriors had not learned to shoot arrows and steer the horse simultaneously. These cavalry rode in pairs, side by side, with one rider holding the reins for both horses, while the other rider fired his weapon. (ibid., 106)

The earliest horse-mounted soldiers acted as "light cavalry." The purpose of light cavalry is to harass and threaten the enemy, largely through the use of superior speed. They have superior speed because they are not encumbered by heavy armor and weaponry. Light cavalry can be used in an offensive capacity, but they more frequently seek to create disorder in the opponent's army. Fast horsemen also hope to induce the enemy into attempting a futile pursuit. "Steppe warfare at its purest is one of travel across great distance, missile warfare and, if it is advantageous, strategic retreat before the enemy until attrition, exhaustion or isolation have made his defeat inevitable." (Hildinger, 39)

The light cavalry of the ancient world also, to a degree, enabled women to become skilled warriors in some armies. Women like Queen Tomyris of the Massagatae led light cavalry forces to victories against large enemies. She defeated King Cyrus the Great of Persia in 530 BC. Such examples led to classic tales of "Amazon women." Defeats brought about by enemy tribes with superior cavalry caused King Cyrus to create more Persian horsemen. He increased the ratio until an estimated 20 percent of his soldiers were mounted. (Kelekna, 86; Gabriel and Boose, 9, 142)

King Darius of Persia purportedly owed his kingship to a horse. Herodotus wrote that six men vied to become the new king of Persia, and they agreed that they would all ride to a certain place the next day to await the dawn, and "He whose horse neighed first after the sun was up should have the kingdom." Darius hired a clever groom, who took a mare in heat to that place and then brought his master's stallion there to breed with the mare. The next morning when Darius arrived at the location, his stallion apparently wished to repeat his performance of the night before, and scenting the mare's scent on the groom's hand, neighed loudly, thus making Darius the new ruler. This trickery did not give Darius any advantage in horsemanship, however. The Scythians invaded his kingdom, and when the Persians pursued, they could never catch the enemy. The Scythians made constant harassing attacks but would never allow the full Persian army to engage. (DiMarco, 126; Smith, 14–15; Hildinger, 2, 37–38)

Horsemen earned little respect during these early years of light cavalry warfare. Though the army loved the speed and flexibility, the cavalry was not yet a battle-winning element of war. Leaders could see the potential benefits of horsemen but had not yet developed the tactics, discipline, and strategies necessary to use them effectively on a large-scale basis.

The Persians, perhaps embarrassed at failing to corner the Scythian cavalry, grew their mounted forces rapidly. Xerxes, the son of Darius, invaded Greece in 480 BC with a massive army, including 80,000 horsemen. Xerxes, a religious man, wondered if the gods might oppose the Persian invasion, so he designed a self-protective test. When crossing the Hellespont between Turkey and Greece, Xerxes sent his 10 white royal horses across first, to see if the gods would drown them. Once they arrived safely across the water, the great king crossed to join the army. The 80,000 Persian horses, along with the huge army, stalled for days at the "Gates of Fire" where 300 Spartans blocked their path into Greece. (Barber, 111; Steiner, 39; Kelekna, 127)

Many traditions of the steppe horsemen passed to the emerging world empires. In many cultures, the horse "served as the steed on which the dead made their journey to the next world." Ironically, the ancient metaphor might taken literally in a reverse manner... horses would be involved in sending millions of souls on their eternal journeys, not just bearing them to this end. (Kelekna, 79)

China started the transition from chariots to horsemen by 484 BC, using equines bought from the steppe peoples. Large-scale road construction became necessary to accommodate the upsurge in cavalry. When Duke Jing of Qi died, the officials dug a large sacrificial pit, killing and burying more than 600 horses with him. Such traditions continue even into modern times among the horse peoples. (Gabriel and Boose, 199; Kelekna, 140–41, 81, 88)

Xenophon, trained as a cavalryman in his youth, led 10,000 Greek mercenaries on a long journey in retreat from Persia in the famous Anabasis. They had been hired to fight on one side of a Persian civil war in about 401 BC, but by the time they arrived, their side lost. The mercenary generals were betrayed and murdered at a fake parlay. The Greeks retreated swiftly, staying ahead of Persian foot soldiers, but under constant harassment by the multitudes of Iraqi light cavalry. Xenophon faced low morale

Cavalry Death-Rituals

When a Persian horseman was killed, his friends shaved off the horse's mane, so that the horse "shared in the grief" over the lost man. This was a very tame ritual compared to Scythian postmortem traditions. When a Scythian leader died, his men killed his horses, gutted them, and built frames so the horses could remain standing. Sometimes grooms were killed and affixed on the back of the framed horses, so the dead leader had a troop of horsemen with him in the afterlife. (Steiner, 39; Hildinger, 34) among his soldiers, as well as exhaustion. He rallied them in part with this speech: "If any of you is despondent because we are without horsemen and the enemy has many, let him remember that ten thousand horsemen are nothing but ten thousand men. Nobody ever lost his life in battle from the bite or kick of a horse. Besides, we are on far surer footing than horsemen. They hang on their horses' backs, afraid not only of us but of falling off. Horsemen do have one advantage over us—retreat is safer for them than it is for us, and faster." (Steiner, 29)

Though commanders may exaggerate the weaknesses of their enemies while trying to improve the morale of their own men, Xenophon's words do correctly pinpoint some of the feelings of infantry regarding their early horsemen. Even in full retreat, outnumbered and often surrounded, the Greek infantry were not completely terrified by their situation. Xenophon is also famous for writing one of the world's first books on the training and riding of horses. It is not clear whether he wrote the horse book before or after the retreat of the 10,000. Xenophon did not despise equines; he loved them, promoting kindness as the only proper way to teach a horse. "Young horses should be trained in such a way that they not only love their riders, but look forward to the time they are with them." Also, "Anything forced and misunderstood can never be beautiful. And to quote the words of Simon, 'If a dancer was forced to dance by whip and spikes, he would be no more beautiful than a horse trained under similar conditions.'" (Morris, Desmond, 72; Podhajsky, 63, 17)

Dancing Horses

Training horses to make highly flexible movements, such as dancing, was believed to make them better warhorses, much like the movements of the modern Lipizzaners. However, in one case, teaching the horses to dance to the music of flutes proved problematic to the war effort. In Italy circa 450 BC, the Sybari dancing horses went to war with their enemies, of Croton. The people of Croton pulled out their flutes to play, and immediately the Sybari cavalry horses stopped their attacks and began their dance movements, leading to a Croton victory. (Edwards, 84)

Xenophon promotes the use of armor on the horse, with a frontlet plate on the head, a breastplate, thigh pieces, and a belly cloth, since the cavalryman who loses his horse is "in extreme danger." For the Greeks a horse was very expensive, perhaps 5 to 10 times the cost of an ox. An average horse might sell for 3 minae, but a racehorse or warhorse went for 12 minae in Xenophon's time. (Morris, Desmond, 67, 76–77)

The Sarmatians, powerful in Eastern Europe from about 500 BC to AD 150, used strong horses wearing heavy armor in an attempt to make cavalry divisions more effective. Heavy armored horses came to be known as *cataphracts*. The horse and rider were heavy enough to charge right through enemy infantry formations, with the rider carrying a heavy lance and broadsword. The cataphract came to be the preferred shock weapon of medieval times hundreds of years later. Sarmatians frequently made scale armor out of horse hooves, split to resemble scales: such armor was sword- and arrow-proof. The heavy charge did intimidate some infantry, but the weight of scale armor on both horse and rider quickly tired the beasts, so that the poor animals could do nothing after the initial shock attack. The use of heavy cavalry enabled the Sarmatians to finally defeat the Scythians. (DiMarco, 128–29; Hildinger, 18, 47–48; Kelekna, 190; Maenchen-Helfen, 242; Everson, 202; Oakeshott, 26)

Though heavy cavalry certainly had an important role in future combat, the armored horse never dominated the battlefield. The mobility and speed of cavalry horses would eventually be recognized as the key to their effectiveness in combat. Great military minds would think carefully about the tactics and strategies necessary to win battles, in order to fit the useful new tool. What they needed to learn is this key truth:

> Battles are most likely to be won by the side which can marshal its forces where they are most needed as fast as possible. The desire for mobility meant that man quickly learned to utilize the speed of horse for his battles, and the horse soon became all-important in early skirmishes and fights. The horse, in fact, must surely defy all comers as top animal in the military league. (Barber, 110)

In a more crass manner, the purported words of Confederate general Nathan Bedford Forrest would sum this up nicely: "Git there fustest with the mostest men!" (*Army Times*, 82–84)

One of the first commanders to make careful modifications to the cavalry arm of service was Philip II of Macedon. In preparing to invade Persia, Philip organized a large cavalry arm to accompany his formidable infantry phalanxes. Many of the horsemen came from Thessaly and were called "the King's Companions." They fought in tight formation using lances as stabbing weapons. Philip united Greece under the Macedonian banner, but his sudden assassination left the budding enterprise to his remarkable son named Alexander. (Kelekna, 129)

Alexander earned his favorite black stallion at age 10. The horse may have been rather unattractive, already 14 years old: the owners named him Bucephalus, or ox-head. Ox-head resisted all efforts at taming, though Philip had paid a small fortune for him. Young Alexander noticed that Bucephalus kept shying at his own shadow, so he turned the horse to face the sun, reducing shadows, then leaped upon his back and galloped off. From that day on (c. 346 BC), Bucephalus would bear no other rider. The stallion learned to kneel so that Alexander could mount while in full armor. Alexander and Bucephalus became primary actors in Philip's cavalry. (Smith, 17–19; Morris, Desmond, 104)

When Philip died, Alexander took command and led the Macedonian army for revenge against the Persians. Alexander led his small but disciplined army from his command position as leader of the Companion Cavalry. One major innovation developed by Alexander was the use of heavy cavalry. The heavy infantry phalanxes would control the center of a battlefield, while heavy horse struck the flanks or weak points of the enemy. The Macedonians attacked in almost every battle, even when vastly outnumbered, and the offensive came first from the cavalry. Alexander pioneered a diamond formation so that his heavy cavalry could drive a wedge into the enemy lines. Alexander liked to charge for the center, chasing the enemy leader. To keep Bucephalus fresh, Alexander rode other horses until battle time. (Ruthven, 38; Gabriel and Boose, 9, 160)

Alexander the Great stamped his name on history by his brilliant tactics. It is beyond the scope of this work to analyze his victories in great detail, but two battles can be considered in brief.

The first engagement between Alexander's forces and Persian armies came at river Granicus in Turkey. Arrian wrote "It was a cavalry struggle, though on infantry lines; horse pressed against horse, man against man, wrestling with one another, Macedonians trying to push, once for all, the Persians from the bank and force them on level ground, the Persians trying to bar their landing and hurl them back into the river." Alexander himself, dressed gaudily and leading the charge, was nearly decapitated by a battle ax that sheared off part of his helmet. The 14-foot-long *sarissa* spears used by Greek horsemen probably forced back the heavy Persian cavalry and won the day. (Gabriel and Boose, 244–45)

Before the battle at Gaugamela in 331 BC, the Macedonians had defeated the Persians at the Granicus River and at Issus. The great king of Persia rallied all of his remaining troops from Babylon to northern India to stop the invaders. The number of troops on the Persian side vary among sources, but there is no doubt that the Greeks were outnumbered by four to one, at a minimum. The great king chose the field of battle; it was prepared carefully for a hundred scythed chariots and 20 elephants. Persian cavalry ranged on both ends of the battle line with infantry in the center. The strategy was to completely envelop the Macedonians and overwhelm them from all sides. The Persian infantry was no match for the heavily armored Greek phalanx. The best, and perhaps only way, to defeat the phalanx was by flank or rear attack. The Persians would surround the phalanx and cut it to pieces. How could 7,000 Macedonian medium and heavy cavalry hold off some 40,000 Persian light cavalry? (ibid., 259)

Alexander did delay for one day, not attacking when the Greeks first approached the battlefield. He needed time to consider the problem, particularly the enemy elephants, with which his cavalry was completely unfamiliar. General Parmenio suggested that Alexander could attack at night, in a surprise assault. It was a somewhat typical and logical solution to the problem, offering hope in the face of seemingly impossible odds. Alexander refused, saying he would not steal a victory. At any rate, the Persians had considered this danger, and they remained in line all night. The night attack would not have won the battle for Macedonia. (Alexander, 176; Cummings, 214)

Alexander created a formation never seen before. Using a wedge-type formation, his men marched at an oblique angle across the battlefield, away from the center and toward the Persian left wing, perhaps to avoid the center elephants and scythed chariots. Alexander left a large cavalry contingent on his left flank to slow down the vast Persian right wing. He used a small group of center cavalry to charge across toward the Persian left, for two possible reasons. One, to create a dust screen to hide the remaining center phalanxes and Companion Cavalry. Two, to tempt the great king to weaken his own center by sending some central Persian cavalry after the Greek horsemen. It worked in both ways. Once the center Persian horsemen pursued the decoy Greeks, the Companion Cavalry charged straight for the center, panicking the great king, who fled. Because Parmenio's cavalry was being flanked and overrun, Alexander and his cavalry had to fall back to protect his army. The Persian army disintegrated without their leaders. The Macedonians conquered the Persian Empire by the judicious use of cavalry against superior numbers of enemy horsemen. Arrian writes that the Macedonians lost at least 1,000 horses in the battle, many of wounds, and many ridden to death. (Gabriel and Boose, 264)

During a campaign near the Caspian Sea, one night, some horse thieves managed to steal Bucephalus and other Greek horses. Alexander sent word to the neighboring regions that if his horse was not returned, he would kill all the inhabitants of the area. Bucephalus was immediately returned. (Smith, 19–20)

After a few years of chasing the great king, Alexander decided to invade India. Here he faced a huge problem, literally. The large Indian army was not the major difficulty. Elephants were the problem. His favored cavalry-charge tactic could not work, because horses will not approach elephants. Crossing a major river, the Hydaspes, in an attempt to flank the Indian army, they faced an early-morning attack by Indian chariots. According to Plutarch, a javelin went into Bucephalus' neck, but "almost drained of blood, he turned, carried his master from the very midst of the foe and then and there fell down, breathing his last tranquilly now that his master was safe." Unable to use the Companion Cavalry against the main enemy force, the phalanxes had to face the elephants alone. The Greeks took heavy losses but did win the battle. Winning the battle does not mean winning the war, however. Learning that other Indian kings had thousands of war elephants, while Alexander's men had barely survived against 200, the Greeks mutinied, refusing to go further. (Smith, 24; Murphy, 111)

Bucephalus died at age 30 after traveling 11,000 miles in eight years. Alexander founded a new town near the site of his death, called Bucephala. (Ruthven, 38)

In China circa 220 BC, Qin ruler Shi Huangdi united the Chinese kingdoms into one imperial state, with much help from chariots and horsemen. The leader celebrated his growing empire by preparing a massive burial army, the famed terra-cotta warriors discovered in recent years, with at least 7,000 life-sized soldiers, 500 horses, and 130 battle chariots. The Chinese had little choice but to increase their cavalry numbers, for reasons of survival. The Xiongnu nomads north of China fielded 300,000 mounted archers by the end of the third century BC. They frequently raided China, or demanded ransom not to invade, so that the Chinese began building the Great Wall to keep them out. (Kelekna, 389, 142–45; Steiner, 46)

As raiders became more troublesome and rode larger horses, the Chinese needed to find bigger horses for their own army. In 102 BC an official named Chan K'iens took 60,000 men on a long journey and managed to purchase 3,000 Iranian horses and acquired the new and superior fodder called alfalfa for the imperial Chinese stables. China could not maintain massive cavalry armies like the northern nomads because the large human population of China kept grazing land to a minimum. The Chinese would always have to import their horse stock. To make up for their equine deficiency, the Chinese invented new weaponry to kill cavalry. By 100 BC, the primary means of opposing horses and horsemen was the crossbow. Crossbows are easy to make and easy to use: even lightly trained soldiers could successfully fight against the cavalry. Though China could not compete with the numbers of horses in the steppes, horses played an important role. Around AD 40, General Ma Yuan sponsored the creation of a bronze horse statue inscribed below "Horses are the foundation of military might, the greatest resources of the state." (Kelekna, 147–49; Hyams, 21; Cotterell, 218)

As China began to struggle with the steppe horsemen of the north, Japan also acquired horses. Japanese acquired equines from Korea around the third century AD. A law passed in AD 682 ordered all officials to practice with weaponry on horseback. (Edwards, 114)

The horse also spread as a weapon of war into Africa and Western Europe, though we have few records to detail their use. In Hispania and Gaul, the Celtiberians had developed a medium-heavy horse from which they used lances. In North Africa, especially Numidia, the tribes used light horse and threw javelins. Most of Hannibal's heavy cavalry were Spaniards with two men on the horse, one to jump off for infantry combat when near the front. (Gabriel and Boose, 291)

Numidians became the mainstay of the Carthaginian army, the rivals of Republican Rome. The Africans' "superb rapport with their horses allowed them to ride without head restraint, leaving both hands free for combat. Riding without bridle, guiding their nimble horses with body movements, a withe around the neck, and taps of a stick, they repeatedly engaged in lethal charge, disperse, and re-form tactics." The Numidians also preferred to ride in the nude with a leopard sash over the shoulder. (Kelekna, 183)

Hannibal Barca made superb use of Numidians, particularly in his first battle with the Romans at the river Trebbia. The light cavalry taunted the Italians early one morning, throwing javelins over the barricade and challenging the enemy to fight. Hannibal knew that the consul in charge was a hothead who might rush into battle unprepared. The consul did not disappoint. The legions skipped breakfast and marched miles across the snow and through a freezing stream to arrive cold and hungry at a Carthaginian ambush. The Romans were almost completely routed. Hannibal's cavalry outnumbered the Roman horse by more than two to one at the Trebbia. In fact, it was the Carthaginian use of horsemen that reshaped Roman tactics, forcing it away from its lopsided reliance on infantry. Polybius wrote, "The Carthaginians owe not only their victory at Cannae, but all their victories to the preponderance of their cavalry." Periodically the Romans would learn this lesson, making their legions more balanced with cavalry contingents, hiring horsemen from North Africa and Hispania. (Robinson, 480; Gabriel and Boose, 300; Kelekna, 184)

Rome required reminders, however. The Italians loved to revert to their infantry-centric ways and quickly forgot that speed of horse protected the legions from encirclement. Early Roman legions deployed a mere 300 horsemen to a 5,000-man legion. In the massacre of Roman legions in the Teutoburg Forest, at the hands of the Germans, about 22,000 infantry had only 1,500 cavalry. They did not scout ahead and so they marched blindly into ambush after ambush. What little cavalry the Italians had proved to be ill-trained and useless. Most of the Roman horsemen fled, to be destroyed by barbarian horsemen piecemeal. Once the Carthaginian and Germanic lessons were forgotten, the Parthians stepped up to provide an effective demonstration. (Gabriel and Boose, 296, 419–24)

In 54 BC a wealthy Roman named Crassus sought to increase his power and reputation in Italy by defeating a foreign enemy, since his victory over Spartacus and the slaves did not gain him a triumphal parade. Crassus had no personal experience in the legions, but he took over a Roman army to fight the Parthians. With at least 40,000 heavy legionary infantry, the Roman force dwarfed the Parthians, but the Parthians were 11,000 cavalry, 1,000 of those cataphracts. In the desert, Crassus made many bad choices. Rather than camp near a water source, he ordered the infantry to pursue the apparently fleeing horsemen. He did not recognize the classic steppe tactic of the feigned retreat. Running away in faked disorder, the Parthians under Emperor Suren drew large groups of Romans away from the central force, then encircled and destroyed them. The Romans were never able to get near the enemy to attack, but suffered days of harassment. The Romans, thirsty and panicking, hoped the cavalry would run out of ammunition, as arrows barraged them incessantly. Camel caravans kept the Parthians fully supplied, and the legions were annihilated. Few Romans survived the Battle of Carrhae. (Hildinger, 46; Sinclair, 21; DiMarco, 71–72)

Carrhae showed that an inferior but speedier force could destroy a vastly superior force of slow infantry. Marc Antony's legions nearly fell to the Parthians in 36 BC. Once again, the Romans redoubled their effort to acquire cavalry for their armies. Their cavalry was rarely used as an offensive weapon. Roman horsemen protected the flanks against encirclement and provided reconnaissance to keep the leaders informed of enemy movements. Indoor riding schools were established to train the men for riding, jumping, and combat. (Lawford, 43; Hamid, 5)

Romans preferred stallions in the cavalry because of their aggressiveness, in contrast to the steppe peoples who liked geldings for ease of training. To maintain order in the "herd" it was best not to mix the equine sexes. In other words, an army needs all stallions, or all geldings, or all mares, lest the sexual call of nature create chaos at inopportune times. (DiMarco, 58)

In the early days of Roman horsemanship, the beasts were imported from many nations within the empire. Each region of the "world" trained and bred horses for specific purposes, with certain qualities. Julius Caesar noticed both good and bad in Germanic horses, for instance. "Those poor and ill-shaped animals, which belong to their country: these, however, they render capable of the greatest labor by daily exercise. In cavalry actions they frequently leap from their horses and fight on foot; and train their horses to stand still in the very spot on which they leave them." (ibid., 64)

The Italians finally started their own horse-breeding programs, seeking to improve the species for various roles. Latin names show the Roman equine roles: *venaticus* for hunting horses, *celer equus* for racing horses, *bellator equus* for war chargers, *manuus* for draft animals, *cantherius* for parade horses, *gradarius* for pacing horses, and there were many more. One way that the Romans chose their breeding horse stock was through the public games. Crowds cheered for the chariot racing steeds, and the winners passed on their genes to speedy descendents. Roman army couriers using fast horses and periodic changing stations could ride 240 miles in a single day. (Edwards, 14; Kelekna, 192, 188–89)

The Romans imported alfalfa from northern Iran to increase the size and quality of their horses. In the summertime, they took the horses to the mountains so that the rocky ground would toughen their hooves. Before the Germans invented iron horseshoes in the second century BC, Romans used a *hipposandal*, a smooth iron plate held on the foot by leather straps rather than nails. The horse hoof is similar to a human fingernail, but thicker, helping the animal to run on hard or soft ground by protecting the foot from injuries on sharp rocks. (Kelekna, 190–91; Johnson, Isaac, 133)

The Romans did not advance the science of horsemanship by creativity and innovation, preferring to simply adopt any useful modifications already tested in other countries. However, the typical Italian love of organization led to institutional advancements in stable design and veterinary procedures. Roman legionary doctors were world-renowned for expertise in the treatment of human wounds, and the treatment of their horses would have been similarly professional. (DiMarco, 61)

Light Horsemen

The Roman attitude of ignoring cavalry—using it only in defense and out of necessity—proved to be a fatal flaw. At the time of Augustus, a Roman legion included 5,300 infantry with a paltry 120 horsemen. The Germanic tribes and steppe peoples, predominantly horsemen, ran circles around the Roman legions in the latter centuries of the empire. In fact, many of the "barbarian" groups who would later attack Rome were hired as mercenary cavalry to protect the legions. Emperor Hadrian introduced heavy horse cataphracts to the legions, but they were few in number. The Goth cavalry slaughtered 30,000 to 40,000 men of the eastern Roman legions and killed Emperor Valens at the Battle of Adrianople in AD 376, so the Romans began hiring Goth mercenary cavalry to fight for them, or bribing the enemy hordes not to attack Roman lands. As time passed and the "auxiliaries" or allied horse learned Roman tactics, they became more dangerous. The most famous of the raiders who toppled Rome were the Huns. "Like sharks, they had become expert predators, honed to fitness by constant movement, adapted to roam the inland sea of grass, blotting out lesser tribes, until they emerged from the unknown and forced themselves onto the consciousness of the sophisticated, urbanized, oh-so-civilized Europeans." (Smith, 26, 29; Gabriel and Boose, 438, 456; Oakeshott, 108; Man, 77)

Unlike many of the empires discussed thus far, who dabbled in horses to improve the speed and flanking ability of their armies, the steppe peoples are cavalry. Horsemen are not a component of the military, they *are* the military. There is no infantry. A Roman of the time described them thus:

> Scarce had the infant learnt to stand without his mother's aid when a horse takes him on his back. You would think that the limbs of man and horse were born together, so firmly does the rider always stick to the horse; any other folk is carried on horseback, this folk lives there. (Maenchen-Helfen, 206)

The horse peoples relied upon equines for transportation and food. Hunting was done from horseback. They collected mare's milk, sometimes fermenting it as a form of alcohol. Russians still made this alcohol, called "koumiss," into this century. When necessary, the rider would make a small puncture in his horse's neck in order to collect a quantity of equine blood, boil it, and eat it. When a horse died, its meat was eaten. (Edwards, 9; Maenchen-Helfen, 220–21)

The most famous of the Huns was Attila. Under his leadership in AD 451, the Huns fielded 50,000 to 60,000 war horses, not counting mares and foals of the baggage train. They used a mixture of heavy and light cavalry, harassing the enemy from a distance with archers and using armored horsemen with lances and swords for close-quarters combat. In a modern study of the bows of the ancient steppe peoples, the estimated ranges of the weapon have been established. The maximum range for the horse-mounted bowman was 1,150–1,475 feet, but their accurate range was closer to 165 or 200 feet. To give the arrows more piercing power and distance, the two wings of Hun cavalry rode in counter-rotating circles, thereby adding momentum to their projectiles. With the added horse-speed momentum, Hun arrows could travel at 125 miles per hour. In 10 minutes, 50,000 arrows were launched. (Maenchen-Helfen, 213, 227; Kelekna, 196; Lajos, 11; Man, 130)

One interesting and lesser-known weapon of the Huns was the lasso. A Roman officer, Ammianus, observed, "While the enemy are guarding against wounds from saber cuts, they throw strips of cloth woven into nooses over their opponent and so entangle their limbs they cannot ride or walk." Later, the Goths adopted the lasso, though in recent centuries it seems to have become a more common method of cattle control than weapon of warfare. (Newark, 29; Maenchen-Helfen, 239–40)

Attila and his Huns never did attack Rome, nor Constantinople, though they threatened both. For the most part, the Huns raided small towns and cities, pillaged, and extorted money from large cities in exchange for not causing trouble. "Civilized people" hated and feared the Huns, calling them "the Scourge of God." The greatest difficulty for all-cavalry forces was the taking of fortified cities, since horsemen lacked siege equipment and the skills of siege-craft. (Smith, 30)

New inventions in China, such as the cast-iron stirrup, spread to Europe by the fifth century AD. One source says that sculptures found in India as early as 120 BC show the use of stirrups. Many modern historians exaggerate the importance of stirrups, implying that horsemen were useless prior to the stirrup. The stirrup did bring more stability to the rider and enabled a more powerful shock attack using lance or sword. (Kelekna, 164, 198; Quammen, 38–41; Oakeshott, 31)

Rome fell under repeated raids by the Germanic peoples. In AD 537 the Byzantines of the eastern empire sent General Belisarius to defend Rome. The Ostragoths attacked, trying to drive the Byzantines from the city. Belisarius ordered his Avar and Slav horsemen to conduct mounted attacks against the Ostragoths. The speedy eastern cavalry earned repeated victories, the archers running easily around the heavy Germanic mounted spear- and swordsmen. At times, light horsemen could run out of weapons, but the troopers of Belisarius carried a large variety. They bore feathered darts for stabbing or throwing; lances, swords, and a bow. This tactic again defeated the Ostragoths 15 years later under Procopius, who lead the Byzantines at the Battle of Taginae. When an Avar horseman was buried, the horse of the dead warrior was shot in the forehead by an archer with a triple-bladed arrowhead, then buried with its saddle and harness along with its master. Such hefty arrowheads could even pierce a steel helmet when striking at the perpendicular. (Newark, 9; Edwards, 95–96; Lajos, 9–10)

The steppe peoples did not keep records and so we have only fragmentary accounts of their lifestyles and tactics, written by their enemies. Fortunately, the Muslim Arabs broke this pattern. The Koran, for instance, offers several legends about the relationship of man and horse.

In Islamic writings, the Arabian horse descended from the horse of Ishmael, the first son of Abraham through his servant Hagar. Once Isaac was born to Abraham's beloved wife, Ishmael was cast into the desert to die. He found a pregnant wild mare in the wastelands, captured her, and tamed her. Then Ishmael mated the colt to its mother, bringing about the pure Arabian breed. More than 2,000 years later, the prophet Muhammad did not trust that Arabian horses were purebred and loyal. As a test, he deprived 100 of these horses of their water for three days, then released them near a lake. As the thirsty beasts charged the lake, he sounded the battle horn to order the horses to return before they drank. Only five mares obediently returned, and these he declared to be *asil*, pure Arabians. From these five horses came the modern line of Arabian equines, says the Koran. (Steiner, 83–84)

The Arabs adored their horses. One of Muhammad's friends, Sidi-Aomar, said, "Love horses and look after them, for they deserve your tenderness; treat them as you do your children; nourish them as you do friends of the family and blanket them with care. For the love of God do not be negligent for you will regret it in this life and the next." Muhammad himself wrote, "As many grains of barley as thou givest thy horse, so many sins shall be forgiven thee." The desert Bedouins kept their horses in or near their tents, hand-feeding them, even with some meat (supposedly inducing courage). It was forbidden to sell horses to the "infidels" (non-Muslims) because potential enemies must not gain access to good horse stock. (Edwards, 35; Quammen, 44)

Islam spread quickly through North Africa and the Middle East in the seventh century AD. Arabs and others did not lead cavalry armies south of the Sahara because the tsetse fly that inhabits these regions kills horses. (Kelekna, 219, 250)

The Berbers took the fight into Western Europe, defeating the Visigoth king, Rodrigo, in Spain. Rodrigo's white horse became stuck in the mud, perhaps from the ridiculous weight of his golden saddle filled with rubies and emeralds. With all of Western Europe in jeopardy, Charles Martel ably defended France. He confiscated church lands and gave it to "retainers" in exchange for promises to train and equip cavalry to fight in his army. Martel's system of raising cavalry would become the major "feudal" system, used for almost a thousand years in Europe. Thus Martel built a significant cavalry force to oppose the Arabs who followed the Berbers into Spain. He defeated them at Poitiers in AD 732. His grandson Charlemagne would drive the Moors (Spanish Muslims) farther back and help to unify Central Europe. Ruy Diaz, El Cid, took Valencia in AD 1094 on his famous gray Andalusian horse Babieca. The horse earned its name when Ruy's father saw the gray horse that his son had chosen and shouted, "Babieca!" meaning "stupid!" The Cid would ride the animal in war for 20 years. The Cid died in Valencia in 1099 while the Moors besieged the city. His men secured the dead man upright in Babieca's saddle with armor and sword, dressed in white and accompanied by his knights in a night departure from the city. The Moors saw the Cid and thought he had risen from the dead, and they fled, giving him a last victory even in death. Babieca lived in retirement for two years, dying at the old age of 40. (Steiner, 79; Kelekna, 238; Edwards, 35, 99–102; Sinclair, 33)

The purity of the Arabian horse breed was kept carefully by the Muslims. Even into the 13th century, all matings and births had to be watched by a committee to approve the pedigree of the parents. Arab mares were allowed to mate only with Arab purebred stallions, and in enemy territory the rider would sew up the mare's vagina to prevent her from mating with local, inferior stallions and contaminating the bloodlines. Foals were not allowed to hit the ground when born; the owner caught the foal and petted it at its first appearance. Mares were the preferred horses for Muslim cavalrymen because they were less apt to challenge other horses. They were fed camel milk and dates, and the rider would often sleep on his mare's neck as a pillow during campaigns. When the Europeans first asked to try competition races against the Arab horses, the desert people were amused that the challengers asked for six weeks to prepare their horses for the short three-mile race. Arabs raced Arabians for days, not a few miles. When Europeans were able to acquire some Arabian horses, they became the preferred warhorse in countries like Poland and Hungary and even spread as far as India. The English Thoroughbred was bred partially with Arabian blood. (Kelekna, 220–21; Edwards, 35–39)

Unfortunately, the Arab love of expensive purebred horses required lots of money. The black African slave trade provided wealth to the conquering Arabs. Fifteen to twenty human slaves was the average price of one good Arabian horse. Perhaps this was justified by one of Muhammad's writings, "Money spent on horses is, in the eyes of God, like giving alms." (Kelekna, 237; Edwards, 34)

The Arab expansion ground to a halt in the eighth century, but the horse peoples had not yet reached their peak of influence. Steppe horses tend to be small (under 14 hands in height), stronger, and thicker, with larger heads and greater stamina. They learned to find food in the snow and under ice, by digging with their front hooves. They rarely wore shoes: they ran on soft ground, and they often fought in winter rather than summer. Nomadic horsemen wore trousers, soft boots, a tunic, a fur-lined coat, and a fur cap or turban. The men hung the bow in a case on the left side, with a quiver of arrows on the right side. Over the centuries, the steppe tribes perfected the art of speedy cavalry warfare. "Tactically, they were unmatched by any other mounted forces. For 2500 years the horse-archer armies of the steppe were virtually unstoppable. Before the invention of gunpowder, no weapons system could stand against the steppe horse archer." (Hildinger, 9, 16–20; DiMarco, 116)

The steppe peoples' personal and public lives revolved around their horses. Mongol children learned to ride no later than age four. Mongol art shows horses. Horsehides were used to make clothing tents and equipment. Bowstrings were made from horsehair. The shamans read omens from charred horse bones, and the men used horse manes and skulls as totems over their tents. (Kelekna, 284; Quammen, 43; Hildinger, 121)

Riders owned multiple horses so they could ride one for a few hours and then trade for a fresh one, so as not to exhaust the animals. The men did not use spurs, just a light whip. Horses learned to come on command, called by the master by whistling. Colts (male foals) were quickly turned into geldings; only the best were kept as breeding stallions. Stallions were too difficult to control on campaign. The horses were "broken" at age two, then trained for three years till strong enough for battle at age five. Once a horse fought in any combat it became a veteran, with a sort of pension. Once a veteran horse grew old or lame, it retired to a grassy pasture until its natural death. A warhorse was killed only if the owner died, and then the horse was buried with its rider. The rider's stallion, mare, and a foal were buried with him so that in the afterlife he would have a riding horse, milk, and means for producing a new herd in the future. The spirits of the horses would go through the gate of the sky to serve their masters in the afterlife, it was believed. The horses wore their saddles and gear, ready for action. One horse was roasted, the meat eaten, and the skin stuffed with straw and propped on poles so it stood watch above the tomb. (DiMarco, 121, 124; Gabriel and Boose, 541; Steiner, 53–54; Ruthven, 27)

The Mongols began to rise as a world power around AD 1000. China desperately sought horses to repel the new enemy. Song Qi wrote in the 11th century, "The reason why our enemies to the north and west are able to withstand China is precisely because they have many horses and their men are adept at riding.... China has few horses and its men are not accustomed to riding...without horses we can never create an effective military force." (Kelekna, 150)

The Mongols had many strengths, with organization among the best of them. For training purposes, the tribes hunted together. Some 100,000 cavalrymen formed a single line 60 miles long. Moving at a controlled pace, the wings moved slightly faster than the center, forming a semicircle that would gradually become a complete circle, trapping all of the fleeing game animals inside. This was excellent practice for synchronized movement, archery, and camaraderie, and simultaneously provided food and hides for the winter. Another method of training was the game of polo. Though partly recreational, polo served also to teach the horses and riders the skills of charging, defending, and riding. Young horses must be slowly acclimated to the bow and arrows and their sounds, so the animal will not be frightened by the rider's weapon. The bow of an archer on horseback is only inches from the animal's eye, and the sound of the arrow ejecting from the string is right next to the horse's ear. It takes months of training for the equine to tolerate and ignore these distractions while riding at a gallop into battle. (Hildinger, 156; Lajos, 28–31; Gabriel and Boose, 541)

In a Mongol army, for every 10,000 soldiers there were as many as 40,000 noncombatants and up to 600,000 animals including the horses. Such a force consumed eight square miles of grassland each day and forced them to keep moving for grazing. The cavalry consisted of about 60–70 percent light horse archers and 30–40 percent heavy horse with laminate armor and spears. The heavy cavalrymen carried 12-foot lances with a hook for pulling enemies from their horses. The remounts followed behind. (DiMarco, 134–38; Gabriel and Boose, 537, 540; Kelekna, 289)

The men carried their rations on the horse. Milk was stored in leather pouches, where it curdled into cheese. They soaked horse meat in salt water and stored it under their saddles, where the rider could tear off a chunk and eat it like jerky. This led some foreign observers to believe that the riders were actually tearing off pieces of the live horse and eating them raw. Such an idea was furthered by the true deed by desperate riders who would drink the blood of the horse by cutting a small hole in the horse's neck. The rider carried tools for leather repair, needle and rawhide thread, fishing line and hooks, a cooking pot, a file for sharpening arrowheads, and one change of clothing. Like the Huns, some Mongols carried a lasso on the saddle to entangle the enemy. (DiMarco, 126; Steiner, 54–55; Lawford, 60)

The preferred season for Mongol military campaigns was winter. This caused major problems for western foes, who rarely prepared for winter defense against invaders: Spring and summer were the campaign seasons. Why not spring, for the steppe horsemen? Because rivers swollen with snowmelt were major obstacles and would require the building of bridges or locating of choke-point crossings where opponents might wait. Mongol campaigns began at the first winter freeze, and the horses could cross the ice. Also, they knew that local farmers stored supplies for the winter, thus Mongol raids stole all of these supplies of grain and food. Their horses learned to forage under snow and ice. To keep them warm in deeper snow, the men tied yak skins over the horses' legs. In AD 1241, Subodai moved his cavalry army 180 miles through the snow in three days. (DiMarco, 141; Smith, 29; Kelekna, 293; Gabriel and Boose, 537–38)

Special horse couriers were called Arrow Messengers. They established stations of fresh horses every 19 miles, and the riders were swathed in cloth bandages to absorb the shock and bouncing of the ride so that they could ride farther. These couriers could carry a message up to 120 miles in a single day. A Mongol army could cover 40 to 60 miles per day, compared to the 20 miles of the famous hard-marching Roman infantry. (Kelekna, 288; Harfield, 13; Hildinger, 17)

Tactically, the Mongols had no peers. Security scouts went forward to find enemy scouts and kill them, so the enemy could never learn of Mongol positions. Small units would harass and distract the enemy, while larger units would attack from the rear. Once archers disrupted a formation, the heavy cavalry charged to mow down the foe. Black and white flags were used for signals in daylight, and flaming arrows for night signals. The horsemen yelled and screamed to terrify the enemy. Practiced archers could launch an arrow every two seconds, by holding arrows in the fingers with the bow hand and pulling them quickly with the right hand after each release. Accuracy is best when the archer looses the projectile "at the top dead center of the galloping leap, during the moment we float through the air before the horse's hoof connects with the ground again." The rhythm of shocks caused by the animal's hooves striking the ground can be anticipated to allow for firing between hoofbeats. (DiMarco, 129, 140; Kelekna, 289; Lajos, 43–44, 57)

The Mongol generals planned ahead carefully for each step of the campaign, even years in advance. For instance, near the Aral Sea they demolished small dams on local rivers to flood the region and destroy the farmers' crops. It was not out of spite. In the next year or two the land would thereby revert to grassland and provide pasturage for the multitude of cavalry. Genghis Khan was so concerned with having sufficient pastureland for his horses to graze that he proposed razing all of China's cities so it might revert to grass. Ironically, during a hunt, Genghis's horse reared up when startled; he fell off and was trampled under his horse's hooves. (Kelekna, 295; Sinclair, 39; Edwards, 117)

The Mongols raced across Russia and Eastern Europe, slaughtering the knights of the Teutonic Order and Knights Templar with their nimble horsemen and their mounted archers. In 1221 the Christian king of Georgia, George IV, took 70,000 men to stop the advance of the light horsemen. The Christian heavy knights charged at the Mongol center, which slowly withdrew, staying out of range, until the western horses were tired out and disorganized. Then a fresh division of Mongol archers barraged the Georgians and encircled them, killing them all. A few months later, 18,000 Mongol horsemen annihilated 40,000 Russian soldiers. The Mongol bow was said to have had twice the force of an English longbow. "By holding one end of the bow between his foot and his stirrup the Mongol cavalryman could shoot in any direction at full gallop, timing his arrows with swift and lethal accuracy in between the pounding hoof beats of his horse." The Mongol carried two bows, one for horseback and one for use on foot. They used a variety of arrow types for varying ranges and penetration depths, with 60 arrows in total, kept in quivers. One innovation was the Mongol fluted arrow that whistled aloud as a signal to the allied cavalry to execute preplanned maneuvers. The Mongols also fired Chinese firecracker-style arrows into the air to startle enemy soldiers and horses. The Mongols terrified everyone because they moved in fast, then destroyed and burned everything. They did not stay, just stole what they wished, raiding and destroying. Christians generally thought the Mongols to be demons, full of evil. Roger Bacon called the Mongols soldiers of the Antichrist come to reap the last dreadful harvest. (Steiner, 56–57; Gabriel and Boose, 524, 528; Lawford, 58, 61; Edwards, 113)

The last army prepared to oppose the Mongol invasion assembled in Poland in April 1241 under King Henry the Pious. It was a great force, but they were no match for Mongol tactics. Using smoke bombs to conceal the movements of the cavalry, the Mongols ripped apart Henry's knights. He tried to escape, but his heavily armored horse grew tired. Henry the Pious was captured. They removed his head, impaled it on a spear, and rode around in triumph with it. The Mongols annihilated the Polish army and gathered nine sacks full of ears as proof of victory. (Steiner, 60–61; Gabriel and Boose, 535)

No large forces remained to block the Mongols from taking Europe. By 1242 they camped on the Danube, ready to push on, but chance or providence ended their campaign. The great Khan Ogedai died in Asia. By tradition, all the Khan's armies must return for his funeral and to determine the next leader. So the vast Mongol cavalry headed east, never to trouble Europe again. (DiMarco, 148)

The Mongols continued to plague central Asia and the Far East. The inventive Chinese, however, were experimenting with a chemical mixture that would eventually doom horses and their riders. Gunpowder trials began in the 1250s, and within a hundred years the explosive mixture would be creating a variety of noisy weapons across Asia and Europe. In Japan a feudal system like the medieval European system had arisen, under a militaristic state with samurai warrior-knights skilled in horsemanship, archery, fencing, and unarmed combat. Only rich Japanese could afford to buy and keep horses and spend time learning to fight effectively on horseback. The weather defeated the great Kublai Khan in 1281. As a huge Mongol fleet prepared to land on the shores of Japan, and the brave samurai stood ready to oppose them, a fierce typhoon struck and sank nearly the whole expedition. (Kelekna, 316, 322; Gabriel and Boose, 570; Edwards, 114–15)

Though the Europeans could never stop the swift Mongols, they met with some success in their efforts to stop the spread of Islam in the Middle East. These adventures became known as the Crusades.

Crusaders and Knights

The Crusades were periodic medieval European responses to the spread of Islam in the Middle East. While the moral aspects of the Crusades are the subject of much controversy and bitterness, the battles and tactics of cavalry of the times are of great interest. The age of knights continued from about the 8th through 16th centuries. The storming of Jerusalem on July 15, 1099, may have been the peak of the military power of knighthood, though the blood from the slaughter in the city was said to have reached the knees and bridles of their horses. (Gies, 2, 35, 43)

After the fall of Roman civilization, how did heavy cavalry become the favorite arm of medieval Europe? With central control and organization, the Romans could train and field a disciplined infantry. Once that control and organization died, cavalry was the only alternative. Historian Andrew Ayton called the Middle Ages "an equestrian age of war." (DiMarco, 115; Baker, 52)

Ancient Egyptian War Chariot. (Engraving by Butler, 1856.) (*An Illustrated History of the Holy Bible,* by John Kitto. Norwich, CT: Henry Bill, 1868, p. 159.)

The Muslim forces, much like the steppe peoples, were chiefly made up of light cavalry, dedicated to speed and endurance. The Europeans preferred heavy cavalry and the single-charge offensive. Crusaders waited for an enemy force to oppose them and charged the heavy cavalry into the enemy, usually routing them. The charge of heavy horse started at a walk, three to seven miles per hour, to a trot of 8–10 miles per hour, a canter of 10–17 miles per hour, and finally the gallop of 20 miles per hour. "The horses knocked down opposing footmen or barged into the enemy mounts. Each knight thrust first his lance and when that was torn from his grasp or he had come to close quarters, he swung his heavy sword. Unless his opponent was similarly mounted, the contest was very one-sided." Cohesion could be a problem for medieval knights because they rarely practiced the charge together. Arabs learned a couple of ways to deal with this tactic. Once the Crusader charge had ended, the heavy horses were too tired to move much farther. Once the European horses tired, the Muslims could attack with impunity. (DiMarco, 83; Baker, 145; Hildinger, 98–99)

The clever Arab leader Saladin used a long-term strategy to overcome his heavily armored foes. Against King Richard of England, the Muslim soldiers targeted the horses rather than the armored men, knowing that the huge horses could not be replaced. By the end of that Third Crusade most of the 300 knights had to ride mules, lacking horses big enough to bear their weight. In 1187 when Sultan Saladin destroyed the Christian army at the Horns of Hattin, the Muslims collected much "booty" but no horses because killing the horses was the only way to kill their armored riders. Before the 11th century the average European horse stood about 14 hands tall, but by 1500 the average horse had grown to 15.2 hands. Both Arab and Crusader warhorses, often chosen from the larger animals, averaged about 15 hands high during the Crusades. Though both armies had horses of similar height, the Crusader horses weighed 1,257 pounds compared to the 750 pounds of the desert equines. The rider and his armor weighed a combined 397 pounds. The Arabs used lightweight saddles and equipment compared to the armored knights. (Reston, 204–6, 297; DiMarco, 90, 99; Kelekna, 242, 263–64; Sinclair, 46)

The knight's armor, though completely encasing his body in metal, was actually not that heavy when compared to the uniforms and equipment of modern soldiers. Of the six complete medieval suits of armor still in existence, they range in weight from 41 to 90 pounds with another 7 to 12 pounds for the helmet. The two remaining sets of horse armor weigh almost 70 pounds.

With horses having such a high value, medieval jousting games had specific taboos against any injury to an opponent's horse. If a knight caused any harm to his foe's equine, he was disqualified from all events. The jousting and other knightly games had an important purpose. As Roger of Hoveden wrote in the 12th century, "A youth must have seen his blood flow and felt his teeth crack under the blow of his adversary and have been thrown to the ground twenty times. Thus will he be able to face real war with the hope of victory." During combat, all rules protecting the warhorse were irrelevant, though capturing a fine enemy steed was always desirable: it could be kept or ransomed. (Oakeshott, 59–60, 102–5; Smith, 40)

Middle Eastern armies wielded brilliant archers. They fired in volleys, and practiced by aiming at a straw target standing in the back of a cart rolling downhill. While riding at full speed, the Arabs held arrows and bow in the left hand, and could shoot up to five arrows in less than three seconds. Accomplished riders could fire with the horse taking only seven steps between arrow volleys. In the last Crusade of 1396, Muslims defeated the Christian knights by letting them charge through weak forward troops who were hiding rows of sharpened stakes. Forced to dismount from their crippled horses, the Christians were destroyed by the Muslim light cavalry. (Kelekna, 265; Hildinger, 158; Sinclair, 47–48)

Many of the Crusaders were knights from Western Europe, but the long journey from the west to the Middle East meant that only a small number of horses and equipment could be taken. The Byzantines, the eastern Roman empire, remained entrenched at Constantinople (modern-day Istanbul) and continued to use ancient Roman methods of horse transport. The ships called *dromons* had a large stern with ramps to embark and debark horses, by backing the ship on to the beach. In the ship were mangers, railed stalls, grass bedding, and underbelly slings to stabilize the horses in case of rough seas. Early vessels held up to 20 horses; later, larger vessels could hold 30 to 60 horses. The hatches were caulked to be watertight. After a long voyage, the equines would need several days of rest. The knights who remained in Europe with a home base provide a better look at the standard equipment and animals used during medieval times. (Kelekna, 261–62)

In the common feudal system of Europe, a wealthy landowner would hire and equip soldiers to protect his properties, and he agreed to send these knights to fight for his regional governor or king when necessary. One problem with the feudal system was the necessary emphasis on money. To obtain horses, armor, and servants required funds. To gain funds, the knight had to win tournament games or defeat his enemies and take their horses and armor. Predictably, when looting became important on a battlefield, soldiers stopped to grab the goods from fallen opponents rather than pursuing the enemy army for a more complete victory. Sometimes, loyal knights who failed to stop to grab valuable loot were publicly reminded by their "lords" not to leave it for peasants to grab. The knightly military orders like the Knights Templar and the Hospitallers became important because they swore to stay together and never leave the group during battle, thus keeping cohesion during combat. A knight owned multiple horses, each with a different purpose, almost all males, with ears and tails docked. The heavy horse capable of carrying the armored warrior in jousting tournaments was called the destrier, often a large breed of equine (up to 18 hands) with hairy legs like a shire horse. The regular riding horse, smaller and more calm, with more stamina and used for war, was called a rouncy or courser. The soldier might also have a parade horse for public display and carrying equipment but not real combat training, called a palfrey. One poor knight named William, when his horse died of injuries, had to sell his robes to buy a smaller replacement. (Smith, 35; Cooper, 25; Gies, 86–87, 127; Oakeshott, 10–11, 65; DiMarco, 91).

The medieval knights relied on a long lance, held in a couched position in the right hand, braced under the arm, to knock an opponent down. The stirrup and high saddle enabled the rider to remain in position on his horse. The soldier required years of training to properly wield the heavy lance at a full gallop. Two opposing knights galloping toward each other would strike each other at 50 miles per hour with the momentum of two small vans, concentrated at the tiny tip of a sharp lance. The danger was so great that horses were often blindfolded so they would not flinch from the approaching danger, working solely under the rider's commands. The stirrup provided a great deal of support to keep an armored rider in place, but in the 13th century, saddles came to include a wide "burr-plate" in front and a wide cantle behind, to give even more stability. Though the majority of jousting experts were males, a few women became champion riders, including the famous Joan of Arc. (Kelekna, 198–99, 337; Oakeshott, 34–35, 40, 97, 116)

Some knightly horses were trained to pick up things from the ground with their teeth, because it was so difficult for the armored rider to dismount to get it himself. A few medieval horses wore armor that included a chamfron headpiece with a sharp spike it could use against an attacker. The major pieces of horse armor were the chamfron protecting the head, a crinet over the neck, and flanchards down the sides. (Coultas, 103; Barber, 112; Oakeshott, 47)

Medieval centuries are popularly known as "the Dark Ages" for many reasons. As people suffered, animals earned no special treatment.

The riding masters of the Middle Ages employed very rough methods. Thinking that punishment proved the best means of education, they did not even try to make their horses submit by normal treatment. The aim of their training was the subjection of the horse. In order to make them obey, the horses were subjected to every sort of punishment, and it was no concern to the trainers how many horses were spoiled or broken down in the course of training. The cruel bits and other instruments of torture employed in those days and exhibited in museums are proof of this fact. Pluvinel, at the beginning of the seventeenth century, was the first riding master to oppose these methods. (Podhajsky, 63)

Military forces could, to a degree, gain better control of their cavalry horses by using painfully shaped mouth bits, rather than improving upon the training of the riding soldiers. Stubborn humans prefer to force compliance by the animal rather than modify their own methods of riding. To a degree, archaeologists can determine the quality of army horses and horsemen by examining the metal bits, since severe bits usually indicate poor horsemanship of the army. A modern and milder way of improving the animal during training is simple: "repeat the exercise until it is finally successful." (DiMarco, 27; Podhajsky, 67)

Another method of control of knightly horses was the spur. Unlike the steppe peoples, who used their voices, their legs, or a small whip to signal desired movements to their mounts, the armored knight could not spare a hand nor perhaps even reach the horse with his feet under his bulky saddle. Thus the long, sharp spur came to be attached to the knight's foot, so he could order the horse to speed up. In modern times, the spur is used in more moderation. If the horse comes to fear the rider, superior control is not gained, and the equine may react nervously or stop responding altogether. "The too constant use of the spurs will deaden the sensibilities of the horse, and render it dull and sluggish. Every saddle horse should be taught to bear the attacks of the spur with complacency, but the occasions when the sharp rowel is required on a well-trained horse are very rare. The schooling of a horse renders it quick and vivacious; some horses show so much mettle and life that their obedience seems wonderful to the uninitiated." (Podhajsky, 58–59; Anderson, 107)

In World War II, the Nazis designed and fielded some remarkable new armored tanks with innovative features, but then discovered that very few bridges in Europe could bear their weight, and thus the vehicles could not reach the battlefield. Similarly, the Europeans of medieval times discovered that the heavy horse and knight were not always the most effective weapon. In 1314 at the Battle of Bannockburn, Robert the Bruce defeated Edward II when the heavy horses became bogged down in marshy terrain and pothole traps and could not extricate themselves. These large battle horses presented other problems as well. The churches of England were horrified to learn that the money needed to feed one warhorse could feed four or five people. (Sinclair, 61–62; Cooper, 26)

Once the heavy horse became the dominant feature of medieval European battlefields, opponents spent time and resources seeking countermeasures to defeat the horsemen. The first major challenge to the knights was improvements to the bow.

The crossbow was the first dangerous weapon to frighten the armored horsemen. In knight versus knight combat, the enemy lance presented the main danger, but it was a visible and expected weapon, wielded by an honorable knightly foe. The crossbow changed the dynamic of chivalric warfare. A bolt from a crossbow was capable of piercing armor, but the real advantage of the crossbow came from its being an easily operated mechanical device, not requiring long years of practice or the creation of hand-fletched arrows. With a crossbow, an untrained soldier could kill a mounted armored knight from a distance. In 1361 a Danish army defeated a Swedish army, and a 1930s excavation of the battlefield found at least 125 bodies wearing mail with the arrowheads gone through the armor, into their skulls and bodies. (Baker, 48–49; Lawford, 50; Turnbull, 43, 166)

About this time the longbow also came to endanger knights on horseback. A longbow was a six-foot-long weapon made of elm, hazel, basil, and yew, firing a three-foot-long missile for hundreds of yards. With it, a skilled archer could launch 12 arrows per minute. The battles of Courtrai in 1302 and Bannockburn in 1314 debuted the powerful weapon, but for the battle of Crecy in 1346 the British equipped thousands of archers against French knights. The arrows fell like snow: up to 24,000 per minute. The French lost 1,500 knights, piling up in heaps with the carcasses of thousands of horses, while the British lost only two knights and 40 infantry. The Battle of Crecy has been called "the death of knighthood in Europe." The knights so hated longbowmen that when captured, the bowmen's fingers were cut off, so they would never pull a bowstring again. Combining archery and ground traps was a recipe for butchering knights. In the 1342 Battle of Morlaix, the first battle of the Hundred Years' War, archers took down the first line of chargers, with trenches and booby traps for the second line of cavalry. (Smith, 41; Steiner, 73–75; DiMarco, 109; Kelekna, 341; Baker, 41; Turnbull, 28)

Other non-projectile weapons, pole weapons, were designed for the infantry to use against knights. A two-meter pole with an ax blade and hook, called a halberd, was used for pulling knights off their horses. These weapons worked just as well for cutting off the legs of horses. Resembling the Macedonian phalanxes of old, infantry formed up using four-meter-long pikes to impale charging horses and their riders. The Swiss used pikes for stabbing at horses' chests, or halberds for pulling knights off their horses' backs. Strangely, while further dangers imperiled the knights, the ratio of cavalry to infantry continued to rise. In England it rose from 2–1 in the 1300s to 10–1 in 1440. (Kelekna, 342; Smith, 43; Gabriel and Boose, 618–19, 630; DiMarco, 84–85)

The next nail in the coffin of heavy horsemen was the coming of gunpowder. A novelty weapon at first, making noise and smoke, the powder weapons became more accurate over time. King Edward III brought the "primitive gunpowder cannon" to England in 1327, though it would be a long while before the cannons became effective weapons. In English and Scottish battles, the first centuries of cannonfire succeeded mainly in scaring away cavalry horses with the noise. At the Battle of Castillon in 1452, the English tried to keep a foothold in France. John Talbot led the British forces but unadvisedly led a horse charge against French cannons. One cannonball struck Talbot's horse, causing it to fall over, and a Frenchman drove a battle-ax through Talbot's head. Cannons would become more and more decisive on battlefields over the next decades. The year 1516 saw Selim the Terrible of the Ottoman Turks use 150 cannons against Mamluk cavalry near Aleppo, Syria, ripping them to shreds. Cannons would soon be miniaturized into handheld weapons called muskets. (Sinclair, 80; Turnbull, 126; Kelekna, 276)

Attempts to keep knights in battle in spite of their growing vulnerabilities led to unusual tactics. The French and Germans attempted to lessen their exposure to enemy gunfire by charging in a long, narrow column rather than a wide line. Ideally, the knights would break through the foes like a wedge so that the armored riders behind could all join in the combat. However, in reality, the charging columns often failed to pierce the enemy, and thus only the two or three men in front did any fighting, while the rest waited in line behind. When the foe possessed cannons, the tightly massed knights were an easy target. On one occasion in the mid-16th century, the Germans charged the French in such a column. Fabrizio Colonna later said that one French cannonball had knocked over 35 men and horses. (Oakeshott, 18)

Horses Return to the New World

For unknown reasons, the horse went extinct on the American continent many thousands of years ago. The American empires of the Aztecs and the Incas were the only significant world powers to control vast areas without the assistance of horses, and both of these empires fell to invaders using horses. Equines did not return to the "New World" until 1493. (Edwards, 10, 23; Steiner, 115; Kelekna, 353)

When Christopher Columbus invaded the island of Hispaniola (modern-day Haiti and the Dominican Republic), the natives were so terrified by his 50 horses (and war dogs) that they fled into the mountains. Once the explorers and conquerors discovered the psychological effects of horses and dogs upon the native inhabitants, animals became key elements of the European forces sent to pacify the regions. The Spaniards came in force when Hernando Cortes discovered that the Aztecs of Mexico owned an abundance of gold. (Kelekna, 352)

Twenty-five years after Columbus arrived, Hernando Cortes sailed from Cuba with 11 ships carrying a small force of a few dozen men, 10 cannons, and 16 horses: 10 stallions, 5 mares, and a foal. The Spanish horses were probably the same breed seen in Renaissance portraits, sturdy, short, but strong Arabian-style animals. The horses had names like King, Little Roland, and Moor's Head. (Kelekna, 356; Sinclair, 149; Thomas, 153)

When the Spaniards landed on the Yucatan Peninsula, word came to the Mayan king, Montezuma, that the white men rode on "deer" as "high

The Horse Latitudes

For the Europeans, getting horses to the New World proved difficult. Only the largest Spanish galleons had space below decks big enough to hold horses, so most animals remained on deck. To keep them from falling during rough weather, a belly girdle supported them. Still, a combination of bad weather, lack of water and food, and disease killed more than half of the equines before they reached the Americas. Quite a few animals became dinner to hungry sailors when the rations ran low. So many carcasses were thrown overboard that one windless region of the sea route became known as "the Horse Latitudes" because of all the floating horse bodies. Even survivors of the long voyage might succumb in the hot and humid climate they had never experienced before. (Kelekna, 353; Steiner, 116–17)

as rooftops." Others called the horses "dragons." One Aztec said of the horses, "They make a loud noise when they run; they make a great din, as if stones were raining on the earth. Then the ground is pitted and scarred where they set down their hooves. It opens wherever their hooves touch it." Seeing the reaction of the locals, Cortes said, "Do you know, gentlemen, I believe it is the horses that the Indians are most frightened of." Cortes then intentionally staged viewings for the locals to show horses to be scary. One trick was to invite an Aztec leader to a meeting and put a male horse nearby with a mare "in heat" so the stallion bucked and snorted excitedly. In battle they put bells around the horses' necks to further confuse the Indians. (Thomas, 168–69, 180, 246; Bernal, 70–71; Sinclair, 147)

Confusion and fear did not keep the Aztecs from fighting against the invaders. The native Mexicans learned that the horses were easier to kill than the armored men, so they intentionally attacked the horses. One town dug holes in the streets with sharp stakes inside to stab the equine feet when they passed. They used long lances for stabbing and volleys of darts and arrows. Cortes ordered any dead horses to be carefully buried so the Indians would not see them to be mortal, but the plan did not work for long. In September 1519, Pedro de Moron was wounded and the natives "slashed at his mare, cutting her head at the neck so that it only hung by the skin. The mare fell dead." The Indians cut her in pieces and sent them to nearby towns, showing that the beasts could be defeated. This became a big problem for Cortes because his horsemen owned their own horses and did not want to risk losing them, with the cost of a warhorse being up to a thousand pesos. The Spaniards formed into groups of three for mutual assistance and were ordered to charge and thrust their lances at the Mayans' faces to keep the Indians at a distance. (Bernal, 124–27, 167, 311–12)

Another Spaniard landed with an army to oppose Cortes, wanting the gold for himself, but the hundreds of soldiers and their horses surrendered to Cortes, providing him with fresh forces. (Steiner, 101)

Cortes's personal horse was a black stallion named Morzillo. In the final push on the Aztec capital, Tenochtitlan, Cortes received a head wound and the enemy pulled him off his horse. He was nearly captured, but Morzillo, with an arrow sticking out of his mouth, fought the warriors off until other Spaniards could rescue Cortes. Later, Cortes had to leave Morzillo behind with friendly Indians when a deep splinter crippled a hoof. The Indians wreathed him with flowers, perfumed him with incense, and fed him delicacies, worshiping Morzillo as Tziunchan, the god of thunder and lightning. They built a statue to him when he died, and it remained until 1692 when an idol-hating Jesuit "filled with the Spirit of the Lord and carried off with furious zeal for the honour of God" destroyed it. (Koenig, 220; Wyman, 48; Ruthven, 174; Edwards, 121)

Many of the Spanish conquistadores with Cortes were Jews fleeing the Spanish Inquisition. Once the Aztecs fell and the Spanish soldiers earned lots of gold, these Jewish men would not return to the dangerous Catholic Spain, and they became horse ranchers in Mexico and the southwestern part of the future United States. Spaniards seeking gold and fortune were shipping so many horses to the Americas that the rulers of Spain had to embargo all horse exports. Thus the conquistadores started up their own ranches. (Steiner, 115)

Hernando Alonso, one of the first ranchers in New World, established a prosperous horse-breeding ranch in Mexico, but the Inquisition found him and burned him alive in 1528. This incident, and others like it, left the numerous ranch horses to the native workers. Slaves and Indians were hired to work the ranches with their Spanish bosses. The workers were called "vaqueros." To keep them from thinking of rebellion, though allowed to ride, they were not permitted to use saddles. Thus the workers learned to ride bareback, and became better riders for it. This is how the American Indians would first obtain horses and learn to ride. As the famous painter Frederic Remington would later write, "of all the monuments which the Spaniard has left to glorify his reign in America there will be none more worthy than his horse." (Steiner, 93, 125–29; Wyman, 27)

In 1531, a new expedition of Spaniards landed to plunder the great empire of the Incas in South America. Pizarro landed 62 horsemen and 102 infantry. The Inca's best troops were routed by a charge of 26 horses. When the Spanish ran out of iron, they started using the more plentiful silver of Bolivia to make shoes for their horses. (Kelekna, 362–65)

The early successes of the Spanish in conquering the Americas did not lead to permanent ownership. Rebellions against European rule began in earnest with the Arauco War in Chile in 1598. The South American Indians used horses and a unique weapon called a bola, composed of two or three thin strips of leather with leather-wrapped stones on the ends. When hurled at a man or animal, it would entangle the legs or body. (ibid., 375)

The North American Indians would again bring the horse to prominence in the Americas.

Warhorses of Renaissance Europe

While longbows and cannons forced Europeans to reconsider their overreliance on heavy horses, an unbelievable amount of stolen New World gold flowed into the continent. This wealth enabled a rapid expansion of the military, with trained infantry, large navies, and the start of colonialism. Countries like England and Spain could afford to send their cavalry forces around the world to take control of lands in Africa and Asia, to exploit their resources. The gold ingots of Peru and Mexico also funded wars against the Islamic armies seeking to advance in Europe. (Kelekna, 371, 399)

The Islamic armies sometimes mingled with the steppe peoples or imitated their light horse tactics. The traveler Pierre Chevalier wrote about the Tatars:

> Their horse, which they call Bacmates, are long, ugly, and lean, have the hair of their neck thick, and great tayls which hang down to the

ground; but nature hath very well repaired their ugliness by their swiftness, and their incomparable and indefatigable service they perform in traveling, being able to carry their riders whole days journeys without drawing bit; they feed at all times, and when in winter the earth is covered with snow and the Tatars make their incursions they live either upon what is under the snow, or upon the branches or sprouts of trees, pine tops, straw, or anything they can find. (Hamid, 6)

The Tatars had such disciplined and well-trained mounts that the army would stop every hour and the horses and men would urinate on command when a whistle sounded. Like the Mongols, the Tatars moved in 10 or 12 groups with orders to meet at a prearranged location, arriving by different paths. This both confused any enemy scouts and enabled each group to find fodder for the horses. Turkomans would starve and sweat their cavalry horses before a campaign, preparing them for hardship so they could ride long distances and go without water for a few days. (Hildinger, 205–11)

The Europeans had begun to see the advantages of light cavalry during the Crusades and in opposing invaders from the eastern steppes. Since technological advances like crossbows and muskets were killing the previously impervious knights, light cavalry became a part of western armies again. At first, cannons were very immobile and heavy, but they gradually became smaller and more portable. By the late 16th century, handheld muskets grew more accurate, with shorter reload times and longer ranges. (DiMarco, 151)

One of the first stud farms dedicated to breeding a specific horse type, strong but agile, was founded in Austria in 1580, and the breed became known as the Lipizzaners. They descended from the Arabian-type horses used in the Islamic invasion of Spain and were trained to jump and turn in the air and lash out with their hind feet at the enemy. Visitors to the Vienna Spanish Riding School see how the jumping of a horse can contribute to the rider's defense in battle: the kicking is for battle, not for show. (Kelekna, 366; Smith, 44)

Part of the training of a horse is balance, since the dynamic is changed with a human rider on the animal's back.

Even a human being needs gymnastic training for smooth and supple athletic action, although it is easier for him than it is for a horse as he is not hampered with a weight on his back and the direction of gravity is vertical over his feet... the weight of the rider throws additional weight on the forehand, which makes matters more difficult for the horse. It is the rider's art to balance the centres of gravity of horse and rider so that the former is not disturbed in his movements. Any rider who has had the opportunity to break in a young horse will see how clumsily he moves when first mounted. The reason is that the horse must readjust his balance to the unaccustomed weight of the rider. (Podhajsky, 40–41)

In England, civil wars broke out between Catholics and Protestants. In the early 17th century some armies experimented with horse-drawn brass cannons set atop a small cart, called horse-artillery. These provided minor support, but so few were available they could take no decisive part in battle. Oliver Cromwell went from captain of 65 horsemen to colonel over a thousand cavalry in 1643. Cromwell was said to be the "best judge of a horse in England." Cromwell, who believed in discipline and always sought prompt payment of salary and adequate provisions and equipment, built Parliament's New Model Army. At Cromwell's headquarters, there were officials such as a Waggon-Master-General and Commissary-General of Horse Provisions. Cromwell wrote that "if a man has not good weapons, horse, and harness, he is as nought." He succeeded against the Royalist forces to make England a Protestant country. (Smith, 52; Lawford, 89–90; Sutton and Walker, 13; Newark, 45)

Rather than using heavy cavalry to plow through enemy formations, light and medium horse were deployed on the field, and they were identified by the types of weapons they carried. Pistols were actually firearms designed to be small enough for a rider to carry in one hand, but firing from horseback never proved to be very accurate or effective. Some of the 17th-century cavalry types included cuirassiers, harquebusiers, dragoons, carabineers, and hussars. Typically the horsemen would gallop toward the enemy, slow to a trot at 11 to 16 yards in front of the enemy line, fire with their pistols, then move away to reload while the next cavalry line moved in. This tactic was called the Caracole; it took much practice and discipline to do it correctly. Since the range of the pistols was a mere 30 feet, the horsemen had to bravely stop a very short distance from the enemy rifles and pikemen. The enemy infantry deployed in squares with pikes, practically impenetrable by horses. Gustavus Adolphus may have started the rejection of the Caracole maneuver, with the British under Marlborough soon following suit. The armies continued to use pistols for the initial assault but then continued the charge with swords, not stopping to reload. (Smith, 44; DiMarco, 157, 205; Oakeshott, 19–20; Gabriel and Boose, 645; Lawford, 73, 97–98; Hamid, 8)

Gustavus Adolphus of Sweden organized his cavalry and infantry into the finest fighting force of the 17th century. Because he had only small horses for the army, standing about 12 hands, there were strictly enforced rules about the riders and their weight and clothing. Not one extra ounce of useless weight was allowed, including tall, gaudy hats or golden-trimmed sleeves, lest the horses be tired unnecessarily. Rather than purchase expensive, huge horses to pull artillery pieces, he strung together a team of 36 horses to pull the cannon. This attention to detail was not repeated among European commanders for almost 200 years, with the Duke of Wellington. Adolphus's victories did much to save the Protestant Reformation from Catholic armies, but he charged into danger once too often. At the Battle of Lutzen, Gustav was shot and dragged by the stirrup, when the enemy realized he was the king and stabbed him to death with swords. (Smith, 49–50)

Very few cavalry charges against infantry squares succeeded. One such victory came in Spain in 1812, when Germans breached a French square. As repeated volleys mowed down the horses, one mortally wounded animal crashed into the front line of the infantry, creating a hole. Some following horses jumped over the bodies and into the square, thus bringing about its disintegration as the footmen fled. (Lawford, 133)

Dragoons were probably the easiest type of cavalry to equip, because dragoons fought with very little armor, and on foot, dismounting and leaving their equines behind. This meant the horses did not have to be large and strong, nor trained to handle shock tactics. The Prussians, for instance, would charge with heavy cavalry to engage the enemy; send the dragoons behind closely, jumping off their horses and acting like a first row of infantry; with the infantry following behind. Cavalry horses had to be trained not be panicked by the sound of gunfire and cannon shot. In a 17th-century training manual, the process is explained. "When he is at his oats (at a good distance from him) a little powder may be fired, and so near to him by degrees. So may a pistol be fired some distance off and so nearer: in like manner a drumme or trumpet may be used." (Lawford, 108–9; DiMarco, 175)

In the late 1600s the Poles continued to use heavy cavalry. The hussars called "winged lancers" wore three-quarters plate armor, a leopard-skin cloak, and a unique attachment on the back of their armor: gilded wooden wings filled with eagle feathers. "In battle, it was said, the wind rushed through the wings of the horsemen making a terrifying wailing sound." Frederick the Great explained how he kept his whole formation in line even with frightened men in his own cavalry. "I make the squadrons charge at a fast gallop because then fear carries the faint-hearted along with the rest; they know that if they hesitate in the middle of the onrush they will be crushed by the rest of the squadron." Speed was an essential ingredient of the charge. Since the infantry would be firing muskets, the cavalry needed to move fast to reduce their exposure to enemy bullets. Further, the speed of the charge had a major morale effect on the enemy. "Hundreds of horses moving in a tight formation at the gallop were a very imposing sight and could literally make the ground shake under the feet." (Newark, 51, 60; Lawford, 95; DiMarco, 203)

The British desired to create tall and strong horses for themselves. King Charles II started horse-breeding programs in the 1670s. By the early 18th century, a mix of Arabian, Barb, and Turk bloodlines brought the new English Thoroughbred. (DiMarco, 209)

As gold from the New World began to dwindle, European nations had to reduce some of their cavalry forces in the 18th century. It cost three times as much to equip horsemen as to equip infantry. Also, severe epidemics broke out among the animal populations of Western Europe in the 1740s. This lead to a widespread need for veterinarians. A French stable-master named Claude Bourgelat started a school for vets in Lyon in 1761. The school won international fame, and the idea spread to other nations to practice horse care. On the other hand, during times of peace, discipline often collapsed. The French cavalry, during times of peace, were required to act as tax collectors and to build roads. Alcohol and womanizing were key components to the cavalry lifestyle of the day. One regiment initiated a potential leader by seeing if he could drink three bottles of champagne, pleasure three willing wenches, and ride three horses a distance of 20 miles in just three hours. (DiMarco, 161; Lewinsohn, 256–57; Lawford, 94; Meistrich, 48)

Frederick the Great not only kept his frightened men together with the charge, he succeeded magnificently with the cavalry charge. Prussian cavalry superiority came through constant drills and patient training. To order his men to begin a charge, the brilliant cavalry general Friedrich Wilhelm von Seydlitz would throw his clay pipe in the air and shout, "My children, follow me!" Even on campaigns the horsemen practiced head-on attacks, wheeling to the flanks, and marching by squadrons in different maneuvers. The 1757 charge at Rossbach is considered by some to be the greatest cavalry victory since Hannibal's routs of Rome. Von Seydlitz practiced with his horse by riding through the blades of turning windmills, and he would stick his clay smoking pipe into the ground and shoot it down with his pistol shot by shot. Some of his men could shoot accurately as well: von Seydlitz would hold his pipe in hand and let them blast it from his fingers. Von Seydlitz ordered his men to rotate in shifts to his home, were there were water troughs for the horses. The troopers had to jump over the railings and depart by jumping out as well, and if any man fell off his horse, he was punished. Not only did von Seydlitz know the arts of combat, he also knew how to hinder an enemy before they arrived on a battlefield. He would study maps to anticipate the enemy's movements and purposely order his own cavalry to graze there so the enemy would have no fodder. Frederick himself was only a mediocre rider and often fell off, but his cavalrymen and von Seydlitz would look away so as not to embarrass the king. Von Seydlitz clinched the victory at Rossbach, where 50,000 enemies lost to 22,000 Prussians. Frederick developed horse artillery a few years later, with horses pulling "six pounder" guns. Of his 22 victories, 15 were won by cavalry. King Frederick was asked once why he did not wear spurs while riding. He replied, "Try sticking a fork into your bare stomach and you will soon see why." Napoleon used the speedy horse artillery to great effect in the early 19th century. He also increased the number of light cavalry hussars from 1,000 to 15,000. These hussars worked in many capacities, including as military police, keeping down desertions as well as catching enemy spies. (Smith,

65–69; DiMarco, 190–91; Duffy, 16–18; Lawford, 12, 110–12; Edwards, 152–53; Kelekna, 393–94)

Though the French used cavalry with excellent tactics, the French horsemen were not kind to their animals. Though they had manuals and regulations on how to care for horses, many soldiers would try to get out of battle by injuring their mounts, putting tacks or stones under the saddles to create back sores. "Probably one of the most graphic condemnations of a French cavalry was the saying that one could notice the approach of a mounted unit by the smell of the infected sores of its neglected horses." In contrast, though the British overloaded and overworked their horses, they also had many veterinarians checking the horses on a weekly basis. (DiMarco, 216–17)

French cavalry of the 19th century was known to be beautiful, on fine horses, dressed and caparisoned in elegance. However, this in itself was part of the problem. So proud were the French of their appearance, they refused to drill or practice maneuvers lest they become dirty. The French hierarchy was designed to promote men based not on their skill, but upon their loyalty to the principles of "the Revolution" and loyalty to current leaders. Furthermore, as a commanding officer would be guillotined if he suffered defeat, the sensible ones were prone to be wary of ever committing to battle. Strange and unpredictable men ended up becoming cavalry commanders. One General Macard, for instance, rode screaming into battle stripped naked from the waist up, which did not improve his charisma or ability in the slightest. During the Revolution, such chaos ruled France that 6,000 cavalry horses starved to death near the Rhine River. Napoleon, fortunately, was able to bring some order back to the French horsemen and find some competent leaders, like the brilliant Murat and clever Lasalle. (Duffy, 22; Johnson, David, 11–17, 45)

Horses became hard to come by, and regiments were forced to use inferior mounts. Napoleon ordered agents to find as many good horses as possible from other countries, like Germany. Regulations on the size of horses had to be relaxed. Napoleon sent money for buying horses, but the local commanders used much of the money to buy the best possible horses for themselves rather than buying a large quantity of equines for the troops. Thus, in 1806, when the French began moving toward Berlin, Napoleon had 5,000 fewer horses than desired. Fewer horses meant longer working of the available animals, and without periodic removal of their saddles and packs, their backs became ridden with sores. Expert tactics and leadership allowed the French cavalry to succeed even when outnumbered and on exhausted mounts. Charles Lasalle commanded light horsemen, and he specialized in letting the enemy cavalry run about until tired, then charging and destroying them. Napoleon would hold back the cavalry reserve until all enemy units were engaged, then unleash the fresh horsemen on the enemy. Joachim Murat led 10,500 reserves against the Russians at the Battle of Eylau in Prussia, turning the tide with one of the most legendary cavalry charges in history. The French horse reserves could also pursue fleeing enemies to keep them from regrouping. As the Allies invaded Spain, Napoleon lost many key cavalry commanders and armies. By 1810 he needed 28,000 horses to give each of his awaiting men a mount. As they prepared to attack Russia, the quality and size of horses decreased so that the animals could not handle the weight of rider and supplies. (Johnson, David, 43, 47, 60–61, 97; Meistrich, 49, 53)

Napoleon's campaign against Russia was an utter disaster. Marching into Russia the French had 80,000 horses. A problem common to all army movements is the lag time between the movement of the front units and the movement of the back units. General Murat ordered every horse to be saddled and bridled during all daylight hours. If the forward element of cavalry left at sunrise, the rear cavalry would not start marching until four hours later. Fully loaded horses get tired even by standing. Summer and autumn that year were especially hot and so forage was scarce. The Russians burned everything in the marching path of the French, so there was little or nothing to be scavenged from the land. Eight thousand equines died the first week, and General Murat alone lost 30,000 horses in two weeks of November from the cold. They arrived near Moscow with 37,000 horses where a battle was fought, but for some reason Napoleon used only infantry and left the cavalry standing in ranks, thus exposing them to horrendous artillery fire. The Russians burned much of Moscow as the French arrived in 1812, forcing the Napoleonic army to retreat in midwinter. The wagons became stuck in mud and ice. On the coldest nights, riders would disembowel their horses to lay down in the warm entrails to sleep. Even small ditches could pose fatal problems. "To get out they had to climb the opposite incline, thickly coated with ice on which the horses' hoofs, with their smooth, worn-out shoes, could find no hold. One after another they slipped back exhausted—horse and drivers on top of each other. Then the famished soldiers fell upon the fallen horses, killed them and cut them in pieces. They roasted the meat over fires made from the wrecked wagons, and devoured it half cooked and bloody." The men preferred the liver and heart of the horse, saying it tasted like chicken, but the rest of the equine meat was stringy. Starving men, of course, will eat anything. They created "black pudding" out of horse blood. During the retreat as men and equines froze and starved, the Russian Cossacks harried them constantly and very nearly captured Napoleon in a surprise attack. In one case a Russian artillery shell "plowed into the body of a horse, exploded, and blew the animal to pieces without wounding the rider, who landed on his feet and kept on walking." Eighteen hundred French horses made it to Smolensk, but only 1,500 reached France alive. One of the few surviving horses, named Cadet, belonged to Private Melet. He bought the horse in 1806 and they became inseparable. During the Russian winter horror, Melet and Cadet would raid Russian lines at night to find food. They remained together until Waterloo in 1815, when Melet was seriously wounded and Cadet was killed. (Johnson, David, 100–110; Cooper, 28; DiMarco, 208–9; de Segur, 164, 190; Meistrich, 49)

The Russian debacle permanently weakened the French army. Sensing their weakness, the Prussians decided to attack. The French scrambled to find horses and recruits. "Some had only mounted a horse for the first time in their lives two weeks previously. Most of them did not know how to handle their horses or their weapons," and in fact some cavalrymen received a horse only on the eve of battle. (Johnson, David, 118)

The Napoleonic Wars, with the French against a coalition of European enemies, completely drained the continent of its horses. The British had a difficult time finding equines as well, but would not leave them to be captured by the French. In the British retreat to Corunna during the Peninsular War, the boats had no room for the horses. The men shot the animals, and when they ran out of ammunition, they used swords. Horses not killed froze solid. (Cooper, 28–29)

After a brief exile, Napoleon rose again. He was able to raise a large army but could not obtain many quality horses for cavalry. In March 1815 the French had only 16,000 cavalry horses in the army. Napoleon said himself,

"It is impossible to carry on anything but a defensive war, covering oneself by entrenchments and natural obstacles, if one has not a cavalry fairly equal in strength to that of the enemy." The French could not adequately scout the enemy nor even protect their own flanks from enemy horsemen. The Duke of Wellington gathered a new coalition of armies to finish the French at Waterloo on June 18, 1815. When Napoleon's infantry and artillery could not force the British to abandon the heights, the French cavalry was ordered to charge. Heavy rain had made slippery, deep mud, and the horses could not gallop. The animals were already tired by the time they reached the enemy, under heavy artillery barrage the whole time. Reaching the heights achieved nothing, because the British cavalry counterattacked. As the bodies of French horses and men piled up, they served as bloody barricades for the British infantry. (DiMarco, 207–9; Meistrich, 49; Johnson, David, 139–40)

During the battle, many horses were horribly mangled but not killed. In his diary, Capt. Alexander Cavalie Mercer records that he saw one horse with the lower half of its head blown off, yet still trying to join the other horses in pulling a cannon. Another horse lost both hind legs, and it neighed for help, but the men were so sick of blood they could not bring themselves to shoot the beast. One commander said the artillery pieces fired against the cavalry became red-hot. "Those who pushed forward over the heaps of carcasses of men and horses gained but a few paces in advance, there to fall in their turn...like grass before the mower's scythe." The cavalry-type to receive the most glory and acclaim for their effectiveness at Waterloo were the lancers, also called uhlans. This led to a brief revival of cavalry lancers in the 19th century as their commanders hoped their long spears could penetrate infantry squares. (Cooper, 31; Sinclair, 236–37; Lawford, 140)

The Duke of Wellington's favorite horse was named Copenhagen. At Waterloo, Wellington rode Copenhagen from 6:00 a.m. to 11:00 p.m., far longer than a normal day. When Wellington dismounted and tried to pet his horse, Copenhagen lashed out at him, broke free, and ran away, upset at the long day. He returned later. The duke never forgot his favorite horse, and when Copenhagen grew old, he was given a stable, rich pasture and was often hand-fed by the duchess herself. When his teeth wore down and oats were too hard, the oats were mashed for him. Wellington often visited Copenhagen on a daily basis. Upon his death, Copenhagen was buried with full regimental honors, shots rang out in salute, and a giant oak tree was planted on his grave. (Roberts, 27; Coultas, 103–4; Kelekna, 399)

Parts of Asia continued to use vast numbers of cavalry horses after the Mongols and their heirs the Moguls diminished. In 1759, one army of India included 50,000 horsemen. Though the opposing Afghans were outnumbered, with their heavier horses they surprised the Indians and defeated them. Such huge battles between the Asian powers made it much simpler for the colonial British to take over in later decades. (Lawford, 124–26)

The British pursued their colonial policy in many lands around the world. Their most valued foreign possessions, South Africa and India, required a large military presence. Permanent garrisons of troops were kept in these lands, but it was not enough for thorough control. The British trained Sikhs and other Indian natives to be cavalry. Amusingly, these auxiliary horsemen were trained to ride their horses well: they were trained to turn right, turn left, and charge. They were not trained to turn about, because the British feared they might run away. Leaving out parts of important cavalry training may have been a poor idea, though. In 1841, a British invasion force of 16,000 men was annihilated by Afghani nomadic horsemen. (Hamid, 29; Kelekna, 395)

The Carnivorous Horse

One unusual story of a horse comes from India in the early 19th century. A British secretary to King George IV was traveling in India when a man-eating horse attacked his caravan. He saw it carrying a child in its mouth, and he saw the body of a woman it had partially eaten. They were able to capture this crazed beast. The governors of India decided to hold a public spectacle to see how the carnivorous horse would fare against a royal tiger. When the horse and tiger were put in a corral together, the horse repeatedly kicked the tiger, breaking its jaw. A second tiger was put in with the horse, but the tiger was terrified of the beast and would not come close to it. Finally the people decided to keep the man-eating horse alive in an iron cage as a curiosity. (Hamid, 171–81)

In 1838, 10,000 Zulu warriors attacked 500 British soldiers under Andries Pretorius and were defeated. The Zulus and other tribes who rebelled in southern Africa could not breed horses of their own because of diseases. One small place where natives could breed horses was modern Lesotho, in the Drakensberg Mountains. There King Moshoeshoe fielded 7,000 cavalry against the British and was able to retain his people's independence. (Kelekna, 393)

The British were involved with the most famous cavalry charge in history. It became famous because of a poem by Alfred, Lord Tennyson, with the recited line, "into the valley of death rode the six hundred."

The British and Russians fought in the Crimean War (1853–1856). The troops from England sought to capture Sevastopol from the Russians, their main base on the Black Sea. Eighty-eight ships carried 33,452 men and 3,349 horses from Britain to Balaclava. Later ships brought another 15,000 horses. On October 25, 1854, the Russians had a far greater force. Early in the day, the British earned a brilliant victory as some 300 to 800 cavalry attacked and drove 2,500–3,000 Russian horsemen off the field. This action became known as the Charge of the Heavy Brigade. ("Balaclava"; Sutton and Walker, 43–44; Newark, 100–1; Sinclair, 244; Maitland, 23)

Some young British officers desperately wanted to prove themselves brave by attacking their enemies. The Russians held all of the ridges of a U-shaped valley, with long cannons at the rear, and smaller artillery and riflemen all along the crest of the hill. When the British commander Lord Raglan ordered the cavalry to "reclaim" some cannons captured by the Russians, his instructions were apparently misinterpreted. He likely intended that nearby guns at the ends of the hills be retaken, but an ambitious young officer said the Light Brigade was ordered to charge through the entire valley to take the big cannons at the far end. Four thousand Russians lined the sides of the canyon. Recognizing it was a suicide mission, the British horsemen put on their best uniforms. (Urwin, "Mad-Brained," 33–36)

Six hundred seventy-three British cavalry started the mile-long trip through the narrow pass at a trot, since they could not gallop the full mile.

Before the second line had gotten half way to the guns, Paget and his men found themselves floundering over a bizarre obstacle course, pulling their reins to the right or left to avoid trampling or tripping over the bleeding forms left behind by Cardigan's two leading regiments. Presently, riderless horses, some crazed with pain, and others driven mad with fear from all the noise and carnage, were rushing into line with Paget's harassed troopers, as they had been trained. Riding out in front, at one point Lord George was surrounded by seven of these terrified, wide-eyed beasts. They seemed to cringe against him for protection, smashing into his legs and covering his overalls with their blood. They nearly unseated him several times, and things got so tight he had to draw his sword and drive them off more than once. (ibid., 67)

As the horsemen approached their target at the end of the canyon, a final Russian salvo swept the British with grapeshot, similar to the pellets from a giant shotgun. The screaming horses collapsed in their tracks and flipped over, "many of them rolling and thrashing and crushing their helpless riders beneath them." Enough British reached the cannons to disable several of them, but then the Russian cavalry counter-charged. The surviving British then had to brave the mile-long gallop back to their own lines through the deadly valley. (ibid., 68)

The battle of the Light Brigade lasted about 25 minutes. Two hundred thirty horsemen reached the Russian guns, 195 returned, and 335 horses died or were mercifully put down. The violent fate of the equines at Balaclava may have been a sort of blessing, since in the next two months, 1,800 out of 2,000 horses in the division starved to death. Lord Cardigan survived the battle and returned with his horse, Ronald. When Ronald died, Cardigan had the animal's head removed and mounted in a glass case in his home. ("Balaclava"; Urwin, "Mad-Brained," 69; Sinclair, 245; Edwards, 155; Felber, 28)

The greatest of the European cavalry battles occurred during the Franco-Prussian War, in 1870. Over three days of August there were numerous small conflicts, with a final large engagement. The new weapons on the scene would change cavalry forever. The British described them this way:

Naturally we have heard about the French mitralleuse, how this gun consisted of an iron cylinder containing more than thirty rifle-barrels fixed in a frame, how it could fire about thirty rounds a minute and required only some five seconds for reloading. We know something too, of the Maxim. Was it not Lord Salisbury who told Sir Hiram Maxim that he had prevented more men dying of old age than any other person who ever lived? The Maxim could spurt 500 rounds a minute and that from a single barrel...One officer tells us that under certain field conditions the whole of our regiment could be wiped out in five minutes by a small battery of Hotchkiss guns properly placed. (Maitland, 29)

On August 6, while the Germans attacked a French division, the French commander called on 1,000 of Michel's Cuirassier brigade and the 6th Lancers of Duhesme's division to cover their retreat. They charged the Germans and were mowed down by breech-loading rifles. A few hours later, the commander sent 2,000 cuirassiers with sabers to slow the German pursuit. In 10 minutes 1,500 of the men were down, and not a single horse returned alive. (Ascoli, 81–82)

The Germans, on a different field, ordered a charge of hussars up a steep hill against a French entrenched position. The French used the new Mitralleuse guns. None of Kameke's fusiliers returned. (ibid., 89)

French general Francois Achille Bazaine sent a cuirassier regiment of Imperial Guards against the Germans in three lines with drawn sabers crying "Vive l'Empereur!" The Germans waited till the enemy came close. One volley dropped the whole first line of horses. The second and third groups of horsemen could not get past the piles of fallen horses and men. (ibid., 152–53)

In one case, the sacrifice of cavalrymen created a victory. A group of 800 German uhlans, dragoons, and cuirassiers under General von Bredow charged against a vastly superior French infantry force. Half of the horsemen were cut down. However, the unexpected attack of cavalry threw the French center into disarray and allowed the Germans time to bring up reinforcements to save the day. "There can be few more singular examples in the long catalogue of war when the action of so small a parcel of men succeeded in throwing so great a body of the enemy into such absolute disarray." The event became known as the Todtenritt, or Death Ride. (Ascoli, 172, 177; Smith, 261; Newark, 114)

The final great cavalry battle near Vionville, also called the Battle of Mars-La-Tour, involved 5,000 men, in 49 squadrons. Over 15 minutes, such confusion reigned that some forces attacked their own men. The Prussians gradually gained an advantage and held their ground, though it was not a decisive victory. When the German bugler sounded the evening call, 602 badly wounded horses struggled back to their line, crawling and shuffling, so that many soldiers wept at the pitiful sight. (Ascoli, 200–2; Cooper, 32)

Over three days of battle in the area, more than 64,000 men lay dead or wounded. The Germans had been outnumbered, but the French badly used their cavalry. Their cavalry doctrine "was still rooted in the distant past when thundering squadrons rode down and pursued a demoralized enemy....By 1870 fire-power had changed the geometry of the battle-field." This was the first major European conflict using the early machine gun and repeating rifle. Neither the Germans nor the French yet recognized how devastating the rapid-fire weapons would be against horses. (Ascoli, 163)

American Indians and the Early United States

The Spaniards did not bother conquering North American natives because they had no gold to steal. European invaders focused on the Mexican Aztecs and Peruvian Incas in search of treasure. The horse had been extinct for many thousands of years on the American continent, and the natives often fled in terror from the Spanish horses and dogs.

Before horses came, the native North Americans used dogs to pull a long travois: two long poles with cloth between, acting like a sled. A dog could pull about 66 pounds in this manner. The people walked while the dogs pulled small loads. The native peoples could not travel far or fast on foot. (Kelekna, 372)

When the Spanish conquered Mexico and then invaded Peru, horses had to be imported by ship. More than half of the horses died on the long trip across the Atlantic Ocean. A shortage of horses in Europe led Spain to embargo the sending of horses to the New World, so the conquistadores had to breed horses on their own. Many Spaniards started stud farms in Mexico in the mid-1520s. They hired Indians and slaves to help work the ranches. Gradually, horses worked their way into North America. By the 1590s, the Comanches were famous horsemen, called the "Horse Indians" by the Spaniards. By the 17th century, horses were common all the way north to Wyoming, and the Native American cultures had been transformed from sedentary hunter-gatherers to nomadic horsemen. Horses could pull a travois with four times as much weight as dogs could, and twice the distance. This enabled the Indians to make longer forays into the plains. (Steiner, 144; DiMarco, 275; Kelekna, 372)

The Spanish controlled much of Central and South America and had even moved up into the regions of California, Arizona, New Mexico, and Texas. In the 1680s, the Indians revolted against the Spanish and forced them out of the region. One Catholic in Sonora, California, named Father Kino cared for the Indians and remained in the region as a rancher. He taught many Indians how to ride, and he gave them horses. The natives of South America also revolted. The Argentines drove out the Spanish in the 1770s, then the Portuguese were driven from Uruguay, and the British from Buenos Aires in 1807. (Steiner, 143–44; Kelekna, 377)

The North American Indians "broke" a wild horse in a unique manner. A brave would lasso and throw the animal to the ground, then tighten a rope around its neck till it nearly choked to death. Then the man breathed into the horse's nostrils, offering his own spirit to the horse. When the horse revived a bit, the man tied its legs so it could stand up but not run or kick. He ran his hands all over the horse's body to soothe and calm it. Native American skill at riding was unmatched in the continent. Plains Indians usually rode with only a thong around the horse's neck rather than a bridle and reins, and a brave could hang low along one side of the horse for protection against bullets and arrows. Some Indians painted art with colored clay on their warhorses or tied tassels and feathers on their manes and tails. A few tribes were said to worship horses. The Dakotas prayed to horses, and the Arikaras believed the souls of horses would "arise in judgment against cruel riders." (Steiner, 154–55; Kelekna, 373; Wyman, 81–82)

The next pressure to come upon the Indians would be from the east rather than the southwest. Europeans formed colonies along the Atlantic seaboard and steadily drove natives to the west. In 1609 a shipment of horses arrived at the Plymouth Virginia colony. The Dutch imported horses to New Amsterdam (later New York City) in 1625. Soon mares and stallions arrived at the Massachusetts Bay Colony. The French in Canada

Col. William Augustine Washington at the Battle of Cowpens. (Drawn and engraved for *Grahams Magazine,* by S. H. Gimber, 148-GW-390.) (Courtesy The National Archives.)

brought horses even earlier, by 1604, and they sold muskets and ammunition to the natives, hoping to hinder British expansion in North America. Mounted troops played only a minor role in the French and Indian Wars because the heavily forested wilderness curtailed their movements. Young Col. George Washington, trying to defend Fort Necessity against the French, asked for reinforcements. An officer Fry on horseback led some troops to help, but he was killed when the horse threw him and broke his neck. A few years later, when General Braddock tried to reach and capture Fort Duquesne in 1755, 300 ax-men had to clear a path for the 150 wagons and 600 packhorses. In eight days they covered only 30 miles. George Washington accompanied the British army as an aide-de-camp and helped in the exhausting march. Some horses, struggling to pull heavy cannons over difficult terrain, died in their harnesses of overexertion. The French and Indians ambushed the British, and General Braddock had four horses shot from under him before he sustained a fatal wound. Washington escaped. (Wyman, 29–30; Kelekna, 373; Sutton and Walker, 18–19; Lengel; Carter, 2)

Some Americans of the 18th century recognized the usefulness of cavalry. Benjamin Franklin, in *Poor Richard's Almanac*, wrote, "For the want of a horse the rider was lost, for the want of a rider the battle was lost." The American Revolution of the colonies against England may have been prolonged because Gen. George Washington is said to have been unenthusiastic about cavalry. Though he may have liked his own horse, Blueskin, he did not see any purpose in cavalry. Lack of mounted support cost him dearly at battles in Manhattan and Long Island. On December 11, 1776, Washington did write to Congress, recommending the establishment of a cavalry corps. Within two weeks the corps started forming, but Washington treated them as minor auxiliaries, good only for running errands. (Downey, 24; *Army Times*, 14; Livingston and Roberts, 37; Urwin, *U.S. Cavalry*, 13)

A few small mounted colonial units acted freely to harass the enemy, causing great trouble for the British. Capt. Allan McLane of Philadelphia, with two or three friends, made numerous surprise attacks. In one case, McLane charged on his horse through the portico of a ballroom during Lord Howe's farewell ball, killing three guards. (*Army Times*, 18)

In September 1777, Polish Count Casimir Pulaski took over the Corps of Continental Dragoons. He died two years later during a reckless charge at Savannah. Comte de Rochambeau brought 280 French hussars, who helped at the battle of York River and the siege of Gloucester. They served until 1783. (Newark, 187)

Capt. Henry Lee of the 1st Continental Light Dragoons came to be called "Light Horse Harry." Lee came from a long line of horsemen going back to the medieval Crusades. Lee was the only non-general to receive a gold medal for gallant service from Congress during the Revolutionary War. Light Horse Harry became a good friend to George Washington. His son Robert E. Lee would later command the Confederates in the Civil War. Col. William Washington commanded the 3rd Continental Light Dragoons, but his horse was shot and he was captured. (Perry; Newark, 187–88)

The British used horses against the Colonials but did not always use them effectively. While preparing to invade Philadelphia, the horses were kept aboard ships for a full month, without exercise, trapped in hot, humid stalls, and without sufficient food and water. The horses started dying and were thrown overboard to prevent disease from affecting the other animals.

When the troops finally landed, hundreds of animals were dead, and the rest emerged emaciated, hardly able to walk. The British dragoons lacked cavalry horses for weeks and thus were practically immobile. (Lengel)

The southern theater of the Revolution saw the most cavalry action. "Over-mountain men" from Virginia, Tennessee, and the Carolinas destroyed Ferguson's Tory Corps at King's Mountain in 1780. Lord Cornwallis used green-coated dragoons under men like "Bloody Tarleton" to terrify rebels. Lt. Col. Banastre Tarleton made long, swift raids against the Colonials, earning his nickname in part when his men "massacred" captured enemies with saber and bayonet. At Cowpens in 1781 Tarleton was finally defeated, in part with Col. Andrew Pickens's mounted militia. Francis Marion, "The Swamp Fox," harassed the British in small raids, often seeking to capture the fine English horses, since the heavy work animals of the southern United States were not good cavalry mounts. Marion captured one horse named Ball and used it throughout the war. Brig. Gen. Daniel Morgan led another rebel force, in South Carolina. (*Army Times*, 27; Lawford, 156; Sinclair, 164–65; Carter, 2)

The Colonial Army did not use cavalry in an organized manner, and the U.S. Congress cut cavalry funding immediately after the war. Whenever troubles arose, they briefly authorized a new cavalry to be formed, and as quickly cut it down.

The Indians soon began to chafe against the U.S. westward expansion. In 1790 near Cincinnati, Ohio, the Indians defeated the state militiamen. A local commander wrote, "Without a regular cavalry, I know not how the Indians can ever be effectively checked." He could not pursue the mounted natives, and Congress did not want to fund cavalrymen. What few detachments of dragoons existed were used mainly for catching deserters from army forts. After a few years and rising public anger over Indian attacks, funding came through. In July 1794, Maj. Gen. "Mad Anthony" Wayne used a flanking cavalry attack to encircle and rout 1,000 Indians at the Battle of Fallen Timbers. (Urwin, *U.S. Cavalry*, 31; Prucha, 31; Newark, 191)

The War of 1812, in which the British allied with several Indian tribes, saw an increase in U.S. cavalry actions. Some horsemen used the 1811 book "Colonel Herrie's Instructions for Volunteer Corps of Cavalry": the first truly American cavalry manual on drill and tactics. Though Congress authorized money to raise two regiments of dragoons, they never formed.

However, Kentucky and Tennessee each provided a mounted militia that served well. (Ottevaere, 6; Carter, 2)

On October 5, 1813, east of Detroit, Michigan, 900 British regulars joined with 2,000 Indians under Tecumseh to attack 3,500 Americans under Brig. Gen. William Harrison at the Battle of the Thames. The American cavalry leader, Col. Richard Mentor Johnson, led the Kentucky cavalry against the redcoats, causing them to flee. The Indians remained in defensive positions in the swamp and led a terrific volley of bullets, forcing most of the Kentuckians to dismount. One native jumped up and wounded Johnson in the arm, but Johnson fired his pistol from horseback and killed the Indian with a hit to his face. Legend has it that the Indian was Tecumseh himself, and Johnson's admirers later sang a chant, "Rumpsey, Dumpsey, Colonel Johnson killed Tecumseh!" This victory ended the British influence in the northwestern sector of the states. Johnson became vice president in the Van Buren administration. (Newark, 191–92; Urwin, *U.S. Cavalry*, 46; Utley and Washburn, 138; *Army Times*, 34)

In Tennessee, the Creek Indians massacred many Americans in the summer of 1813. Maj. Gen. Andrew Jackson led his Tennessee state militia of 1,500 mounted riflemen. The militia made a night encirclement attack on the main Creek village of Tallushatchee on November 3, killing 186 braves. A few months later, the last 1,200 Creek Indians made a stand against Jackson's army, but a cavalry attack from the rear finished them off. (Urwin, *U.S. Cavalry*, 48)

Andrew Jackson used his cavalry to hold New Orleans against a superior British force at the end of the war. The cavalry had many victories in the war, though most of their opponents had been on foot, not mounted. In spite of the effectiveness of U.S. horsemen, Congress again unfunded them in 1815 when the war ended. (*Army Times*, 37–38; Urwin, *U.S. Cavalry*, 49)

From 1815 to 1832 the United States had no cavalry. Indian depredations finally forced Congress to reestablish the U.S. cavalry, with President Andrew Jackson choosing leaders for them. The U.S. Mounted Rangers of 1832 did not fare well. Pay was minuscule; the men had to furnish their own horses, clothes, and weapons. Young Abraham Lincoln led the 1st Regiment of the Brigade of Mounted Volunteers during the Black Hawk War of 1832 in Illinois, but he and his men found only scalped victims,

Blackfoot Indian on horseback, circa 1833. (Painting by Karl Bodmer.) (Courtesy National Archives.)

no Indians to fight. In 1833, a federal force called the 1st Dragoons was created, and it included a "who's who" of famous future leaders including Winfield Scott, Stephen W. Kearney, Nathan Boone (son of frontiersman Daniel Boone), and Jefferson Davis. While the leaders may have excelled, the general condition of the cavalry units did not. Recruiters told ridiculous lies to raise troops quickly, keeping none of their promises. These units often had no horses or weapons; far more Indians died of smallpox during the 1830s than died during engagements with U.S. cavalry. (Urwin, *U.S. Cavalry*, 51–60; Utley and Washburn, 148, 167; Prucha, 240–41; *Army Times*, 41)

Some leaders tried to cooperate with the Indians to keep the peace. Sam Houston, when president of the Republic of Texas, worked with the Comanches. At Fort Chadburne, Texas, a Comanche Indian participated in horse races, challenging the three best U.S. Army riders. He defeated them in three consecutive races, and in the fourth race he rode backward so he could make faces at the slower competitors. The soldiers said that the Comanche's horse looked like a dog. By contrast, the expensive, well-bred horses bought by the army, accustomed to the green fields of Kentucky or Tennessee, wilted in the Texas heat without their fine eastern alfalfa. Browsing on scrub brush and the occasional handful of corn could not sustain "fine" horses. Smart cavalrymen learned to seek local, hardy mounts, like the Indians did. Recruits were taught to watch for any sores on their horses, since blowflies could turn the sores into serious wounds. They learned not to allow the horses to eat the same field too long, lest they eat the grass to the roots and consume some clay, plugging their kidneys and killing them. Officers had to ensure that individual soldiers cared properly for their mounts. As for Sam Houston's idea of cooperating with the Indians, the sentiment did not sit well with the next governor of Texas. Mirabeau Buonaparte Lamar completely reversed this policy and alienated the Indians. Four hundred Comanches raided Texas, burning Linnville, sacking Victoria, and stealing thousands of horses and mules. In 1843 the Comanches drove off most settlers in Austin. ("Great Indian Wars," DVD, 5; Steiner, 146; Arnold, 61, 98, 107)

The 1st and 2nd U.S. Dragoons became a tough and disciplined force in the late 1830s, fighting Indians and riding the Great Plains. They would play a decisive role in the Mexican War (1846–1848). The Mexicans had at least 20 regiments of mounted regulars and militia cavalry. Sgt. Jack Miller of the 2nd U.S. Dragoons was leading a small patrol when they stumbled across a large enemy force near Monclova. His men grabbed for their carbines, but he roared, "No firing, men! If twenty dragoons can't whip a hundred greasers with the saber, I'll join the Doughboys and carry a fence rail all my life!" They charged and bowled over the Mexicans, killing 6, wounding 13, and capturing 70, with no casualties among his horses or men. The Mexican horsemen were often superior to the U.S. Army troops, as was the case at the famous small Battle of San Pasqual near San Diego, California. Brig. Gen Stephen W. Kearney's cavalry force was nearly destroyed by 100 Mexican lancers. They used a lesser-known weapon called the "reata," or lasso. The Mexicans would toss a rope over the U.S. riders and yank them from their horses. Only the lucky arrival of an artillery piece saved the U.S. cavalry from destruction on December 6, 1846. (Urwin, *U.S. Cavalry*, 79; Regan)

When the Mexican War ended in 1848, the U.S. cavalry had taken California, Nevada, and Utah, plus portions of New Mexico, Arizona, Colorado, and Wyoming from the enemy. "Never in modern history, had mounted troops accomplished anything of comparable lasting value." (Urwin, *U.S. Cavalry*, 89)

1848 saw the end of a war but the rise of another major movement in U.S. history. The discovery of gold in California inspired 100,000 settlers to head west in 1849 and 1850. This mass invasion of whites across the Great Plains rekindled the simmering conflict between Indians and whites. Thousands upon thousands of settlers and their animals moved westward, so that cavalry detachments said they had to avoid emigrant caravans just to find forage for their horses. In spite of periodic raids by various Indian tribes, the U.S. Army garrisoned a huge proportion of infantry in western forts, rather than cavalry. In Texas. for instance, in the 1850s, 20 of the 28 companies of troops were infantry. A headstrong cavalry officer at Fort Laramie, Lt. John Gratton, tried to arrest a Sioux Indian accused of killing an ox in Wyoming in 1854. When tribal leaders refused to turn over the suspect, Gratton shot the chief dead. The tribe slaughtered Gratton and his whole 29-man patrol. Secretary of War Jefferson Davis claimed the "Gratton Massacre" was a devious plan for an Indian uprising, and he sent reinforcements to the region. ("Great Indian Wars," DVD, part 2, 5; Prucha, 389; Utley and Washburn, 205; Arnold, 16)

In 1857 the Cheyenne again rose up in arms. Colonel Sumner led the U.S. cavalry to subdue the Cheyenne at the Solomon River. When a chief wants to go to war, he mounts his horse, holds a long pole with red flag tipped with eagle feathers, and rides through the camp singing a war song. The warrior's lance was a 4.5-foot wooden pole with 2.5-foot tapered steel blade, often painted red and adorned with yarn and beaded cloth. He would have a brightly painted shield of wicker with deer skins and buffalo hide, decorated with feathers and human scalps or bear claws. One of the tribe's medicine men had the 300 warriors bathe in "magic water," promising that they were thus protected against all bullets. Though Sumner probably did not know this belief of the Cheyenne, he ordered his horsemen to put away their rifles and charge with sabers. The Indians seemed confident before the battle when bullets threatened, but the magic water did not promise protection against blades, so most of the warriors fled. Nine

Indians died, versus only two cavalry deaths. One of the cavalrymen at the Battle of the Solomon River was J. E. B. Stuart. He saved his friend Lomax and received one gunshot wound to the chest, but it bounced off a rib and he recovered after a few weeks. Stuart invented a couple of useful cavalry tools including a saber bracket and a horse hitching device while convalescing. Stuart would become a feared Confederate cavalry general a few years after his wounds at Solomon River. The U.S. cavalry learned that in combat against Indians, the best way to win was to separate the braves from their horses. Attacking the Indians' camp and driving off the ponies made the braves much less dangerous to face in battle. (Urwin, *U.S. Cavalry*, 98; Arnold, 60, 95; "Long Knives," DVD; Davis, 40–43; Essin, 51)

The Indians were not the only troublemakers in the western lands. The Mormons of Utah sought to create their own nation called Deseret, and the 2nd Cavalry moved to the Rocky Mountains in case force would be required to keep Utah part of the United States. As the cavalry forces moved into the mountains, terrible snowstorms swept down on the troops and their lines of wagons. At 20 degrees below zero, the axle grease froze and the horses, mules, and oxen fell by the hundreds. Happily, no civil war ensued and the United States made peace with the Mormons without bloodshed. (Arnold, 168–69)

Horses in the American Civil War

The American Civil War and its use of cavalry horses completely changed the U.S. military. From sporadic use in the American Revolution, to limited use in the War of 1812, to heavy use in the Mexican War, cavalry would be a dominant force in the bloodiest years of our history. The United States had the largest horse population in the world in 1860, with 4,504,852 horses according to the census: most in the north. (DiMarco, 240)

The Union possessed the major advantages of manpower, industrial capacity, transportation capacity, and money. The North also had more horses, but these animals were used almost exclusively for pulling carts, plows, and streetcars. Northerners used carriages and had little experience with horseback riding. The North began the war with over 3 million horses and 800,000 mules, compared to 1.7 million horses and 100,000 mules in the south. The South, or Confederacy, had the advantages of experienced leadership and experience on horseback. The southern states had few roads suitable for wheeled vehicles, using horse paths instead. Because southerners loved their equines and used them for work and show, they kept close watch over the breeds and qualities of both stallions and mares. One of the South's favorite riding songs said, "If you want to smell hell, if you want to have fun, if you want to catch the devil, jine [join] the cavalry." (Carter, 3; Koenig, 7–8; Downey, 24–25; Smith, 116, 128)

The northerners not only lacked cavalry, they did not wish to create any. On April 15, 1861, when President Abraham Lincoln called for volunteers to fight the southern rebellion, the governors of Indiana, Minnesota, and Pennsylvania all offered mounted regiments. The War Department said no, there would be no need for cavalry; the war would be short. Similarly, the Union offered 90-day enlistments for infantry soldiers, expecting a quick and easy victory. Gen. Winfield Scott thought cavalry outdated in modern warfare and advised states not to accept many cavalry volunteers. In the first three years of the Civil War, the Army of the Potomac sent only five mounted charges against the enemy during major battles. This army also fielded so few horses that the cavalry-to-infantry ratio never amounted to more than 9 percent, while armies like that of Napoleon used 20–25 percent cavalry. For this reason, the early years of the cavalry war relate mostly to the Confederacy. (Urwin, *U.S. Cavalry*, 108–9; Lawford, 158; Downey, 13–14; Griffith, 61–63)

Though the southern experience of horseback riding did bring a great advantage to their cavalry units, not every man or horse arrived battle-ready. One Texas regiment arrived in Rome, Georgia, in their saddles. The riders were superb horsemen, forming up in the center of town before heading to war. At dinnertime, a black waiter working for a Chinese restaurant came outside and struck a big copper gong to announce mealtime. "Horses reared, plunged, and turning like goats, stampeded in all directions, leaving many riders on the ground, and creating more excitement than the fire of a Federal battery would have done." Though Texas and all of the southern states would provide cavalry units, Virginia ponied up the most, with 27 regiments and 17 battalions. (Morton, 219–20; Carter, 5)

One problem with having multiple elite cavalry leaders is their tendency to compete with each other. Two Confederate commanders, Turner Ashby and J. E. B. Stuart, became angry when it seemed that one might be promoted over the other, so each had to be given a separate command. Col. Thomas "Stonewall" Jackson took Ashby for his cavalry, while Stuart worked independently under Robert E. Lee. (Carter, 17)

On April 28, 1861, Thomas Jackson asked Turner Ashby to gather information on General Patterson's positions north of the Potomac River. Ashby dressed up like a country veterinarian and rode from one Union camp to another, treating their wagon horses with liniments. He returned to General Jackson with volumes of detail about the enemy dispositions. Ashby hated to retreat. When Jackson's 4,600 men were faced with 37,000 advancing Union soldiers, the southerners had to retreat through Winchester, Virginia. Ashby remained in town as the last man. Two Union cavalrymen lunged ahead to capture him. Ashby charged them angrily, killing one with a bullet through the chest and seizing the other by the throat, pulling him from the saddle and carrying him away as a prisoner of war. As the retreat continued with the Union closing in, Turner Ashby remained behind to set off explosive charges on a bridge. A running Union soldier shot Ashby's horse, a snow-white Arabian. Ashby cut down the soldier with a sword stroke, and the stallion carried his rider safely back to his lines, but once there, it collapsed. One of Jackson's staff assistants, Henry Kyd, wrote, "Then Ashby knelt beside it stroking its mane and looking into its eyes until it died. Thus the most splendid horseman I ever knew lost the most beautiful war-horse I ever saw." Not long after, Ashby would lose another horse, and his own life. (Carter, 39–43; O'Ferrall)

J. E. B. Stuart, who had fought against the Cheyenne, now fought a new enemy but continued to innovate. His rival Ashby had tried using small artillery pieces to give his cavalry more firepower, and Stuart perfected this with the Stuart Horse Artillery, a three-gun battery. Stuart's first defeat was suffered at Dranesville, largely by enemy artillery, so he was eager to have guns of his own. He also started "Camp Cripple," keeping a separate area behind the troops where wounded men and horses could recuperate and receive treatment. They changed the name from Camp Cripple to Company Q, but rumors got around that some of Stuart's men were faking injuries to get out of fighting. After the loss at Gettysburg, with other generals looking to pass blame, Stuart had to nix Company Q. (Davis, 56, 83–85, 356; Carter, 20–21)

During the first major battle of the war, Bull Run, Stuart's horsemen were not called until late in the combat. They were waiting near a Confederate hospital watching, and retching, as doctors cut off the wounded arms and legs of soldiers. Finally ordered forward, the 500 horsemen charged at the New York Zouaves, who panicked and ran. As the Union retreat became widespread, the cavalry pursuit terrified the fleeing federals, and Confederate horsemen came to be called "the Black Horse" by the northerners. One of Stuart's captains, Blackford, pursued the enemy for many miles. He and his horse became very thirsty. The river was red with blood, but they were so thirsty they drank from it anyway. Blackford saw some wounded horses following the battery of cannons they had been pulling and saw what he thought was a rider being dragged behind one of the horses. Going over to free the man he found that the horse was dragging its entrails, not a rider, from a gaping cannonball wound. "On many battlefields my pity has been so touched by the sufferings of wounded horses that I would stop and put them out of their pain by a friendly pistol shot," wrote Blackford. After the battle, Gen. Jubal Early commended Stuart for his actions. On the other side of the lines, the rout and flight forced the Union to reconsider its refusal to start cavalry units. Within a month, the northerners began drafting horsemen. (Davis, 62–64; Downey, 34–35; Urwin, *U.S. Cavalry*, 110)

STUART'S CAVALRY CUTTING TELEGRAPH WIRES.

J. E. B. Stuart's cavalry cutting down telegraph lines, American Civil War. (*Pictorial History of the United States,* by Henry Davenport Northrop, vol. 2. Philadelphia: National Publishing Co., 1901, p. 752.)

Like the ancient Romans, northern soldiers frowned on horsemen, calling them "buttermilk rangers" and "critter boys." Even the Union leaders looked on cavalry as nothing more than messengers or a light screening force. It would be almost two years before cavalry was taken seriously. It took time to shape them into a decent fighting force and for the leadership to learn how to deploy them. One infantry soldier wrote to his father about watching the new cavalry recruits in training: "It was comic to see the cavalry splashing around and hear the taunts and jeers of the infantry. Cavalry never has and never will fight and is heartily despised by the men who do the fighting." During the first two years of the war, 284,000 chargers were delivered to federal regiments, yet no more than 60,000 troopers were mounted at any one time. Aside from suffering battle wounds, "thousands [of horses] were needlessly crippled by the inattention of inexperienced riders and the lengthy hare-brained raids that were so frequently sanctioned." Men with no understanding of horses more easily brought the animals to harm. One frequent illness of horses is "foundering," a swelling of the hooves that has many causes. Commonly, this happens when riders allow the animals to overeat young grass or to drink a lot of cold water when they are overheated. (Carter, 4–5, 250; Urwin, *U.S. Cavalry*, 113; Smith, 118–19)

One early problem for the raising of Union cavalry was that their inexperience with horses enabled "horse traders" to take advantage. During the war, a horse cost $150–$185: 6 times as much as a repeating rifle, and 10 times as much as the monthly pay of a private soldier. In 1861 and 1862 the Union horse buyers were defrauded en masse, purchasing many blind and lame horses. In a Saint Louis shipment of horses, only 76 out of 411 animals sold to the army were fit for service: 330 were undersized, "overaged, stifled, ringboned, blind, spavined, or otherwise crippled." Also, the states raising Union cavalry had no idea what sort of requirements they should ask of volunteers, and they sometimes recruited men too small or too huge to ride well on a standard-sized horse. (DiMarco, 241; Griffith, 63; Downey, 21–22, 27)

In the Fall of 1861 the governor came for a parade review of the newly formed 7th Indiana Cavalry. "The horses having been but recently drawn, had never been exercised in drill. Some of them had never been backed…The men were as green as the horses. Some of them never having been on a horse's back, did not know how to mount. Those who had wild steeds, had great difficulty in maintaining their positions in the saddle, and some in attempting to mount suddenly found themselves on the ground. However, after great effort, the horses were sufficiently quieted, so as to stand in reasonable proximity to each other. The hour having arrived for the review, the companies were marched to the parade ground, and the regiment, after long and patient effort, formed in a reasonably straight line. Governor Morton and his Staff, accompanied by Colonel Shanks, took their positions in front of the regiment. Colonel Shanks, in genuine military style, gave the command 'Draw Sabres.' The men obeyed the order. The sabers in being drawn made a great rattling and clatter, and waved over the horse's heads, the sight and sound of which greatly frightened them. This was more than they could bear. Some of them reared and plunged, depositing their riders on the ground; others darted over the commons, their riders hatless, holding on with both hands to the horses' manes, or the pommels of their saddles, presenting pictures not in keeping with accomplished equestrianism…So ended the first grand review of the regiment." (DiMarco, 244)

The Confederates were not without their own institutional problems. The South lacked funds, manpower, and horseflesh. The difficulty was exacerbated when the Union captured much of Kentucky, Missouri, and Tennessee, where the best horse-breeding grounds lay. Perhaps related to these shortages, the Confederate war department required all cavalry applicants to provide their own horse. If the soldier's horse was killed, the government paid him a fair value so he might buy another animal, but if the horse was just wounded or disabled there was no reimbursement. Then, the soldier must join the infantry until he could find another horse. This caused much absenteeism, as horseless troopers scoured the countryside looking for a replacement. Thus, southern cavalry units spent a significant amount of time raiding and trying to capture Union horses. Not only horses, but supplies of every kind: fodder, clothing, and even weapons were sought by the Confederate raiders. J. E. B. Stuart and his men would personally stop to remove bridles, reins, saddles, and any other useful equipment from dead men and horses. "It was a common sight to see his riders bearing the amputated hooves of animals slain in the North's cause to rebel farriers for removal with nippers and then reuse of precious horseshoes." Of course raids not only equipped the southerners but disrupted and confused the enemy. An eyewitness wrote, "Much of the Southern cavalry was ridiculously equipped. In one regiment I have seen four or five different kinds of rifles and shotguns; all sorts of saddles, some with rope stirrups, many of the saddles without blankets; all sorts of bridles, and in fact a conglomerate getup fairly laughable. The horses were usually fed on raw corn on the cob. Baled hay, sacked corn and oats, such as the Union army had, was a rarity on the other side." (Downey, 25; Smith, 137; Jacobs, xi; Davis, 266–67; Eisenschiml and Newman, 79)

Col. John Hunt Morgan and his raiders drove the Union army to distraction in Kentucky in 1862. Many of the cavalry actions had no military value except to annoy the enemy and force them to commit more troops for defense. Morgan's raiders would tap telegraph wires, intercepting communications and sending false messages. He would capture enemy gunboats, set them ablaze, and run them into docks and other boats. When Morgan faced large enemy forces, he would ride up under a white flag of truce and demand that the enemy surrender. It was just a ploy so he could get a closer view of the foe's positions. Skill and cleverness cannot change the weather, however. During Morgan's third Kentucky raid in late December, the cold was so intense that the horses were "stupefied," with icicles hanging from their manes and dangling from their nostrils. (Carter, 54; Walsh, 104)

Morgan's raiders rode into a small Indiana town where 300 home guards had gathered and were trying to train horses. Morgan told the men that his unit was Union cavalry from Kentucky and would be pleased to help the men break in the animals. So Morgan and his raiders took all of the nice fresh horses and rode away with them. (Seguin, 83–84)

Always struggling to bring fresh troops to the field, the Confederacy even created some cavalry regiments out of Indians. The 1st Indian Brigade worked under Gen. D. H. Cooper for the last three years of the war, and Cooper said, "I have never heard of a Choctaw or Chickasaw Indian forsaking his company, country, or cause." (Jacobs, 165)

While small southern cavalry forces ran the Union infantry ragged, President Lincoln sought to find generals capable of stopping the Confederates and invading the southern states. Gen. George B. McClellan had spent time in Europe and admired the Polish lancers, so he set up the 6th Pennsylvania Cavalry with 10-foot-long spears. Other regiments teased the 6th mercilessly, nicknaming them "the turkey-stickers." The 6th horsemen hated the lances too, because in wooded country they became entangled in branches. They quickly abandoned the spears in favor of pistols and sabers. General McClellan received orders from President Lincoln to attack the South, but he refused, saying that his new cavalry horses were "sore-tongued and fatigued." Lincoln wrote back sarcastically that the cavalry could not be fatigued because they had never been used, and McClellan was replaced. Though McClellan had little direct success in the war, he did design the famous saddle bearing his name that would be the standard seat for hundreds of thousands of equines from 1859 to the 1950s. Just a few months later, McClellan's replacement, General Rosecrans, claimed he could not start attacks as Lincoln ordered because his 19,000 draft horses were starving and only 3,700 were usable. Perhaps this problem arose because Union horsemen routinely overloaded their horses. With the weight of the soldier, 50 pounds of uniform and weapons, and more than 70 pounds of extra baggage (including plunder), the northern equines probably were exhausted: not from battle but from inexperience and greed. One well-meaning recruit felt sorry for his horse having to carry so much weight, so he put the bags over his own shoulders while he rode, not recognizing that the weight was still on the horse. One way of judging the experience and wisdom of a horseman was looking at the load: the lighter the load, the smarter the horseman. (Downey, 38–44, 59; Seguin, 60; Ottevaere, 109; Essin, 82)

Meanwhile, in December 1862, 3,500 Confederate cavalry captured 1,500 Union troops and destroyed and stole more than $1 million in provisions and munitions from Grant's base near Vicksburg. The "running joke" of the time was that if you saw Union cavalry moving toward the rear, there must be a battle coming. (Longacre, 64; Carter, 108; Smith, 143)

J. E. B. Stuart was promoted to brigadier general and worked directly with Gen. Robert E. Lee. General Johnston said that Stuart "is like a yellow jacket. You brush him off and he flies right back on." He rode a big bay gelding named Maryland but owned other horses including Sky Lark and Lady Margrave. Unfortunately, during one of his unit's deep raids, Stuart's mulatto servant named Bob got drunk, fell asleep, and was captured along with Sky Lark and Lady Margrave. Equipment was always in short supply for the Confederacy, so the cavalry would stop to strip dead horses of their leather gear, horseshoes, and even nails for future needs. (Ruthven, 160; Davis, 72, 83, 235, 266–67; "Horses," DVD, 1)

Long cavalry raids behind enemy lines were exhausting and stressful. It was frequently necessary for riders to sleep in the saddle, and the horses learned to walk while sleeping. When they did have a few moments to rest at a stop, "the column in front would halt, every trooper dismounting, and thrusting his arm through the bridle rein, would fall down directly in front of his horse, in the road, and fall into a profound slumber. The horses too would stand with drooping heads, noses almost touching their riders' faces, eyes closed, nodding, but otherwise giving no sign, and careful not to step on or injure the motionless figures at their feet." Sometimes the tired riders would tie the horse's reins round their wrist and lie in the grass to sleep while the horse ate. It was said that when the rider awoke the horse had consumed everything around the man, leaving his shape in the uneaten grass. The hungry horses would strip the bark off of trees at times. Some officers received issues of hay to soften the floors of their tents, but they would usually give it to their starving horses instead. Long marches could be fatal to a horse. Generally, two days and two nights marching without food or rest caused the beast to die of exhaustion. (Kidd, 45, 62; Smith, 150, 157; Jacobs, 62)

After a deep raid behind Union lines, Stuart joked with General Longstreet, saying he had left a general in the rear of the enemy: "General Consternation." Stuart taught his men that the horses should be galloped only during a charge, never during a retreat, since galloping in reverse is unbecoming to a soldier. One of Stuart's men, Heros von Borcke, enjoyed saber combat. He said, "I had a happy feeling riding out of the battle and wiping the blood from my sword on my horse's mane." (Davis, 130, 58, 167)

The first major attempt of the Union to use cavalry to disrupt the Confederate rear came in the spring of 1863. Gen. Joseph Hooker sent a large force of horsemen under Gen. George Stoneman on a raid behind Lee. It did cause some disruption, but the Union army without cavalry was struck by J. E. B. Stuart's horsemen and Stonewall Jackson's infantry. (Lawford, 158–59)

In June 1863, as the South prepared to invade the North, came the "greatest" cavalry engagement in U.S. history, at the Battle of Brandy

Station. While J. E. B. Stuart's cavalry held a river position to keep enemy scouts from seeing the vast southern army forming behind, the Union was looking to test its own growing numbers of horsemen. Generals Buford and Gregg were ordered to use a pincer movement of 10,000 cavalry against Stuart's cavalry across the river. It was not a complete surprise, and the Union lost 1,000 men, but it showed that the northerners could finally make significant attacks on horseback. Though the Confederacy lost fewer men, their horse casualties were high, and the animals could not be easily replaced. Perhaps worse, the strong Union showing at Brandy Station caused southern states to withhold reinforcements from Robert E. Lee during the Gettysburg campaign. Days after the battle, with the dead soldiers buried, flocks of turkey vultures gorged themselves on the horse carcasses piled on the fields of Brandy Station. (Carter, 159; Lawford, 159–62; Downey, 143–46)

The cavalry charge was a very risky venture for anyone involved. "Trooper Henry R. Payne of the 1st New Jersey Cavalry, described a saber charge he witnessed which ended in disaster. 'Pressing upon one another, strained to the utmost of their speed, the horses catch an infection of fear which rouses them to frenzy. The men, losing their places in the ranks, and all power of formation or hope of combined resistance, rush madly for some point of safety upon which it may be possible to rally. Each check in front makes the mass behind more dense and desperate, until horses and men are overthrown and ridden over, trampled on by others as helpless as themselves to rescue or to spare." At other times horses learned the courage of their riders. "A horse, even with a foot shot off, would not drop. He might be fatally wounded but he would hobble on or stand with drooping head until loss of blood brought him down. They became attached to their riders and to one another and kept their places in the ranks, even when riderless.... In battle the horses became as excited as their riders, sometimes becoming quite uncontrollable and carrying them beyond where they wished to go." (DiMarco, 239; Downey, 32)

A key loss for the Confederacy came in May 1863, when the skilled General "Stonewall" Jackson rode reconnaissance on his favorite horse, Little Sorrell, late at night. Some sleeping rebel sentries heard the horse's hooves and roused themselves, shooting at the movement, fatally wounding Jackson. Little Sorrell survived and lived till old age at Virginia

Military Institute in Lexington, where "he reportedly would run up and down the lines of cadets, snorting loudly, whenever they fired rifles or cannons." He died in 1886 at the Confederate Soldiers Home. (Koenig, 299–300)

The loss of Jackson put new pressure on Robert E. Lee's offensive into the north, and when J. E. B. Stuart led a longer-than-planned raid behind Union lines it left Lee's army without information about enemy movements. In one small skirmish, Stuart lost half of his mustache to an enemy bullet that closely shaved his lip. On the way to meet up with Lee in central Pennsylvania, his units captured 125 full wagons of Union supplies, including oats. His famished horses ate for hours, and his men enjoyed the food and whiskey. Usually the cavalry would take what they needed and burn the wagons, since it slowed them down. This great bounty delayed his units as they kept the wagons and thus slowed their pace, so that General Lee was furious and unprepared when the Union army ran into the southerners at Gettysburg. Perhaps if Stuart had done reconnaissance rather than slurping up Union wagons, Lee would not have forfeited the high ground at Gettysburg. (Davis, 147, 328; Walsh, 233; Smith, 154)

Though both armies approached Gettysburg at about the same time, Union cavalry under General Buford dismounted and held back the early southern advance, allowing the northerners to entrench on the best high positions. (Carter, 165)

The youngest brigadier general in U.S. history, George Custer, age 22, would show that Union horsemen had learned to fight. His grandfather Kuster was a Hessian cavalryman paroled after the Battle of Saratoga in the American Revolution. The 5th Michigan Cavalry formed in September 1862. They organized in an intriguing manner, choosing their horses by colors, so that Troop A owned all bays, Troop B brown horses, Troop C grays, and Troop D black mounts. This made their parade lines quite impressive, though in later years as they took replacement horses, they could not keep the strict color separation. Custer, with his long, blonde curls, loved to dress up in a black velveteen uniform with frilly gold lace and, a broad-brimmed hat. Like many cavalry leaders, he led from the front, charging courageously and not lingering behind to watch the action. He had great instincts for locating enemy weaknesses and exploiting them. Custer was tasked with finding and halting J. E. B. Stuart's movements. (*Army Times*, 110–11; Kidd, 17; Urwin, *U.S. Cavalry*, 122)

The first two days of battle at Gettysburg saw the Confederates try to push the Union soldiers off of their hilltop positions with flanking movements, but this failed. General Lee ordered a final desperate timing maneuver for the third day to capture the hills. Stuart's cavalry would flank the Union's right and harass the northern rear. When the Union cannons and units turned, General Pickett would lead thousands of men up the long slope and take the hills. (Smith, 149–50)

Stuart's cavalry rode around to the Union right, but Custer's Michigan Brigade surprised them, charging out of a wooded area. Custer's men adored him and leaders like him, who called, "Come on, boys!" from the front, rather than "Go in, boys!" from the rear. There were charges and counter-charges as North and South tried to gain an advantage. (ibid., 152)

A Union soldier wrote about the experience of a cavalry charge.

> Who can describe the feelings of a man on entering a charge? How exhilarating, and yet how awful! The glory of success is intoxicating! One forgets everything, even personal safety, in the one grand thought of vanquishing the enemy. We were in for it now, and the nerves were strung to the highest tension....Then followed an indescribable clashing, banging and yelling.... On they went, amid a perfect tangle of sights and sounds, filled with such a rare, whole-souled excitement as seldom falls to the lot of man to experience; and thoughts of danger were for the time furthest from their minds. Even the horses seemed to enter into the spirit of the occasion, and strained every nerve to do their full duty in the day's strange deeds, obeying the least motion of rein of spur with unusual promptness, as if feeling the superiority of their riders in this terrible commotion. (Carter, 157–58)

Custer led a counterattack, but many of the 7th Michigan riders blindly galloped into a stone wall, where men and horses became "a mass of pulp." Still, Custer rallied them and stopped the Confederate momentum. Though in casualty numbers the action might have been called a draw, in fact, this was a major Union victory. Stuart could not make the rear feint ordered by Lee, and thus Pickett's infantry marched up the hillside into the Union artillery and sharpshooters and were mowed down. (Smith, 153; Urwin, *U.S. Cavalry*, 122)

Gettysburg proved to be the turning point of the war, when the South lost any hope of capturing the North, and the Union gained confidence to push into the Confederate lands. An estimated 72,000 horses were used at the Battle of Gettysburg, where at least 5,000 of them died. Gettysburg was actually comparatively easy on horses, since there were few cavalry actions. After the battle of Antietam, the dead horses and mules in piles bloated and burst in the heat. Brig. Gen. Oliver O'Howard said they tried piling rails and tree limbs on the bodies to burn them, but it only made the stench more widespread. Over all, as many as 50 percent of the animals used for service during the American Civil War perished. ("Horses"; Seguin, 114–15; DiMarco, 302)

After the battle of Gettysburg, hundreds of wagons carried wounded Confederates southward in retreat. Union cavalry and even local citizens harassed the wagons. At Greencastle, "citizens chopped down the wheels of the wagons of the wounded, and were beaten off only by a cavalry squadron." Not all of the up and coming Union cavalry commanders were honorable soldiers. "Kill Cavalry" Kilpatrick had the reputation of a criminal and regarded no rules of "civilized" warfare. It was Kilpatrick who would lead Sherman's cavalry on a path of destruction through the South, earning the undying hatred of the southern states. (Davis, 344; Smith, 155)

One of J. E. B. Stuart's scouts, John S. Mosby, was given command of the 43rd Virginia Battalion of cavalry in 1863. He operated largely in the area of Washington, DC, and Baltimore, making raids on railroads and gathering supplies for the Confederacy. Mosby was especially hated by the northerners because his raiders were so effective and within their own territory. Fifty or so Confederates would surprise a town or encampment and make off with fresh horses, food, and equipment. On January 4, 1864, the cavalrymen staged a raid in one foot of snow and subzero temperatures. When the cold was this bad, the men rode with the reins held in their teeth and their hands under the saddle blankets against the horses for warmth. They captured 45 Union soldiers with no losses except for a few fingers and toes to frostbite. (Crawford)

Both North and South practiced the "impressment" of local horses as needed, meaning they took any horses they wished. When any enemy cavalry troops were known to be in a region, the local people would try to hide their horses in the woods or caves, or even in their houses, to keep from

Cavalry Captures a Cake

In one of the strangest stories of the Civil War, Confederate commander John Mosby's horsemen crossed the Shenandoah River to raid a federal garrison on July 3, 1864. They captured a gigantic eagle-shaped cake, intended for July 4 celebrations. The pastry had glass eyes and measured 25 feet tall, with some sort of machinery designed to shriek like an eagle whenever a knife cut into it. Perhaps hoping to share it with their compatriots, Mosby's men cut it into five huge pieces and put them on a raft across the river, then transferred them to a huge six-horse wagon. Five escorts followed the wagon, but they got drunk and fell asleep. The wagon driver, a Union sympathizer, hid the cake and eventually got it back to the Union army. Unfortunately, the wagon overturned on the bridge over the Shenandoah and the cake fell into the river and sank. (Crawford)

---

losing them. Though both sides appropriated horses, food, equipment, and so on, the Union did not view "raiders" as real soldiers and gave them none of the protections of normal military prisoners. Mosby's men, when captured, were often hanged as thieves. (Smith, 179; Crawford).

A few months after Gettysburg, the Union cavalry under Philip Sheridan charged up Missionary Ridge to help capture Chattanooga, Tennessee. Sheridan was promoted to major general and put over most of the Union cavalry. President Lincoln described Sheridan this way: "Chunky little chap, with a long body, short legs, not enough neck to hang him, and such long arms that if his ankles itch he can scratch them without stooping." Sheridan came to the east to help with General Grant's campaign, pushing into Virginia. Sheridan reported to General Meade, under Grant, and hated it. Meade continued the old tradition of using cavalry only for guarding wagon trains, guarding prisoners, standing picket lines, and running messages. Sheridan personally complained to General Grant, saying that if he had "free rein," he could kill Stuart and drive the Confederate cavalry off the field. Grant appreciated this boldness and unleashed the Union horsemen. In May 1864, Sheridan and Custer caught Stuart's units at the Battle of Yellow Tavern, and the legendary J. E. B. Stuart was wounded and soon died. On his deathbed, Stuart gave away his favorite horses to other soldiers, along with his spurs. (Davis, 384, 414; Smith, 164; *Army Times*, 60–61; Urwin, *U.S. Cavalry*, 125–26)

Now that Confederate ability to take the offensive was over, the southerners had more difficulty finding horses and equipment. In order to protect their horses, more dismounting tactics had to be employed, with the soldiers getting off the horses and leaving them in the rear during combat. This, of course, changed the dynamics of warfare. At their Lynchburg, Virginia, horse depot, diseases broke out, particularly the deadly horse disease called glanders. Union horses had the same malady, with glanders killing some 200,000 animals. Some northerners thought this outbreak of glanders was a deliberate infection carried out by enemy spies. (Cooper, 33; Koenig, 7–8)

The northern system of gathering horses became so efficient that the Union had horses to spare. In fact, they knew that the South was running short of horses, so they took precautions to ensure that the Confederates couldn't capture many. In earlier times, when a horse became too tired to continue, the beast might be left behind to recuperate. In 1864, Sheridan ordered that when any animal showed exhaustion, it must be immediately shot in the head. These orders were followed. Cavalryman James H. Kidd wrote about following Sheridan's troops. He said that the road was hot and dusty, and there was nothing worth recalling "unless it be that the road after the cavalry had passed over it was dotted at regular intervals with the bodies of dead horses, the order having been given that when horses gave out and had to be abandoned they must be shot." During one movement, when southerners followed Sheridan's troopers, they found at least 2,000 dead horses along a 100-mile stretch of road. Long strings of dead horses came to be known as "Sheridan's Milestones." Capt. C. F. Adams believed the best choice was just to ride the horses to death. Though the riders regretted doing so, the animals could not be left to the enemy, nor was there time to rehabilitate them. In just eight months of 1864 the Union averaged 500 dead horses per day. Adams wrote, "The air of Virginia is literally burdened today with the stench of dead horses, federal and confederate. You pass them on every road and find them in every field, while from their carrions you can follow the march of every army that moves." (Kidd, 221; Swank, 79, 126; Smith, 179; Downey, 32–34)

While the Union could replace horses, the Confederates could not. In 1864 the shortage of horses was so great in the southern states that a good

Gen. P. H. Sheridan, the key commander of
Union cavalry during the Civil War. (*Pictorial
History of the United States*, vol. 2, p. 916b.)

horse cost between $2,000 and $4,000. They did not as policy shoot tired
animals. One of J. E. B. Stuart's captains, for instance, left his favorite horse,
Comet, on a local farm, hoping the horse would recuperate, after a shellburst
put shrapnel into its neck. According to witnesses, when shrapnel or bullets strike horseflesh, it sounds like a "pebble squishing in mud," but when
bone is hit it sounds like a hollow crack. If enough shells land close to the
horse it might lose all confidence; the riders called such a horse "corked."
(O'Ferrall; Davis, 188; "Horses," DVD, 1; Smith, 187)

In June 1864, Sheridan made a bold advance, hoping to clear a path for
Grant toward Richmond. The Confederate cavalry beat him to a strategic
spot in the road called Trevilian Station. Though the Union had the numeric
advantage, the Confederates beat the Union cavalry back. In Little Phil's
most famous moment, he rode his steed Rienzi 20 miles to rally his fleeing
troops at Cedar Creek. They rallied and forced the Confederates back, but

they could not rapidly pursue because the southerners had planted mines called "torpedoes" in the roads with trip wires, similar to modern "improvised explosive devices." These devices were large artillery shells set off by passing horses. Nevertheless, the victory by Sheridan came shortly before a new presidential election that Lincoln was in danger of losing. Some analysts believe that if Sheridan had not won this battle, Abraham Lincoln would have lost the election. One magazine titled an article about Rienzi "The Horse Who Elected a President." Forty years later, Gutzon Borglum, the sculptor of Mount Rushmore, made a statue of Sheridan on Rienzi for a monument in Washington, DC. (Longacre, 276; Smith, 185–86, 193–95)

Sherman's march through Georgia could not be stopped. His army included 35,000 animals and 2,700 supply wagons. Food was short for such a huge force, so Sherman sent his 12,500 cavalry under Gen. James H. Wilson to raid and forage separately from the main army. Wilson's horsemen

General Grant at the siege of Vicksburg (1863), where victory gave control of the Mississippi River to the Union. (*Pictorial History of the United States*, vol. 2, p. 832b.)

made "what was called the most successful cavalry operation in American history" at Selma Arsenal, capturing 65,000 prisoners, factories, steamboats, locomotives, artillery, and more. Sherman's other cavalry, under "Kill Cavalry" Kilpatrick, burned and pillaged. Any horse or animal found that was not edible or usable by the Union army was killed with an ax blade between the eyes. Perhaps to show that Christianity had no power to stop his army, Kilpatrick used church organs for butcher's blocks and stabled his horses in church buildings, using baptistries for watering troughs. (Swank, xv; Sinclair, 171; Smith, 202–10)

One of the few Confederate horse leaders to survive the Civil War was Nathan Bedford Forrest, whom General Grant called "the ablest cavalry general in the South" and others called "The Wizard of the Saddle." Being wealthy, Forrest raised his own battalion of mounted troops in Bedford County, Tennessee. Forrest harassed Grant constantly during the 1862–1863 Vicksburg campaign, and then shadowed General Sherman's Atlanta push in 1864. When Sherman sent almost 8,000 horsemen to destroy Forrest's 3,500 men, Forrest routed them, killing 400 and taking 1,600 prisoners. The Confederates then went to Tennessee, destroying Union gunboats, steamships, and barges on the Mississippi River. Sherman started calling Forrest "the very Devil." (Longacre, 283–87; Urwin, *U.S. Cavalry*, 126)

Forrest was enthusiastic and harsh in battle. The enemy so feared him, by reputation, that he could sometimes bluff superior forces into surrendering. One Union force three times larger than his unit gave up before a fight. A legendary statement attributed to Forrest, on how to win a battle, was "Git there fustest with the mostest men!" (*Army Times*, 82–86). While General Forrest, better known as "Old Bedford," may have loved his horses, they did not live long. In fact, "to be ridden by Old Bedford, it was generally agreed, was the kiss of death for any horse throughout the war." In the Battle of Fort Pillow, he lost three horses in five hours. During his war career, Forrest had 29 horses shot from under him. Though many were short-lived, the horses apparently loved him. One of his horses did survive the war, an animal named King Philip. After the war while Forrest worked in his corn field, a Union cavalry unit rode by. King Philip had been grazing, but seeing the Union horses he attacked them with "teeth bared and front feet flailing." Forrest was able to restrain the horse. The Union captain said, "General, now I can account for your success. Your ... horses fight for you." (Carter, 34, 318; Seguin, 122; *Army Times*, 85–86)

Sheridan and Custer, and the rest of the Union army, closed in around the southern army until Robert E. Lee surrendered. Lee's father had been the famous "Light Horse Harry," cavalry major during the Revolutionary War, so Robert knew well how to care for horses. During his own service in the Mexican War, Lee was careful to provide food and safety slings for his horses during the ship voyage to Mexico. For many years Robert showed his children the seven scars received by his horse Grace Darling during the Mexican conflict. Lee owned several horses during the Civil War. One "Lucy Long" was an 1862 gift from J. E. B. Stuart. But the most famous horse of the 1860s was Traveller. Lee bought him in 1861 for $200, and later praised Traveller for "sagacity and affection and his invariable response to every wish of the rider." One day Traveller was spooked badly. Standing beside the horse, Lee grabbed his reins to try to calm the animal, but the strength of Traveller sprained both of Robert's wrists badly. It took months for his hands to heal. After the war, Lee built a brick stable for his horses, and he rode Traveller every day, though Traveller became nervous around people, because admiring southerners kept pulling out his tail hairs for souvenirs. Traveller died of lockjaw in 1872, and his bones were put on display at a university museum until buried in the 1970s. (Koenig, 6, 299; Ruthven, 266; Perry; Seguin, 56–57, 140–41)

Many lessons were learned about cavalry during the Civil War. The U.S. Army learned how to procure horses and train men to ride them; how to deploy them effectively; and that the new repeating rifles gave infantry an important edge in battle. No longer could cavalry dominate the infantry, if it was armed with fast-firing and accurate weapons. (DiMarco, 262)

The Late Indian Wars

In early conflicts with settlers, Native Americans fought with leather armor and lances but primarily with the bow, with a range of 100 yards or less. In the French and Indian Wars, and the War of 1812, European powers assisted the Native Americans by arming them with rifles. As fur trappers, hunters, explorers, and gold-diggers moved west, the Indians obtained even more modern weapons, sometimes having better equipment than the U.S. cavalry that opposed them. Though tactically superior in every way to most U.S. units—using mobility, feigned retreats, and ambushes—the natives had no cohesion or strategic level planning. (Kelekna, 373; DiMarco, 273–74)

During the Civil War, many Native American tribes took advantage of the lack of military patrols in the west. Though westerners demanded action, the easterners needed all their troops for the war, and the west was unprotected. In 1862 the Sioux led the "Santee uprising" in Minnesota, slaughtering civilians and farmers. Kit Carson led some U.S. troops to pacify the Navaho. The Cheyenne, Comanches, and Kiowas ravaged the central plains. In 1864 Arapaho and Cheyenne joined the Sioux to raid trails and settlements throughout Nebraska and the region. The Plains Indians would fight almost constantly, in almost 400 separate actions between 1866 and 1890 in Montana, Arizona, Oklahoma, Wyoming, New Mexico, and South Dakota. ("Great Indian Wars," DVD, 2–3; Urwin, *U.S. Cavalry*, 134–37, 152; Brown, 9; DiMarco, 272)

Immediately after the Civil War, the Union army sent some war heroes west to pacify the natives. Fifteen hundred Cheyenne laid a trap for a zealous cavalry captain named Fetterman. Fetterman boasted that with a company of regular cavalry (80 men) he could whip a thousand "untrained" Indians. Weeks later, his whole 80-man force was annihilated by an ambush of 1,500 Indians: the worst defeat of the frontier army to that date. Some of the Indians used extreme methods of torture, like burning, skin removal, burial alive, and staking out of a victim to be eaten by ants and birds. Cavalrymen learned to save one bullet in the revolver, for themselves. By late 1866, George Armstrong Custer took over the 7th U.S. Cavalry at Fort Riley, Kansas, under the command of Gen. Winfield Scott Hancock. In 1867 Hancock tried to "overawe" the hostile red men, but all it did was antagonize the neutral tribes and lead to wider war. Hancock hated Custer and had him court-martialed for trivial offenses. When General Sheridan was put in charge of the overall western campaigns, he reinstated Custer, and he recognized that the best time to catch Indians was during the winter, when they camped. (Leckie, 19; Brown, 17; Utley and Washburn, 241; Smith, 221; Hoig, 3; Urwin, *U.S. Cavalry*, 152–53)

General Sheridan and later General Sherman, both trained in "total war," saw that the Indian Wars would be vicious. The Indians were already acting brutally.

They almost always scalped dead soldiers, and often mutilated their bodies in a variety of "unspeakable" ways. If they did take prisoners, it merely was for the purpose of torturing them to death by means that cause the victims to wish they never had been born. Atrocities begot atrocities, massacres produced massacres, and savagery incited savagery. The older image of the frontier regular typified by John Wayne contains no more truth than modern cinematic portrayals of Plains Indians as peace-loving sages living in mystic harmony with nature. (Goodrich, xi)

Custer, remembering his Michigan Cavalry days of the Civil War, decided to sort the cavalry horses among the companies by color. The soldiers resented this because they had already become attached and accustomed to certain mounts, and here in 1868 the animals were randomly redistributed for no apparent reason except Custer's aesthetic pleasure. In winter, the tribes had stocked up on their meat and hides and went into camp to await spring. Sheridan's plan, like the brutality of the Civil War, was to destroy the enemy by any means necessary. Custer surprised a village of Cheyenne on November 27, 1868, killing 103 men and boys and capturing 57 women and children and 875 ponies. Fearing that other nearby tribes would counterattack and recapture the ponies, Custer ordered his men to kill the 875 ponies. At first they tried cutting the animals' throats, but the horses fought viciously and reinforcements had to be brought in. Some of the animals were not dead but had broken legs. When the cavalry returned several weeks later, they found that wounded horses had eaten all the grass within reach of them before they finally died. (Philbrick, 132, 136; Urwin, *U.S. Cavalry*, 154; Goodwin, 143)

According to one source:

The hardest thing about fighting the red man was not the actual fighting itself—but finding him.... They only gave battle on their own terms—or when their women, children, horses and other property were in danger. Indians carefully avoided sizable concentrations of troops—who could do heavy damage.... The Indian was admirably suited for hit-and-run guerrilla warfare. He traveled and fought half-naked, carrying only his weapons, ammunition and a few other bare necessities. His small, swift pony could outdistance anything on the Plains, and as he normally owned at least two or three—he always had a fresh mount to put plenty of miles between himself and his pursuers. Both man and animal could live on whatever nature had to offer, which greatly increased an Indian's mobility. The average horse trooper weight 140 to 150 pounds, and even when he was stripped down for action, he burdened his horse with 100 pounds of indispensable clothing, equipment, rations and forage. The American soldiers could not live solely off the country, and had to pack enough rations to last as long as he planned to be out on campaign. His larger, heavier horse was unable to survive on prairie grasses and required a diet supplemented by oats and other grains. The Indian-Fighting Army was a conventional army, and it needed a wide logistical base. The men had to have access to a wide range of extra items—from bullets to horse shoes—to keep them on the trail of the wily "Redskins." These unalterable facts tied the Bluecoats to long, lumbering supply trains, which restricted their movements. (Urwin, *U.S. Cavalry*, 148–49)

Custer was not leading the only cavalry in the American west. The 9th and 10th Cavalry units were the black soldiers, called "the Buffalo Soldiers" by the natives. In their early years, they received "mean and worn-out horses" and "trail-weary nags" and often had to tailor their own uniforms. Despite discrimination, the buffalo soldiers were disciplined, loyal, and brave, and they rarely deserted. Eleven black soldiers would earn the Medal of Honor for valorous fighting during the Indian Wars. The famous artist Frederic Remington rode with the 10th Cavalry in Arizona, which inspired many of his western paintings. (Leckie, 26; Urwin, *U.S. Cavalry*, 161–62; Newark, 211)

The Indians kept two types of horses: war horses and "squaw ponies." Warriors kept war horses, and chiefs usually had several horses ready to be mounted at a moment's notice. Squaw horses were not strong or fast enough for warfare and so were used by the women for carrying burdens. An Indian would never sell his favorite war pony: "neither love nor money could convince him to part with it." These horses were so well-conditioned to long journeys that U.S. cavalry pursuits were futile. Army horses often died trying to catch native horses. Custer and other army officers considered the Indians to be the best horsemen in the world. (Goodwin, 166–68; Leckie, 131; DiMarco, 279)

It took time for the army "to recognize its own self defeating rituals that the Indians knew so well. One Kansas homesteader complained how the army could never catch Indians because every morning they blow the bugle announcing them leaving the fort and blow it again when they go to bed, so the Indians always knew where they were." The horses also had to be trained to disregard bugle-calls or shouts and focus only on the rider's commands, because if another man or unit made calls, the horse might obey those signals at inopportune times. (Newark, 205; Goodwin, 94; Anderson, 16)

In 1874 in New Mexico, the 4th U.S. Cavalry under Col. R. S. Mackenzie brought an end to the Red River War. They found several hundred Comanche, Cheyenne, and Kiowa encamped in the Palo Duro Canyon. Most of the warriors escaped, but the camps and ponies were captured. About 1,700 horses were taken: the army kept a few hundred, but killed the rest. Mackenzie ordered the 1,400 animals shot and pushed over a precipice. Many of the youngest troopers had nightmares about the slaughter for many months after. Without horses, the Indians could do nothing but surrender and walk to the nearest assigned reservation. (Goodwin, 190; DiMarco, 287; Smith, 246; Great Indian Wars, part 5; Newark, 206–7)

Many cavalry missions were less successful. In the summer of 1875, one expedition ran out of water. The men became so dehydrated that they could not even swallow food. When one of the horses died, the soldiers drank its blood. They started saving the urine of men and horses, adding sugar to make it more drinkable. Twenty-two more horses and four mules died, and the men drank their blood too. The expedition went 86 hours without water. (Leckie, 160; Arnold, 323)

In early 1876 the army captured 700 Indian ponies. While returning them to the nearest fort, the Indians counterattacked and recaptured all but 180 of the ponies. Fearing that the rest might be retaken, General Crook ordered that the horses be killed. His men shot 50 and used axes to crush the skulls of 50 more. The other 80 had their throats cut. One witness wrote, "it was pathetic to hear the dismal trumpeting (I can find no other word to express my meaning) of the dying creatures, as the breath of life rushed through severed windpipes." (Goodwin, 221)

Gen. George A. Custer, the youngest general in U.S. history. (*Pictorial History of the United States*, vol. 2, p. 908b.)

1876 was the turning point in the Indian Wars, when two defeats humiliated the U.S. Army and gave the government the excuse or will to annihilate the Native Americans.

On June 17, Chief Crazy Horse, with less than a thousand Sioux and Cheyenne warriors, fought General Crook and his 1,300 soldiers to a draw at the Battle of the Rosebud. Out of supplies, Crook's force had to retreat to a fort; en route many horses died of exhaustion. The soldiers shot the dying horses in the head, then skinned and ate them, from whence came the phrase "horse rations." (Urwin, *U.S. Cavalry*, 152; Goodwin, 179)

Less than two weeks later, Custer led one of the cavalry columns intended to converge against the united Lakota and Cheyenne tribes. Each column included Indian scouts, mule drivers, and translators. Custer was overconfident, believing the enemies to number less than a thousand warriors. He was sure that his 650 men could handle them without waiting for the other army columns to arrive, and he even turned down an offered Gatling gun: an early machine gun. Custer himself rode with two "magnificent" horses, named Vic (for Victory) and Dandy, riding them in three-hour shifts to keep one fresh at all times. On Sunday, June 25, 1876, when his column encountered the enemy encampment, the hilly terrain restricted Custer's view so that he could not see the whole number of 2,000 to 4,000 Indians nearby. (*Army Times*, 115; Philbrick, 39; Urwin, *U.S. Cavalry*, 158–59)

The Only Survivor

None of Custer's men on the hilltop survived the Battle of the Little Bighorn. One creature did survive, however: Comanche, the horse of Capt. Myles Keogh. The 13-year-old Comanche, so named for a Comanche arrow wound he had survived, was shot by seven bullets and arrows in the neck, lung, and groin. After the battle Comanche was led to Fort Lincoln, North Dakota, where he was treated and recovered from his wounds. He had freedom to wander the fort; sometimes he waited near the officers' quarters for someone to give him sugar, or he hung around the bar, where he might be given a drink of beer or brandy. Sometimes when the bugle sounded, Comanche trotted in formation, but orders said he would never be ridden or worked again. He lived 17 more years, and when he died his body was stuffed and put on display at the University of Kansas. (Smith, 235; Ruthven, 57; Roberts, 26)

More than half of Custer's units tried to flee when they saw the huge number of the enemy: most were pursued and killed. Most of the U.S. cavalry used single-shot rifles, while many of the Cheyenne warriors had purchased the new Winchester 17-shot repeating rifle. Custer's remaining 264 men rallied on a hill and formed a circle for protection. In one hour, Custer, his 13 officers, 193 soldiers, and four civilians were shot or cut down. Custer's horse, Vic, was reportedly seen being ridden by an Indian in later months. (*Army Times*, 118; Urwin, *U.S. Cavalry,* 158–59; Livingston and Roberts, 38)

The other columns of cavalry, later in the year, captured 3,000 horses from the Sioux and Cheyenne. Rather than shoot the animals, the army drove them into a blizzard so that most died of the cold. Colonel Mackenzie defeated the last of the Cheyenne and forced them to reservations; he took all their horses and weapons to ensure they could not rebel. (Steiner, 147; Hoig, 32)

The Cheyenne, upon reaching the reservations of Oklahoma, found none of the white men's promises to be true. There were no buffaloes to hunt, there were no farms and cows, and the weather was more extreme than they expected. Within a year, many Cheyenne obtained horses and weapons and fought their way toward home in the northern Rockies, with the cavalry hot on their trail. The U.S. riders, not knowing the land well, fell into many traps and made errors that made the pursuit more difficult. They and their horses became sick drinking from salty water sources. The Cheyenne set ambushes in canyons where the army horsemen had no water supply for the horses. One advantage the cavalry had was the ability to get supplies and reinforcements from forts, while the Indians were starving to death. To keep the Indians from eating their own dead and wounded horses, the army burned horse carcasses to cinders. (Hoig, 59, 66–70, 183)

Col. Wesley Merritt came to typify the U.S. cavalry leaders who would finally track down and kill the last of the warring tribes. With daily hard training, Merritt enabled his men and horses to travel an average of 50 miles a day. Once, a three-day trip averaged 62 miles per day without harming the men or horses. With this level of hardiness, the army could finally match the Indians' horsemanship and catch up to them. (DiMarco, 284)

In 1890, the Sioux on a reservation in South Dakota were convinced by a shaman that the white invaders would soon be exterminated. They started a small rebellion. At the so-called Battle of Wounded Knee, the 7th Cavalry killed most of the men, women, and children with four artillery pieces, bringing an end to the Indian Wars. (Urwin, *U.S. Cavalry*, 163)

War Horses from 1880 to World War I

The major world powers learned the hard way that cavalry, for thousands of years the master of the battlefield, had new vulnerabilities. The crossbow and longbow of medieval times first endangered the horses and their riders. Early gunpowder weapons were grossly inaccurate and slow to reload. By the 18th century the rifles became more accurate but remained slow. In the mid-19th century, the American Civil War and the Franco-Prussian War tested new rapid-firing guns capable of decimating cavalry divisions.

While the practice of colonialism and worldwide empire held promise of wealth and power, the British discovered that rebellious foreign lands would cost a fortune in manpower and lives. By the late 19th century, their holdings in India had stabilized, and the British came to use Sikhs and Indian cavalry in many foreign wars. Institutionally, however, there was little improvement in animal husbandry. For example, the 8th King George V's Own Light Cavalry of India, around 1880, managed their horses so badly that after one campaign all of their horses had died and they had to fight as a dismounted regiment. (Hamid, 134)

British officers in India did not learn the Urdu language very well and so often made a verbal faux pas. The Urdu word for cavalryman, "sowar," is very similar to their word for pig, "suwar." Thus British public speeches about their cavalry pigs were a cause of constant amusement to the Urdu listeners. (ibid., 67)

One interesting method of training by Indian cavalrymen was called tent pegging. In ancient times, they say, horsemen would attack enemies still encamped in their tents for the night. The men would ride through quickly and yank up the tent pegs by leaning down from horseback, causing the tents to fall on the enemy and create confusion. This became a training game, usually held on Thursday mornings. The competitions were judged or measured by the height that the pegs projected from the ground. A normal height for the pegs was six inches, but winners often had to yank the pegs sticking up only two inches out of the dirt, riding at a gallop. Even more competitive were the night games with only torches to light the pegs. (ibid., 88, 91)

In 1898 the British general Lord Kitchener was sent to retake Sudan from dervish forces. Using Maxim machine guns to mow down thousands of African infantry, the cavalry was sent in pursuit, under the impression that the enemy would flee. The 21st Lancers charged with 320 horsemen but were ambushed by 2,000 dervishes hiding in a dry riverbed. One of the cavalrymen, Lt. Winston Churchill, accompanied the offensive. Churchill loved the cavalry. "The stir of the horses, the clank of their equipment, the thrill of motion, the tossing plumes, the sense of incorporation in a living machine, the suave dignity of the uniform—all combine to make cavalry drill a fine thing in itself." The British lost 70 men and 119 horses dead and wounded in the initial charge, then they dismounted and fired with carbines. After the Battle of Omdurman, the lancers led the heavily wounded animals to the river for a drink before shooting them. (Newark, 114–18; Smith, 265; Lawford, 168–69; Cooper, 32)

Pack horses carrying artillery shells through the mud, World War I. (Mary Evans Picture Library.)

The British became embroiled in South Africa in the Boer Wars. The First Boer War in the early 1880s saw the British defeated in two key battles. A cavalry retreat is quite different from a cavalry charge. "Pressing upon one another, strained to the utmost of their speed, the horses catch an infection of fear which rouses them to frenzy...officers wild with shame and rage, shouting themselves hoarse with unavailing curses, and the bullets of the enemy whistling shrilly overhead, the mingled mass sweeps on, until utter exhaustion stops them." The Dutch forced the enemy to offer a good peace settlement. The British would not honor the peace for long; when diamonds were discovered in Dutch lands, they returned in force. (Downey, 115; Newark, 219)

The Second Boer War lasted from 1899 through 1902 and was far more brutal on men and horses. The Boers used German Mauser magazine rifles, machine guns, and artillery. They employed men from ages 16 to 60, who were usually familiar with the land and could live with hardships. British invaders were not prepared for the climate or hardships.

The two opposing sides in the Boer Wars resembled those of the Indian Wars in the United States. The mobile Boers under commanders such as Botha fought a defensive war against relatively immobile but well-organized British in an area half the size of Europe. (Newark, 219; Sinclair, 222)

One advantage held by the defenders was their tough little ponies. A British leader described them as "wretched little brutes."

> He will triple and amble on, week after week and month after month, with a heavy man on his back, and nothing to eat but the pickings of sour, dried-up veld grass and an occasional handful of Indian corn….All the imported breeds will gradually languish and fade away and drop and die, worn down by the unremitting work and the bad, insufficient food; but your ragged little South African will still amble on, still hump himself, or make an occasional hearty meal off the straw coverings of a case of whiskey bottles. With an action that gives the least possible exertion; with the digestion of an ostrich and the eye of a prairie dog for any stray morsel of food; with an extraordinary capacity for taking rest in snatches and recouping himself by a roll whenever you take his saddle off. (DiMarco, 302)

The invaders had to import their animals. For the first several months of the war, the British had only two blacksmiths and a few veterinarians. Commanders doled out only a starvation level of food. The horses and mules arrived by ship after a long voyage from Europe or the United States, in poorly maintained stalls aboard ships with no medical care. Around 5 percent of the equines died aboard ship. Once they arrived in port, the animals were moved into train cars without a minute to rest or adjust to the hot climate. The British Army began experimenting with tractors for moving supplies because horses died so quickly; the tractors worked well only in flat areas, close to cities. There were so many dead animals piling up around Pretoria, however, polluting the water supply and threatening to spread disease, that the tractors spent much time just getting rid of the bodies of horses, oxen, and mules. A future field marshal of World War I, Allenby, wrote that the British generals of the Boer Wars "don't care a

British horse team trapped in mud, World War I. (Mary Evans Picture Library.)

straw about the horses." During the course of the war, the British horses suffered a 70 percent mortality rate, as 326,073 horses died out of the 520,000 brought to South Africa. (DiMarco, 302–4; Koenig, 42–43; Lawford, 14; Sutton and Walker, 66–67; Cooper, 36–37)

Many soldiers and civilians killed the horses to eat because they had no supplies for themselves. The soldiers seemed to think that horses, mules, and equipment were in easy supply and so were disposable. One British unit had 610 horses when they took a 14-mile march. There was a small raid; they lost 35 dead and 40 wounded horses. They left all of the 75 saddles and the wounded horses behind to die. There were no veterinarians to treat or even kill the sick or wounded horses. The one bright side to the situation is that the British public was outraged, and the British set up a permanent military veterinary corps for the future. (DiMarco, 305; Koenig, 42–43; Cooper, 36–37)

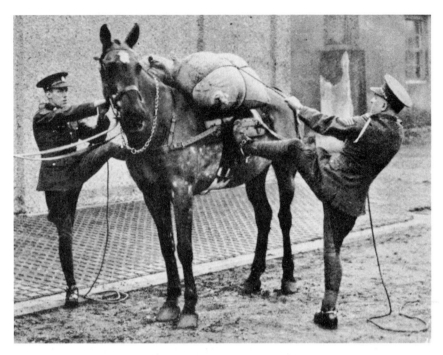

Securing a load to a packhorse. Manual of Horsemastership, Equitation and Animal Transport, 1937. (Crown Copyright His Majesty's Stationery Office, 1937, plate 25.)

As the Boers used typical hit-and-run tactics, the British eventually countered with some specialist horsemen of their own, including some Royal Canadian Mounted Police and some Australians. Even the better cavalry probably would not have won the war. The decisive factor in British victory seems to have been "total war"–style brutality. They captured Boer women and children and put them in concentration camps until the enemy surrendered. (Newark, 224–28)

One participant in the war, Arthur Conan Doyle, wrote a history of the Boer Wars. He wrote that the British cavalry needs many reforms. "Lances, swords, and revolvers have only one place—the museum. . . . We must teach the trooper to use his rifle on foot and dress him so that he can do so. So in an automatic and unavoidable way he becomes mounted infantry. . . . Let a man be a fine rider, a trained horsemaster, a good skirmisher, and a dead shot, and he becomes more valuable than any mere cavalryman can be." The British set up a memorial in Port Elizabeth, South Africa, to the 326,073 horses lost in that war. (Newark, 241; Gardiner, 186)

In the years between the Boer Wars and World War I, the British cavalry saw many changes, some desirable, some less so. Francis Maitland of the hussars hated the new "ugly, utilitarian battledress," preferring the colorful panoply and plumes of earlier decades. Some things never changed when horses and men were together. "We set about mucking out and grooming our horses. It is good to be with the early-morning odours of stables, the ammoniac tang which never becomes offensive to a lover of horses; the feel the sleek, warm flanks of a favourite troop horse; to run a duster over a saddle which shines like old mahogany; to see the blue burnish on bits and stirrup-irons; and to note the hardly-concealed pride in the eyes of the boyish Troop-officer." (Maitland, 15, 19)

The U.S. cavalry finished off the Indians in 1890 but returned to war in 1898. The Spanish-American War was fought largely in Cuba and the Philippines. This meant that the horses had to be shipped to the battle fronts. The U.S. Navy was woefully unprepared for the carrying of cargo, particularly horses. They found one ship to carry all the officer's horses, but there were no piers at the landing place. Expecting the horses to swim to shore, the sailors pushed the animals off the deck into the sea. The horses swam in the wrong direction and drowned. In Cuba, though Theodore Roosevelt and his famous Rough Riders were known for their cavalry skills, there was no room on the transport ships for horses, so most had to fight on foot. Only Roosevelt himself had a horse, while the rest of the Rough Riders marched up the San Juan Heights to victory. Confederate cavalry general Joe Wheeler came out of retirement to lead some horse engagements in the Philippines. (Urwin, *U.S. Cavalry*, 169; Smith, 238; Newark, 215–16; *Army Times*, 122–23)

While Europe fought in the early years of World War I, the United States again invaded Mexico, this time in retaliation for the raids of Pancho Villa in 1914–1917. General Pershing led the invasion with 10,000 cavalry. One of his fine cavalrymen on the expedition was the young George Patton. The Mexican invasion also saw the U.S. Army's first use of motorized trucks. The army thought that these vehicles would make cavalry and pack mules unnecessary, but in fact, in this early attempt, the trucks had difficulty in rough terrain, and mules had to carry the fuel. The Punitive

Expedition in Mexico was the last large-scale use of U.S. cavalry in the field. (*Army Times*, 124, 130–31; Essin, 141; Urwin, *U.S. Cavalry*, 178–79; Koenig, 156)

World War I Cavalry

Between 1908 and 1911 the U.S. Army opened three depots to gather and train horses and mules: Fort Reno, Oklahoma; Fort Keogh, Montana; and Front Royal, Virginia. General Pershing had recognized the logistical problems of obtaining and transporting horses during the Spanish-American War, and he pushed for major improvements in the system. Front Royal became the main staging point for all military equines east of the Mississippi River, from whence they were sent to Western Europe to support World War I before the United States became involved. The sale and transport of horses to Europe would become one of the most interesting stories in the history of military animals. Recent documents have shed light on this story, presented ably by Robert Koenig in the book *The Fourth Horseman*. (Koenig, 41, 44–45)

Germany began World War I with 4.5 million horses, including pack and wagon horses, far more than any other nation except Russia. The Germans would use some 14 million horses through the war. Badly trailing the Germans, the Allies relied heavily on the neutral United States for horses and mules. Even when the animals arrived, they did not live long. The French, for instance, were infamously lazy, leaving horses saddled for weeks. By 1914 more than two-thirds of French horses died from lack of care or from exhaustion. The British vets were simply ignorant: deciding that mange was more dangerous than weather, they ordered all horses to be shaved bare so that insects and diseases couldn't hide in their hair. Most of these horses froze to death. Of 256,000 horses lost by the British on the Western Front, only 58,000 died from enemy fire. Most died of the winter cold. Their provisions were so scarce that many horses died from eating their own blankets, choking to death on the buckles. In South Africa there were no supplies for the 60,000 wounded horses at the veterinary depots. Thousands were shot out of mercy, so that vets came to say that the only skill necessary to be a veterinarian was accurate marksmanship. Some battlefields were littered with the carcasses of dead horses "like stepping stones on battlefields." The British bought nearly three-quarters of a million horses and mules from the United States in World War I, all sent by ship. Almost all of the animals came through the Front Royal army horse depot. (Koenig, 44, 61; Livingston and Roberts, 32; DiMarco, 327; Cooper, 43–45, 52–53)

The German government was furious that the so-called neutral United States provided obvious war materials—horses and mules—to England and France. In just a nine-month period of 1914–1915 the European allies bought 200,000 horses from the United States. When diplomatic pressure failed to change the policy, Germany sent spies to covertly hinder the U.S. production of horses, by any means necessary. (Livingston and Roberts, 31)

Journalist Basil Clarke investigated reports of sabotage in the United States and Canada. Rail lines were blown up; buildings were burned. In one case, the Germans used tiny steel "spikes, each of them barbed at the sides like the end of a fish hook . . . mixed with oats intended for horse food. These, if swallowed by a horse, were calculated to perforate the stomach and bowels." These sort of physical devices could be spotted by the men feeding the horses, and so extra guards were posted to keep out unauthorized persons. The spies also tried to dump disease germs in the horses' and mules' food bins or water supplies, but few incidents resulted in actual equine deaths. Only one act of physical sabotage caused great damage: a fire at the stockyards in Kansas City killed several thousand animals, and a German suspect was apprehended. For the most part, the spies and saboteurs were ineffective, but the Germans soon found a brilliant volunteer. (Koenig, 105, 170–71)

Anton Dilger was an American born of German ancestry who grew up on a farm and horse ranch right next door to the Front Royal depot. Dilger trained as a doctor and spent months in Germany treating wounded civilians during the early part of the war. He grew angry about the U.S. support of Britain and France and offered to help the Germans stop it. They gave him pure cultures of several nasty diseases, which he took to a house in Chevy Chase, Maryland. In the basement, Dilger built a biological weapons laboratory and grew microbe cultures of deadly horse diseases. (ibid., 89)

As a doctor and a horseman, Dilger knew more effective means of infecting horses than just dumping germs into feed bins. He gave several henchmen vials of nasty diseases and trained them to rub the germs into the horses' nostrils and inject the animals with syringes. "This German sabotage campaign had the distinction of being the first systematic use of germs as a tool of modern warfare." The French also tried to spread glanders during World War I, but the attempts were unsuccessful. (ibid., 96–97, 278)

Diabolically clever, Dilger convinced dockhands at Newport News, Virginia, to infect horses that were waiting at the docks to board ships to Europe. On average, one ship full of horses and/or mules left the docks every 1.5 days. Each vessel held 500 to 1,000 animals. The equines were given physical exams and tested for all diseases at the depots, then branded and put on trains for the port of Newport News. Dilger knew that if he infected the horses at the docks with glanders, the sickened animals would spread the disease to others in the ship's hold. Once at sea, if any horse or mule showed symptoms of illness, the sailors shot it in the head and dumped the body overboard, hoping to contain the sickness. The Germans later claimed, while trying to convince Adolf Hitler to approve biological warfare programs, that a World War I saboteur had killed every horse in a transport ship with glanders, probably referring to Dilger's work. Though uncommon in the early years of the war, outbreaks of glanders and anthrax became common later in the war, likely thanks to the tireless efforts of Dr. Anton Dilger. Some suspicions had been aroused so that Dilger fled the United States. Spies followed him to Spain, where he died mysteriously in 1918. (ibid., 44, 99, 107, 122, 173, 281)

The Germans used more direct means to kill horses on the seas. In 1916 a German submarine, U-202, sank a British vessel, killing hundreds of horses and mules. Overall, nearly 7,000 horses and mules died by German submarines. (ibid., 116)

In the European theater, when the war began, German horse regiments carried 10-foot-long steel lances and wore heavy breastplate armor. On August 12, 1914, the Belgian infantry held a river crossing in Haelen. German uhlans, dragoons, hussars, and cuirassiers made repeated charges down a road but were cut down by rifle and machine-gun fire. At this "Battle of the Silver Helmets" at least 150 soldiers and 400 horses died. One cavalryman, Baron Manfred von Richthofen, saw his regiment destroyed because their horses were easily shot. He left the cavalry to become a pilot, later to be known as "The Red Baron." In France just three weeks later, the

Germans horses charged at Nancy. The first wave of cavalry was mowed down, and the second wave of chargers couldn't jump over the six-foot pile of horse bodies. These hard lessons taught the Germans that the days of lances and breastplates were over. Cavalry did still have some uses on the Western Front, just not in the frontal charge. General Scheffer's reserve corps was saved from annihilation during a retreat by an intervention of German cavalry in November 1914. By war's end, East Prussia alone had lost 135,000 horses. (Koenig, 59–62; DiNardo, 90; Clough, 17)

The foes arrayed against Germany faced the same hazards and challenges. The British 9th Lancers charged a German infantry group at a gallop but ran into lines of barbed wire. Some 128 men and many more horses were killed. A group of 150 Canadian cavalry attacked 100 Germans with machine guns: only four horses survived. The Allied cavalry did have some moments of glory. The Canadian Cavalry Brigade was nearly wiped out by the German offensive heading toward Paris, but they stopped the enemy and saved Amiens in the battle at Moreuil Wood. At the Somme on July 14, 1916, Gen. Douglas Haig ordered two British squadrons each from the Twentieth Deccan Horse and Seventh Dragoon Guards to charge up a hill through wheat fields to capture a German infantry and machine-gun position. Losses were heavy, but they did capture the hilltop before being forced to retreat the following day. (Cooper, 57–58; Newark, 243–45; Quammen, 37)

The commanders of the various armies had hoped that the infantry would punch holes in the enemy lines, so that the cavalry could charge in behind. This strategy rarely worked because barbed wire and trenches hindered any such movements. Another hazard to horses and mules were the craters formed by artillery shells. The larger craters were so deep that an animal might fall into the hole and sink, never to be recovered. In some cases a whole team of horses and wagon were trapped when one horse of the team fell into a muddy crater. The wagon was sometimes saved by shooting the trapped animal in the head and detaching it from the harness team. Sydney Smith remembers on the Somme, "I had the terrible experience to witness three horses and six men disappear completely under the mud. It was a sight that will live for ever in my memory, the cries of the trapped soldiers were indescribable, as they struggled to free themselves. The last horse went to a muddy grave, keeping his nostrils above the slush until the last second. A spurt of mud told me it was all over." (Hamid, 53; DiMarco, 310–11; Cooper, 43)

As the war dragged on, the veterinary services of the Allied powers, at least, grew stronger. In part this was due to the intervention of public exasperation and contributions. The British Royal Society for the Prevention of Cruelty to Animals (RSPCA) held fundraisers to pay for warm blankets, grain-grinders, veterinary advisers, and horse hospitals. They built 13 animal hospitals behind the front, each with an operating section, forage barns,

Poison Gas

The most infamous weapon of World War I affected animals as well as men. In the summer of 1916, Germans attacked with 110,000 artillery shells full of phosgene gas, killing or injuring more than 10,000 men. In 1917 they used mustard gas. Mustard gas was worse than phosgene for horses and mules because of its oily property: it stuck to their hooves and legs, causing blisters, and it burned their eyes and groins. Sometimes the horses' eyes were permanently scarred. Ten to twenty percent of horses stricken by gas died. Gas masks for the animals, invented toward the end of the conflict, were so much like the nosebags used for feeding horses that the hungry animals ripped them up searching for the nonexistent oats. (Koenig, 70–71; Gardiner, 51)

German lancers in gas masks, early World War I. (Mary Evans Picture Library.)

and dressing sheds. The Blue Cross was formed as a veterinary mercy service. Horse fodder was the item in greatest demand in World War I. Organizational improvements helped the treatment of the animals. Each wounded beast received a paper with his serial number, unit, and reason for the hospital visit. A green paper was used if surgery was needed. Red paper indicated contagious diseases like mange. White paper meant that only basic medical treatment was needed. According to records, at the veterinary hospitals behind the Western Front, 2,562,549 horses and mules were treated, with almost 2 million of them cured and returned to duty. (DiNardo, 1; Koenig, 296; Gardiner, 159; Cooper, 48–49, 55)

In the western sector of the war, cavalry horses could not prosper thanks to barbed wire, trenches, and machine guns. On March 30, 1918, while pursuing the fleeing Germans at Moreuil Ridge, the Australian and Canadian cavalry charged. "The air was alive with bullets. . . . It was strange to see the horses roll over like rabbits." They lost 300 men and 800 horses in just 90 minutes. In the two eastern sectors of the war, horses were able to commend themselves as weapons more ably. (Gardiner, 18; Sinclair, 250–51)

In the north and east, the Germans faced the Russian Cossacks. The Cossacks were descendants of the Mongol Tatar hordes of southeastern Russia. By the 15th century they were hired to protect Russia from invaders. The word Cossack is a corruption of Kazak, meaning "free warrior." The different Cossack tribes usually took their names from the rivers where they camped, so there were the Don Cossacks, Ural Cossacks, Kuban Cossacks, and others. Being independent by nature, the light horsemen were difficult to control, and they sometimes rebelled to become brigands. They designed their equipment specially to create no noise during their movements. A British captain observing the Cossacks said, "A hundred cossacks make less noise than a single regular cavalry soldier." They remained cavalrymen practically all their lives, joining for a 30-year term, which few would survive to retirement. (Newark, 119–26)

The small and sturdy Cossack ponies could survive on a little grass dug from under the snow, and they could carry a rider 50 miles a day. They ran low to the ground as if slouching and tired, even when fresh. Cossack horses were treated like pets, beloved and adored, their riders weeping openly when the animals fell to enemy bullets. Cossacks claimed that the horses took the emotions of their riders, becoming angry at enemies and kicking at enemy horses. Their "ponies were as fat as butter and looked as contented as kittens," said one observer. Some Cossack riders practiced trick riding called *dzhigtovka*, a sort of circus vaulting or trick riding with sabers held in their teeth. The riders wore a tall cylindrical hat of black Astrakhan wool, a gray overcoat, and a waterproof and windproof cloak. For weapons they carried a carbine, a saber, a dagger, a flintlock pistol, and a bandalero. The Cossacks employed the lasso just as the Huns had done more than a millennium earlier: they would lasso a prisoner and drag him back for interrogation. (Newark, 129–30, 136–37; DiMarco, 320; Sinclair, 50)

Most of the time, the Cossacks were loyal to the czar. To join in service for the czar, a Cossack brought his own horse, and the Russian government issued him a rifle and ammunition. In 1914, 10 Cossacks were attacked by a large German cavalry group. The Russians rode sideways down on the far side of their horses so the Germans could not see them. The Germans approached to capture the apparently riderless horses. As the incautious invaders came close, the Cossacks cut them apart with sabers. Not all skirmishes succeeded so well. Unaware, perhaps, of the new weapons of war, many Russian Cossacks died as German machine-gunners aimed at the horse's legs and then finished off the fallen men. (DiMarco, 312–13; Axell, 138; *Army Times*, 126–27)

Horse-drawn sleigh ambulances in Russia, World War I. (Courtesy John Kistler.)

The Cossacks fought loyally for the czar, but when the Communist revolution split Russia, they also split and fought some for each side. After emerging victorious, the Communists would not trust the Cossacks, and most of them were killed in the "purges." The Communists then withdrew from the war altogether. (Newark, 147)

The other eastern theater of World War I lay more to the south, in Turkey and the Middle East. In 1915, hoping to take Constantinople quickly, the British landed at Gallipoli to drive out the Turks. Instead, the Turks held them at bay, on a beachhead less than two miles deep. Though the orders for New Zealanders to leave their trenches to charge the Turkish machine guns are remembered in legend and cinema, the fate of the horses is less known. At Gallipoli, the horses and mules came under constant enemy artillery and machine-gun fire. For three days, under sniper and machine-gun fire, the veterinarians could only occasionally run out to shoot the wounded animals. Harder still, though, was any attempt to bury the bodies because of the shallow sand beaches present. They tried to float the bodies out to sea, but the carcasses would not sink. On a few occasions the British navy ships lurking nearby mistook the dead horse hooves floating above the water for U-boat periscopes. (Sutton and Walker, 101–4; Cooper, 51–52)

Edmund H. H. Allenby worked as the inspector general of cavalry from 1910 to 1914, then commanded a cavalry division in France in 1914. His lifelong nickname, "the Bull," grew from Allenby's infamous temper: officers were known to faint under his screaming. In June 1917 he was given command of the Egyptian Expeditionary Force, which had been stopped by the Turks near Gaza. His knowledge of cavalry enabled him to successfully deploy horsemen in the Palestinian desert. Lack of water was the main problem for the horses. Desiring water four times per day, they often went 60 hours without drink, with the Worcestershire Yeomanry once surviving 90 hours without water. The Australian Light Horses charged the Turks to capture Beersheba. In 38 days Allenby's men advanced 350 miles, destroyed three Turkish armies, and captured 100,000 men. On some long marches the horses were so tired that they could not eat, but their riders would make little balls of moistened grain and feed them by hand. The Egyptian Expeditionary Force lost about 20 percent of its horses, but only 782 men died. Allenby was able to take Jerusalem before Christmas. (Kelekna, 400; Cooper, 59; Smith, 278; Newark, 245–47; Edwards, 158)

German transport column passing through a town destroyed by fire, in Poland, World War I. (*Collier's Photographic History of the European War*, New York: P. F. Collier & Son, 1917, p. 65.)

While the British drove the Turks from the Middle East, the Americans abandoned neutrality and joined the Allies on the Western Front in 1918. Recognizing that the trench warfare did not work for cavalry, the United States converted a majority of its cavalry forces into artillery and mortar battery units. The U.S. Army did use thousands of horses in draft capacity, pulling wagons and ambulances. After the war, only a few hundred American horses returned home. Some became workers on European farms, but the majority were slaughtered. The official policy of the U.S. Army was to chalk a line down from between the ears and one between the eyes, and where the two lines crossed the farrier sergeant placed the barrel of his revolver and shot through the animal's brain. "Their reward for years of military service—for enduring the gunfire, poison gas, and knee-deep mud—was to be served as a main course on French dinner tables or chopped into hash spooned out to German prisoners of war." General Pershing rode his horse Kidron in the victory parade through Paris, and Kidron was one of the few equines to return to the United States. The British Army made similar sacrifices, of horses that is. Of a million equines sent to war, only 62,000 returned to the island nation. (Urwin, *U.S. Cavalry*, 180; Smith, 286; Koenig, 291–93; Morris, Desmond, 5)

Just as industrialization led to mass production in the 19th century, so had the engines of efficiency taken over the military of World War I. Between 1916 and 1919 the British Army let nothing go to waste. The British shipped 40,000 horse and mule hides to England from the French veterinary hospitals, to be used for leather. When the public learned that the dying horses were becoming a profitable business, the publicity forced the British to bring home 100,000 horses after the war, rather than rendering them for leather and glue. A dead horse had substantial value. Hair was used for mattresses; hides, for leather. Tendons became glue and gelatin; hooves made buttons. Intestines were used for sausage wrapping; fat, for lamps; blood, for potash. Though the value of a horse carcass might be only 20 to 60 shillings, the cumulative value of masses of equines was vast. (Lankester, 159; DiMarco, 323)

Australia sent 160,000 horses called walers for service, mainly to the Egyptian Expeditionary Force. After forcing the Turkish surrender, orders were given to destroy all horses over eight years old. The leadership said it was too expensive to send them home by ship, and they might take diseases back to Australia. All the younger animals would be sold to the Arabs. The

Horse-drawn artillery wagons. (Courtesy National Archives.)

Officer's horse delivered to Gallipoli from transport ship, World War I. (Courtesy John Kistler.)

Australian cavalrymen had seen the cruelty of Egyptians to their animals, and would not see them treated badly. They held a race day, fed the horses a last bag of grain, and then shot them down. More than 10 years later, Mrs. Dorothy Brooke, the wife of a British general stationed in Cairo, saw that many of the horses working on the streets bore the brand of General Allenby's famous cavalry. Mrs. Brooke sent a letter to a newspaper in England mentioning that she would like to buy back and care for the poor horses. Britishers sent in lots of money, and she started the Old War Horse Fund. She would eventually find 5,000 war horses, sending the semi-healthy ones back to England and giving the doomed animals a few days of rest before a painless death. Mrs. Brooke was also able to extract a promise from the British War Office that they would never leave their horses overseas again. The charity Brooke Hospital for Animals still operates in several nations, helping animals afflicted by war. (Koenig, 294–95; Smith, 287–89; Gardiner, 160)

One horse team called the "Old Blacks" included a horse that had served in the Boer War and then throughout all of World War I. Four British officers collected enough money to bring the team back where the horses retired to green pastures. (Koenig, 296)

The Russians, once the Communists took power, sent a huge army toward Poland with 150,000 cavalry, including many Cossacks, but the Polish cavalry under Marshal Jozef Pilsudski defeated them decisively in 1921. (Sinclair, 232–33)

In 1921 Gen. Willard A. Holbrook of the U.S. Army dedicated a bronze tablet in Washington, DC, donated by the Red Star Animal Relief, to honor American horses that died in the Great War. Holbrook said that horses were "as indispensable to the successful prosecution of the war and to final victory as were shot and shell…[yet] no white crosses, row on row, mark their last resting places." (Koenig, 293)

World War II Horses

Twenty years separated the two world wars. In the 1920s, the German cavalry leader Maximilian von Poseck wrote that cavalry horses would still be needed in future conflicts because motor vehicles required good roads. Gen. Heinz Guderian disagreed and led Germany instead to building tanks and smaller armored vehicles. Guderian was quite annoyed that the German Army was training cavalry riders and reportedly grumbled, "Why don't they learn to be mechanics?" (DiNardo, 90)

India, under British control, began the conversion of horse units to mechanized units. Many riders despised the change, missing their horses, and chose to retire rather than become drivers or mechanics. (Hamid, 56)

In 1931, Chief of Staff of the U.S. Army Douglas MacArthur judged that firearms had eliminated the horse as a weapon. He ordered that mechanized cavalry would "fulfill the normal cavalry role, substituting the vehicle for the horse." The romantic image of the cavalry dimmed in 1932 when 213 horses of the 3rd U.S. Cavalry broke up the protests of 20,000 World War I veterans camped in Washington, DC. MacArthur's hopes to upgrade from horse cavalry to gas-powered vehicles failed not for lack of will but for lack of funding. As the Great Depression spread and deepened, the cost of tanks and armored cars was far higher than horses and their riders, and so the old-style cavalry continued. Fort Riley, Kansas, remained the main training center for U.S. cavalry until World War II. Each student was issued four horses in different levels of training, so the men learned all levels of training and care. Each man had an untrained remount, a "green" (inexperienced) jumper, a green polo pony, and an experienced old jumper. They learned leadership, tactics, supply, maps, and so on. The men used sabers until the weapon was retired in 1934. (Clough, 27; Urwin, *U.S. Cavalry*, 182; Yeide, 21–22)

Though the United States and other countries kept minimal cavalry forces, the world's population of horses sank rapidly. Lewinsohn notes that equines became less important in the world as trains and automobiles became human transporters, but "Horses have suffered another setback, too, in the military sphere, a loss of face both material and moral. No longer are they used as chargers on the battlefield. . . . True animal lovers will not much regret this change, and the horses themselves will certainly manage nicely in their unheroic role, for they have never been as combative as the bards would have us believe. This loss of prestige, however, can have material consequences, for the use of horses for military purposes has been one of the most important motives in breeding them." At the end of World War I there were 150 million horses. As World War II began, their number fell almost by half, to 80 million. (Lewinsohn, 386–388)

Germany under Guderian committed itself to exchanging cavalry for mechanized vehicles and yet remained economically far behind the rest of Europe in motorization. Lacking steel capacity and oil, Berlin could produce few tanks or trucks. In a 1935 article, Guderian wrote that Germany had perhaps one vehicle for every 75 people, compared to one in five in the United States. Adolf Hitler never liked horses. He was enraged at a Reich parade in Berlin when the people mildly cheered at passing tanks and artillery but fervently applauded the two leftover horse regiments marching past. However, since Hitler started combat operations long before the army and navy had reached their intended numbers of tanks and ships, the Germans had to hurriedly gather huge numbers of horses. In 1935 the army was buying so many horses that Italian peasants had to go back to using oxen as draft animals because horses were becoming scarce. Between 1938 and 1939 the German Army mobilized 400,000 horses, reaching a total of almost 600,000 by September 1939. (Dinardo, ix, 3–6, 10, 17–19; Smith, 11; Cooper, 66)

The German Army started a horse's training at age three, although the animals were not fully developed physically until age five. For two years they were exposed to loud noises, for a taste of battlefield conditions. The army sought three types of horses: warm bloods, cold bloods, and mixed bloods. Warm blood horses are for riding; cold bloods (bigger and stronger), for draft work; and mixed bloods were an attempt at balancing the two for a multipurpose horse, which did not work well. The difference in size created varying logistical needs, since a normal horse wanted 12 pounds of food per day, while a heavy horse could require 20 pounds per day. Fodder for the horses was of the greatest importance. Even if grass was available for the animals to graze it for themselves, it would take eight hours of grazing to meet their daily needs. If the horses are supposed to work hard much of the day, they cannot be grazing very much. The German fodder included oats, hay, and straw, with oats being preferred. Horses could also be strengthened quickly with corn feed. The heaviest draft horses were saved for pulling heavy artillery pieces. (Dinardo, 8–12)

Fortunately for the German horses, the army organized its veterinary workers well. A German army in the field had three army-base horse hospitals, two parks for training replacements, and one veterinary examining station. At a lower level, each infantry division had a horse hospital able to care for 500 horses. A German infantry division required 4,000 to 6,000 horses just to haul artillery pieces. The large number of blacksmiths and veterinarians were not hard to find, since Germans had long worked with horses. Horses are subject to many diseases. The most common ailment, mange, comes from mites or ticks that burrow under the animal's skin. Mange is very contagious and can become seriously infected if untreated, but it is easy to treat if sulfur dioxide is available and applied. (Dinardo, 8–9, 12–13, 20; Gardiner, 68)

There could be many reasons why the Nazis chose to invade Poland first. One reason was certainly that Poland was a huge source of horses. The Poles completely relied on horse power for both military and personal use. In 1937, the Poles had 40 cavalry regiments. The Germans were ordered to leave untouched all horse-breeding establishments and stud farms, since these would be a future source of new equines. By 1940 Poland was providing 4,000 horses each week to the German Army. ("Animals in the Polish Army"; Dinardo, 21, 25)

The Poles have unjustly become the butt of jokes for purportedly charging the panzers on horseback. What actually happened is far less grotesque, at least in intention. The Polish cavalry charged a German infantry unit, but shortly after the horses began to gallop, armored Nazi reinforcements arrived and cut the horses to pieces. General Guderian was kind enough to order his men out of their tanks to shoot the dying horses with revolvers to end their misery. Stuka dive-bombers probably killed more horses than tanks did. The Pomeranian Cavalry Brigade lost 2,000 horses, out of 3,000, from Stukas in a mere 30 minutes. As the Germans moved toward Warsaw, the Polish cavalry horses worked so hard that many horses died of exhaustion. They had no veterinarians or farriers, so the men wrenched the shoes off dead horses to put on their own mounts. The rapid fall of Poland's cavalry arm to the German advance, and a war game in the spring of 1940 where tanks overwhelmed the horsemen, were the last proofs needed for the U.S. Army to stop raising cavalry regiments. (Piekalkiewicz, 8, 16; Sinclair, 253; Edwards, 159; Smith, 305; Urwin, *U.S. Cavalry*, 186; Yeide, 23–24)

The 1940 German invasion of France succeeded but suffered 90,000 horse casualties, mostly from sickness, but many from French artillery shells. The Germans used trucks to evacuate wounded horses back to their hospitals. As they approached Paris, the Germans laid some minefields to keep French forces from counterattacking. The French sent a large number of horses into the minefield, lacking any other way to clear the explosives. "Dozens of horses, driven frantic with pain and terror, were racing madly hither and thither through the minefield, till one after another they were blown to pieces. Moments later, the entire field was carpeted with a bloody, seething mass of horses' bodies." The Nazi invasion of Norway

German artillery horses killed by dive-bombers. (Courtesy John Kistler.)

proved difficult because the sea transports were not ready for horses. In the first two waves of ships only 1,700 horses arrived. The merchant ship *Ionia* took a British torpedo near Oslo, killing all 150 animals aboard. (Dinardo, 22–23, 29; Piekalkiewicz, 32)

In April 1941 the Italians began to falter in Greece, so the Germans invaded to assist. As the Greek and British forces retreated, the Greek cavalry "hurled themselves against the artillery of the German elite troops, showing immense courage as they faced their enemy on horseback, armed only with sabers and rifles. The effect of shrapnel was horrific, mowing down the horses and tearing their riders to shreds in their saddles. Here and there, horses, with their entrails pouring from their mangled bodies, wandered crazily, trotting towards the surrounding hills. The entire valley was strewn with horses' carcasses. The cry of the dying animals sent shivers down one's spine. Horses rolled on top of each other in agony, or lay on their mutilated hindquarters, beating madly in the air with their forelegs." (Piekalkiewicz, 39)

The Russian campaign was the true disaster for Germany, both men and horses. For the offensive the Germans amassed 3 million men, 600,000 vehicles, 3,350 tanks, 2,000 aircraft, and 600,000 to 750,000 horses. The march across Eastern Europe was long, hot, and humid. Though the Soviets had few aircraft, they used them to target the lines of horses. Pushed constantly, the horses got worn out quickly. German military commanders received only two hours of training on horses, their limitations, speeds, and workloads. This ignorance led officers to work horses to death. Replacement horses were sent, but shortage of train cars meant the horses had to walk 120 to 285 miles to the front, and by then, they were also exhausted. Their cotton feedbags wore out, so they shared wooden troughs, but this promoted the spread of contagious diseases. The Germans tried to use locally captured horses, but these were small and weak, unable to pull heavy carts, so the Germans actually had to build smaller wooden carts that little horses could pull. From September 16 through November 30, 1941, one division's veterinarian company hospital had dealt with 1,072 horses, 117 from wounds, the rest from exhaustion. At times, German tanks or trucks ran horse wagons off the roads and into the mud as they raced by, not seeing the need to share the path with lowly animal vehicles. (Clough, 61; Dinardo, 39, 42–49, 128; Malaparte, *Volga*, 28)

In November near Moscow, the 44th Mongolian Cavalry Division charged the German 106th Infantry and artillery lines at a gallop with sabers. In 10 minutes, Nazi machine guns had killed 2,000 Mongols and their horses in the snow, without a single German casualty. Thirty riderless horses reached the German lines. This would be among the last events for the Germans to cheer about in the Russian lands. (Kelekna, 401; Cooper, 69)

The winter of 1941–1942 was the worst in over a century. The horses stood shivering in temperatures of –50 degrees Fahrenheit. The horses got mange, pneumonia, and frostbite. Hospitals designed to care for 500 equines instead had thousands needing help. There was very little fodder, so the horses ate rotten roof shingles or decaying straw from the eaves of peasant shacks. Though the Germans had retained some cavalry early in the war, in November 1941 the Fuhrer disbanded all cavalry units, shifting the horses to haulers of artillery and wagons. From June 22, 1941, to March 20, 1942, the Germans lost 265,000 horses in the Russian campaign alone. On average, 865 horses died each day for the Reich. Just as Napoleon and his French army had retreated from Moscow, so did the Nazi armies. (Dinardo, 51–52; Piekalkiewicz, 4, 43, 47)

Losing a quarter of a million horses in the Russian invasion, the Germans imported 400,000 more. Each year, Germany became more reliant upon horses and mules because of the lack of trucks and fuel. At Stalingrad the Germans brought in about 90,000 horses, but soon all of the food was gone. They captured a grain elevator full of grain on September 20, 1942, which provided several weeks' worth of horse fodder. As the soldiers became hungry, horses became food. The Germans saved 7,300 horses for the retreat from Stalingrad. On December 23, Army Group Don notified headquarters that they needed 22 tons of fodder to be air dropped for the last 7,000 horses. The requested food did not come. On January 19, 1943, General von Paulus wrote to headquarters again: "The last of the horses have been eaten up." (Overy, 216; Dinardo, 55, 60, 64)

Their enemies on the eastern front, the Soviets, used horses also. The Germans would use about 2.7 million horses. The Soviets used as many as 21 million equines in 30 cavalry divisions, with millions of pack horses as well. The British RSPCA set up a War Aid to Russia Fund, with Winston Churchill's wife Clementine as its president, providing significant help to the Soviet veterinary services, mainly for horses. (Sutton and Walker, 137;

DiMarco, 343; Piekalkiewicz, 4; Sinclair, 253; Livingston and Roberts, 33; Gardiner, 68, 159, 162)

The Soviets invaded Finland in 1939, but the Finns repelled the attackers and forced a peace treaty in 1940. However, the Soviets attacked again in late 1941. A major body of water, Lake Ladoga, formed a natural barrier between parts of Finland and Russia, and thus became a focal point of combat. The Finns, short of supplies, ate dogs and used the skins to make warm gloves. Having no grains with which to feed their horses, the Finns converted paper into cellulose paste as horse fodder. One story, offered by an Italian journalist who traveled in Finland at the time, became famous from his book *Kaputt*. Curzio Malaparte was the pen name of Kurt Erich Suckert, a journalist sent by Mussolini's Italy to observe the Germans and their allies on the eastern front. Although *Kaputt* may not be a strict work of nonfiction, it is a stylized account of what Suckert saw. Since his stories are not confirmed by multiple sources (he was the only reporter on hand), they must be taken with some skepticism, but the famous story about Lake Ladoga is beautiful and horrifying. The lake spans some 125 miles in length and 80 miles across. (Malaparte, *Kaputt*, 53; Salisbury, 484)

As the Finns counterattacked the Soviets at the beginning of winter, a forest fire began in the Raikkola forest, trapping Soviet forces against the western shore of Lake Ladoga. The Soviet soldiers were saved by climbing into boats and withdrew to safety behind their own lines, but there was no room for the horses left behind. About a thousand Soviet horses escaped the flames and machine guns. They reached the lake shore and took refuge in the shallow four-to-six-foot deep water.

The horses clustered, shuddering with cold and fear, their heads stretched out above the surface of the water. Those nearer to land were scorched by the flames and struggled to hoist themselves onto the backs of others, tried to push a way open by biting and kicking. And while still madly struggling, the ice gripped them. The north wind swooped down during the night. (The north wind blows from the Murmansk Sea, like an angel of doom, crying aloud, and the land suddenly dies.) The cold became frightful. Suddenly, with the peculiar vibrating noise of breaking glass, the water froze....In such instances, even sea waves are gripped in mid-air and become rounded ice waves suspended in the void. On the following day, when the first ranger patrols...cautiously stepped over the warm ashes in the charred forest and reached the lakeshore, a horrible and amazing sight met their eyes. The lake looked like a vast sheet of white marble on which rested hundreds upon hundreds of horses' heads. They appeared to have been chopped off cleanly with an ax. Only the heads stuck out of the crust of ice. And they were all facing the shore. The white flame of terror still burnt in their wide-open eyes. Close to the shore a tangle of wildly rearing horses rose from the prison of ice. (Malaparte, *Kaputt*, 57–58)

The following spring the Finnish Army realized that the stinking bodies of decomposing horses would be unbearable, so the Finns used axes to chop through the ice and dismember the beasts so they could be buried. (ibid., 61–62)

The Soviets used 1,100 horses on Lake Ladoga during the early part of the war with Germany, as they attempted to supply Leningrad with food and ammunition to withstand the Nazi siege. During the winter months when the waters were frozen with at least four to eight inches of ice, trucks and horses pulled sleighs and wagons across its surface. The Soviets had to improvise, creating a cleated shoe for the animals to keep their footing while crossing the treacherous ice. (Salisbury, 487)

Most of the true Russian Cossacks, the feared descendants of Mongols who served the czars for centuries, had been executed by the early Communists. Stalin forced the surviving Cossacks to work in factories, and many became tank drivers. Some Cossacks left the Communists and joined the Germans against the Soviets. Gen. Hellmuth von Pannwitz commanded the first German Cossack division in Yugoslavia against partisan rebels, with enough success to form a second division in 1944. In December 1942, von Pannwitz, with 1,000 Cossack cavalry, destroyed a huge Soviet force and earned a medal. The Soviets hanged Cossacks as war criminals, when captured. Recognizing the value of the Cossacks' fearsome reputation, the Communists of World War II sought to rebuild the Cossack divisions of old. There is much argument as to how many of the Soviet cavalry were "real" Cossacks, not just Cossacks in name. Some of the heroics and deeds of Soviet cavalry do imply a long tradition of horsemanship at least among some of the Russian troopers. (DiMarco, 344; Huxley-Blythe, 32–34; Malaparte, *Kaputt*, 42; Dinardo, 94–97)

The 50th and 53rd Cavalry divisions of Soviet Cossacks under Gen. Lev Mikhailovich Dovator traveled hidden in the forests and spent weeks behind German lines. The cavalry was effective at flanking the Nazis in part because German armor needed roads, while horsemen could travel without roads. General Dovator and his 3,000 cavalry routed the 430th German Infantry regiment; destroyed four armored cars, two tanks, and four artillery pieces; and killed 2,500 soldiers during a 12-day raid, with few casualties. This raid near Smolensk caused the German Sixth Army to flee at the rumor of "one hundred thousand Red Cossacks" attacking their rear. (Piekalkiewicz, 43; Dempewolff, 208–11; Axell, 156–57)

When German bombers or fighters pursued Cossack cavalry from the air, the horsemen rushed into forests. The horses were trained to lie down on their sides while their riders threw snow over them as camouflage. At Shtepovka, the 1st Guard Cavalry Corps flanked the German 9th Tank Division and 25th Motorized Division, capturing hundreds of trucks, cars, motorcycles, and other vehicles. In early 1943 the Cossacks led the effort to recapture Taganrog on the Sea of Azov. German fortifications were pierced by Soviet infantry, and the Cossack cavalry shot through to hit the rear of their defenses. Their general said that they enjoyed playing cat and mouse, even with tanks. To destroy tank units, the cavalrymen would cut off communications, steal their fuel and supplies, and finally kill the tank crews. At Rostov on the Don River, the Germans blew up the bridge. Cossack cavalry tried to cross the ice-covered river, but the horses kept slipping. An old Cossack veteran told the men to take off their cloaks and throw them over the ice, and thus the horse regiments crossed and continued the pursuit. (Dempewolff, 212, 234; Hindus, 16–19; Axell, 140–41)

The Soviets learned to use cavalry in concert with tanks. As Capt. Nicholas Caratneff of the Soviet Army said, "Tanks and infantry for a breakthrough. Tanks and cavalry for a breakthrough and encirclement." Tanks would punch a hole in the line, then cavalry rushed through the hole to flank the enemy. (Livingston and Roberts, 170)

In October 1943 the German Seventeenth Army defended the Crimean Peninsula against a vast Soviet army. On May 8, 1944, after 80,000 Nazi casualties, Hitler finally allowed his troops to evacuate Sevastopol. There

Cossacks and their Ponies

A World War II Cossack general was interviewed and gave some insight into their training and relationship with horses.

> You must appreciate the relationship between the Cossack and his horse. The two must trust and love each other. They are not only companions but comrades in arms. The life of the one depends on the skill and devotion of the other. The horse must be sensitive to the will of the man on its back. It must not only fulfill but anticipate the right move, the right step, the right prance, the right maneuver. Quickly and faithfully it must respond to every sound, every gesture, every poke, every nudge of the man in the saddle. To rouse such response the Cossack must never, never neglect his horse. If there is only one piece of sugar, the horse gets it. If there is bread only for one, the horse comes first. If there is only one swallow of water, the Cossack himself goes thirsty and offers it to the horse.... The horse appreciates such attention and will fight for the Cossack to his last breath. Mistreat the horse, be negligent in your care of it, and it will throw you down or do just the opposite of what you want it to do in a critical moment, and then you and the horse are lost...The horse gives the Cossack his most precious asset—dependable mobility. Where the tank cannot pass, where the human foot cannot tread, the horse can make its way. (Hindus, 15–16)
>
> The same general also said that a Cossack youth has achieved perfection in the use of the saber "when, leaping on horseback over a stream, he can swing down his body from the saddle and cleave the water with the saber without stirring any spray." (Hindus, 13–14)

was no way to get out the 30,000 German horses, and the Reich could not leave the animals behind to be absorbed by the Soviet armies. The Germans lined the horses in long rows near a 300-foot cliff above the Black Sea. Each German rider was ordered to shoot his own horse and push its body over the cliff to fall into the Bay of Severnaya. Many riders could not bring themselves to do it, and some of the horses were getting nervous about the deepening blood on the hillside and the noise of dying animals. Machine guns were brought in to mow them down. "The bay was afloat with thousands upon thousands of horses' bodies, surging in a gruesome tide in rhythm with the waves." (Dinardo, 100; Piekalkiewicz, 227–28)

Between the diseases, exhaustion, and machine-gunning of their own horses, the Nazis were running low on horses, particularly trained horses. In June 1944, as the Allied forces pushed inland from the D-Day landings, the Germans discovered that their new artillery-pulling horses were not properly broken-in. Worse, the Allies owned the skies, strafing any Germans or horses on sight. This forced the Germans to move mainly in the darkness, and disrupting the horses' normal sleep patterns caused even more problems. By August, the Germans were in full retreat, with wounded and dead horses blocking their roads of retreat. Germany would have little time remaining to use equines as the Allies pushed from the west and the south while the Soviets rushed in from the east. (Dinardo, 107–8)

The Japanese had even fewer trucks and tanks than the Germans and thus relied upon horses to a greater degree. They used 300,000 horses in China and 75,000 more in their Pacific island offensives. In 1939 Japan kept three cavalry brigades in Manchuria and two in North China, mainly intended for use against Soviet Russia. Each brigade consisted of 2,300 men with 3,000 horses, equipped with carbines and a few machine guns, artillery pieces, tanks, and armored cars. The Japanese homeland had poor horseflesh resources and so scavenged other lands for horses. The two Japanese North China cavalry brigades fought in battles near Kalghan and Suiyang against Chinese forces, apparently in envelopment movements including armor and infantry. Their efforts were considered ineffective with weakness of firepower, though Japanese propaganda trumpeted cavalry successes. An April 1939 *Tokyo Gazette* article wrote that Japanese horsemen carried out "successful daring attacks upon enemy positions, particularly in battles on the rugged steeps and in the narrow passes of the Chinese mountains." Fearful of enemy horses, particularly the Soviets in Mongolia, the Japanese army funded massive biological weapons programs to infect horses with glanders, anthrax, and other diseases (see chapter 4 for more details). (Overy, 221; Benitez; Dempewolff, 221)

The British used cavalry in the Syrian campaign of 1941–1942. These equines were not trained as warhorses, they were simply drafted hunting horses. The RSPCA had asked the British public to open their empty garages (cars had all been requisitioned by the army) so that horses could hide inside when Nazi aircraft dropped their payloads. For shipment of the horses from Britain to Palestine, the horses had to be carefully secured lest they slide back and forth during storms and break their legs. Some horses had a shorter journey, from India to Burma, for instance. The last charge of British cavalry came on March 18, 1942, when Capt. Arthur Sandeman had his 60 Sikh cavalry of the 2nd Frontier Forces in Burma counterattack a Japanese ambush. They were mowed down by the Japanese guns. (Barber, 113; Cooper, 67–68, 158; Gardiner, 31)

The United States, as it had done in World War I, tried to remain neutral as war raged in Europe and Southeast Asia. General MacArthur had demanded that the army move away from horses to motor vehicles in the early 1930s, but the Great Depression kept funding down and thus vehicles were not affordable. One movie and book, citing an anonymous witness, claim that General MacArthur ordered that the horses be gunned down and buried en masse, but there is no evidence of this. In fact, the military scrupulously sold its unwanted horses to gain funds: machine-gunning horses in the desert would be a huge waste of materiel. The number of horses and mules did gradually dwindle since military commanders had concluded that there would be no need for equines in future wars: aircraft were better for reconnaissance, tanks were more powerful, and trucks were faster. They ignored the heavy usage of horses and mules in China, Ethiopia, Spain, and other countries. By 1940 the U.S. Army had only 17,000 horses and 3,500 mules in service. (Livingston and Roberts, 81, 150; Brophy et al., 315–16)

What little remained of the U.S. cavalry was stationed in the Philippine Islands. The 26th Cavalry Philippine Scouts were a scout regiment under "Black Jack" Pershing remaining overseas after the Spanish-American War of the 1890s. About a thousand men, mostly Filipino regulars under American officers, were stationed at Fort Stotsenburg, 60 miles north of Manila. Their average length of service was 13 years, so many veterans remained on duty. This cavalry practiced the horse charge, though it had not been done in battle since the days of Pancho Villa, 35 years earlier. In

February 1940, Clinton Pierce, an instructor of the Cavalry School at Fort Riley, Kansas, transferred to the 26th. Pierce was promoted to colonel in October 1940. (Ramsey and Rivele, 26, 36–37; *Army Times*, 135–37)

The Japanese forced the United States into World War II by attacking Pearl Harbor on December 7, 1941. American government officials assured the U.S. forces in the Philippines that the Japanese would not be able to invade the islands for months. This assurance was completely false. Japanese bombers came in quickly and wiped out the U.S. Army Air Forces, then started landings in Luzon on December 22. The 26th Cavalry used delaying tactics to slow the Japanese movement toward Manila, falling back slowly and contesting each hill. Imperial Japanese fighters and bombers killed many horses and their riders. The U.S. cavalry held off two enemy armored regiments and two infantry regiments, then counterattacked on December 24, forcing the enemy to bring up reinforcements. The 26th Cavalry had 830 men before the war

M5 gas mask for cavalry horses, 1943 (side view). (Courtesy National Archives.)

M5 gas mask for cavalry horses, 1943 (front view). (Courtesy National Archives.)

started, but their number had fallen to 450 men, and fewer horses, by Christmas day. Food became so scarce that the quartermaster ordered most of the remaining horses to be slaughtered, to feed the soldiers. Col. Edwin Ramsey did spare enough horses to make the final mounted cavalry charge in U.S. military history. On January 16, 1942, as the Japanese invaded a village called Morong, his horsemen charged into the enemy, causing them to flee. In moments, however, mortar shells fell in town near one of their horses. "It reared up on its hind legs with a horrible scream, and I watched its belly peel open, the steaming contents slithering out, and then the horse crumbled onto its haunches in a hypnotic slow motion." On March 15, 1942, the remaining 250 horses and 26 baggage mules were slaughtered and cooked for the starving U.S. troops. (*Army Times*, 142–44; Urwin, *U.S. Cavalry*, 186; Gardiner, 31; Ramsey and Rivele, 51, 66–67, 73)

Most remaining U.S. troops in the Philippines surrendered to Japan on April 9, 1942. General Wainwright credited the 26th Cavalry, "this gallant little band of horsemen," with enabling the troops to withdraw to Bataan before the surrender. However, Colonel Ramsey and a handful of other soldiers did not surrender but became a guerrilla movement. They had no cavalry, just a few pack horses. (Livingston and Roberts, 151; Urwin, *U.S. Cavalry*, 186)

By 1943 the U.S. military no longer acquired horses, just mules. The army sent 3,900 of its horses to the Coast Guard for beach patrols. Cavalrymen trained the Coast Guard patrolmen to ride so they could detect enemy ships or shore parties. The patrols lasted from the start of the war until 1944, when the German U-boat threat was ended. Other army horses were used at POW camps in the United States for patrol and guard duty. Though many U.S. commanders asked for horse cavalry throughout the war, the War Department denied all such requests, saying that shipping space was too important for horses and grain. The last World War II use of horses by the U.S. Army was when the 10th Reconnaissance Troop of the 10th Mountain Ski Division moved with 60 horses and a pack train of mules across Italy in 1945 as the army moved north toward Germany. (Brophy et al., 317–19; Livingston and Roberts, 153–54; *Army Times*, 148–49)

Gen. George S. Patton approved an unusual mission in 1945, behind German lines. As the Soviets streamed across Eastern Europe, the Lipizzaner stallions and brood mares of Czechoslovakia were threatened. Advance Soviet units were already stealing and eating some of the famous "dancing" equines. Col. Alois Podhajsky, director of the Spanish Riding School in Vienna, called Patton with an urgent request to rescue the white stallions. American troops raided the region and saved the horses, sending most of them to Spain and a few to the United States. After the war, Patton himself took the opportunity to ride one of these horses, named Favory Africa. This horse had been chosen personally by Adolf Hitler as a gift for Emperor Hirohito of Japan as a war trophy. (DiMarco, 347–48; Dolenc, 20; Livingston and Roberts, 146, 187)

Along with the Lipizzaners, other famous and fine German breeds of horses were endangered by the Soviets and had no assistance from Patton. About 56,000 equines of the Trakehner line of East Prussia, longtime cavalry horses for the German Army, found their stables under increasing artillery shelling and tank fire. The Trakehners, also known as East Prussian Warmbloods, originated by breeding large English animals with sturdy Arabians. Some caring individuals led small groups of the horses westward ahead of the Soviet juggernaut. The winter of 1944–1945 saw German refugees fleeing west, in such numbers that the bridges became choke points. Horse-drawn wagons spaced themselves properly to cross ice-covered rivers, but strafing by Soviet aircraft

German artillery horses killed by American artillery shells, 1944.
(Courtesy John Kistler.)

caused a panic. As the heavy wagons clattered across the ice, the ice broke. Hundreds of people and horses drowned in the freezing waters. At war's end, only a thousand East Prussian Warmbloods survived. (Clough, 12–14, 122–23, 162)

Horses after World War II

After World War II, only the Soviet Union continued with organized horse cavalry units. The Soviets kept large numbers of horsemen and equines through the 1950s, until mechanized units completely supplanted the animals. (DiMarco, 350)

The Portuguese used horses for counter-insurgency efforts in Angola in the 1970s, while Rhodesia utilized mounted units like the Grey Scouts to track and attack antigovernment guerrillas in the 1980s. (Lawford, 9; DiMarco, 351)

The longtime battlefield of Afghanistan saw the mujahideen of the 1980s countering Soviet invaders from horseback, but in recent years even

Reckless the Korean War Horse

During the Korean War, the U.S. military did not officially use horses, but some soldiers acquired them anyway. Lt. Eric Pederson of a U.S. Marine Recoilless Rifle Platoon bought a small Korean racing mare in October 1952 for $250 to help carry the unit's heavy ammunition. Having no horse fodder at first, the horse's "first Marine meal consisted of a loaf of bread and uncooked oatmeal," though in the future she came to love beer and chocolate provided by her soldier friends. The bazooka-like recoilless rifle startled her for the first several shots, but she grew accustomed to its firing. Named Reckless (a nickname based on "Recoilless"), the horse earned a promotion by her unit to the rank of corporal. She made 51 trips up a steep 45-degree slope, on a narrow, muddy, winding trail, hauling more than 9,000 pounds of ammunition (386 recoilless rifle rounds) to the front in just two days. The men yanked up clumps of grass for her food. During times when the heavy weapons were not firing, Reckless worked more leisurely at stringing communication wire between units. The soldiers hired a Korean tailor to make Reckless a red silk parade blanket trimmed with gold, bearing the globe and anchor symbols of the U.S. Marine Corps, and the general came to the ceremony and pinned her new sergeant stripes onto the blanket. Her story appeared in the *Saturday Evening Post*, and the marines sent her aboard a ship to retire to Camp Pendleton, California, in late 1954. (Ruthven, 216; Geer, 292–307)

---

the U.S. military has come to use Afghani horses and horsemen against the Taliban and Al Qaeda sympathizers. (Livingston and Roberts, 36; Gardiner, 31–32)

On September 11, 2001, when Al Qaeda terrorists struck New York City, the Taliban had nearly destroyed the Northern Alliance of Afghanistan. The United States had ignored the situation, but the attack by Al Qaeda, with its ties to Afghanistan and the Taliban, led it to intervene. The Bush administration considered a full-scale invasion, but it would take six months to get 60,000 troops into Asia, by which time the Taliban would probably have total control of Afghanistan. Instead of sending an army, the United States sent a handful of U.S. Special Forces soldiers to join the Northern Alliance. These soldiers mounted horses for the first time: there is practically no other way for people to travel in the mountainous terrain. Afghans ride shaggy, strong, short-legged ponies, with primitive saddles made of boards covered with goat skin. One American described the horses' eyes as "full of misery." The animals were always overloaded and underfed, with cracked hooves and no shoes. Because of the mountainous terrain, with thousand-foot-drops along a narrow path, the men learned that if the horse bolts and you cannot dismount, you must shoot the horse in the head, or you will fall to your death. The Northern Alliance soldiers camped in high caves where they could not be pursued by the mechanized Taliban forces. For warmth in the cold mountain caves, they plastered horse and mule dung onto the cave walls as primitive insulation. (Stanton)

Guard patrol duty at a U.S. naval base. (Courtesy National Archives.)

Horse hoisted to U.S. Navy transport vessel. (Courtesy National Archives.)

The horses did not suffer because their riders wished them harm, but because supplies were so scarce. Northern Alliance soldiers had only one blanket, and they tied it over the horse outside the cave; if they had only one biscuit, they fed it to the horse. Frustrated at their inability to force their enemy out of the mountains, the Taliban planted mines at every known watering hole, hoping to kill the horses where they came to drink. They learned mine tricks from the Soviets, who were estimated to have left between 10 million and 30 million mines in Afghanistan: perhaps 100 per square mile. Most of these mines exploded with the force of a small hand grenade, designed to maim rather than kill. They used different-colored mines to camouflage them better, with light brown devices in sandy areas and gray ones in riverbeds. These devices were plastic and hard to see or detect. Afghans are thankful for occasional hailstorms (called "Allah's Mine Sweeper") because hail will often detonate the small explosives. (Stanton; Kaplan, 2–5, 122)

U.S. soldiers could not help the Northern Alliance in any straight-forward numeric manner but became a technologically advanced artillery system to assist the rebels. The Taliban forces owned Soviet tanks, personnel carriers, and anti-aircraft guns (ZSUs). ZSUs were particularly dangerous to the Northern Alliance because 4,000 rounds a minute could tear up the cavalry forces. The Americans used high-tech communication equipment to call in precision airstrikes from B-52 bombers miles overhead. The combination of a primitive cavalry strike force and laser-guided bombs proved potent against the Taliban. (Stanton)

A typical Northern Alliance attack on a Taliban stronghold would occur late in the afternoon around 2:00 or 3:00 p.m., thus allowing for a retreat under cover of darkness if the offensive failed. More than a thousand light horsemen would use low hills to screen their movements from the enemy, getting as close as possible without coming under enemy artillery fire. They formed in lines about one-quarter mile long, and sometimes a few forward riders intentionally created dust clouds to help hide the allied force. When within a mile of the target, the cavalry would charge, firing only when they came up on the crests of hills. At a quarter mile, the front line would dismount near a hillcrest to provide covering fire for the second line galloping past. Then the first line remounted and charged. The American troops, meanwhile, called in coordinated bomb strikes from bombers or fighters to hit the enemy armored vehicles just 30 seconds or a minute before the cavalrymen arrived. If any vehicles remained, a few of the Northern Alliance horsemen carried rocket-propelled grenades (RPGs) to knock them out. Very few prisoners were taken, because Taliban commanders in the rear shot their own men for cowardice if they raised their arms to surrender. The "shock and awe" of huge munitions blasting their position, followed by the quick arrival of mounted foes, brought several significant victories to the Northern Alliance and nearly destroyed the Taliban. (ibid.)

A Special Forces soldier, Capt. Mitch Nelson, in Afghanistan, summed up the situation in late 2001.

I am advising a man on how to best employ light infantry and horse cavalry in the attack against Taliban T-55 tanks, mortars, artillery, personnel carriers: a tactic which I think became outdated with the invention of the Gatling gun. The Mujahadeen have done this every day we have been on the ground. They have attacked with less than ten rounds of ammunition per man, with snipers having less than one hundred rounds, little water, and less food. I have observed a PK gunner who walked ten plus miles to get to the fight, who was proud to show me his artificial right leg from the knee down. We have witnessed the horse cavalry bounding over watch from spur to spur to attack Taliban strongpoints, the last, several kilometers under mortar, artillery, and sniper fire. There is little medical care if injured, only a donkey ride to the aide station. I think the Mujahadeen are doing very well with what they have. We could not do what we are doing without the close air support. (ibid.)

Small, poor nations often use cavalry because horses require neither gasoline nor parts for repairs. The most infamous cavalry force in the world today must be the Janjaweed ("Devils on Horseback") of western Sudan. The Islamic government in Khartoum claims to have no relationship with these raiders who massacre villagers throughout the Darfur region bordering Chad. (Kelekna, 404)

There remains one last group of cavalry in the U.S. Army. The Caisson Platoon, H Company, 3rd Infantry Regiment, best known as "The Old Guard," consists of about 35 horses with riders for use in ceremonial parade maneuvers at military funerals in Arlington National Cemetery, Virginia. (*Army Times*, 150; Livingston and Roberts, 273)

4

Insects and Biological Weapons

Some creatures have become unwitting participants in the militias of men, whether tossed into a fray without training or direction, or purely by accident. One of the most common insects useful in warfare is the bee, though historically writers have not always distinguished between bees, hornets, wasps, and other stinging creatures.

Egyptians were already cultivating honeybees and their sweet honey-laden hives by 3000 BC, though who first "harvested" bees is unknown. In Mesopotamia, one of the first projectile weapons, dating to Neolithic times, was the beehive bomb. Anyone who has frantically tried to shoo away a dozen buzzing insects can imagine how distracting a weapon a thrown hive of angry bees could be. (Hyams, 104; Mayor, *Greek,* 177–79; Lockwood, Jeffrey, 16)

Philip of Macedon's engineers designed the first catapults capable of hurling large rocks and beehives. The Greek word *bombos* means "bee," from which English developed the word "bombardment," alluding to the threatening hum coming from projectiles filled with angry bees. (Lockwood, Jeffrey, 24)

Not only may bees cause confusion when they are intentionally tossed at the enemy, but their honey may be poisonous. As Xenophon and 10,000 Greek mercenaries made their famous march out of Persia, the soldiers rested in a region where many wild hives seemed free for the taking. Thousands of men became ill, "like intoxicated madmen," staggering about, when able to walk at all. Most began to regain their senses the next day, but

Mayan Bee Weapons

The Mayans of central America created special containers for the weaponizing of bees and stinging bugs as early as 2600 BC. The book *Popol Vuh* describes invading soldiers wearing war bonnets with gourds full of bees, so that when the men scaled the walls they could toss the gourds into the city and let the insects distract the enemy. These "bee grenades" were created quite ingeniously by leaving the portable casings in areas where bees liked to swarm. Once the insects inhabited the gourd, grass was stuffed in the entrance hole to trap them inside, for later use in battle. (Mayor, *Greek,* 177; Lockwood, Jeffrey, 17)

---

it took three or four days for the men to fully recover. This toxic honey is known in the region today as "mad honey," made by bees collecting nectar from local poisonous rhododendron blossoms. (Mayor, *Greek,* 146)

Perhaps the master of ancient bee weapons and poisons was Mithridates VI of Pontus (134–63 BC), the famous enemy of Rome, who often found biological means to harm his foes. When Roman legions under Pompey the Great invaded his territories, Mithridates ordered local tribes to gather beehives from that same area where Xenophon's men indulged. He set the hives intentionally in the path of the Italians, knowing they could not resist a sweet snack on the march. At least a thousand Romans died when the army of Pontus attacked the drugged invaders. Later, when Romans laid siege to his city and dug tunnels under the walls, Mithridates drilled holes down to the tunnels, then dropped beehives and other wild creatures (including bears, it is said) into the tunnels, routing the underground attackers. A thousand years later, Britons would defend the town of Chester against Danish invaders by plopping beehives down into their sapper tunnels in similar fashion. (Mayor, *Greek,* 153–54, 181; Lockwood, Jeffrey, 21, 35)

Medieval and Renaissance times are replete with stories of cities saved by bees or the slaughter of the enemy after tricking them into drinking drugged mead (honey alcohol). In the 17th century the town of Wuppertal, Germany, cleverly drove out marauders when the nuns toppled all the

Honeybee at work. (Mary Evans Picture Library.)

local beehives. The town actually changed its name to Beyenburg, "Bee Town," in honor of the deliverance. During the Thirty Years' War (1618–1648), Swedish warhorses fled from swarms of stinging bees loosed by the enemy. (Lockwood, Jeffrey, 22–23; Mayor, *Greek*, 154, 180–81, 197)

During the American Civil War, at the Battle of Antietam, the 132nd Pennsylvania Volunteers were routed when they sought cover in a field full of beehives, and cannon rounds disturbed the hives into attacking the men, who were then shot by the enemy. In a much smaller conflict, Yankee soldiers foraging in Kentucky were driven away while stealing honey from beehives. Apparently a resident in the home had attached a rope to some of the hives and pulled them over when intruders came visiting, so the soldiers fled. (Lockwood, Jeffrey, 74; Morton, 267–70)

The Tiv people of Nigeria, like the Maya of ancient times, found clever ways to direct bees at the enemy. The Africans kept bees in special large horns, with a toxic powder perhaps helping to calm the bees. In battle, the horns were pointed at the enemy and the bees sent forward. (Mayor, *Greek,* 179)

The creative use of bees has continued even into the most modern of times. Both the Axis and the Allies of World War I used beehives set up with trip wires, set to fall when enemies passed. Near Mombasa, Kenya, during a battle between Germans and British, machine-gunners unwittingly destroyed several hives of large bees, which attacked and drove away the British. (Mayor, *Greek,* 180; LeChene, 215–16)

One very unusual use of insects during World War I came with the newly invented armored "tank" vehicles. An officer would walk ahead with jars full of glowworms to guide the tanks to their positions in the early morning darkness. (Cooper, 211)

When Mussolini invaded Ethiopia in 1935, the Italians used poison gas. The locals responded by dropping beehives on Italian tanks, causing many crashes. During the Vietnam War, the Vietcong used giant Asian honeybee hives, and scorpions, as booby traps for American troops. At the same time, the Pentagon began playing with a secret bee weapon: apparently a pheromone would be somehow attached to the victims, attracting swarms of bees to attack them. The U.S. Army also tested assassin bugs as primitive human detectors to try to find the Vietcong. These insects can detect a human up to two city blocks distant, and they make a "yowling sound" when they sense a person. No one knows if the device was used in the war. (Mayor, *Greek,* 180–87; Denega, 47; Lubow, 110–12)

DARPA, the Defense Advanced Research Projects Agency, calls projects seeking to use living creatures in war "vivisystems." Vivisystems include the attempted creation of cyborg-type robotic insects. The science is called "biomimetics," an "extreme version of the technological exploitation of the living world," trying to capture the essential workings of a living organism via machine. DARPA has trained bees, with their incredible sense of smell, to correctly detect 99 percent of mines planted within 200 yards of their hives. Moth antennae are very sensitive to the molecules in explosives, but moths are not easy to train. However, even detached from the animal, moth antennae can still sense explosives for hours. Scientists are trying to rig the antennae to computers as a means of finding explosives. (Lockwood, Jeffrey, 5, 206, 283, 288–89)

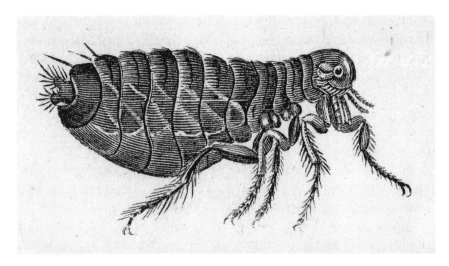

The flea, purveyor of disease, especially during World War II by Japanese Army biological warfare in China. (Courtesy John Kistler.)

Rather than stealing the antennae from moths, or the excellent legs from cockroaches, DARPA and similar organizations seek to build robots capable of imitating the living forms. One desirable application of this research is the race to construct "Micro Air Vehicles" that imitate insects, for use in spying or reconnaissance. A 2007 *Washington Post* article reports that many people have seen "large black dragonflies" hovering near important political events since 2004, with many flying in formation or pulling small spherical objects behind. (Lockwood, Jeffrey, 294–96)

The bees and other insects used by armies described in the earlier part of this chapter were used in their "natural state." Bees sting because they naturally do such things. However, with specific modifications, or by people's using some feature possessed by an insect, such as poison, some insects can become biological weapons. Known from ancient times, the Paederus beetle of India exudes toxins more potent than cobra venom. Simple contact with human skin causes blisters, but if eaten or injected into the bloodstream it can kill. Putting such toxins on an arrowhead or sword blade can add the poison to an enemy's wound. (Mayor, *Greek,* 74)

Tricking enemies into eating or drinking a toxin can sicken or kill them. As early as the Peloponnesian Wars (431–404 BC) in Greece, armies would pollute a water supply by dropping in dead human or animal bodies. Thus, microbes and disease could decimate a foe. In 1710, the Iroquois Indians dropped flayed animal skins into a French army water supply, killing at least a thousand men. This was a common tactic during the American Civil War. An estimated two-thirds of the half-million soldiers who died during the Civil War died of disease, mainly from insect-borne pathogens. Five million became sick and 150,000 died in this manner. (Mayor, *Greek*, 106–7; Lockwood, Jeffrey, 67)

Early attempts at biological warfare were crude and only sporadically effective. By World War I, medical and technological advances enabled scientists and armies to create more deadly bioweapons.

Russia and the newly emerging Soviet Union fought frequently with Japan in the Far East in the early 20th century. When the Soviets began large-scale biological weapons programs in the 1920s, the Japanese Army ramped up its own studies. The man who would take these "germ weapons" from the theoretical and into practical and usable weapons forms was Ishii Shiro, born in 1892. (Harris, xi, 22–23; Williams and Wallace, 5)

Trained as a doctor but recognizing that the growing military might of Japan could bring power, Ishii made bacteriological warfare his main study. As Japan took Manchuria and larger sections of China in the early 1930s, and possible dangers (and opposition) arose in Japan itself, in 1932 Ishii arranged for the biological weapons programs to be moved to mainland Asia. In Manchuria, far from prying eyes, Ishii had unlimited money, manpower, and resources to advance his tiny weapons. His base took the public name "Water Purification Bureau" but was called "Unit 731" by the military. To test his new chemical and biological toxins, Ishii had an endless supply of local Chinese people. One euphemism for the human guinea-pigs in the heavily fortified water purification bureau was to call them "logs" for use in the lumber mill. The unfortunate captives were infected with "anthrax, yellow fever, plague, typhoid, typhus, smallpox, tularemia, jaundice, gangrene, tetanus, cholera, dysentery, glanders, scarlet fever, undulant fever, tick encephalitis, hemorrhagic fever, whooping cough, diphtheria, pneumonia, brysipelas, meningitis, venereal diseases, tuberculosis, salmonella, frostbite and many other diseases." Some captives had their blood drained and replaced with horse blood in plasma experiments. Some U.S. and British prisoners of war were also experimented upon by

Ishii. Before World War II had ended, Unit 731 produced hundreds of millions of infected insects and dispersed them across China, where they may have caused more deaths than the atomic weapons detonated over Japan in 1945. (Harris, 21–23, 33, 47, 59, 124–25; Williams and Wallace, 49; Lockwood, Jeffrey, 2).

By 1940, Unit 731 had developed bombs and spraying devices capable of carrying biological weapons. A missionary's diary tells of a single Japanese plane flying over the city of Ningbo, spraying wheat, rice, and sorghum down on the starving city. The people were quick to gather the food, not knowing that it was infested with fleas infected with bubonic plague. "The onset is abrupt, with chills, high fever and extreme weakness. The eyes redden, the face becomes congested and the tongue coated. Victims can become maniacally delirious and death may be rapid, sometimes within one day." The Japanese hoped the disease weapons would spread into enemy armies and overload their medical facilities. Because bubonic plague is "natural," it would be hard to prove that it started in a weapon form, to turn public opinion against the Japanese Army. At Ningbo, when people started dying, masons built a brick wall around the six blocks in the center of the city, and no one could leave without being cleansed in decontamination sheds. They burned the city center. This thorough work did not end the plague, however, which would return five times in Ningbo over the next 15 years. (Williams and Wallace, 21; Lockwood, Jeffrey, 110–11)

The flea became the ideal method of spreading bubonic plague because the bacillus itself is fragile and cannot survive "in the elements." Inside a warm, living body the bacillus can remain fresh and dangerous, and the flea itself injects the disease into humans naturally and without training. Ishii's older brother took over the animal house and supervised the gathering of rats to speed production of the plague fleas. When asked why Japanese soldiers fanned out in villages capturing rats, they answered, "to make hats" with the pelts. The flea factory had metal jars full of fleas, with a restrained white rat dropped into each jar to feed the insects. Ideally for the Japanese, fleas could also be dropped from airplanes and still survive the fall to earth. (Williams and Wallace, 24–25)

Another Unit, Unit 100, started in 1936, was devoted entirely to creating animal diseases such as anthrax, glanders, and other cattle killers intended to disable enemy horses and food supplies. They ran tests along

Soviet territories north of China, contaminating lakes and streams with anthrax and other germs. Unit 100 never had the manpower and resources of Unit 31, however, and did not have the same impact. (Williams and Wallace, 74–75)

The successful spread of bubonic plague led General Ishii to travel to Berlin in 1941 to promote bacterial warfare schemes to the Nazi regime. Hitler hated such ideas, and he rejected the notion. The Fuhrer had a phobia about bacteria and forbade any bacterial research, thus stunting the German pursuit of such weapons. The Nazis did some minor insect research, especially the idea of sending beetles to destroy enemy crops. The crop-eating beetles escaped and began eating up German farms, so the Germans, to hide the truth, accused the Allies of dropping the creatures. (Koenig, 282; Lockwood, Jeffrey, 128–29, 134)

The Soviets did not share Hitler's compunctions about bacterial weapons. Soviet spies captured in 1935 in Manchuria purportedly carried ampoules full of anthrax and cholera to use against Japan. Soviets planted lice infected with typhus among German troops in the Karachevo region, causing almost 3,000 casualties. In 1941, the Soviets tested diseases in Mongolia near Ulan Bator by chaining prisoners of war in their tents with cages of plague-infected rats and fleas. One prisoner escaped, spreading the plague throughout the region. Soviet bombers leveled the nearby towns and burned the bodies of thousands of Mongolians, either to stop the outbreak or to hide their experiments. In 1942 an outbreak of tularemia, never before seen in Stalingrad, may have indicated a Soviet biological weapon attempt in the region. (Williams and Wallace, 63; Lockwood, Jeffrey, 140)

Unimpressed by the Nazi beetles, the Japanese continued with the slaughter of the Chinese people. On May 4, 1942, some 54 bombers hit Baoshan in Yunnan Province. Most of the buildings collapsed into rubble, and 10,000 people died. Some of the fallen bombs seemed to be "duds" since they did not explode. Inside the casings was a "yellow waxy substance" full of flies. These devices came to be called *yagi*, or maggot bombs. That substance was a bacterial slurry of cholera. The bombers returned for four more days, driving the infected people to flee to other towns, thus spreading the cholera. In a few weeks the disease had spread 125 miles. In two months, 200,000 people were dead across an area the size of Pennsylvania. Much of the Chinese resistance, the Nationalist Army under Chiang

Kai-shek, was destroyed. The army in Yunnan Province was gone. Japanese soldiers had been vaccinated against cholera and so were not affected by the disease. (Lockwood, Jeffrey, 114–15)

Word of the cholera weapon reached U.S. President Franklin Delano Roosevelt in 1943. He threatened Japan with retaliation if such methods continued to be used in China, but his threats were ignored. In fact, in March 1942, the Imperial Army planned to drop 200 pounds of Ishii's plague fleas on the American troops defending Bataan in the Philippines. Because Japan conquered Bataan so quickly, the plan was called off. Ishii did send 17 officers on a ship to Saipan with drums of plague fleas to sprinkle on runways, but the ship was sunk by a torpedo. Roosevelt himself may have been opposed to biological weapons, but the U.S. Army started a secret biological warfare program at Detrick Field, near Frederick, Maryland, in 1943. Before the huge invasion of Iwo Jima, officers pressured Roosevelt to authorize the use of poison gas against the Japanese defenders, but the president refused. (Lockwood, Jeffrey, 116, 119, 299; Williams and Wallace, 81, 94)

Unit 731 experimented with many delivery systems for the germs, including artillery shells and bombs that continued to be discovered in the ground even into the 1990s. Ishii and his men modified fountain pens and walking sticks that were encrusted with bacteria. Contaminated wheat and millet cargoes were sent by train to regions all over China, carrying typhoid, cholera, and plague. Germs were dumped into reservoirs, ponds, lakes, and wells. Aircraft dropped rice balls and colored paper for children, coated with plague virus. When Ishii moved Unit 731 to Nanking, Maj. Gen. Kitana Masaji took over the older water purification facility, and he perfected spraying techniques for aircraft. He even filmed parts of the plague operations near Shanghai in 1944. (Harris, 60–61, 66–67, 78–81; Williams and Wallace, 29)

As reports of the effective disease-weapons reached the United States, the thousands of Japanese balloons launched over the Pacific became a greater concern. What if the incendiary bombs were replaced with bubonic plague fleas? Ishii developed a plan called Operation Cherry Blossoms at Night, to hit the United States with biological weapons. The plan was finalized on March 26, 1945, for one of Japan's newest mega-submarines to launch its three seaplanes with bubonic fleas along the California coastline. Fortunately, one Japanese general realized the intense retaliation that the United States might send, and he called off the plan. Increasingly desperate for any means to stop the advance of the U.S. troops toward Japan, Ishii ramped up production of plague fleas. He hoped to have one billion infected fleas, and he hurriedly bred rabbits and rats for flea food. These efforts were delayed when one of the prisoners killed a guard, and freed all the prisoners, starting a riot. They could not escape the cell block, however, and were killed with poison gas. (Lockwood, Jeffrey, 120; Williams and Wallace, 82–84)

As the Soviets began to push toward Mongolia in early 1945, the Japanese prepared to use their biological weapons. They purchased many cows, horses, and sheep, injected them with anthrax and other cattle-borne diseases, and sent the animals behind Soviet lines to infect cattle and spread

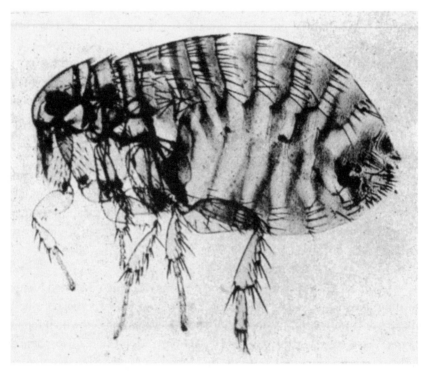

Bubonic plague flea taken from a rat. (*Wonders of Animal Life*, J.A. Hammerton, ed., vol. 4., Waverley Book Co., p. 1695.)

diseases. When Ishii learned that the atomic bombs had brought an abrupt end to the war against the United States, his men destroyed evidence, killed the prisoners, and released all of the infected animals and insects. In August 1945, as the Japanese troops retreated, the Soviets found a mass grave near Hailar with at least 10,000 Chinese and Mongolian bodies. Also in the area were released monkeys, camels, rabbits, and guinea pigs: perhaps from the Unit 731 experimentation cages. The released infected animals caused bubonic plague to erupt in Pingfan in 1946. (Harris, 4, 96; Lockwood, Jeffrey, 122; Williams and Wallace, 86)

Although the post–World War II world included the famous Nuremburg Trials, in which war criminals were prosecuted, some escaped justice by volunteering to help the victors with their own fledgling weapons programs. Ishii survived by taking an immunity deal, providing the U.S. Army with entomological and bacterial warfare expertise in exchange for freedom. He traveled often to the United States and received a "generous" pension. Because most of the information was destroyed or kept confidential, Japan has continued to deny any Unit 731 atrocities. Ishii died of natural causes in 1959. (Lockwood, Jeffrey, 123–27)

With Ishii's help, the U.S. Army set up "Unit 406" in Kyoto, Japan. The work of Unit 406 remained secret, though a 1952 leftist organization in Tokyo distributed pamphlets claiming that insect weapons including plague, cholera, scarlet fever, meningitis, and dysentery were being produced in the lab. In the United States, similar programs worked at Camp Detrick. (Lockwood, Jeffrey, 160–61)

The Korean War began in 1950. By early 1951, smallpox and typhus were spreading through the region. China claimed that the United States was using biological weapons, which the United States denied. The North Korean foreign minister officially informed the United Nations that on January 23, 1952, American planes dropped large quantities of diseased insects over North Korea. China added details, that 448 aircraft in 68 sorties dropped the bugs. Though the United States insisted this was propaganda, the Chinese did mobilize a "massive defensive response" of epidemic-prevention campaigns, vaccinations, and other measures to reduce diseases. They claimed that flies, mosquitoes, spiders, ants, bedbugs, fleas, and 30 types of bacteria-laden insects were dropped in the north. (Lockwood, Jeffrey, 164–68)

The most detailed claims purport that an F-28 fighter plane flew over the village of Kan-Nan in the early morning. When the villagers awoke, they found voles dying everywhere, all laden with fleas, and at least one had bubonic plague. One villager, Kum Song Li, reported to have heard a plane circling at about 4:00 a.m., and later the townspeople found fleas floating on the water in wells and open water jars, so they had to have fallen from the sky. Later, some captured U.S. pilots "confessed" to dropping the fleas, though U.S. authorities said these were coerced confessions. Documents found in 1998 do prove that the U.S. Air Force lectured the pilots about germ warfare at the 3rd Bomb Wing at Kunsan air base in 1951, and that they were ordered to drop propaganda pamphlets after the bombs. Some say that these pamphlet drops may have included biological weapons. (Lockwood, Jeffrey, 178–79, 184–85)

In 1952, Camp Detrick built Building 470 as a pilot facility for producing biological pathogens, including anthrax. The half-million infected mosquitoes created each month were not enough, so the army built a new mill in Pine Bluff, Arkansas, in 1960, capable of weekly batches of 100 million mosquitoes. When Building 470 stopped producing germs, it took years to decontaminate the area; cleanup was finally finished in 1988. (Lockwood, Jeffrey, 198, 201)

In 1954 the United States began testing air-drop containers that would burst at 1,000 feet and spread fleas over a region. A successful test over Utah was marred when one of the canisters malfunctioned and burst inside the plane, causing flea bites of the crew. Fortunately these were not biologically infected fleas. The following year the air force dropped mosquitoes on rural Georgia and Florida, to see how far the insects would travel. The results of those experiments are still classified. (Lockwood, Jeffrey, 195–99)

In 1972, the Biological and Toxin Weapons Convention banned biological weapons. The United States and the Soviet Union signed in 1975, but it seems that the ban was not really obeyed. The Soviets continued to produce anthrax and smallpox. An accidental tiny release of anthrax spores from a Sverdlovsk bioweapons factory killed 66 people in 1979. (Lockwood, Jeffrey, 209; Harris, xi)

The state of the United States' biological weapons programs is an open question. Officially it may not exist; unofficially, some say that it does. One of the most interesting cases comes from Cuba, in 1996.

On October 21, 1996, a U.S. State Department plane left Patrick Air Force Base in Florida, and flew over Cuba. Officially it was going to dump herbicides on cocaine fields in Colombia. Cubans, however, claim that a gray mist fell from the plane. Later, the United States said that the pilot released a smoke signal, fearing a nearby aircraft might collide with the plane. Cuba claims that the mist was in fact a cargo of "thrips," a crop-destroying pest, dropped on the fields near Havana. Two months later, there was a huge plague of thrips. Two months is precisely the time it takes for thrips to breed and spread over an area. The United States denies having anything to do with the plague of insects, claiming the bugs must have flown there naturally. The nearest known locale of thrips is an island 400 miles offshore. (Lockwood, Jeffrey, 223–25)

Crop-destroying bugs like thrips are a major economic threat. In 1989 the state of California received threat letters from "ecoterrorists" planning to spread medflies and other fruit pests over crops to crush the economy, if pesticides were not discontinued immediately. The state ignored the threat, and soon there were outbreaks of medflies and oriental fruit flies. Whether local terrorists' biological weapons are military weapons is open to debate, but the impact of such infestations can be large. Forty-three non-native insect species have settled in the United States between 1906 and 1991, causing $93 billion worth of damage. (Lockwood, Jeffrey, 235–36, 243)

The onset of West Nile virus in the United States in 1999 came with rumors and claims from Iraqi dissidents that it had been planted there by Saddam Hussein. It is true that the U.S. Centers for Disease Control did send samples of West Nile virus to Iraqi scientists, at their request, in 1985. (Lockwood, Jeffrey, 260–62)

One of the many dangers to nations in the future of warfare is the specter of insect-borne biological weapons.

5

Pigeons

Pigeon Messengers of Olden Times

Pigeons, loved and hated, are among the least likely military heroes. Modern city-dwellers despise the common rock dove because of its numerous droppings, but just 60 years ago Great Britain passed laws to protect these feathered creatures as messengers of martial secrets.

Ten thousand years ago, soon after humankind trained dogs as sentries and companions, we started breeding pigeons. Their peaceful demeanor and high reproductive rate made them excellent livestock (for eating) and common victims of religious sacrifice. But pigeons were destined for greater things. (Blechman, 10)

The book of Genesis in the Bible, with other parallel stories of history and literature, hints at the marvelous pigeon discovery. When Noah and his menagerie of animals floated above the mountains in the Ark, he released a dove to scout around. In the story, the dove returned with an olive branch, proof that the Great Flood waters were receding. Though many animals have an instinctual ability to find their way home, the pigeon's homing instinct surpasses the rest. Over the centuries, through breeding and training, people created the "homing pigeon." (Harter, 17; Bonner, 8)

By 4500 BC people had discovered pigeons' ability to fly home. The birds do not need training to "home"; it is instinctual. However, by training, the pigeons can be taught to add small rituals to their journeys that improve their usefulness to humans. For instance, the bird can be taught to peck at a small bell when it arrives at its pen, thus alerting the owner that the bird has returned. A pigeon owner could carry the bird in a pouch or box for hundreds of miles, release the bird, and watch it fly home. Obviously, the simple act of flying home would do little practical good for the human owner. Once a message could be attached to the bird, a superfast messenger service came into being. (Lubow, 27)

Exactly how the homing pigeon accomplishes this journey remains a mystery. The bird's journey home is not based solely on landmarks. One theory is that pigeons can orient their travels based on magnetic fields in the Earth, sensing the movement of iron particles in their beaks. Some doves have flown thousands of miles across continents to find their own nests. (Peduto, 26)

Pigeons have remarkable eyesight. Because of the placement of the eyes on opposite sides of their heads, they have a vast field of vision, almost 360 degrees. Pigeons even possess an extra pair of transparent eyelids called "blinkers" to protect their eyes from dryness and dust particles in flight. Though the rock dove sees with great precision, the birds can probably perceive only four colors: ultraviolet, blue, green, and red. (Bonner, 40–41; Harter, 118; Grandin, 44)

The legendary King Solomon probably used carrier pigeons during his reign, around 950 BC. Archaeologists have found underground pigeon coops from that era, capable of holding more than 100,000 birds. Though a majority of the birds would be for the Temple sacrifices practiced in Judaism, some might have been messenger pigeons. (Blechman, 11)

Egyptian Pigeons

Pharaoh Ramses III, upon ascending the throne as ruler of Egypt, used pigeons to deliver the news across long distances. In 1204 BC homing pigeons carried the royal news to cities all over the Egyptian empire, probably on tiny papyrus notes tied to their legs. Although the birds notified his people about the coronation, the pharaoh did not spare them from religious rituals on the occasion. Ramses sacrificed 57,810 rock doves to the god Ammon in Thebes for the celebration. (Blechman, 14)

The first Olympic Games were the biggest event in Greece in 776 BC. As the races and competitions ended, with anxious fans awaiting the results, pigeons sped the news to the Greek cities. (ibid., 4)

China used messenger pigeons by 650 BC. A Chinese emperor received regular reports from the outer provinces by bird mail in 500 BC. The Chinese had problems with their pigeon mail system because hawks often caught and ate the messengers. But they soon figured out that if they dangled little bells and bamboo whistles from the pigeons' legs, the noise frightened off birds of prey. (Roberts, 27; Blechman, 12; Bonner, 19)

Hannibal, the famous North African who invaded Italy with his elephants, received secret messages from his spies carried by pigeon. The information told the Carthaginians which roads were clear of Roman legions. His enemies the Romans were quick to adopt the swift messenger service as well. Julius Caesar learned of Pompey's opposition in 49 BC by pigeon. (Harter, 18–19)

Caesar's assassin Brutus, surrounded by Marc Antony's forces at Mutinia, needed a way to get messages to his allies. The historian Pliny wrote, "What service did Antony derive from his trenches and his vigilant blockade, and even his nets stretched across the river, while the winged messenger was traversing the air?" Antony's siege could not stop Brutus's bird squadrons flying overhead. (Webb, 9; Bonner, 9)

During the Crusades of medieval times, many Crusader knights carried homing pigeons in the baggage train, so they could send news home about their exploits. Still, it was the Arab armies of the Middle East that used pigeons most effectively. Crusader troop movements were known by the Saracen leaders because their scouts lofted pigeons with the news on papyrus notes strapped to their legs. However, sending message by bird is not completely safe. During the siege of Jerusalem in 1095, the Crusaders had no lumber to build ladders for scaling the city walls and were discouraged. They intercepted a pigeon from the Muslims, which carried a message promising that reinforcements were coming to relieve the city. This news of the enemy inspired the knights to hurry, and they managed to conquer the city. (Hyams, 40; Webb, 11; Dempewolff, 177; Cooper, 97; Harter, 21–22)

Genghis Khan made frequent use of homing pigeons. He encouraged the Mongol soldiers to keep pigeons and race them between battles, as both training and fun for the troops. These birds carried battle plans to

Mongol leaders fighting in distant areas or in separated columns. (Harter, 76; Denega, 44)

The greatest single military victory prepared by pigeons came in Holland in 1574. The Spanish had ruled the Netherlands but the Dutch rebelled under the leadership of William of Orange, with several Dutch cities declaring independence. Spanish ruler Phillip II laid siege to the city of Leiden hoping to capture William and end the war. Completely surrounded, the Dutch rebels could do very little, but they used pigeons to send and receive secret messages, including the plan to end the Spanish siege. With careful timing enabled by pigeon messages, Dutch spies coordinated the release of the dikes so that a raging wall of water rushed in, destroying the Spanish siege camps and breaking up the whole enemy force. The hero pigeons, upon their deaths, were stuffed and mounted in the Leyden Town Hall. (Webb, 12; Bonner, 10)

In similar fashion, pigeons soared to heroic heights during the siege of Paris during the Franco-Prussian War. With Germans encompassing the city in 1870–1871, birds became the only means of communication with the outside world. One difficulty with the pigeon messenger process is that the birds fly from outer locales and return home, so first the birds had to be sent out of Paris in order to come home with news. Under siege, the French could not get homing pigeons out of Paris for their flights. Germans searched all people leaving the city and certainly confiscated any pigeons found. Defiantly and cleverly, Parisians found ways to circumvent the German pigeon hunts. Hot-air balloons lofted high above rifle range and brought the messenger pigeons to French towns so they could carry messages back. (Webb, 8)

One problem with pigeon mail used to be that the amount of information that could be carried by a small bird was relatively small. Traditionally, a tiny handwritten or typed message was rolled into a small metal tube attached to the dove's leg. A large package of mail could not be carried by a pigeon. The French solved this problem by using incredibly tiny mail: the latest 1860s technology we now call "microfilm." Up until the digital age, the best way to fit lots of data in a small space was by shrinking it down and capturing it on film. On February 3, 1871, a pigeon carried 40,000 messages on one tiny microfilm. Unfortunately, the success rate of the pigeons arriving with their mail was very low. Out of 302 tossed pigeons, only 57 arrived in Paris. Contemporaries claim that these birds

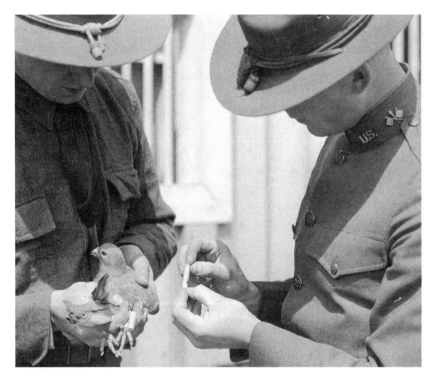

Soldier slides a message into a pigeon leg tube, 1919. (Courtesy National Archives.)

were not well trained, but the Germans may have also shot down some of the pigeons with accurate rifle fire. (Harfield, 91; Cooper, 97)

After the Franco-Prussian War, Europeans recognized the usefulness of homing pigeons. Governments published articles encouraging civilians to take up the hobby of breeding and racing pigeons, hoping to have a ready supply in case of war. Although the British used a few messenger pigeons during the Boer Wars, especially in the siege of Ladysmith (1899–1900), it was not until World War I that birds became indispensable to the world's armies. (Harter, 31; Gardiner, 98)

World War I Pigeons

For thousands of years, the world's armies used pigeons for sending messages. In the 20th century, humankind perfected the large-scale use of messenger birds. By that time, however, telegraphic wires allowed for long- and short-distance communication in quick fashion. In theory, that meant Europe's armies would send and receive orders by telegraph. Great Britain, for instance, canceled all military pigeon programs in 1908 expecting telegraphs to provide all necessary service. In the reality of war-time conditions, early electronics did not work as well as hoped, and the British had to scramble to confiscate pigeons for help when the war began. (Harter, 40–41; Cooper, 97)

Telegraph wires became key military targets, sought out for cutting, blasting, and even tapping to steal signals. Systems to power the sending and receiving of telegraphic messages, often hand-cranked devices, were easily affected by extreme weather conditions to be found in the infamous Western European trenches. Pigeons became the main backup communication system.

Major General Fowler, of the British Army Department of Signals and Communications, wrote:

> If it became necessary immediately to discard every line and method of communications used on the front except one, and it were left to me to select that one method, I should unhesitatingly choose the pigeon. It is the pigeon on which we must and do depend when every other method fails. During the quiet periods we can rely on telephone, telegraphic signals, dogs, and various other ways in use on the front by British Armies. But when the battle rages and everything gives way to barrage and machine gun fire, to say nothing of gas attacks and bombing, it is to the pigeon we go for succor. When troops are lost or surrounded in the mazes on localities, then we depend absolutely on the pigeon for our communications. Regular methods in such cases are worthless and it is at just such times that we need most messengers that we can rely on. In the pigeon we have them. I am glad to say they have never failed us. (Harter, 42)

As the Germans invaded Belgium and neared Antwerp, Commander Denuit, the head of the Belgian Pigeon Service, could not allow the enemy to capture his 2,500 homing pigeons. With tears running down his face, he set fire to the base, burning the birds alive. Early British pigeon messenger services ran into surprising problems. Soldiers love pets and mascots, and the men often fed the pigeons so much that the birds could not fly well!

Pigeon messenger being released from a
tank, World War I. (*Wonders of Animal Life,*
J. A. Hammerton ed., vol. 4, London:
Waverley Book Co., n.d., circa 1930, p. 1465.)

It was also discovered that rats developed a taste for pigeons, so that the birds had to be protected from varmints by other means. The standard wire-mesh pigeon coop with one-inch gaps between the wires could effectively keep sparrows and mice from coming in to steal the birds' food, but a large rat could break in to the lightweight pens and eat the pigeon as well as its bird food. Cat and dog mascots kept with the men in the trenches often served as rodent-killers as much as morale boosters. (Cooper, 103; Harfield, 92; Bonner, 21)

The pigeon does not look like a speedy bird, but they can fly at speeds from 30 to 75 miles per hour (and faster in a dive). The pigeon likes to fly only in daylight, and they can go as far as 600 miles in a single day. (Webb, 10)

Pigeon handling became a full-time military job for many soldiers when birds were used by the hundreds of thousands. The Germans used at least 100,000 birds in World War I, though they started with none. The Allies fielded at least 300,000 pigeons in the war years, with the French using 4,000 birds in one battle alone. One cheeky Australian, tired of sending pigeon messages, proposed "crossing these birds with cockatoos and teaching them to deliver verbal messages." The handlers did not just train and release the birds with messages. These men had to provide proper nutrition for the pigeons, with proper proportions of grains, fruit, and seed, about half a pound per week per bird. Keeping the pigeon fodder dry was a key component of care: soaked bird food loses its taste and nutrition value. The pigeon itself has a natural means of keeping its body dry in the rain. The birds produce a powdery milt that dries their feathers, and a layer of soft feathers allows the bird to dry while in flight or flapping its wings. (Harter, 41; James; Cooper, 100–101; Bonner, 32–33, 40–41)

The pigeon handlers also became experts on pigeon health, even with limited equipment. Paper clips became effective splints for birds with broken legs, enabling them to walk while healing. (Dempewolff, 197)

Pigeons did not live only in the trenches, because they were used in so many ways. The massive British armored trapezoidal tanks had no communication equipment and were prone to break down, but the men inside could not safely climb out and run for help. A round door opened at a fist-sized hole at the right front side panel of the tank so that a messenger pigeon could be pushed out to fly home, calling for a maintenance crew.

Though small, pigeons are hardy animals. The birds often arrived with their messages at headquarters in sad shape, with multiple gunshot and shrapnel wounds. One bird named Mocker lost an eye and bore several other bullet wounds but brought the exact coordinates of enemy guns that Allied artillery was able to batter into silence. Mocker survived the war, lived to a ripe old age, and was buried with full military honors. (Harter, 47)

Artillery officers on forward observation duties needed pigeons to relay coordinates for the big howitzers to fire. Thus, mobile lofts were invented. The shifting nature of battle lines meant that a bird could not be trained to arrive at X house on Y Street. X house might be leveled by artillery or taken by the enemy. Rather than static buildings, large wagon-style lofts were designed, mounted on a horse-drawn wagon. Toward the end of the war a few trucks joined the 150 mobile lofts. Stationary lofts were permanent buildings. Wagons and trucks carried mobile lofts. Another type, much more varied in implementation, was the mobile combat loft. Basically the mobile combat loft was any possible means of getting a few pigeons to a battlefield for use. Frequently, a messenger dog filled this role. A basket on each side of the dog's back brought two or four birds to the desired unit. Horses, or even camels (in the Middle Eastern sector), might deliver baskets full of homing pigeons to the troops. Bicyclists, too, bore birds to the front lines. (Harfield, 94; Webb, 3; Cooper, 98)

Occasionally the Allies captured a German pigeon. Pigeons had become targets for riflemen, but wounded birds could often be rehabilitated and trained to serve whichever army provided the bird a happy nest. One German bird named Kaiser served the Allies well. He was strong and fast, so he was kept as a breeder. He lived at least 28 years (to 122, in pigeon years) and fathered many valiant birds for the Allies in future battles. (Harter, 49; Bonner, 12)

At least 20,000 pigeons are estimated to have died while flying in combat in World War I. Improved accuracy of rifles enabled sharpshooters to bring down many homing pigeons, which prefer to fly low to the ground. Just as the French of 1870 used balloons to carry pigeons out of Paris, the Allies tried similar strategies on the Western Front. To get the pigeons to Allied troops who were cut off from help, pigeons were put in baskets attached to balloons with timers. When the timer went off, the balloon dropped the basket and instantly deployed a small parachute. It was hoped that the pigeon would then float down to allies unharmed, where the troops could send the birds back with information about the enemy deployments and Allied soldiers' needs. (Blechman, 32; Harter, 36–39)

Late in the war, hoping to destroy the Allies before the United States could put many troops on the Western Front, the Germans launched a major offensive. The United States used only about 20,000 pigeons due to its late arrival in the war. In the Saint Mihiel drive, American troops used 567 pigeons, 202 of them in tanks. Ninety messages were delivered, but 24 birds were lost or shot down. One pigeon named Big Tom flew 25 miles in 25 minutes with two bullet wounds, delivering an important message during the Meuse-Argonne offensive. (James)

On October 3, 1918, the U.S. 77th Division was surrounded in the Argonne Forest and communications were cut. After a long silence, the Allies assumed that the division had been annihilated, and they ordered artillery to barrage the region. Survivors of the 77th sent several human runners to try to break through for help, but German sharpshooters picked them all off. Seven pigeons took flight with messages; all were sniped by the enemy too. The last pigeon, named Cher Ami, carried a desperate message saying only, "For God's sake lift your fire!" The bird traveled a short distance but was hit and plummeted to the ground. After a moment, Cher Ami launched again and disappeared from sight. He arrived at headquarters, falling to the ground on his back, with one eye and part of his skull blown off, his breast ripped open, and the message dangling from a sinew of his mangled leg. Message received, the artillery redirected its fire to enemy targets, and reinforcements rushed in to save the remnants of the famous "Lost Battalion." Cher Ami healed temporarily and survived for one year, but died of injuries in 1919. He was stuffed and put on display in a museum in Washington, DC. (Harter, 45–47; Blechman, 33)

World War II Pigeons

As always, between wars, the promise of new technologies prodded armies to forget the lessons of the past. Reliable and necessary pigeon messengers seemed "old fashioned," even though it is estimated that 96 percent of messages sent by pigeon in World War I arrived in timely fashion. (Bonner, 37)

When the speed of battlefield communications was tested, pigeon against radio, the results were surprising. In a U.S. Army test at Fort Sam Houston in Texas, a homing pigeon competed in a 22-mile race against the new radio. The pigeon message came in 42 minutes, while the radio signal and the time for decoding required only 34 minutes. Of course 22 miles was a long distance compared to most battlefield conditions, and a pigeon would likely arrive long before the coded signals at range of 10 miles. (James)

The new wireless radio systems would not suffer inconsistencies of telegraphic equipment, it was believed. Once again, the newest electronics brought only sporadic successes. World War II would field perhaps 1 million pigeons, though it started with very few birds. Some nationalities did not even know about homing pigeons in the early 1940s. One British commander gave a Portuguese commander a pair of homing pigeons as a gift. The next day, the Portuguese commander wrote back his thanks, saying that he and his staff had "enjoyed them very much indeed," meaning they were served for dinner. (Dempewolff, 204)

England required that homing-pigeons be registered, to help catch enemy spies sending pigeon messages. The one flaw with this solution was that some German spies in Britain kept unregistered pigeons and thus received no visits from the British spy hunters. To combat the secret Nazi pigeons, the British drafted peregrine falcons to catch and kill them. MI5,

Nazi Pigeon Spies

Early in the war, Nazi German spies were using pigeons to send secret messages from England, across the English Channel. Pigeon-racing and pigeon breeding were popular hobbies in England, so there were more than 68,000 registered pigeon owners present in Britain. How could the British Army quickly root out the German spies from among the innocent hobbyists? With a simple and clever tactic. The British sent soldiers to the homes of all 68,000 pigeon owners and made one simple demand: release all of the pigeons while the soldiers watched. The English pigeons flew around the house for a few minutes and then came back to their nests. Any German spy pigeons flew directly for Germany and never came back. Thus, in a brief period, many Nazi spy birds were gone for good. (Dempewolff, 180)

---

the British secret service, learned that the Nazis were using pigeons to send invasion plans into England. The falcons deployed along the English Channel beaches in two-hour shifts, killing all pigeons found flying back and forth to mainland Europe. (Denega, 22–23)

As the British then tried to train and deploy their own pigeon messenger services, a domestic problem arose, in contrast to the enemy plots of earlier months. The U-boat and Luftwaffe raids had blockaded England for more than a year. Many people were hungry and took to hunting to supplement their meager diets. Unfortunately, hunters were blasting pigeons out of the skies or using falcons to catch them. Britain had to raise the fine for shooting pigeons from 2 pounds to 100 pounds and/or three months in jail and disallow falcons from the skies. Along with a public-relations program explaining the importance of pigeon messengers, these measures put an end to the major pigeon losses in early World War II Britain. (Dempewolff, 204–5)

Perhaps the single most important change in warfare between World War I and World War II occurred in aviation. World War I introduced aircraft mainly in a reconnaissance role, watching enemy troop movements and harassing enemy troops with small machine guns. The early aircraft had very limited range, however. They had to return to base often to

Pigeon with camera for reconnaissance photography, World War I. (Mary Evans Picture Library.)

refuel. Over the next 30 years, aircraft grew larger, with long-range fuel tanks and heavier caliber guns and/or bombs. Perhaps the least-known aspect of pigeon heroism came in their services to the air forces of World War II.

Radio systems, even when they worked, were easily intercepted by enemy listening posts. For this reason, "radio silence" meant turning off radios whenever aircraft traveled toward or through enemy airspace. Fighter planes could find and destroy bombers once their positions were determined. Even after a crash, if radio emergency signals were sent, the enemy might come to capture the downed crews. The best way of providing "silent" aircraft communication with allies? Homing pigeons. This began in a small way in World War I, with seaplanes and some ships carrying homing pigeons to request rescue. (Cooper, 102)

In 1942 alone, the British Royal Air Force used nearly 500,000 pigeons. Two thousand birds per day launched with British aircraft. Each bird capsule was watertight, containing 2 pigeons, food, paper, and a pencil. These pigeons required some extra training because pigeons prefer to fly over land and not water, but they learned quickly. One crew member was in charge of the pigeons (along with other duties, no doubt). The capsule remained open during the flight, but if a crash seemed imminent, the bird capsule was shut so it would float in case the plane ditched in the ocean. The closed capsule contained one hour's worth of air for the pigeons. Once the crew got into a lifeboat, they would open the capsule and send one pigeon with a small rescue message, keeping the second bird for later. If they crashed at night, the men were usually to wait until daylight before tossing the homing pigeon, since pigeons do not like to fly at night. One pigeon, officially named NEHU 40 NS1 but nicknamed Winkie because of a droopy eyelid, flew 350 miles over the North Sea from a crashed Royal Air Force bomber, bringing the rescue request to Dundee, Scotland, and saving the crew. For this act of valor, Winkie won the first Dickin Medal. (Dempewolff, 200; "Pigeons Save Life"; Webb, 1; Gardiner, 128–29)

British pigeon lofts in France. (Courtesy John Kistler.)

When an aircraft received heavy damage but remained aloft, a pigeon could be sent homeward during flight. This might be done in anticipation of a crash, with fuel leaking or steering destroyed, or for many other reasons. Bombers fly at hundreds of miles per hour, so launching a bird out into the heavy, buffeting winds around the aircraft could easily kill or wound the animal. The earliest strategy for reducing pigeon injuries for midflight homing missions was simply to wrap the bird in a few sheets of newspaper. By hurling the bird out in a newspaper, the heavy initial winds tore up the newspaper and reduced the bird's speed. By the time the wrapped bird was freed from the paper, its speed had slowed and the pigeon could fly safely. Many other contraptions and methods were tried, but in the end, the standard Number 12 brown paper bag, a common lunch sack, proved best. The handler simply stuck a pigeon in the bag, twisted the opening shut, and tossed it into the slipstream. By the time the wind tore up the bag or the bird climbed out of the bag, its speed was tolerable. Even from altitudes over 20,000 feet, pigeons could fly home. When released at high altitude, the bird instinctively dived quickly to the more oxygen-rich lower atmospheric levels. (Webb, 8; Dempewolff, 201–2)

Homing pigeons are believed to have saved thousands of aviators in World War II. (Bonner, 8–9)

Clearly, this sort of pigeon rescue mission could apply to more than just aircraft. The British also sent homing pigeons out on all sorts of ships both naval and civilian. It became normal practice for all ships departing British waters to carry homing pigeons, so that if torpedoes or storms caused distress, the birds could call for help to save the crews. Warships or spy vessels might carry baskets of pigeons, carrying regular reports and even photographs of enemy positions to base. The British Royal Navy operated small torpedo boats off the coast of occupied France and relayed messages home by bird. (Webb, 7; Harfield, 99)

Pigeons flew missions for air forces, navies, and ground forces. Resistance groups in occupied territories sometimes had to use pigeons when their radios were confiscated or tracked by enemy detector vehicles. Often these resistance fighters received their pigeons by air drop, with bombers or gliders releasing parachuted crates full of birds at designated sites for the rebels to find. Out of 16,544 pigeons dropped for spies behind enemy lines, only 1,842 ever returned, implying that more than 10,000 died in their dropped capsules. Because the Germans would kill peasants found to have pigeons, assuming the people to be spies, families would often kill pigeons on sight lest they become a liability. One key message returned by spy pigeon brought the Allies the exact location of the V1 flying bomb station in Peenemunde, Germany. Tiny aluminum cameras could be attached to a pigeon's breast, with a timer setting off the shutter periodically, to gather photographs of enemy positions. The British Office of Strategic Services (OSS) also parachuted spies in the India Burma Theater with pigeons, to return information on Japanese troop dispositions to the Allies. (Cooper, 103, 109; Gardiner, 103; Harfield, 99; Bonner, 10–11; Harter, 63)

The United States came into World War II when the Japanese launched a surprise air attack on Pearl Harbor, Hawaii, in late 1941. At that point, the U.S. Army had only one pigeon company active. Volunteers were requested from American pigeon hobbyists, and the birds came in droves to help the war effort. The United States did not employ nearly as many birds as Britain did. The U.S. Signal Corps used 54,000 birds overall, but only 36,000 actually served actively in the war. Even some submarines carried pigeons. (Webb, 6; Harter, 54)

Baby pigeons are called "squeakers." Ten days after birth they are given an aluminum leg band for permanent identification. They start learning to fly at three to four weeks, and they begin their training at 28 days of age. Pigeons retire from frontline military service by age four years, but then they are used as studs for mating. The homing instinct of pigeons is dramatic, even if the bird is rendered unable to fly. During World War II training of pigeons at Camp Meade in Maryland, a homing pigeon failed to return from a 100-mile flight. Trainers presumed he had died or decided not to return. About a week later, the bird arrived home. He had stopped to drink from a water source that was coated with oil, which rendered him unable to fly, so he had walked the hundred miles home. (Dempewolff, 184; Webb, 5; Harter, 116)

The Pacific Theater proved to be a difficult region for the use of messenger pigeons. The Signal Corps experimented with using pigeons during the Asian island-hopping offensive of 1944. Mosquitoes were the biggest problem. Mosquitoes attacked even the pigeons' eyes, and the finest mesh could not keep the insects out. Pigeon messengers did not work well in the tropical climate, so the army instead used dogs in the Pacific campaign.

American efforts in Europe and North Africa used pigeons to great effect. (Lemish, 58–59)

In late 1942 and early 1943 the U.S. Army landings and campaigns in North Africa included homing pigeons. Forty-five secret and urgent messages delivered by bird earned the congratulations of Major General Harmon. These birds learned that their home nests were crates on the backs of Jeeps. One improvement in pigeon mail came when the Signal Corps invented a new breast-tied pouch system that increased the load capacity to three ounces, far more than the little aluminum leg capsule could hold. (Webb, 2–4; James)

The only true relationship between the U.S. military and falcons was a negative one. To keep falcons from eating Signal Corps pigeons, handlers were issued 12-gauge shotguns to blow raptors out of the sky near their pigeon lofts. Nazis used trained hawks to kill pigeons, particularly in the Pas de Calais region of France. (Webb, 10; Cooper, 109)

The North African campaign was just a warm-up for the huge invasion of mainland Europe, starting with Sicily and then Italy. The greatest pigeon success of World War II may have been the saving of Allied troops at Colvi Vecchia.

Parachute-Tearing Falcons

One remarkable controversy related to the U.S. Signal Corps pigeon program erupted when the actor Burgess Meredith did a radio interview during World War II. In the program, Lt. Thomas McClure of the Fort Monmouth pigeon section of the Signal Corps claimed that he was training falcons to intercept Nazi pigeons in the air, and that his falcons could dive upon and tear enemy parachutes to shreds, thus killing Nazi soldiers. The program brought a huge number of phone calls and letters from falconry hobbyists, offering to donate their birds to the anti-paratrooper crusade. Apparently McClure's comments were personal and had nothing to do with the U.S. Signal Corps' official programs, and the army had to scramble in putting down the rumors of murderous falcons deployed by the United States. (McClure and Meredith, 22–23)

During the offensive in Italy, the Allied strategy was to heavily bomb Colvi Vecchia to soften up the opposition before the troops entered the city. The plan was based on coordinated timing between air and ground forces. Unexpectedly, the German and Italian armies withdrew from the city, and Allied forces marched in quickly. With their victorious entry came the nauseating realization that friendly bombers would soon be leveling the city. (Harter, 51)

G. I. Joe, a U.S. pigeon, took to flight immediately, having to cover 20 miles with its desperate message to call off the airstrike. The Allied bombers were taxiing on the runways when the message arrived and the strike was called off. It is estimated that between a hundred and a thousand U.S. soldiers might have been killed if G. I. Joe hadn't brought the urgent communiqué. Joe was the first non-British animal to receive the Dickin Medal. (Roberts, 27; Gardiner, 129)

Two other pigeons figured prominently in the Italian campaign. Geronimo, born in Italy in 1943, flew more than 30 combat missions with no mishaps, delivering 81 messages to Allied troops near Naples. Anzio Boy, a pigeon from the 209th Signal Pigeon Company, provided excellent service and garnered his unit a Meritorious Service Unit plaque from Gen. George S. Patton. (Harter, 62–63)

Even in defeats, the pigeon could provide valuable help to the troops. William of Orange, a British pigeon, set a flight record on September 19, 1944, during the failed Operation Market Garden. William flew 260 miles in 4.5 hours with vital intelligence. (Harfield, 99)

B. F. Skinner, a famous psychologist who studied animal behavior, first thought of using pigeons for missile guidance in April 1940 when he heard about the Nazi bombings of Warsaw. He trained the pigeons to peck at a bull's-eye in order to receive a kernel of corn, while they were secured in a sock or snuggie. By neck movements the birds could control their platforms in three dimensions, raising them to various levels for food. Eventually the pigeons could propel themselves toward pictures of ships or other bomb targets with 99 percent accuracy. At first the army rejected the idea. (Blechman, 37)

By 1943 the army had second thoughts and considered using Skinner's pigeons in the experimental Pelican Missile system, a wing-steered glider bomb. The army loved the idea of organic rather than mechanical piloting

Taxidermied President Wilson, who had been attached to tank corps. (Courtesy National Archives.)

because it meant that electronic jamming would be ineffective. The pigeons would peck at a target projected on a light plate in the nose cone to direct the payload to its target.

Worried that one pigeon might make bad decisions, they designed a three-bird nose-cone where each of the trio got one vote in choosing their target, if multiple targets were available. Some birds were specifically trained for factory targets, others for sea targets. By December 1943 the program was ready, but the army sent the whole plan to MIT scientists for a second opinion. The scientists rejected the idea out of hand, and the army then abandoned the project. The U.S. Navy took a look at the project in 1948 but decided that since pigeons could guide only to objects in visual range, electronics offered much better long-range systems. (Peduto, 28–29)

After World War II, many nations dropped their war pigeon programs, but pigeons did not completely vanish from martial applications. In 1947 British intelligence proposed training a fleet of pigeon bombers with tiny bombs to fly to enemy targets. (Denega, 45)

The U.S. Army officially closed its pigeon courier program in 1957. In 1966, military scientists experimented with using pigeons as sentries, to detect enemies in a manner similar to patrol dogs, but the tests didn't work very well. Not until the Gulf Wars (1990–1991 and 2003–) in the Middle East did the United States think about pigeons again. Reportedly, Saddam Hussein used carrier pigeons after his communication systems were destroyed. U.S. troops simply used pigeons as the proverbial canary in the coal mine, setting pigeons in cages around troop tents to die first, if chemical weapons settled in the area. (Lubow, 87–90; Blechman, 38–39)

Messenger pigeon that lost an eye to shrapnel in France, 1918.
(Courtesy National Archives.)

Taxidermied Cher Ami, hero pigeon, shot but delivered rescue message. (Courtesy National Archives.)

Motorcycle carrying messenger pigeons. (Courtesy National Archives.)

In recent years, the Swiss Army finally discharged its 30,000 homing pigeons after 77 years of military service. Since the end of pigeons in military service, the bird species is viewed only as a bane to human societies, not a help. In the United States, the Department of Agriculture interprets the Animal Welfare Act as excluding rats, mice, and birds from its rules concerning animal treatment. And South Africa announced that all pigeons will be shot on sight in diamond-producing areas, since diamond smugglers supposedly fly illegal gemstones out of the mines using homing pigeons. (Kohut and Sweet, 77–89)

Pigeons have gone from heroes to targets in just a few decades.

Animals in Support

6

Camels

Ancient Camels

Camels are among the lesser-known of the animal warriors. This seems to parallel the general feelings of humans toward camels: they are just not popular beasts. Says one writer in regard to a group of camels, "there was a supercilious, haughty expression of disdain about the hump-backed, splayed-footed, knock-kneed, long-necked, unwieldy creatures which chilled right from the beginning any feelings of intimacy that might be desired between a camel and his rider." Later he adds that the camels were "blowing grubs a yard long out of their noses" and were covered with ticks and mange. (Reid, 11, 53)

Further alienating cultured humans is camels' unattractive practice of chewing the cud. "After partially digesting whatever they had eaten, they regurgitated their food into their mouths for further chewing or spitting. The cud was a foul smelling, sticky mass that soldiers were sure caused terrible sores." Another observer describes the smell of camels as "a combination of rancid butter under a hot sun, a glue factory, and a field of fresh fertilizer." (Essin, 59; Dempewolff, 25)

With all of these factors set against the camel from the outset, it is remarkable that humans ever started domesticating them. However, people came to cooperate with the creatures because they were simply indispensable, in certain regions of our planet. No other cargo-bearing creature can cope with the extremes of climate in arid regions, both hot and cold. Camels from the desert can instinctively sense when a sandstorm is about to erupt. The animal hurries its pace, thus warning its driver of a coming danger. (Toperoff, 33)

The scientific name for members of the camel family, which includes camels, llamas, and vicunas, is camelids. There are two species of domesticated camelids in the Old World. The one-humped dromedary of North Africa and the Middle East seems to have been trained first, circa 2000 BC in Arabia. The two-humped Bactrian camel, tolerant of colder Asian climes, worked for men before 1000 BC. Why did horses come to be domesticated thousands of years before camels? Perhaps because climactic changes that created the current arid conditions in the Middle East and Asia did not occur until 2000–1000 BC. Horses are easier to tame and utilize but cannot handle the dry conditions as well as camelids. Wild dromedaries no longer exist; they became extinct shortly after humans began domesticating them. (Kelekna, 212–13; Steiner, 3; Hyams, 127, 122)

"The camel is in the East what the horse is in other parts of the world, the useful servant of man, and his able assistant in a variety of works which, without its aid, could scarcely be performed at all." How does the camel provide such services? Regarding food, the camel's hump (or humps) are basically fat, and the animal can live many days without food by internally consuming the fat packs on its back. For water needs, the camel, like cows and sheep, has multiple stomach compartments. Its second stomach can hold a large amount of water and can drink that water when it becomes thirsty. (Johnson, Isaac, 171–74)

Midianites and other biblical figures in the book of Genesis used camels for roaming around the Middle East, in stories dating from before 1000 BC. These dromedaries spread into Persia and the Sahara Desert over time. Throughout history there have been unconfirmed rumors and stories of "superfast" camels with extraordinary endurance: specially bred and trained. In the 19th century these were called *delouls*, purportedly able to ride 9–10 miles per hour for two days without stopping, covering 500 miles. If true, this would be about triple the speed, endurance, and distance covered by a normal camel. Mail-carrying camels did travel from Cairo to Suez, a distance of 84 miles, in 18 hours. (Worcester, 39; Carroll)

The first major battle known to have included camels came at Karkar in 853 BC when the Assyrians faced a coalition of Palestinian rulers including King Ahab of Israel. Ahab brought 2,000 horse-drawn chariots, but an Arabian ally, Sheikh Gindibu, arrived with 1,000 camels. The camels' role in the conflict is not known, though the Bedouin riders of the time did fight directly from camelback using long lances. Most future cameliers simply used the camel as a transport through the desert, then switched to a horse for the actual fighting. At Karkar, the coalition fell to Assyria, and the Assyrians went on to destroy the Bedouins of Arabia and capture many camels. King Sargon used camels and mules to help his Assyrian army cross steep mountain passes with supplies; even chariots were dismantled and hauled across the rough terrain during the Urartu campaign. (Steiner, 84; Hyams, 127; Gabriel and Boose, 111)

Around this time, Queen Semiramis of Assyria supposedly attacked India with hundreds of camels disguised as elephants. The event is shrouded in myth and legend, but even the legends admit that the camel disguises failed, and the elephants of India defeated the Assyrians. Though the ancient Indians did not fear camels, they held an unusual superstition. They believed that by killing pregnant camels and roasting their fat, and smearing the fat on soldiers' shoes, the soldiers could walk for hundreds of miles without fatigue. (Kistler, 16–17; Mayor, *Greek,* 92)

Though the key usefulness of camels always lay in their cargo-carrying ability in dry regions, the military could not fail to notice one aspect of camelid presence on the battlefield. While soldiers tended to despise camels, horses hated them even more.

In 546 BC, King Cyrus of Persia attacked King Croesus of Lydia, who possessed a strong cavalry. Cyrus ordered the camels in his baggage train to be unloaded and put in the front line of battle. Herodotus the ancient historian explained the Persian plan: "the horse has a natural dread of the camel, and cannot abide either the sight or smell of that animal." The Lydian cavalry horses pivoted and fled, running right over their own infantry. After this debacle, armies dependent on horse cavalry tried to keep a few camels around so the horses would become familiar with their sounds and smells, to avert panicky routs of the Lydian kind. The Persian king Darius later tried this camel strategy against elephants, adding flaming packs on his camels, but the ploy failed. (Hyams, 128; Mayor, *Greek,* 198; Gabriel and Boose, 230–31; Higham, 153)

Cambyses of the Persian Empire, son of Cyrus, invaded Egypt, using caravans of Bedouin camels to carry water for the army across the Sinai desert all the way into Libya. The Persians continued to utilize camels, even under Xerxes. (Kelekna, 122; Hyams, 129)

Camel transport became more efficient with improved saddle designs. The dromedary proved to be much faster than the Bactrian camel. A dromedary could carry 440 pounds at less than two miles per hour, but unloaded, it could travel 40 to 50 miles in one day. When horse domestication brought larger and hardier horses, the horse became the preferred desert battlefield mount. Henceforth, the camel became a support vehicle. A rider would ride a camel, with his horse tied to the camel, throughout the desert journey. The camel carried not only the man, but the food and water supply for man and horse. By using female camels, up to 22 pounds of milk per day could be taken for human or horse consumption. Approaching the battle front, the rider left the camel in the baggage train and rode the equine into combat. (Kelekna, 212–13)

Camels provided more services as well. Camel meat could be eaten, if necessary. Woven camel hair is said to be waterproof, used for making tents, saddlebags, and sandals. Camel dung could be used as fuel for fires,

---

Extreme Camel Journey

One extreme example of camel usefulness to Arab militaries came in AD 630. Khalid ibn al-Walid was ordered to travel quickly across the desert to attack an enemy. The Bedouins did not have enough water skins to carry water for the men and horses. Before the trip, the Bedouins withheld water from the camels until the beasts became thirsty, forced the camels to drink copious amounts of water, then tied the animals' mouths shut to prevent cud chewing. During the desert journey, each day, when the men and horses needed water, they killed several camels, sliced open their stomachs, and drank the fluid therein. By this tactic, the force did reach the battlefield on time and in good condition. (Kelekna, 216–17)

and in fact the smoke and soot produced by camel urine and feces produces "sal ammoniac" (used in jewelry-making and metallurgy). Camel milk was often used to boil rice and flour. (Coultas, 68; Toperoff, 33)

The Arab armies continued to use camels for their supply train even during the Crusades under Saladin. Camels served as personnel carriers, with one soldier in a seat on each side of the animal, with the baggage. When the Crusaders captured a few camels they were amazed, never having seen such creatures before. (Sinclair, 45–46; Baker, 146)

The camel must be trained to kneel down to receive its rider, since climbing up the six-to-eight-foot-tall animal is nearly impossible from its standing position. The camel also kneels to receive cargo or have its cargo unloaded. (Toperoff, 33)

The famous Mongol armies of Genghis Khan and his descendants used large numbers of camels to carry supplies among their horse-armies. They successfully bred camels as pack animals. (Gabriel and Boose, 543–44)

The vicious Tamerlane, during the assault on India in AD 1398 purportedly loaded camels with bales of straw, intending to light the flammables and send the burning beasts into feared enemy elephant squadrons. In this case it was not necessary, as the elephants posed little threat in the battle near Delhi. (Mayor, *Greek,* 204)

As the Spaniards tried to conquer all of South and Central America in the 16th century, a Biscayan named Juan de Reineza tried to introduce camels to Peru. Peru is an arid, mountainous country, already inhabited by llamas and vicunas (of the camelid family, but much smaller). The camels must have been intended to be large pack animals for the conquistadores, but in the end just a few camels survived around Lima in the Andes Mountains. (Lesley, 5)

The Spanish found greater success with their importation of camels into the Canary Islands in the 16th century. When the Dutch invaded in 1599, the authorities were able to withdraw from the port city with several cannons, hauled by camels. The Spanish thus defended their positions and sent the Dutch sailing home. Camels were used as mobile shields against English pirates in 1740 and 1762, with mixed results. The camels thrived in the dry Canary Islands, so that the locals exported camels to Australia from Tenerife in the late 19th century. (Del Castillo and De Lugo)

Egyptian Camel Corps patrolling in the desert, 1896. (Courtesy John Kistler.)

With the advent of gunpowder, Asians found that a large animal like an elephant could wear a small cannon on its back. In 1722, Afghans invented a cannon for use on camelback as well, attached to the wood-framed saddle. The key was to train the camels not to flinch or panic when the loud boom echoed from their backs. The Afghans persisted, and in a major battle of 1761, a thousand Afghan camel swivel-gunners charged against their foes from India. Camel handlers recognized quickly that a camel "saddle" could not put weight on the beast's hump or humps. This fatty hump grows or shrinks rapidly during times of feast or famine. Saddles cannot grow and shrink that way. So the saddle was a frame of wood or metal bars with padded or tiered platforms on top, built around and over the hump. Wooden saddles were preferably built from hard woods like teak, because "a camel will at unexpected moments indulge in a sand bath, with disastrous results to any faulty equipment." In other words, soft wood camel saddles just wouldn't survive the camels' joyous frolics in the dirt. (Barber, 119; Lawford, 127; Cooper, 116; Manual of Horsemastership, 64–65)

British soldier on camelback, 19th century.
(Mary Evans Picture Library.)

During the war between Russia and Turkey in the late 1870s, Russian general Mikhail Skobelev used 12,000 Bactrian camels in his army's baggage train. Only one camel returned alive. Most died of the cold, it was said. (Cooper, 114)

U.S. Army Camels

Camels of the Asian and African variety are not native species in the Americas. The Spanish dropped a few dozen camels in Peru in the 16th century, but the species did not propagate. Two species of camelids are native to South America: namely, the llama and the vicuna.

The first Old World camels to arrive in North America may have come in 1701 to Virginia on a slave trader's ship. Whatever the owner had in mind for these animals, they did not long survive. A more thorough attempt to use camels in North America would come about 150 years later. (Carroll)

The first official suggestion that camels could be a useful addition to the U.S. military came during the Second Seminole War (1835–1842) in Florida. Maj. George H. Crosman proposed using camels, but nothing came of the idea. The more natural locale for camels, in North America, was the arid southwestern United States. (Lesley, 4)

By the 1840s, newspapers often proposed the importation of camels for carrying the mail through the parched lands of west Texas and the American southwest. The Secretary of War, Jefferson Davis (later, president of the Confederate States of America), submitted official requests for funding from Congress to experiment with camels as draft animals. In 1855, $30,000 was allotted for the test. Davis's orders read, "The object is at present to ascertain whether the animal is adapted to the military service, and can be economically and usefully employed." (ibid., vi–vii)

Maj. Henry Wayne and Lt. David Dixon Porter traveled to the Middle East to find camels. They discovered that good, healthy camels were scarce and expensive, because the British were sending camels to the Crimean War against Turkey. The Americans sailed to Balaklava and spoke to the British quartermaster who gave glowing reports of camel performance. It took some searching, but the U.S. Army officers purchased 33 healthy animals and started their return voyage on February 15, 1856. To enable different kinds of testing, they acquired a variety of camels. Nine were fast-running dromedaries; 22 were draft camels. Two Bactrian males would be used for breeding with some of the dromedaries. The father, Tuilu, was huge: over 10 feet long, 7 feet tall, and 9.5 feet at the girth, weighing a ton. They had to cut a hole in the upper deck of the ship because Tuilu could not stand up in the camel stable on the lower deck. By cross-breeding a Bactrian male with a dromedary female, a "booghdee" one-humped camel would be born. These hybrid camels are heavier and stronger than either the dromedary or Bactrian, but cannot breed, much like the mule. (Carroll)

Several Middle Eastern men were hired to care for the camels, including three Egyptian riders, two Turkish saddle-makers, and a Syrian named Hadji Ali, whom everyone in America called "Hi Jolly" for short. Jolly would continue working for the U.S. government for 30 years. When he died in 1902, Hadji Ali was entombed under a pyramid-shaped stone with a camel on top. (Lesley, vii)

Lieutenant Porter created a fastidious military regimen for camel-care aboard ship, including perfect cleanliness. Four of the beasts were Pehl-evans, camels taught to wrestle, a gambling sport in some countries. The animals learn to raise a front leg over their opponent's neck and force him/her to the ground with their weight. Injuries or illnesses, the Arab handlers believed, could be cured by tickling a camel's nose using a chameleon tail. (Froman, 37)

One of the Arab riders trained a baby camel, named Uncle Sam, to wrestle with people. While perhaps it was humorous to watch, the young camel came to enjoy this too much, at least in the opinion of his keepers. Uncle Sam would suddenly rush up at men, throw them to the deck, and pin them down. (Carroll)

One camel died, but two were born, during the voyage. Thirty-three camels arrived healthy at Indianola, Texas, on May 14, 1856. The animals were so happy to be on dry land again, they "became excited to an almost uncontrollable degree, rearing, kicking, crying out, breaking halters, tear-ing up pickets, and by other fantastic tricks demonstrating their enjoyment of the 'liberty of the soil.'" Before long, the locals made a sport of teas-ing the camels and their drivers, mocking that the whole affair was a great waste of time. One day Major Wayne was "greatly annoyed" and offered a challenge to the townsfolk. He brought in two of the best camels, had them kneel, and ordered two bales of hay weighing 314 pounds each to be placed on their saddles. The bystanders jeered, believing that the beasts could never rise with such a load. Then Wayne had two more bales put on top, for a load weight of 1,256 pounds on each camel (not counting the saddles), and the camels stood up and walked back to their corrals. This put an end to the jokes. Hybrid camels could carry 2,200 pounds, it was said. (Carroll; Arnold, 172)

Soon the camels were moved to the larger army post at San Anto-nio, Texas, including an additional shipment of 41 camels to join them. Other army units in the region were none too pleased with the new spe-cies. "Our mules and horses were very much frightened at the approach of the camels. They [the horses and mules] dashed around the corral, with heads erect and snorting in wild alarm. They were so much excited, that the whole camp was aroused and put on watch." Troopers who disliked the camels called the menagerie "Little Egypt." Perhaps this conflict with the main army corrals of horses and mules at San Antonio led Major Wayne to move the camel herd to Green Valley, about 60 miles distant. (Lesley, 43; Arnold, 173)

The first actual test for the unit was to compare mule work to camel work in bringing supplies from San Antonio to Green Valley. They sent six camels and three six-mule wagon teams to bring back fodder. The camels carried 3,648 pounds of oats, while the mule wagons bore 1,800 pounds each, so three camels were equal to a six-mule wagon team. Furthermore, the camels returned in only two and a half days, while the mule wagons needed five days. The camel tests proved very successful under Major Wayne. (Carroll)

The new Secretary of War, John Floyd, authorized a long-distance test for the camels. He assigned 20 of the Texas camels to Lt. Edmund Fitzgerald Beale to pioneer a trail to California. The beasts ate food that horses and mules would never touch, like cacti and bitter bushes. "They went without water from six to ten days and even packed it a long distance for the mules, when crossing the deserts. They were found capable of packing one thousand pounds weight apiece and of traveling with their load from thirty to forty miles per day all the while finding their own feed over an almost barren country. Their drivers say that they will get fat where a jackass would starve to death." (Lesley, 156, 122)

For more than three years, Lieutenant Beale explored paths through New Mexico, Arizona, and California, with Hi Jolly as chief camel driver. Beale's early reports were so positive that the Secretary of War asked Congress to purchase 1,000 camels for military use in the Southwest. Congress ignored the request. (ibid., 124)

In every measurable way, camels seemed to be ideal for working in the arid regions of the United States. So what happened to the experiment, and the idea?

Americans and soldiers loved horses, and they tolerated mules. Horses and mules worked everywhere, and most people knew how to use them and how to treat them. Plus, the horses and mules hated the camels, causing difficulties in mixed baggage trains, since the camels had to work separately or at a distance from the rest. Only the Middle Eastern camel drivers would accept them. American mule drivers despised them, and since only one Arab, Hi Jolly, remained with the camels, lots of American muleteers were ordered to work with the beasts, unwillingly. (Essin, 59)

Lieutenant Beale saw the hatred of the mule skinners. He demanded that they stop their cruelty and even started hiring Mexicans to train to replace them. One of the supposed cruelties may have been keeping the camels from water. One myth that was popular in the time was that camels stored water in their humps, and so as long as the animal had a hump, he didn't need water. (Froman, 96)

The other major factor that doomed the camel experiment was bad timing. The American Civil War began in 1860. The camels that accompanied Lieutenant Beale to California never returned to Texas; they were sold at auction to miners from Arizona and Nevada.

Confederates captured the several dozen camels stationed in Texas in 1861, but the army couldn't think of any use for them. Opening the corrals, they released the camels into the wild to wander off into the hills. Three of the animals wandered far enough to be captured by Union troops. The Yankees were just as stumped in trying to find a job for the beasts, so they gave the camels to a Mr. Paden in Iowa. (Lesley, xii–xiii; Carroll)

One camel was not set free during the Confederate camel-release in Texas. The 43rd Mississippi Infantry under Col. William M. Moore kept a camel mascot named Douglas. Douglas died from a 'minie ball' during the siege of Vicksburg. (Seguin, 11)

In 1865 when Union forces retook Texas from the Confederacy, they found more than 100 camels wandering the region. They had apparently enjoyed their free time and bred prolifically! An auction was held and the beasts were sold to one man, who then sold them to circuses and miners. Most of the camels toiled in the mines until their deaths. (Lesley, xii–xiii)

Not all of the U.S. military camels died of hard work. Lieutenant Beale of the 1850s California expeditions became a general during the Civil War, then retired to California and started a ranch. He bought several of the old camels still in the area and enjoyed showing them to his descendants for many years.

The only visible remains of the U.S. Camel Corps experiment is a camel skeleton that was donated to the Smithsonian. The camel was killed

The Red Ghost

One of the most interesting stories of the Old American West regards the infamous "Red Ghost." Many rumors of a gigantic red creature arose in southeastern Arizona. Miners named it the Red Ghost and said it carried a "grisly demon rider." In 1883, a witness saw her friend killed and trampled by a giant beast, and red hairs were found in nearby bushes, along with giant cloven hoof prints. Not long after this, a rancher named Mizoo Hastings shot a beast in the dark for eating his turnips. On examination he discovered it to be an old camel with tight rawhide strips wrapped around its body. Some theorized that Indians had captured a man and tied him to the camel, thus explaining the "demon rider," though no body was found with the camel. No one saw the Red Ghost again. (Froman, 35–36, 98)

during a vicious musth (mating season) fight, and an officer at Fort Tejon, California, sent the skeleton to the museum. (Carroll)

The U.S. Army did one more brief trial with camels, but not on American soil. During the 1899 Boxer Rebellion in China, the army dabbled with Bactrian camels, but again decided that it preferred mules. (Essin, 135)

British War Camels

Napoleon used camels during his Egyptian campaign, and the British and Egyptians used camels in the 1798 Sudan conflict. In the 19th century, the British military seemed very hopeful about using camels throughout the empire. In India, camels proved most capable. (Sinclair, 217)

A contest to conquer Afghanistan erupted in the 1830s. The Russians tried to capture Afghanistan with 60,000 soldiers and 30,000 camels carrying provisions. When the British tried to march 1,000 miles through tough terrain to capture Kabul, they did not properly care for the pack animals. Of the 32,500 camels, almost 27,000 died of starvation. The Russians may have fared even worse. (Sutton and Walker, 41; Sinclair, 217)

In the 1850s, when the U.S. Army sent officers to the Middle East to acquire camels, the British quartermaster greatly exaggerated the abilities of the camel. He said that 25,000 camels accompanied Gen. Sir Charles

Napier during his invasion of Pakistan in 1842. Napier mounted each corps of 1,000 soldiers on 500 camels. The average dromedary, he claimed, carried 600 pounds of cargo for 25 to 30 miles per day, but, when needed, 70 miles in just 12 hours. When a corps arrived to fight, the men dismounted and put the 500 camels in a hollow square, using the camels as breastworks for firing their rifles. The camels were kept in place (from standing or running) by tying a hobble to their forelegs. The quartermaster also said that during the current Crimean War, the camels were so efficient that more were being brought to the field. While there are elements of truth in that summary, the numbers are exaggerated. (Lesley, 9; Carroll)

As for the actual use of camels in the Crimean War, not much information is available, and one rather brief summary says that many of the British dromedaries died of the cold. (Barber, 119)

In India the British used camels for carrying baggage. "A common sight was a 'thunder box' tied on the top of a camel and a clock or a lantern hanging from its neck. Fast camels or horses were used for carrying the requirements of the mess, especially drinks, which were available at all times." A "thunder box" is a portable toilet. Presumably the thunder box was removed from the camel's back and put on the ground before use, since the user could hardly perch on top safely! (Hamid, 62)

The British Army learned a lot about camels because in the colonial era, the British had many foreign territories to manage. Their army wrote field manuals, and though camels weren't common enough to have their own instruction book, they figure prominently in the horse-care manuals of the 19th and 20th centuries. New recruits from England thrown suddenly into the Suez region could read the book and learn some helpful tips about the camels they would have to learn to tolerate. In 1898 at the Battle of Omdurman, the enemy Sudanese charged British forces on camels, but were mowed down by machine-gun fire. (Sinclair, 177)

According to the British manual of the late 19th century, a light load for a camel to carry is 250 pounds; a heavy load is 350 pounds. A camel company has 1,500 camels with a 20 percent reserve for sick or wounded animals. Each company carries small suction pumps and canvas troughs, because many desert wells are deep. The average pace for a camel is two and a half miles per hour, with a maximum safe march distance of 20 miles per day. Every hour, the camel line must be halted for a 5-to-10-minute potty break. Camels should not cross a stream or river more than four feet deep: they can swim but will not do so voluntarily. (Manual of Horsemastership, 198–201)

Camels proved their worth for the British Army in the 1903 Somaliland Field Force. The Telegraph Battalion included 45 men, 58 mules, 50 camels, and 26 camel drivers. The camels were found to be much better than the shorter animals at telegraph work because they could carry wooden poles on their sides more easily, and they needed less water. The battalion installed 432 miles of air lines and 504 miles of laid cable. (Harfield, 61)

The camel can pull far more weight than it can carry on its back, but camels are more handy for negotiating difficult terrain, so they spent more time as pack animals. A British Army manual describes some typical 350-pound camel loads: six cases of meat, two chests of tea, four boxes of tobacco, four boxes of rice, four bales of hay, or two fantasses of water. The camel carried double the average horse or mule load, but camels were a bit slower. (Manual of Horsemastership, 205, 254)

Manual of Horsemastership, Equitation and Animal Transport, 1937. (Crown Copyright His Majesty's Stationery Office, 1937, plate 13.)

Camel Ambulances

Perhaps the most unique use of camels was in carrying wounded soldiers in devices called cacholets. The cacholet camel is basically a camel ambulance wearing a covered canvas stretcher on each side. Occupants were known to complain, particularly when one soldier was heavier than the other, causing violent bouncing described as "the very refinement of torture." However, some wounded soldiers claimed that the camels recognized the sad condition of the men and walked more quietly and took frequent rest stops for the men. (Reid, 76; Dempewolff, 54)

Camel carrying cachalot ambulance for wounded soldiers, circa World War I. (Artwork by the author based on antique photograph.) (Courtesy John Kistler.)

In India from the 1880s through 1910 camels bore four big guns for the 8th King George V's Own Light Cavalry. Indian Sikhs often worked the British mobile artillery. One such company carried six nine-pounder mountain cannons and included 140 veterinarians. (Hamid, 134; Reid, 29)

The psychology of the camels themselves is an intriguing puzzle. Though most short-term camel handlers despise them, it seems that a majority of long-term handlers adore them. Whether it is the lengthy term of the relationship that causes camel and man to "bond," or if the human and animal simply learn to tolerate each other, is an open question.

Camels show strange contradictions in their reactions to stimuli. For the most part, even radical noises and physical contact with a camel will be ignored by a camel. Soldiers once lit a small fire under a camel to rouse it from lazy lounging, and it did get up but seemingly unworried by the flames. One camel did not flinch as it was hit by 23 bullets, and it remained steady as a man removed the bullets; yet another camel panicked when someone popped a paper bag, and it could not work for two weeks due to jitters. Camels are very noisy, vocal animals. "He complains loudly about everything, and of all the creatures in existence the camel is equipped with the best apparatus for oral complaints. He is a great talker. He can grunt, gurgle, chortle, chuckle, whine, sigh, chirp, bark, yelp, squawk, scream, groan, grumble, and mutter. But most of the time he grumbles and groans." (Reid, 53–54; Dempewolff, 26, 37–38, 32)

Psychologically and physically, camels require a lot of care. "The mixed stones and sand of the desert would ruin the feet of almost any animal, and it is necessary that the camel should be furnished with a foot that cannot be split by heat, like the hoof of a horse, that is broad enough to prevent the creature from sinking into the sand, and is tough enough to withstand the action of the rough and burning soil. It consists of two long toes resting upon a hard elastic cushion with a tough and horny sole...in consequence of this structure, the camel sinks less deeply into the ground than any other animal....It is popularly thought that hills are impracticable to the camel, but it is able to climb even rocky ground from which a horse would recoil." (Worcester, 38–39)

The most important truth for working with camels is ensuring their footing. While camelid feet are ideal for marching through sand and even rocky heights, slippery surfaces can cause a camel's death. Sailors on board ships carrying camels had to watch out for this. "The strict regulation against wetting the camel deck was necessary, because the camel can travel over any kind of surface except one that is slippery. In Asia Minor, Syria, Persia, North Hindoostan, and Tartary he travels loaded across valleys and mountain ranges and deserts alike, exhibiting no hesitancy except when he encounters ice or mud. Here he loses control of himself, spreads his legs wide apart, and if not helped generally ends by the dislocation of shoulders or hips or by literally splitting himself up, an injury which is, always fatal." (Carroll; Reid, 150)

Purchasing camels for the army required experience and a sharp eye. Dealing with horse and camel traders is dealing with professionals of deception, who would love to make money by selling aged, sickly animals. Agents for military camels sought beasts aged 7 to 10 years, with a high-domed forehead, clear eyes, and long eyelashes for protection against sandstorms. Skin infections, mange, and other maladies could be hidden by an unscrupulous seller, however. (Dempewolff, 30)

Female camels are always preferred to males, for many reasons, but especially for their temperaments. One man rubbed his female camel's ears consistently and she followed him around like a puppy, chirping and drooling on him. By gelding the males some aggressiveness can be removed, but they still go into musth, though the gelding may reduce the frequency of their musth. Just as in elephants, camel musth is a crazed male condition that strikes about once per year. A musth camel stops eating and drinking, it makes horrible sounds, its mouth swells up, and it becomes vicious and may kill people and other animals. Such a crazed animal must be muzzled, staked far from other animals, or shot. (ibid., 28, 34–45)

Camels can be dangerous, even when not sexually active. The British Army often filed down or cut off the tips of the camel's canine teeth. The camel is an expert kicker. The most serious kick is a powerful roundhouse maneuver. The camel leans away for balance, thus freeing a back leg to swing around and smash its target. Riders learned to deal with the vengeful proclivity of the offended camel. Purportedly a camel may hold a grudge for months, so it is best to cure the problem without either camel or rider suffering a major injury. Experienced camel riders discovered that allowing the camel to "feel" that it has had its revenge will satisfy the beast. Thus if their camel is angry, some riders will wear an extra cloak or two and walk close to the angry animal, knowing it will bite. The loose top piece of clothing is torn from the rider, and the camel happily stomps and tears up the rider's garment. Within minutes the grudge is gone and the rider is safe from future retribution, they say. (Dempewolff, 26, 44; Carroll)

Similar psychology can be used on the camel for more simple tasks, like getting the beast into the back of a truck. Camels are just as stubborn as mules. Without using a crane, the best way to get the camel in the truck is by trickery. British soldiers discovered that you can blindfold the beast, spin her around until dizzy, and then try to force her *away* from the truck.

The camel will fight and pull herself right up the ramp and into the back of the vehicle. (Reid, 176)

World War I saw organized and effective use of camels, mainly in the Middle Eastern sector. Nearly 125,000 camels served, with 50,000 of them under the British fighting the Turks. (Dempewolff, 29)

Though the British had learned much about camels over the centuries, getting troopers and leaders to abide by the understood "standards" was difficult. Though the enemy Turks killed hundreds of camels with their biplanes, a vast majority of British camels died from forced marches, malnutrition, lack of water, and disease. After one battle, when the camels' saddles had been left on for eight straight days of marching, the flesh literally tore from the camels' bodies when the packs were finally removed. (Reid, 176–77)

Camels carrying cannons to war in Sudan.
(*Illustrated London News*, cover, March 29, 1884.)
(Courtesy John Kistler.)

The standard daily ration for a camel was 20 pounds of grain, barley, and vegetables, along with 20 gallons of water. The standard ration was never available: the camels could hardly carry enough water and food for the men riding, let alone themselves. Soldiers did not fight from camel-back; they left the beasts behind with the baggage and proceeded on foot to the battle. Soldiers commonly complained that upon returning to camp, the camels had eaten everything in sight: rope, clothing, tent canvas, tree bark, anything they could fit in their mouths. The handlers were warned never to put camel food on the ground, but to put it in a trough or even on a tent canvas, because otherwise the camels licked up sand with their food and got sand colic and stomach ulcers. (Dempewolff, 43–44; Cooper, 118)

Most soldiers tried to care for their camels as best they could, under the conditions of war and desert. The men loved baby camels and would not let harm come to them. Toward the end of the war during a time of need, the British bought a group of 3,000 camels without careful inspection,

Bikaner Camel Corps from India used in World War I. (*Wonders of Animal Life*, J. A. Hammerton, ed., vol. 4., London: Waverley Book Co., n.d., circa 1930, p. 1475.)

not realizing that many of the beasts were pregnant. During their first major caravan duty, baby camels were being born all along the route. The soldiers referred to the gangly creatures as "anthills on sticks" and the mothers would not let the babies fall behind, but the young ones were slowing down the military supplies. Unwilling to kill the little fellows, soldiers folded them up in nets and carried the babies on the mother's sides. The native camel drivers were not so kind. The common practice was to kill the baby, skin it, and carry the baby's skin ahead so the mother was deceived into following the scent of the baby. (Cooper, 123; Dempewolff, 45–46)

Poor care, insufficient food, and little rest meant that the "10 percent" of camels kept in reserve to fill in for sick and injured camels was never enough. Some sources estimate that at least half of the camels were sick at any one time, but they were used anyway. General Allenby oversaw the Palestinian campaign against the Turks, with 50,000 camels under his command. Less than half survived that final year of World War I. When heavy rains slowed the advance near Jerusalem, camels were sent along the coastal sand dunes, but many sank into the wet sand and were lost. (Dempewolff, 39–40; Sutton and Walker, 112–13)

More than the dangers presented by machine guns and bombs, it was the invention of motor vehicles that supplanted the usefulness of camels in desert battlefields. Camels saw much less action in World War II, though the North African campaigns did include some camelids. Native Tuaregs were hired to ride their camels up to Rommel's positions as reconnaissance for the Allies, which they accomplished with great success. The British Somaliland Camel Corps heroically delayed the Italian invasion of East Africa in 1940 with a mere 1,500 men. Later in the war, when Italians and Germans were being driven back by the Allies, the exiled ruler of Ethiopia, Haile Selassie, led a large force from Sudan to retake Ethiopia. His baggage train included 15,000 camels. Sadly, the men had no idea how to treat the animals. Only 50 arrived in Addis Ababa; the rest died in the forced march. (Dempewolff, 39–40, 50–51, 55; Cooper, 44; Gardiner, 78; Sinclair, 231)

The Soviets used Bactrian camels to haul war equipment during World War II for battles at Stalingrad and Kuybyshev, by dragging heavy sleds. (Dempewolff, 55)

Camel delivered from transport ship, World War I. (Courtesy John Kistler.)

Camel pulling a cart in front of barracks in Egypt in 1944. (Courtesy National Archives.)

The British Army continued to use camels to carry heavy radio equipment and men in Arabia even into the 1960s. (Harfield, 64)

The most recent and continuing use of camels in warfare is in Sudan, where the Janjaweed militia in Darfur uses camels to raid enemy tribes of the region. Though the word Janjaweed means "the devil on a horse" because most of them ride on horseback, a significant number of camels are included in their light-cavalry-style units. The Janjaweed are "willing to die for their camels," and some of their actions may be retaliation for camels stolen by rebel groups (though rebels claim the camels were stolen by the Janjaweed first). During raids the Janjaweed soldiers ride two on a camel, dismount outside the town, and proceed on foot. The militiamen feel that camels cannot maneuver well between huts and in small places, though riders on horseback often remain on their animals in close-quarters attacks. (Sinclair, 254; Steidle and Wallace, xiii, 130–32, 149, 164)

7

Mules and Donkeys

Mules and Donkeys before the 19th Century

Mules and donkeys, relegated always to the rear echelons of armies, receive none of the glory and praise rained upon men or horses who participate in combat. Without the help of pack animals, however, few armies could move. The old military adage, "the army moves on its stomach," correctly notes the importance of cargo-laden beasts throughout history.

The wild African ass, Nubian subspecies, was likely the first equine to be domesticated. This animal became the domestic donkey, used in Sudan and Egypt, first trained to carry cargo in the 4th millennium BC. In these early centuries, the donkeys were too small to carry riders well. The body types of donkeys around the world depend on the climate. In general, colder climates produce animals with heavier bodies and shorter limbs, while warmer regions bring taller and lighter donkeys. Mesopotamians hitched donkeys and onagers (Asian wild asses) to battle wagons by 2800 BC. Yokes enabled the onager to pull wagons, but they used no reins, just a rope looped through each animal's nose ring. Two to four onagers were required to pull the heavy cart. Such wagons were the earliest type of chariot, a four-wheeled heavy cart, useful only on level ground, and used as archery platforms and command posts. The evidence for these dates comes from ancient art and pottery found during excavations in the Middle East. The Rig Veda of India also refers to asses pulling chariot-like vehicles in early times. (Kelekna, 23–24, 52, 95, 172; Hodges, 87, 101; Hyams, 13–15; Cotterell, 166)

Early literary references to asses in domestic use come from the Bible book of Genesis, which says that Abram traveled with sheep and cattle and donkeys. Around this time, circa 2000 BC, Egyptian inscriptions tell of caravans with up to a thousand donkeys, and Assyrian documents record ownership of several thousand donkeys. Ancient officers had discovered the same surprising truth that World War II commanders learned thousands of years later: "that such ill-shaped creatures, too long in the leg and with sickle hocks, should in fact be such excellent workers." (Steiner, 3; Gardiner, 71)

The modern donkey is a descendant of the ancient wild ass. The male donkey is called a jack, while the female is known as a jinny. The mule is a hybrid animal, a cross between a horse and a donkey. Offspring from the mating of a male horse (stallion) and a female donkey (jinny) is rare. The much more common modern mule comes from a male donkey (jack) and a female horse (mare). Mules are born sterile, and so cannot breed. Mules are considered to be stronger and perhaps more intelligent than horses and donkeys, thus making an ideal combination of the two. The earliest reference to mules comes from a document circa 500 BC, calling the Mysians the inventors of mule breeding. A contemporary Bible reference in Ezekiel 27:14 also mentions mules (not donkeys) as contrasted with horses. Some allies of the Medes and Persians, called Karmanians from the Kerman province of southern Iran, rode on donkeys and mules because of a shortage of horses. (Koenig, 104; Hyams, 27; Sinclair, 17)

Mr. Wood (perhaps J. G. Wood, naturalist) remarks, "It is a very strange circumstance that the offspring of these two animals should be, for some purposes, far superior to either of the parents, a well-bred mule having the lightness, sure-footedness, and hardy endurance of the ass, together with the increased size and muscular development of the horse. Thus it is peculiarly adapted either for the saddle or for desert country...The mules that are most generally serviceable are bred from the male ass and the mare, those which have the horse as the father and the ass as the mother being small and comparatively valueless." Another writer says that mules are more calm and hardy than horses, but also show less cooperation and flexibility than horses. (Worcester, 28–29, 35)

On at least one occasion, army donkeys did save an army from destruction. The Scythian cavalry pursued King Darius I of Persia in about

520 BC, but the "hard braying" of Persian donkeys upset the Scythian horses. Darius then moved all his donkeys to the rear, and they effectively covered his retreat from the enemy. King Philip of Macedon forbade the use of wagons and adopted pack mules and pack horses to speed up the movements of Greek armies. (Mayor, *Greek,* 198–99; Gabriel and Boose, 158)

Though the Roman legions were famous for their relative independence from any supply trains—the soldiers carried a majority of supplies and equipment on their own backs—the legions did use a fair number of mules. Marius increased the speed of the legions by removing all oxcarts and switching to pack mules and horses. The Romans started their own mule-breeding industry to support the legions on campaign. Breeding stock became very expensive. One Roman senator purportedly paid 400,000 sesterces for two pairs of work donkeys, roughly enough to pay 400 Roman soldiers for one year. (Kelekna, 191; Gabriel and Boose, 359; Hyams, 16)

With the fall of Rome and the dearth of large armies during the Middle Ages, donkeys and mules are little mentioned in that time. The greatest change that would affect the future of military draught animals came in the 14th and 15th centuries with the invention of more practical wagons. The two-wheeled cart could carry very little cargo, but the heavier four-wheeled wagons required many animals to pull and could not traverse rough terrain. Newer, "dished" wheels enabled carts to cope with rockier roads with less breakage, and with these, animals could draw heavier loads. Having horses and mules pull cargo in wagons rather than just hanging it over their backs enabled the animals to haul almost three times as much weight, since pulling requires less energy than lifting. The new wagons could carry up to 13,225 pounds. Such capacity became necessary with the advent of hefty artillery pieces and cannons that weighed as much as 5,000 pounds. Such guns sometimes required a 20-horse team for pulling. (Kelekna, 344, 369)

Though donkeys and mules attained some modicum of respect, horse lovers never completely accepted these hard workers. An obvious example came from King Ferdinand of Spain, who believed it to be "effeminate" for a man to ride a donkey or mule: only women could ride on mules. His legal orders that men should ride only horses helped lead to the conquistador style of thinking and the growth of chivalry as an ideal of the 16th century. (Steiner, 111)

Mules and Donkeys in the Early 19th Century

Ancient armies came to rely heavily on donkeys and mules for toting needed supplies to battlefields. With the rise of modern weaponry and capacities for larger armies, mules became even more indispensable.

The first modern British commander to discover the importance of military supply trains during a campaign was the Duke of Wellington. In India he learned how an overly large and disorganized caravan could slow and hinder an army. When Wellington took command of the British force in 1810, he did not forget the lesson. Landing in Portugal and crossing Spain to attack Napoleon from the west, the British army consisted of 53,000 men. Wellington hated the slow and noisy bullock (oxen) carts, so he obtained 9,000 mules. Since these were not able to carry enough supplies, he had 800 specially designed carts built for the mules to pull, increasing their effectiveness. By 1812 Wellington had liberated two-thirds of Spain, and by 1813 the Peninsular War had ended. He invented the concept of the wagon train and taught its use among Great Britain's troops. By 1833, however, the army had completely forgotten logistics and mule-train supplies. (Sutton, 34–36)

While the Europeans experimented with mule trains, it was the Americans who adopted the idea and brought it to perfection during the 19th century. The U.S. Army constantly experimented with improving upon logistics of moving supplies. The Second Seminole War of 1835–1842 provided the first major test. The army used about half horses and half mules as pack animals, and decided that mules proved better on campaign. This led to the adoption of "mule skinners," the men in charge of teams of mules in military caravans. The nickname was earned because these fellows often used weighted whips that would literally strip the skin off of disobedient animals. Though not all mule drivers practiced cruelty, a high enough percentage of muleteers harmed the beasts to make the moniker stick for posterity. (Essin, 24; Froman, 95)

In 1845, "Old Rough and Ready" Zachary Taylor led the U.S. attack on Mexico. Perhaps because of his age, Taylor preferred to ride side-saddle on a mule rather than astride a horse. The army relied heavily on mules, and 2nd Lt. Ulysses S. Grant was one of the quartermasters in charge of mule trains for the war. Grant hated cruelty. During the Mexican War, Ulysses attended a bullfight, where he saw several bulls and a horse killed. He wrote, "The sight to me was sickening. I could not see how human beings could enjoy the sufferings of beasts." (Smith, 108; Essin, 25–26; Woodward, 98)

In September 1846 when Zachary Taylor approached Monterrey, Mexico, a battle ensued, and rather than remain far behind the lines, as most quartermasters would, Grant rushed his mule teams ahead to provide frontline supplies to the beleaguered troops. Interestingly, Grant the quartermaster met Capt. Robert E. Lee during this conflict. Grant's experience with mules became much exaggerated by his loyal soldiers during the Civil War. They claimed that Grant could easily communicate with mules and make stubborn animals move merely by swearing at them. (Woodward, 87, 95; Essin, 70–71)

Since few U.S. Army quartermasters received thorough training, simple procedural steps could be taken to simplify matters for them in the field. The U.S. Army began to label mules with a brand, intended to show the troops how much training, if any, a mule had received. Mules that were already trained for packing supplies received a letter "P" brand on the left front hoof. If the mule had learned to pull a wagon, it earned the "W" for its front hoof. This reduced the number of injuries and difficulties suffered in trying to hitch up an untrained animal to a wagon, which could disrupt an entire wagon train. In 1846, the army shipped 459 horses, 3,658 mules, and 14,904 oxen to the Army of the West for the Mexican War. An official supply train usually consisted of 28 "escort wagons" each pulled by four mules, with five or six animals in reserve as spares. The caravan included a wagon-master, a farrier, a cook, and watchman. The procedures for improving logistics did not reach equally into all areas of army life, however. President Polk ordered an amphibious landing of troops and animals on the east coast of Mexico in March 1847. The move was poorly organized from the beginning; there were few good ships for transport and no landing sites where the ships could gain close entrance to the shoreline. Most of the horses and mules were pushed overboard so they might swim to shore. Many drowned in poor weather and high surf, but at least 500 animals made it ashore alive. (Smith, 108; Essin, 28, 38, 54)

One strange episode of the Mexican War came on December 6, 1846, at the Battle of San Pasqual, when Brig. Gen. Stephen W. Kearney had arrived in California with only 100 soldiers. He had been told by scout Kit Carson that Mexico had no troops in California, and thus he took only a small force of his own, leaving the rest in New Mexico. Tired and ill-supplied, Kearney arrived near San Diego to discover Mexican general Andres Pico camped there with a hundred fresh lancers: soldiers on horseback carrying long spears. Kearney's horses were nearly starved and useless. While trying to scout the Mexican position, Kearney's small force of perhaps a dozen soldiers on mules was discovered and attacked. The lancers charged, killing and wounding nearly 50 Americans, and they would likely have destroyed Kearney's group, but a U.S. artillery piece arrived in time and its firing caused the Mexicans to withdraw. The small hill where the mules had stood firm came to be called Mule Hill. (Essin, 31; Regan)

Mules had proven to be valuable to the army, so the breeding of mules became a valued service. By 1850, more than half a million mules had been bred in the United States. The key mule-breeding regions were Georgia, Alabama, Mississippi, and Louisiana in these years. A new technique for gathering and controlling stubborn mules was discovered in the 1850s. The mule driver or leader would choose a female mule (jinny) as his mount, ride it, and hang a bell around the jinny's neck. This animal was called a "bell mare." The whole herd of mules could be rounded up easily by riding the bell mare back to camp, as this moving bell came to be associated with dinner, and upon hearing it the animals rushed home for oats or other treats. The herd would even follow the bell mare across rivers. To make it easier to find and see the bell mare, white jinnys were preferred. (Edwards, 129; Downey, 25; Essin, 50, 95)

Though 1853 saw the first official U.S. Army request for trained veterinarians to care for expensive horses and mules, it was not until 1916 that the first U.S. Army veterinary services began. This long delay was a tragedy in military history for the millions of animals lost due to inadequate care. The winter of 1857 would be the first example, though the Civil War would prove the point more emphatically. (Essin, 57; Riley, 1)

In 1857 Brigham Young and the Mormons were causing problems and threatening to form their own independent nation of Deseret in the Utah Territory. When the president of the United States sent troops, the Mormons burned all of the grasslands, harassed army troops, and destroyed or stole supply trains and caches. One U.S. Army force that neared Utah in

November 1857 was caught in a brutally cold winter storm. The mules had less than half-rations of food, and they began eating ropes, wagon canvas, and even wood. Some died of the cold; most starved. Of 144 horses, 130 died; hundreds of mules were found frozen solid. Twenty-four hundred mules were sent from a nearby fort with supplies; 588 of these died in one month and less than 500 were usable on arrival. A negotiated settlement was reached with Brigham Young and war was averted. (Essin, 63–65)

Mule breeding moved into the states of Kentucky and Missouri during the Civil War period, providing the Union army with more than a million mules for the war effort. The Union had such an abundance of mules that the animals were badly treated and poorly fed because it was so easy to replace them. Officially, the army estimated that on an average day, a horse should eat 26 pounds of hay and grain, a mule should have 23 pounds, and a soldier should have 3.5 pounds. In reality, however, the horses and mules received less than half of this ration, with the army saying the animals could forage effectively for the rest of their needs. Some regions, obviously, provided better foraging opportunities than others. The Confederates had the opposite problem: a major shortage of mules. To keep the South from obtaining mules, the Union would pay ridiculous prices just to keep sellers from providing any to the enemy. President Lincoln signed General Order No. 300 forbidding any export of riding animals, including donkeys, mules, and horses. The southerners, thus, ended up buying mules far too young or too old. Young and old mules are incapable of much work, and thus most died quickly. Female mules or gelded males were preferred by the armies, because stud mules caused a lot of problems. (Essin, 8. 69–75; Carter, 133)

In 1861, a French military veteran, Monsieur Chillon joined the Confederate 3rd Louisiana and brought his pet donkey, named Jason, along. The man and donkey actually slept together for warmth, but one night Jason mistook the Confederate commander of the 3rd Louisiana for Chillon and lay down and snuggled up to the startled man. (Seguin, 52)

In 1862, Col. Abel D. Streight of the Indiana infantry proposed taking 2,000 men on a cavalry raid into Alabama and Georgia, to cut railroad supplies to Chattanooga. General Rosecrans liked this plan but did not want to weaken his cavalry, so he authorized Streight 800 mules instead of horses, and told him to steal more from the enemy during the operation. The Indiana infantry had no riding experience, and the mules were unbroken.

They did acquire 400 more mules by foraging, but many of the animals panicked under gunfire and ran into a river, drowning. Eventually Colonel Streight did acquire enough mules to mount all 2,000 of his soldiers, but by then Confederate general Bedford Forrest was in pursuit. The constant harassment by Confederate cavalry wore out both the Union soldiers and their mules, until the animals could no longer be ridden due to sore backs and tender feet. Streight surrendered to Forrest, though outnumbering the southerners by a large margin. In prison, Streight said that if he had been provided with horses instead of mules, he would have succeeded in his mission. (Carter, 134–35; 146–47; Longacre, 66–90)

In the 1862 Battle of Shiloh, a Confederate courier had a horse shot from under him, so he grabbed a captured mule. The men then watched as he charged toward the Union lines, taking heavy fire. One of the soldiers said, "Just look at that brave man, charging right into the jaws of death!" The courier yelled back, "It arn't me, boys, its this blarsted old mule. Whoa! Whoa!" (Seguin, 104)

Both Union and Confederate raids proved effective, but on cavalry forays, few captured goods could be kept. One 1863 expedition captured several Confederate supply trains: the Union burned 1,160 wagons and slaughtered 2,000 mules. A southern raid near Chickamauga under Joe Wheeler captured a huge 800-wagon federal caravan. The rebels sabered thousands of Union mules and torched the vehicles. General Rosecrans's campaign in Tennessee went badly. Federal horses and pack mules ate bark, hitching posts, wagon-wheel spokes, and the tails off of neighboring animals. More than 10,000 Union mules died of starvation, and many thousands were captured by the Confederacy. (Carter, 253; Essin, 85; Longacre, 207–8; Jacobs, 67–68)

Union captain James Graydon came up with a scheme to kill Confederates with suicide mules. They packed 24-pound howitzer shells in wooden boxes on the backs of two Texas mules. At dark, some Union soldiers led the two mules within 150 yards of the enemy, then smacked them on the butt so the animals would run into the enemy camp. However, the mules turned and followed the fleeing Union spies. The bombs exploded prematurely, killing the mules. A similar attempt was made in Afghanistan in 2006, with a Taliban rebel loading a donkey with 70 pounds of explosives and landmines on a donkey, intending to blow up the animal at a U.S. base

Mule Promotion

On October 27, 1863, during a Confederate attack, 200 Union mules became frightened and disoriented, fleeing toward the charging infantrymen rather than away. In the confusion of battle, the southern footmen heard the hoofbeats and feared that Union cavalry was charging. The rebels fell back into retreat, only later to discover their error. The Union quartermaster wrote to General Grant in good humor: "I respectfully request that the mules, for their gallantry in this action, may have conferred upon them the brevet rank of horses." One Union soldier wrote a poem about the event. "Half a mile, half a mile onward, right through the Georgia troops broke the two hundred. Forward the Mule Brigade! Charge for the Rebs!" The poem imitates the famous Alfred Lord Tennyson classic, "Charge of the Light Brigade." (Seguin, 105; Essin, 86)

---

near Qalat. Regarding dead mules, some Union soldiers thought that their beef ration was actually mule meat. One Connecticut soldier wrote that "the commissary at Annapolis has give [*sic*] us so much mule meat that the ears of the whole regiment have grown three and a half inches since their arrival at the Maryland capital." A Union army muleteer wrote in 1867 that two-thirds of the mules he saw die during the Civil War died because they were too young to work: animals under age three are not strong or developed enough for the hard work of military life. (Seguin, 104, 132; Riley, 13–14; Afghan Police)

The Battle of Gettysburg is viewed as the turning point in the American Civil War. Part of the Union victory must be attributed to logistical supply for the northern troops. General Meade had some 4,300 wagons with 21,628 mules, along with 8,889 draft horses and 216 pack mules during the battle at Gettysburg. He used a "flying column" formation, meaning that the troops themselves traveled fast and light, with most baggage and supplies in the rear, thus reducing obstructions to the roads. ("Horses," DVD, 1; Essin, 80–81)

The famous "Reb" cavalry leader J. E. B. Stuart did not like mules, especially their untimely and noisy braying that gave away their position

British marine on pack mule at the Dardanelles, World War I. (Courtesy John Kistler.)

to enemy units. He used mules to pull ambulances for his wounded men, but when in enemy territory, he also stationed a soldier beside every such animal with orders to beat it into silence if it brayed. Perhaps the ambulance mules had their revenge, in the end. Stuart was mortally wounded by a gunshot. His men laid him in the back of a mule-drawn ambulance for transport to the nearest Confederate hospital. Under fire, the mules panicked and threw him around the carriage, almost tossing him out the back. Stuart spent hours in the back of that wagon before a place was found for him to get medical attention, but he died soon after this Battle of Yellow Tavern. (Davis, 364, 408–10)

During the 1864 Battle of the Wilderness, with the Union soldiers of the Wadsworth Division running out of ammunition, mule wagons were called forward. The mules heroically rushed forward, though battered by

Burros carry food to U.S. marines in Verdun, France, 1918.
(Courtesy National Archives.)

Confederate artillery. General Hancock later said that this was the first mule-train charge he had ever heard of, and he praised the men and animals for their efforts. In a similar manner, at the Battle of Trevilian Station, with the army desperate for ammunition, a "wagon came rattling down the road with the mules on a full run, the driver lashing and cracking his whip. He continued at the same furious pace along the line in plain view of the enemy, a man in the rear of the wagon throwing out the packages, which are instantly caught-up, and the contents quickly found their way into the hungry cartridge-boxes." ("Horses," DVD, 1; Swank, 76)

Summing up the role of mules in the American Civil War and later Indian Wars, a mule driver wrote, "Probably no animal has been the subject of more cruel and brutal treatment than the mule, and it is safe to say that no animal ever performed his part better, not even the horse." (Riley, 1)

Mules and Donkeys in the Indian Wars and World War I

Though mules proved themselves as valuable allies during the American Civil War, they earned more of a reputation (or notoriety) for their work during the later Indian Wars. In the vast western United States, where roads were scarce and railroads even scarcer, horses, mules, and oxen were the only available means of transport.

Experienced mule drivers came to learn the blessings and curses of mule behavior and passed on their knowledge to comrades. In 1867 James Riley, a longtime worker with mules, produced a manual with practical advice. Riley notes that there are some mule problems that just cannot be fixed, like their proclivity to kick. Mules like to kick, so just be careful around them, he wrote. Avoid using narrow bits in their mouths because

Live pack mules pass dead horse teams, World War I. (Mary Evans Picture Library.)

their mouths become sore, thus keeping the animals from eating and drinking properly, and even creating breathing problems. Never whip a mule in a team, since the whip spooks all of them. Try to avoid white or cream-colored mules, as they are usually poor workers. Small Spanish and Mexican mules are very good pack animals but horrible in teams, so do not hook them up to wagons. Never use young mules (under age three) since they are weak and undeveloped and will just get sick or die when worked hard. Mules also tend to die in service because they stubbornly refuse to show their pain or illness, and thus may perish from infections or illness if the driver is not watching the animal carefully. On long expeditions when the work is heavy and rations are low, the mules lose weight and thus their collars become too large and create sores. Riley explains that a muleteer can cut chunks out of the collars to accommodate the shrinking animals and reduce sores. (Riley, 2–28)

Mule team pulling ammunition wagon, World War I. One mule has died. (Mary Evans Picture Library.)

After the Civil War, mule packers had become specialists, and some joined the Indian Wars, loving their jobs and their mules. Emmett Essin writes, "Mules responded to kindness and would recognize by sight and sense of smell the individual who had shown it to them." A packer could lead a mule anywhere just by placing his hand under its chin. The animals grow accustomed to routines, learn their equipment and their place in line, and might balk if someone tried to harness them with unfamiliar harnesses or changed the routine. Improved treatment also brought benefits to the logistical services of British armies. In the 1867–1868 Abyssinian Expedition, the British army left Suez with 40,000 animals, including 13,000 mules, and lost less than 20 percent during the whole Ethiopian war. By 1874 the British were seeing the advantages to mules over horses in their army system. (Essin, 101–4; Sutton, 55–56; Harfield, 25)

North America is where mules took the greatest role in warfare. Brig. Gen. George Crook earned decades of fame in the Indian Wars for his ability to pursue and capture or destroy hostile native bands. By using pack mules rather than wagon trains for supplies, his units could freely move in territory lacking roads, and at great speed. Crook also recruited Indian (usually Apache) scouts from rival tribes to help track their elusive quarry. His Arizona campaign succeeded against the Apaches mainly because the U.S. cavalry pack-mule system enabled the troops to surround the renegade tribes in remote canyons. One benefit of pack mules, doubtless unintended by the army, was that Apache scouts loved mule meat, so there was no need for burial if a pack animal died during the journey. (Urwin, *U.S. Cavalry*, 149; Utley and Washburn, 325; Essin, 99–100; Brown, 157)

To make it easier for army packers to identify untrained rookie mules from more experienced animals, they would cut off the hairy ends of the tails of the rookies, calling them "shavetails." By the time their tails grew long again, they would have had months of experience and were then called "bell sharps," meaning that the mules had at least learned to follow the sound of the dinner bell. Experienced pack mules carried 200 pounds each, for 10 to 25 miles per day, at six to eight miles per hour, for three to seven days. Rookie mules carried less, and were tied by harness rope to the tail of a more experienced mule. Throughout the Indian Wars, scouts and soldiers moved away from the army horse, which needed constant forage, and adopted the jackass, which could travel long distances with little food and water. Furthermore, the army horse typically feared the Indians, while donkeys seemed unworried about the enemy. (Essin, 95–96, 105–6; Goodwin, 78)

There is a story from 1883, believed by many writers, of a gray mule that worked for the U.S. Army during the Mexican War, and again in the Civil War, that was being sold at market. William Tecumseh Sherman ordered that the animal be kept, fed, and not worked until it died naturally. If the backstory of this animal is true, the mule lived at least 65 years, about three times the average lifespan of a mule. (Essin, 120)

With the end of the Indian Wars, the army reduced its troops and animals to economize. When the Spanish-American War began in the last few years of the 19th century, the U.S. Army had only 2,000 mules. It was able to quickly obtain 19,550 more animals; however, lack of shipping space kept most of them from being deployed to the field. It took more than two years to get 3,259 mules to the Philippines for military use. One bright side to the shortage of mules was that the army recognized their importance. Most officers had to take classes on mule care and packing. A few infamous tragedies at sea overshadowed the better care of the animals on land. In July 1900 the cargo ship *Siam* suffered through a typhoon and lost 300 of its 400 mules due to "flimsy stalls." Stalls were then improved by padding the walls of the stalls, but the padded ship *Leelanaw* with 570 mules lost every animal, apparently killed by their hard food troughs, the only unpadded part of the stalls. (Essin, 124–25, 129–31; Livingston and Roberts, 31)

While the Americans fought against the Spanish, the British were engaged in the Boer Wars in South Africa. Apparently the British navy had much better capacity for carrying animals in ships, as they bought and shipped more than 55,000 mules from the United States for that conflict. For World War I, England obtained 186,000 mules from the United States. The United States became the mule-producing capital of the world, breeding 4,200,000 animals in 1910 and 5,681,000 in 1925. (Essin, 147, 137)

As mule production became a major economic boon, big money drew big deceptions. Mule dealers learned many tricks to hide the poor health or age of a mule. A mule's wheezing breath could be muted by sponges in its nostrils. Putting ice in a mule's rectum might hide its fever temperature. Drugs and stimulants were fed to the animals to make them seem more lively and spry. Aside from deception, there was the problem of transportation fatigue. Once horses or mules came aboard a train car, there was no way to feed and water them properly. Laws had to be passed so that animals were not left in sweltering train cars for more than 28 hours straight. Army buyers had to inspect the animals closely lest they purchase decrepit or sickly mules. (Essin, 148–49)

Mules proved once again to be hardier than horses. Aboard ships heading to World War I battlefields in Europe, the death rate of mules was only half that of horses, and they ate only three-quarters as much as the horses did. A British war correspondent wrote that American mules were "weighed anew in the scales of battle...and not found wanting. In warm winter coat and with long, inquisitive ears flopping back and forth in the breeze, he marches up among the roaring guns with a steady nonchalance that lends confidence and faith to the fighting men who depend so much on him." When he visited a vet hospital he found hundreds of horses and only one mule—the vet said that mules rarely needed repair. In the trenches at Vimy Ridge, no mules even became ill, while the horses died en masse. The only drawback to mule use was a propensity to be "spooked" by odd things. When poison gas started to be used, a French man put on an early model of a gas mask for protection. This panicked all of the mules in the area, scattering them hopelessly throughout the region; it took two days to round them up again. (Essin, 149; Cooper, 128–29)

Abdul, a Greek burro, was used by James Simpson Kirkpatrick, an Australian stretcher-bearer in World War I, to carry the wounded after the disastrous Gallipoli landing in 1915. Day after day, Kirkpatrick, who became known as the "Good Samaritan of Gallipoli," set one soldier after another astride Abdul to be carried down the dangerous "Shrapnel Gully" to aid stations on the Turkish beach. Kirkpatrick was killed but the little donkey kept going. Abdul was later adopted by the 6th Mountain Battery and taken to India. "The Men with the Donkey" a statue by Wallace Anderson of Kirkpatrick supporting a wounded Anzac on Abdul's back, was placed in the Shrine of Remembrance at Melbourne, Australia. In 1964, the statue was reproduced on three postage stamps, commemorating the fiftieth anniversary of the Gallipoli landing. (Ruthven, 1)

Mules were used not only to carry supplies to the front lines, but also to carry the wounded back to hospitals. They used a travois, the same system used by American Indians, with two long poles and a canvas sheet acting as a stretcher. The British also used mules to pull artillery. To hinder Allied advances, the Germans scattered sharp iron spikes on the ground to pierce the animals' hooves. Many horses and mules and men perished when they sank into deep mud pits. (Gardiner, 39, 128)

1916 may have been the worst year of the war, for animal casualties, and perhaps for human casualties as well. As a British advance forced the Germans to retreat in East Africa, General Von Lettow intentionally moved through areas filled with diseased flies and tainted water. All 4,000 of the British donkeys and horses died within three weeks from tsetse flies. Eight thousand reinforcement animals arrived with 2.5 million antibiotic-type pills to keep these animals alive, but the soldiers were too lazy to grind up the pills, so the mules refused to eat them, pushing them aside in their food troughs. Of 34,000 animals used in the East African campaign, less than a thousand survived. Lacking horses and mules, the British had to hire 120,000 Africans to carry the army's supplies. (Cooper, 199–201)

Europe saw a nasty 1916 as well. The mules and horses got so hungry in the winter that handlers had to use chains rather than ropes for harnesses because the mules were eating the ropes, along with the manes and tails of nearby animals. This winter was made far worse by an "insane" British Army Corps order that all animals be shaved completely bald to keep down insect problems. Now bare, these animals died of the cold. Though the order was not rescinded for two years, many commanders refused to enforce it, to keep their animals alive. Many men worked hard to keep the animals alive. Short of combs to groom the mules and horses, the soldiers discovered that "empty bully beef tins" from their ration kits were excellent at cleaning mud off of the animals. Each army group had specialists like farrier sergeants (called "Shoey") and saddler sergeants (called "Waxey"). Farriers were trained to shoe horses and mules at the veterinary hospitals, using a dead horse's foot. Several dead horse's legs were available for practicing at nailing shoes into place. Whenever an animal could not be cured of its wounds or disease at the hospital, it was killed with a "Greener's cattle killer," a sort of short-range bolt gun that pierced the skull instantly through the forehead. (Gardiner, 42–48)

In the Middle Eastern theater under General Allenby, thousands of mules carried supplies for the British army. The more-famous "Lawrence of Arabia" is known for his camel-warriors, but he also had a mule-cavalry detachment. One of Lawrence's men begged for 50 mules, and soon he had 50 mule-riding soldiers. King Feisal's army had pack mules carrying old Krupp artillery guns. (Barber, 116; Lawrence, 49)

For various reasons, the United States stayed out of World War I for several years. General Pershing had led an invasion of Mexico, the "Punitive Expedition" against Pancho Villa, in 1914. Here the U.S. Army tried out the use of small trucks, but many mules were needed as well. Though the United States had provided hundreds of thousands of mules to other countries for World War I, the when it entered the war it could bring very few mules for itself to Europe, for lack of shipping space. In 1918 the American Expeditionary Force instead bought mules on-site in Western Europe from the Spanish and French. These animals were quite small compared to American mules, and so could haul only small machine-gun carts rather than big artillery pieces. Frustrated at the small animals, perhaps, the U.S. Navy redoubled its efforts and managed to send 29,000 mules to France. However, because the U.S. military overseas lacked even basic veterinary services, thousands of the animals died. The British and French offered to let the Americans use their veterinary hospitals, and thus saved many dying animals. The dead mules became meat for the hungry, and skins went to tanners for leather. (Essin, 141, 150–52)

By late in the war the opposing armies had been shelling some areas of terrain for years. The pocked earth proved a formidable obstacle to early trucks and even wagons. Pack mules could easily skirt these difficulties. During the Meuse-Argonne Offensive the U.S. Army utilized some 90,000 animals to carry supplies and still asked for more. Mules had a special role in the battle. Communications were down and trucks could not get through the mud, so ten mules carried spools of communications wire. The Germans aimed artillery at the animals, killing five, but the other five succeeded in finishing the job. (Essin, 154–55)

By the end of World War I, the U.S. Army owned 80,000 pack mules. Nine years later, it would have only 2,700, due to peacetime reductions. The British removed all horse and mule transport by 1930, favoring trucks.

Few of the world powers saw that war was again brewing on the horizon and that mechanized vehicles could not carry the load alone. (Essin, 156; Sutton, 127)

Mules and Donkeys after World War I

The promise of new technology, namely the internal combustion engine and the coming of trucks, led armies to dismantle the majority of organized pack animal units. Between 1920 and 1930 the number of mules in the U.S. Army dropped from 80,000 to 2,700, while the British emptied their stables. Fortunately for the British, the Animal Training Center at Aldershot remained intact; they would need it for the coming conflagration. (Essin, 156; Sutton, 127, 134–37)

The overly optimistic military plan to build fleets of trucks for transporting supplies had not yet succeeded. When the Nazis spread through Europe and the Japanese advanced through Asia, mules were called upon to carry the burdens of the army. Once again the U.S. Quartermaster department began purchasing mules and had to learn that living burden-bearers require different care than mechanical ones. "They cannot be stored like hams, trucks, shoes and pants. They must be provided for every hour of the day because they are animals of flesh, bone and blood." Far more mules were deployed than horses, because it was packing, more than speed, that was needed. Because shipping animals across the oceans was difficult, most mules and donkeys were procured locally. On April 23, 1941, the transport ship *Santa Clara Valley* came under German dive-bombing and sank, killing more than 500 mules aboard. (Brophy et al., 313–15, 322–23; Cooper, 135)

During the North African campaign, frontline Allied commanders begged for more packing mules to tote supplies and ammunition in the desert through difficult terrain. The animals carried dead and wounded soldiers back to roads where Jeeps could take them to hospitals. The Atlas Mountains were a great obstacle to vehicles. Not having enough animals, American troops rented 218 mules and 28 horses from local Arabs for a dollar a day, and bought 95 outright. (Livingston and Roberts, 154–57)

A British example of a properly packed mule. Manual of Horsemastership, Equitation and Animal Transport, 1937. (Crown Copyright His Majesty's Stationery Office, 1937, plate 33.)

Patton's Seventh Army utilized at least 4,000 mules during their drive near Mount Etna in Sicily. They had little or no veterinary care, and it was easier to shoot wounded animals than to find medical help, so many animals died unnecessarily. Packers stopped to salvage the old shoes off of dead mules' feet to nail onto the live animals' hooves. In one famous incident, General Patton himself shot a team of mules in the head with his pearl-handled pistols when the animals stalled on a bridge and delayed the army. The carcasses were thrown over the side. Patton later explained that he feared Luftwaffe fighters might strafe the troops stuck there in line. (Livingston and Roberts, 159; Cooper, 136; Essin, 162–63)

The U.S. Quartermaster department purchased 10,200 mules in 1943, and over 14,000 in both 1944 and 1945, using them in nearly every region of conflict. Other animals were captured from the enemy. Many mules acquired by the army came from the Middle East and had gray coats. The Americans thought their light coloration too conspicuous for enemy guns, and so dyed the animals' coats brown as a sort of camouflage. The quartermaster at an Italian remount depot invented a 5 percent potassium permanganate solution that could be sprayed on the mules to darken them. Once Sicily had been conquered, the surviving mules boarded Landing Ship Transports (LST) for the short trip to mainland Italy. Each LST could carry 355 animals. (Brophy et al., 322–23; Livingston and Roberts, 159–60; Essin, 167; Cooper, 136–37)

The German Tenth Army in Italy fielded some 26,212 animals in 1944, over a quarter of which were mules. The Germans had very little mule breeding of their own, so they acquired most of the beasts locally. The British used two troops of pack mules with their 5th Division near Reggio for carrying supplies in mountainous terrain. Mules, however useful, could make nuisances of themselves at times. An Allied Bofors gun had been hidden nicely on a hill and behind a haystack one afternoon. The No. 35 Indian Mule Company rested nearby. When dawn arrived, the haystack had completely vanished—the mules had eaten it, thoroughly infuriating the artillery major in charge of the gun. (Dinardo, 86; Sutton, 146; Cooper, 138)

Far in the rear of the fighting, mules also bore important burdens. At Maison Blanche Air Field in Oran, Algeria, a major hub of supplies for the Allies in Europe, mud hindered trucks from operating well. Capt. Chan Livingston leased three-mule wagons to meet the C-47 cargo planes for loading and unloading. They could find no oats, but discovered that oatmeal fattened the animals. For two years this "Light Brigade" worked without trouble at the airfield. (Essin, 170–71)

The war against the Japanese in Asia required mules, especially since the islands had no good roads for mechanized vehicles. As the Japanese forced the U.S. troops to retreat southward in the Philippines before the 1942 surrender, two mules were wounded and tied to bamboo trees. Japanese Zero fighter planes kept strafing the mules. The veterinarian in charge devised a camouflage green paint, which put an end to the strafing, but camouflage did not hide the animals from starving soldiers, who killed and ate them. (Livingston and Roberts, 151–52)

In the first major American offensive, at Guadalcanal in late 1942, a shipload of mules from Oklahoma landed for packing duties. Liberty ships designed for cargo could carry 320 to 400 mules in a load, cared for by 60 men in five stable areas. The mules lived on the lower decks, so the men had to carry manure up and dump it over the side. However, they only dumped manure at night so that Japanese submarines would not see the floating detritus and know that an enemy ship steamed nearby. During storms the animals were miserable, and they could remain upright only by spreading their legs out with hooves against the stall-walls. Some mules improved in condition, though, since most parasites died during the voyages, and the animals got a lot of rest. Once they landed at a battlefield, however, the new environment caused illnesses, hoof problems, sunburn, and skin infections among the animals. These beasts carried howitzers and supplies, and provided other unplanned services to the U.S. Army and marines. They "not only survived the heavy loads, the heat, humidity and the noise of battle well but were quick to detect dangers. Enemy snipers, booby traps and unsafe ground were all detected by the alert animals. Handlers learned not to drink water that a mule would refuse." (Essin, 171–72, 181; Livingston and Roberts, 162)

The China-Burma-India Theater (CBI) provides the best examples of mule usage during World War II. In 1942–1943 Gen. Orde Charles Wingate with 3,000 British and Gurkha soldiers (named "the Chindits") and a thousand mules harassed the Japanese in Burma. In the first year of guerrilla-style warfare, the Chindits used many mules, but because they rarely received supplies, they ended up eating most of the animals. Wingate himself taught the soldiers how to tie a mule's feet, roll it over, sit on its head, and cut its carotid artery. One muleteer begged General Wingate to let three mules live, but Wingate said no. The man talked to his favorites all night, prayed with them, and then they were killed and eaten. The muleteer wept for three days. The Chindits ate mule three times a day for six days before running out, then they ate the horses. General Wingate insisted that more mules be sent by airdrop. (Livingston and Roberts, 163–64; Essin, 173–75)

Specially modified U.S. Army Air Forces C-47 Dakota cargo planes could carry four to six mules, their handlers, and ten soldiers, while gliders trailing behind could hold two mules and six men. Coconut mats covered the floors of the plane to keep the animals from slipping, and many nervous beasts received sedatives to keep them from kicking holes in the sides of the aircraft. Only four out of 3,000 mules flown to the front had to be shot for panicking and running amok inside the airplanes. When airstrips

Pack mules guided across river in Burma,
World War II. (Mary Evans Picture Library.)

were not available, mules and horses were drugged and pushed out of the plane at an altitude of 600 feet and a speed of 130 miles per hour, strapped to a six-by-four-foot wooden platform and its parachute. The Chindits received some 3,134 mules and 547 horses and 250 bullocks by air. Some of the gliders crashed, killing 90 men and an unknown number of animals. (Essin, 185–86; Gardiner, 76; Cooper, 138–39)

The key problem with mules, thought General Wingate, was their noisy braying. Fearing that the loud calls would alert Japanese troops to the British position, he ordered the veterinarians to find a way to silence the animals. With use of a general anesthetic, 5,563 mules had their vocal cords cut. The vets averaged 70 to 90 operations per day, and only 53 of the animals died, most from maggot infestations of the wounds. The animals needed 10 to 14 days to recuperate from the surgery, and then they seemed "as good as new" except for their new braying sound. A 1944 Chindit veteran described the nonvocal mules as having a "voice like the gasping of a water-starved tap going on and on with decreasing pressure until ending at last with a prolonged rasping sigh." (Cooper, 139; Essin, 176; Gardiner, 78)

The army mules had difficulty crossing big rivers. Equines swim very well, but many had never done it before and refused to try. In some cases motorboats had to drag them into the water and across. A messenger dog named Judy learned to help mules cross rivers by swimming alongside and directing their heads toward the correct side of the river. Another problem for the animals was not the fear of swimming but the loads on their backs during the transit. Lazy or tired men did not unload the mules before dragging them across the streams, and many animals drowned. (Essin, 184–86)

In 1944 the Americans started a Burma offensive under the overall command of General "Vinegar Joe" Stilwell and the direct local command of Gen. Frank Merrill. The 5307th Composite Unit (provisionally) became better known as Merrill's Marauders. Stilwell insisted on only mules, no horses, saying, "Mules are dependable and steady while horses are all prance, fart, and no sense." The Marauders planned on getting 700 mules, but one of the two transport ships fell victim to torpedoes in the Arabian Sea, killing 340 mules. They accepted 360 Australian horses (called Walers), hardy animals, instead. Merrill's men never did bother cutting the vocal cords, saying that the animals were always too exhausted to bray. On one occasion, a mule saved the day. A Japanese infiltrator was sneaking into an American camp by hiding behind a mule and walking it along. Almost to his target, the mule slowed, and impatiently the spy used a bayonet to poke the animal to continue. The mule berserked loudly, and the infiltrator was captured. When the hard campaign ended, all the horses had died, and only 41 mules remained. (Essin, 177–78; Livingston and Roberts, 165)

The other major role of mules in the CBI Theater came in China. The U.S. Army and Air Force provided munitions and help to the Chinese throughout World War II to keep the Japanese busy in China. In just three months—December 1944 through February 1945—the United States packed 2,500 mules into C-47 cargo planes for the famous high-altitude flight over "the Hump," the tall Himalayas. The planes could carry four to six mules each, tied to the walls and standing on plywood with tarps and straw. (Livingston and Roberts, 35, 167)

On the Ledo-Burma Road, a system was designed to allow six or seven mules to carry a 1,300-pound, 75-millimeter mortar gun, with other mules carrying ammunition. (Essin, 179)

As the Japanese retreated, by May 1945, there was no longer the need for so many mules in the Allied armies. One detachment of 900 animals was ordered to march across the Himalaya Mountains to China, on foot. In August 1945, as the war ended, the mules were getting sick and exhausted from the march, and so orders came for the animals to be shot. The beasts were led to a ravine and shot in the head, toppling into the valley below. The official reasoning was that "disease was spreading," but in reality they just could not be transported anywhere useful. Thousands of left-over mules at the remount depot in India were given to other countries to use. Only 125 sick animals remained at the depot; these were shot, with a farewell rifle volley fired over their grave out of respect. (Essin, 187–88; Livingston and Roberts, 169–70)

In 1946, some tests were done to see how mules could handle high-altitude flights, presumably to see if they could be quickly transported to distant battlefields. At 12,000 feet the mules were doing fine, but by 18,000 feet they were reacting badly to the altitude. In 1949, perhaps just to get

Mule 08K0

The long journeys of one U.S. Army mule came to light during the Korean War. When the Chinese Communists drove the Nationalist forces out of the mainland, many American-donated mules that had been flown over the Hump (the Himalayas) were captured. The Communists later sent some of the animals to Korea for the conflict. Mule number 08K0 had worked in Burma during World War II, flew to China, and then was recaptured by U.S. Army troops in Korea. The soldiers named him Francis, and he became the "prototype" for the later television series "Francis the Talking Mule." (Livingston and Roberts, 35, 225–26) rid of them, the U.S. Army sent 12,000 mules to Greece for use in fighting Communists. The world's armies again abandoned most mule-training programs, believing that helicopters and trucks would end the need for the animals. (Livingston and Roberts, 36; Essin, 190, 192)

On December 15, 1956, at Fort Carson, Colorado, the U.S. Army deactivated the last two operational mule units. The 35th Quartermaster Pack Company and Battery A of the 4th Field Artillery Pack Battalion were represented by two mules, 583R and 9YLL, also known as Trotter and Hambone. "Trotter, an Army mule mascot from 1957 to 1972, came from Fort Carson, Colorado, where he was famous as the only mule ever known to have mastered four gaits—walk, pace, canter, and trot—and to maintain a gait for eight hours, or about 50 miles. He was the last serial-numbered

This Missouri mule named Shrapnel worked in Southeast Asia in World War II. (Courtesy National Archives.)

Army mule, with the number tattooed on his ear and on the inside of his lower lip. Retired from West Point to a farm in Otisville, New York, Trotter was about 51 years old when he died in December, 1981." (Essin, 1; Ruthven, 267)

The British have continued to use mules, sporadically, for various small conflicts around the world. From 1952 to 1956 the British mules carried loads for soldiers through the Aberdare Range of Kenya against the Mau Mau tribe, working at an altitude of 10,000–12,000 feet. At this high altitude, their loads were reduced to 100 pounds, and they got a little energy boost in their rations: a spot of rum in their grain. British operations in Cyprus in 1955 also included animal transporters. Though mules are no longer officially a part of the British military, British did use the animals in 1973 against Arab rebels in Oman. (Sutton and Walker, 206–15)

The famous Democrat lawmaker Charles Wilson worked hard to keep the Soviets from taking over Afghanistan in the 1980s and helped to supply the rebels with some 1,500 mules flown in 747s from Pakistan. After the war, in 1987, Wilson said that "the mules have been absolutely vital" in driving out the Soviets. (Livingston and Roberts, 230–31)

Austria still uses pack mules for mountain patrols, but the hardy mule has largely vanished from the armies of the world. (DiMarco, 354)

8

Sea Lions and Dolphins

Most animals used in human warfare have been land dwellers, because a majority of conflicts were fought on land. For centuries, military leaders dreamed of finding sea creatures that could assist in naval warfare.

Ancient peoples encountered marine mammals for only brief periods of time. The Roman writer Pliny told of a famous dolphin near Carthage in North Africa that would socialize with bathers and allow people to ride on its back. Until the 20th century, humans did not spend enough time in the water to form relationships with sea animals to train them. In the last century, *Homo sapiens* began to form close ties with marine mammals and train them for naval operations. (Wood, 11)

Most studies of military history view the work of the U.S. and Soviet navies in the late 1950s and early 1960s as the pioneering work in this area. However, an almost-forgotten trial in Great Britain, with sea lions, precedes those dolphin experiments by 50 years.

In the early years of World War I, Britain found itself in desperate straits due to the success of German submarine warfare. U-boats sank commerce vessels and warships with regularity, choking off vital supplies. In the days before sonar, submarines were very difficult to detect. The Board of Invention and Research turned to the British public for suggestions on methods of locating enemy subs. One clever plan, proposing the use of seagulls, is discussed in chapter 12. The idea of using rowboats to patrol the coastlines, with swimmers wielding hammers with which to smash in periscope lenses, was rejected. The suggestion that came closest to success was from a Joseph Woodward. Woodward gave popular shows in music halls using sea lions. He volunteered to train his animals to find U-boats. (Wilson, "Sea Lions," 430–32; Gardiner, 107–8)

Joseph Woodward took three animals for the naval training. It seemed logical that sea lions should be able to detect submarines. The unknown element, and key to success or failure, was whether a sea lion could find a submarine and then communicate the vessel's approximate position to the navy.

Woodward's plan was to teach the sea lions to locate a submarine sound and reward them with food snacks. Food is the main ingredient of positive reinforcement work in marine mammal training. In pools 20 to 40 feet deep, Woodward taught the sea lions to signal the source of the underwater sounds. As a reward, they received fish. The pool trials were a success.

Next, the sea lions moved to Lake Bala in Wales: four miles long and almost a mile wide. At first the animals feared the sounds made deep in the lake by naval simulator machines: the three creatures literally leaped out of the water in a panic. Over time the sea lions became accustomed to the faux submarine noises. For more realistic experiments, the navy finally moved the tests into the English Channel.

In the Channel, several problems cropped up. The sea lions were easily distracted by non-submarine sounds; they could not swim fast enough to keep up with moving subs; and they could not hear slow-moving or stationary subs. The Admiralty canceled the program. The convoy system of sending packs of vessels together for protection worked well enough to reduce losses substantially. The brief dalliance of the British navy with marine mammals in World War I long preceded any other Western programs of that type. (Wilson, "Sea Lions," 434–35, 442–43; Gardiner, 107–8)

The Swedish navy may have attempted to train dolphins to locate enemy submarines during World War II, but only rumors exist about that program. In 1946 a curator at the Miami Zoo proposed the revolutionary idea that dolphins used sonar, or echolocation, to navigate underwater. He was later proven right. Dolphin calls "originate in special air sacs in the dolphin sinuses. The sounds are then focused in a sort of tunnel through the melon, the bulbous reservoir of fats and oils atop the dolphin's head. The dolphin points and shoots a volley of sound waves at whatever it is trying to see. The waves bounce off the target, and the returning echoes hit an acoustic window of thin bone in the dolphin's protruding lower jaw. The sound travels along the jawbones to another fat deposit at the base of the jaw, and then to the middle ear. Eventually the sound is translated into a three-dimensional picture in the brain." (Lubow, 125; Benyus, 307)

The U.S. Navy acquired its first dolphin in the late 1950s, hoping to improve torpedo performance by studying hydrodynamics. The movements of the dolphin, along with mucus from its eyes and a layer of oily skin cells that reduce drag on its body, enable the animal to move at almost 20 miles per hour. At first, the navy sought only scientific data, but by 1964 dolphins were being trained for specific practical tasks. (Gardiner, 108; Benyus, 300–301; Wood, 126–27)

Because sea lions, dolphins, and small whales were used for similar operations over the last 50 years, the rest of this chapter will treat the subject more topically than chronologically.

Diving work presents many difficulties for humans. Man is ill-equipped to function below the surface of the water. He can hold his breath for only a few minutes. His muscles and body structure are designed not for swimming but for walking and running. . . . Even with flippers a diver's swimming speed is only about two knots for short distances. Below 30 feet, a diver using conventional scuba gear risks the bends unless he limits the length of his dives or returns to the surface by stages so that he decompresses slowly. Below 150 feet, a diver has about five minutes of working time if he wishes to return to the surface directly, without decompressing, and according to Navy decompression tables he cannot safely make another such dive for 12 hours. (Wood, 125)

While human abilities are limited under the water, dolphins and other sea mammals swim swiftly and dive deeply. The bottlenose dolphin can hold its breath for six to seven minutes, while some whales submerge for over an hour. (Wood, 126)

The first complex task learned by navy dolphins was to help human divers by carrying tools and supplies up and down to Sea Lab II at a depth of 200 feet. Tuffy succeeded as the first navy sea mammal to work in the open ocean, in 1965. (Leinwand; La Puzza)

Tuffy and his companions soon learned greater tasks. The training process begins by using hunger (or food-drive) as a tool. The human trainer hand-feeds the animals and becomes its trusted leader. Though the trainer can use voice commands, hand and arm signals are better ways of giving orders to the creature. The dolphin learns to push buttons or perform simple tasks for rewards of fish. Gradually the tasks become more complex. San Diego Bay is the dolphin's final home, as he or she prepares to work in the open sea with a trainer. The animals learn to follow the trainer's boat and to jump aboard (on a wet mat) when ordered. To call the creature back to the boat, a pinging noise-device is lowered into the water. Veteran dolphins or sea lions may live in pens with less experienced animals to help them learn more quickly. Tuffy and dolphins like him graduated to complex operations, including the locating of mines and retrieving dropped munitions. (Lubow, 117–19, 148; Presnell, 26)

Dolphins and porpoises are basically small whales that use sonar for precise sensing of their environments. Sea lions see better in low-light and underwater situations than human divers, but perhaps no creatures can see as precisely as dolphins. SONAR is an acronym for SOund NAvigation and Ranging. Even blindfolded, a dolphin can locate a tiny vitamin pill at the bottom of a pool: experiments showed the animals detected 7.5-centimeter water-filled spheres at a range of 100 meters. The dolphin lives in a world very different from our own. A dolphin's world is probably seen only in shades of gray, with fewer and less-varied visual images than we experience. It is a world lacking odors, which, for all our own modest olfactory sense, are so important to human beings in so many ways. It is three-dimensional in a way that man's world can never be, for a dolphin can dive and rise as effortlessly as it can swim in a horizontal path. But it is a world of sounds encompassing a range and possessing a significance beyond our powers to comprehend. Using sound waves, the dolphin can sense objects hidden under sand, and they may even be able to sense the moods or stress levels of other animals in the water. A bio-acoustics expert from the University of Hawaii says that dolphins have the best sonar on this planet. They can not only find objects like mines that may or may not be buried into the seabed, but they can distinguish them from clutter such as coral rock and man-made debris. (Wood, 69, 83; Pickrell; O'Barry, 58)

With such exquisite underwater vision, marine mammals can locate mines and dropped munitions. Tuffy started learning this in the mid-1960s, and it has been a routine task for the naval marine mammal program.

When the navy searches for lost items at sea, about 90 percent of the cost involves locating the item, and only 10 percent goes toward actually raising the item from the sea floor. If a ship sinks, man-made mechanical sonar devices might locate the large object quickly. Discovering smaller objects like torpedoes and bombs is far more difficult. When properly trained, the sea lion may find the desired item in just a few minutes. Their physiology allows them to dive deeply and quickly without suffering the pressure dangers that affect human divers.

When marine mammals first located objects, they would simply lead human divers to an object. Later, the navy invented a balloon device that the animal could deploy above the object for a later mission to retrieve. One system now in use is a bite plate recovery or grabber device. Sea lions, dolphins, and a few whales have learned to bite this device. It looks something like the pincers on a soldier ant: with two curved arms reaching out to the front. When an animal presses the bite plate device against a torpedo or other object, the arms close tight against it and lock the device in place. A crane on a ship above can later reel in the object using a cable attached to the bite plate. (Lubow, 121–22, 222–23; Wood, 9; LaPuzza)

Sea lions have been used for such recovery operations down to 1,000 feet below the surface. Killer whales and pilot whales can use the grabber device at greater depths of almost 1,700 feet but have not been used for recoveries for more than 30 years.

One of the greatest obstacles to training the animals to find lost munitions was teaching them how to distinguish between important objects and mere clutter or unimportant objects that litter the sea floor. The trainees must also learn to generalize: to recognize that a torpedo is a torpedo no matter what colors are painted on its shell. (Lubow, 122)

A similar but more controversial task is using marine mammals to locate mines. Dolphins, whales, and sea lions are popular animals with people of all ages: no one wants to think of such "friendly" creatures being accidentally blown to bits. In reality, there is practically no danger of mines going off unexpectedly and harming sea creatures.

Unlike the work with retrieving dropped munitions, the marine mammals used for mine-hunting are specifically taught not to touch or even go near the objects. Even if a dolphin or sea lion bumped against a mine, however, the device would not explode. Most land mines are designed to kill humans, and thus any large animal stepping on a land mine will set it off. There are explosives intended to destroy large vehicles like trucks or tanks; these bombs would not go off with a single soldier stepping on them. Likewise, sea mines are deployed to sink ships. The creators of mines do not want sharks or orcas accidentally setting off the explosives. Sensors or devices within the mine are triggered by more specific events, like the magnetic fields disturbed by a metal hull passing above. The navy spends four to five years preparing a dolphin for mine-hunting. A Navy SEAL or other worker uses a laptop computer to map radio marker devices that the dolphin places near the mines, while human divers plant remote-controlled explosives near the mines for distant detonation. (Milloy; Presnell, 27–29)

Though dolphins have better "vision" thanks to their highly developed internal sonar, sea lions have other advantages and are easier to use for some tasks. Cost is perhaps the biggest factor, relating to the ease of maintenance and transportation. Bringing the animal to the desired location is, in itself, a large task. A dolphin lives in the water, though it can survive for hours suspended in a sling in a small tank of water, with water sponged over it to keep it cool and calm. A sea lion, on the other hand, lives naturally both in and out of the water, and simply seeks its food in the sea. In general, the U.S. Navy uses sea lions more for munitions retrieval and swimmer interdiction, while the dolphins seek mines and enemy divers. (Lubow, 222)

Another reason dolphins and sea lions are not in danger from sea mines is that, until recently, they were not hunting for loaded mines. The United States and its allied navies play war games with helicopters and ships dropping inert mines while others try to locate and disarm the fake mines. Such games prepare forces for real wartime conditions.

Because recent naval exercises are classified, many sources cite anonymous sources and unverified reports; thus their accuracy is questionable. Starting in 1998, U.S. Explosive Ordnance Disposal Mobile Unit Three began work in the Baltic Sea to help Latvia, Estonia, and Lithuania remove an estimated 30,000 underwater mines left over from the Cold War. The U.S. Navy says that the dolphins were hunting not for old mines but simply for training mines intentionally placed for the exercise. Another source says that the dolphins located 83 mines, probably the training mines, and not real explosives. The *Washington Post* claims that the dolphins failed to find any mines, and in fact one dolphin went AWOL (absent without leave) for three days. The navy, on the other hand, says that Baltic waters were not salty enough, so the animals could remain in the water for only a few hours at a time. In 2001 through 2004 the dolphins worked to clear practice mines off the coast of Norway and Denmark during three exercises called Blue Game. The navy says these were just practice mines, though one newspaper source claimed they were looking for 80,000 World War II mines dropped by the Nazis. The U.S. Navy will not provide details but says that the dolphins were very effective at locating practice mines and would be equally skilled at finding real explosives. (Linden, 113; Pickrell; LaPuzza; "Dolphins Find")

Caring for dolphins while on maneuvers, far from their pens in California or Hawaii, is a complicated project requiring the work of many sailors. If plans include remaining at a location for many days or weeks, the navy can set up shipboard inflatable pools inside a large vessel. The pools are large enough for the dolphin to swim around, and have filtered, temperature-controlled water, reducing the danger of bacterial infections or chemical exposure. Amphibious transport vessels like the U.S.S. *Tarawa* can partially submerge their lower deck. This has enabled the dolphins in the Persian Gulf to deploy much more easily. The dolphin jumps out of its pool on to a beaching mat, which is then placed in a small boat, carrying the animal to the sea where it slides off of the beaching mat. They are returned to the ship in the same manner. The most recent invasion of Iraq, to overthrow Saddam Hussein, brought dolphins to seek mines. In 2003 as the allies sought to bring humanitarian aid to the port city of Umm Qasr, numerous mines were found in the passage. The navy dolphins worked with divers to clear at least six devices from the waters of the Kwhar Abd Allah river. The U.S. Navy officially has no comment regarding how many of the mines were found directly by the dolphins, though civilian sources estimate between 3 and 22. The navy will not reveal the names of the animals used during deployments, but two of the dolphins are believed to be Makai and Tacoma, both bottlenose dolphins. Makai and Tacoma placed markers or electronic receiver devices near the mines so that human divers could later dispose of the devices. Another source names Kahili and eight other dolphins as working to clear the passage to Umm Qasr. An undesirable side effect of dolphin deployment to the Middle East was the suspicion of enemy nations about the animals. One Internet discussion group claims that sailors aboard Iranian patrol boats machine-gunned every dolphin they saw, fearing that American animals were laying mines and spying with cameras. (LaPuzza; Milloy; Gardiner, 110; Denega, 31–33; Gasperini, 28–29; Silvers; Puck)

The earliest publicity black eye for the U.S. Navy Marine Mammal Program came in 1966 through a piece of journalistic conjecture printed in a major newspaper. A reporter saw a brief video of Tuffy working in the open sea, and then heard about a conference where a naval scientist mentioned that dolphins' acute sonar abilities might be able to distinguish between metals. The reporter decided that dolphins might be learning to distinguish between Soviet and American ship metals, and then they might plant mines on enemy ships. Readers of the article were outraged, believing the navy was creating suicide bombers. Angry letters flowed in from all over the world. In reality, the idea is outlandish. Even if dolphins could correctly distinguish between Soviet ship hulls and allied ship hulls, would naval commanders really trust the animals to attach powerful explosives to vessels? One mistake could sink an expensive warship and kill many allied sailors. (Lubow, 211–14; Cooper, 210)

The next imaginative worry for the American public regarding U.S. Navy mammals involved nuclear weapons. Dolphins, sea lions, and whales had learned to recover munitions that had fallen into the sea. In 1976 a scientist claimed that the CIA and the navy used dolphins to retrieve a nuclear bomb lost near Puerto Rico. Soon, a better version came out, purporting that the navy trained orcas to drag nuclear weapons onto enemy beaches. Using whales to tow hydrogen bombs to enemy territory is a silly idea. By the late 1960s such weapons could be sent by missiles or dropped from bombers or brought by submarines: the killer whale offers no advantage to these delivery platforms. Orcas and beluga whales were acquired in 1968 for the navy training programs, though never in large numbers like dolphins or sea lions. (Cooper, 210; Lubow, 123–24; Johnson, William)

Only one Canadian newspaper cited named sources, claiming that during the Vietnam War, the U.S. Navy used dolphins to plant mines on Vietcong piers. The diver, an ex–Navy SEAL named Ken Woodal, says that the dolphins were taken close to their targets in small boats, then

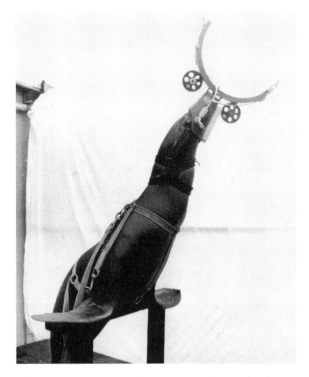

U.S. Navy sea lion with recovery device for lost ordnance, 1971. (Courtesy National Archives.)

planted the explosives using detachable moorings, thus returning safely to their handlers. The navy denies that its cetaceans have ever been used to plant explosives. (Helvarg)

The other accusation with a small amount of documentation, though unproven, is that some naval marine mammals killed enemy divers. During the Vietnam War, five dolphins searched the waters around the Cam Ranh Bay army ammunition pier for enemy divers. According to the U.S. Navy, the animals would locate a potential enemy diver and lead sailors to the intruder for capture. Critics claim that the dolphins actually killed the enemy divers. Dr. Michael Greenwood says that the Swimmer Nullification Program had dolphins wearing knives on their snouts and fins to cut up enemy frogmen, or the dolphins used hypodermic needles, killing some 40 Vietcong divers, and also killing two U.S. sailors by accident.

Zak, a 375-pound California sea lion, swims near some pier-side ships during one of many training swims taking place in the Central Command AOR. (Courtesy U.S. Navy.)

The navy denies any such lethal training. In the recent Gulf War, the navy was pleased at the fearful reaction of the local populace when they learned that navy dolphins would patrol the shipping lanes. In other words, disinformation that serves to reduce potential threats may be welcome, even if the dolphins had no deadly intentions against swimmers. If enemy divers feared the dolphins or sea lions, they might stay out of the water.

The U.S. Navy has publicly demonstrated two marine mammal systems. The Swimmer Defense System uses dolphins to mark enemy divers with a floating beacon device, then brings in boats and men for further investigation or capture. The Swimmer Interdiction Security System (SISS) uses sea lions to deploy a grabbing device to a diver's leg. So two systems may be used, with dolphins locating and marking swimmers or divers, followed by a sea lion to attach a leg clamp to the intruder. These systems are now being implemented at the Bangor, Washington, base for Trident submarines. Such complex systems were not used at more public security events, such as the 1996 Republican National Convention in San Diego. Here dolphins worked with their handlers and the Secret Service to ensure the safety of the waterline near the convention center. (Linden, 110–12; Johnson, William; Gardiner, 109; Silvers; LaPuzza)

The popular public image of marine mammals is distorted by wishful thinking and Hollywood portrayals of dolphins as harmless creatures, incapable of violence. In fact, studies from recent years show that many dolphins aggressively attack and kill smaller dolphins, sometimes without apparent reason. That is not to say that dolphins should be thought of as murderous, just to say that training a dolphin to be aggressive would not be entirely against its abilities or nature. (Grandin, 150–52)

The U.S. Navy trained a few orcas in the 1960s and 1970s. (Courtesy National Archives.)

Zak, a 375-pound California sea lion, leaps back into the boat following harbor patrol training. (Courtesy U.S. Navy.)

As for the swimmer-detection efforts of the U.S. Navy, an interesting distinction for species' deployability or usefulness has been found. Dolphins do not like working in shallow water with shadows (under piers and docks), though harbors are not a problem, as in 1987 when they protected the U.S.S. *La Salle* near Bahrain. Sea lions, on the other hand, naturally gravitate to shallow waters and piers. Sea lions easily comb the shallows. The navy became concerned when terrorist chatter indicated that divers might try to attach explosives to the hulls of ships in the Middle East. Sea lions deployed for the first time to a war zone in 2003. They were tasked with protecting ships and docks in Bahrain against divers, representing Space and Naval Warfare Systems Center Pacific in San Diego. One of the animals, named Zachary, also clowns around for photographers and for fish treats when not on duty. (LaPuzza; Leinwand; Sullivan)

Some of the more radical ideas attributed to the U.S. Navy marine mammals may have come from information leaked about Soviet parallel programs. Since the fall of the Soviet Union, more information has come out about these experiments, but it is difficult to prove any of the claims. The Soviets captured hundreds of dolphins in the Black Sea in 1956 for training.

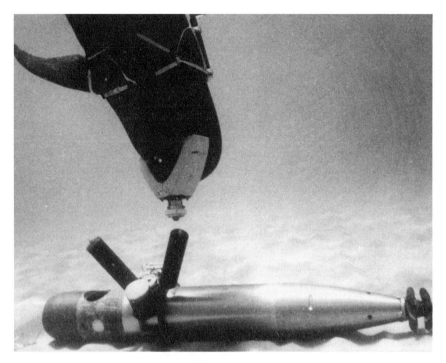

Pilot whale gets fish snack training to find torpedoes and ordnance, taken 1972. (Courtesy National Archives.)

Richard O'Barry says that the Soviets trained these dolphins not only to find stray missiles but also to plant mines and kill enemy divers. Doug Cartlidge of the British Whale and Dolphin Conservation Society wrote that 300 dolphins died in tests as suicide bombers, presumably as sort of a poor man's torpedo. He saw a secret facility at Sevastopol with models of dolphin parachute harnesses for dropping the animals out of helicopters to attack their targets. A History Channel documentary, *Inside the Soviet Military Machine*, claimed that dolphins were trained by traumatic methods, such as draining water out of their pools, food deprivation, and isolation tanks. A Soviet trainer named Boris Zhurid made several remarkable claims to Soviet newspapers. Zhurid says that his dolphins and one beluga whale were trained at a Pacific island naval base to attack enemy frogmen with harpoons, and to carry mines to enemy ships as kamikaze torpedoes. Their whole operation moved to a station in the Crimea in 1991. (Kohut and Sweet, 86; Linden, 111–12; Silvers; BBC)

With the fall of the Soviet Union, the main Sevastopol base shut down, along with the Russian Black Sea Fleet. To keep the marine mammals alive, the trainers opened a tourist and recreational center for paying customers to swim with the animals. The dolphins' names include Diana and Vakh; the administrators are all ex-navy personnel, and they deny that the animals were ever trained in dangerous or lethal missions. (DeMares, 47; Piper; BBC)

Not all of the animals remained in the Black Sea. Desperate scientists needing money and homes hired or sold their marine mammals to foreign powers. Iran, for instance, purchased 27 animals including dolphins and a few walruses, sea lions, seals, and a beluga whale. They were transported from Sevastopol to Iran by Russian military transport aircraft in late

Porpoise takes a line from experimental rescue reel for lost diver rescue system, Pasadena, California, 1968. (Courtesy National Archives.)

Staff Sgt. Justin Roberts escorts K-Dog, a bottlenose dolphin belonging to Commander Task Unit (CTU) 55.4.3, in a Rigid Hull Inflatable Boat (RHIB) back to the well deck and holding areas aboard the USS *Gunston Hall* (LSD 44) in the Persian Gulf. (Courtesy U.S. Navy.)

1999 or early 2000. Boris Zhurid said that Iran had built a nice aquarium and that Russian scientists would help Iran to continue research with the animals. The price of a trained ex-Soviet dolphin was about $60,000. (Sullivan; Kohut and Sweet, 86)

As of late 2009, the U.S. Navy Marine Mammal Program reports keeping about 80 dolphins, 28 sea lions, and one beluga whale. Though animal-rights organizations have claimed that the animals are mistreated, repeated naval investigations have dismissed the claims. Over the decades, with hundreds of thousands of opportunities to escape during open-sea exercises, fewer than 10 animals have left on unplanned excursions. Some have gone away for a couple of days, but then returned.

Critics say that the only reason the dolphins do not escape more frequently is because they are forced to wear a device that would cause them to starve. The navy uses a strip of Velcro called an Anti-Foraging Device, wrapped around the dolphin's snout. Since most mammal training involves positive reinforcement by the use of food fish, the handlers do not want the dolphins eating a lot of wild fish. The band is not tight: it is intentionally loose so that the animals can still eat small reward fish thrown by naval handlers. A spokesman for the navy says that this neoprene strap has a dissoluble link so that the dolphin would be free to eat within a few hours, and would not starve, if it did not return. (LaPuzza; Pickrell; Hoff; Gardiner, 109; Lubow, 222)

Replacements have not been wild-captured since 1989; dolphins have bred successfully in captivity in the naval program, and sea lions are purchased from Sea World in Orlando, Florida. Each dolphin has an estimated working life of 20 years.

Every few years, some administrators predict the end of the U.S. Navy Marine Mammal Program, saying that mechanical submersibles will soon supplant dolphins and sea lions as mine-detectors and munitions-retrievers. Thus far, robotic submarines have not been effective at replacing the tasks performed by naval mammals. Dolphins and sea lions are among the few remaining animals to work for the military. (LaPuzza; Silvers)

9

Oxen

The animal we know as the ox in Western countries is called a bullock in Asian lands. The ox is a bovine creature, and most domestic oxen are castrated males. Males are often chosen for work because their larger size gives them more strength for pulling loads. Oxen were probably the first beasts of burden to be domesticated by humans, thousands of years before Christ. Before the invention of the wheel, circa 3500 BC in Mesopotamia, pairs of oxen pulled carts that resembled sleds, designed to slide over the ground. With wheels, heavier loads could be moved more easily. (Hodges, 83; Hyams, 19; Kelekna, 45–46)

Ox-drawn carts and wagons spread quickly throughout the world. With solid wooden wheels of great weight, the carts moved very slowly, at less than two miles per hour. A pole and yoke harness connected a pair of bullocks to the wagon. With the domestication of horses and mules, people were eager to use the faster animals to speed up their carts, but this failed, early on. The problem was not the horses or mules themselves, but the structure of the yoke. For a thousand years, the yoke frame around the necks of oxen worked perfectly. It never occurred to anyone that the favored yoke shape, fine for oxen, was choking the horses and mules. The yoke circle reduced the power of the slender-necked horses by cutting off their air supply: the harder and faster they pulled, the less they could breathe. Only a newly designed collar system would enable faster creatures to pull wagons. (Kelekna, 45–46; Smith, 6)

Persians used teams of 16 oxen in four lines to pull gigantic 24-foot-tall mobile towers. Twenty archers could stand on top along with commanders, with an excellent view of the battlefield or city under siege. (Gabriel and Boose, 231–32)

The invention of the contoured collar harness and the iron horseshoe enabled horses to bring new strength and speed to the wheeled cart. Horses can work two hours longer than an ox each day, with 50 percent more traction force. "Thus, the ox could move a thousand-pound load only ten miles per day, while the horse team could move the same load thirty-two miles per day on half the food." Farmers increased crop yields, and all of human civilization grew. Though horses gradually replaced oxen in most areas of the world, many people could not afford horses. As the various empires created chariots for rushing about battlefields, horses were too valuable for relegation to farm work. Peasants and civilians continued to plod along with mules and oxen for thousands of years, even into modern times. Few armies could avoid using oxen, since someone or something had to bear the cargo trains of supplies that fed the soldiers. The first to succeed in dropping the bullocks from baggage trains was Philip of Macedon, circa 350 BC. He prohibited the use of oxen and wagons because they slowed down Greek armies; they used mules and pack horses instead. (Kelekna, 334–35; Gabriel and Boose, 135, 161)

Occasionally, brilliant tacticians like Hannibal of Carthage used oxen in other capacities than simple cargo-hauling. In 218 BC, Hannibal stampeded a large herd of cattle at a Roman force, driving them back. Actually he may have learned this tactic from his own foes: 10 years before, in Spain, the tribes used oxcarts full of burning materials to cause panic in the Carthaginian lines. The Romans used oxcarts to carry cargo for their legions, until Gaius Marius replaced carts with pack mules and horses in the century before Christ. (Mayor, *Greek,* 188, 203; Gabriel and Boose, 359)

During the Middle Ages, an ox cost only one-fourth as much as a horse to maintain, and the people loved the ability to eat the cow if it got old. (Edwards, 161)

In AD 1453 the Turks took Constantinople largely with the help of an 8.5-meter bombard cannon that was hauled by 60 oxen, lobbing half-ton balls from a kilometer away. Bullocks were viewed by the British as better than horses for cart-pulling on rough roads or places without roads, with an average speed of just over two miles per hour. Their prime working age was six, and they needed little specialized care. (Man, 186; Harfield, 25–26)

During the American Revolution, as Gen. George Washington hoped to attack the large British garrison in Boston, he awaited large cannons that had been captured at Fort Ticonderoga. Eighty teams of oxen dragged the big guns for over 300 miles, and one cold day in January they were able to pull sledges across the frozen Hudson River. Three hundred sixty oxcarts carried fortifications to the hills that helped force the British to abandon the city by sea. (Lengel)

The British Empire expanding into southern Asia needed lots of bullocks. The army of the time was "hopelessly overencumbered," as the officers and even enlisted men thought nothing of bringing along their wives, children, and miscellaneous possessions on military campaigns. Col. Arthur Wellesley, later known as Wellington, hated this ungainly mob that followed his troops everywhere. In 1799, his 31,000 soldiers had 150,000 followers with 120,000 oxen, camels, horses, mules, and elephants, marching in a pack some three miles wide and seven miles long. The vast number of animals forced the group to take a zigzag course when marching, just to find enough fodder. Wellington wrote about the poor treatment of the oxen, in particular. "A bullock that goes one day without his regular food loses a part of his strength; if he does not get it on the second day, he may not lose the appearance of being fit for service, but he is entirely unable to work: and after these animals have once lost their strength and condition, so much time elapses before they recover that they become a burden upon the army. . . . The drivers hired . . . are entirely unaccustomed to the care of cattle." As the 19th century progressed, trains became a major mode of transport, and bullocks ran in panic from the great iron beasts. (Sutton and Walker, 24, 30; Hamid, 61)

Wellington insisted that all unnecessary baggage be left behind so the army could move faster, and while he remained in India this discipline worked. Within a few decades, the Afghan War of 1839–1842 showed a return to the old, undisciplined ways. The British forces tried to march a thousand miles through hard terrain to take Kabul. Thousands of horses and bullocks died with thousands of camels on the journey. (Sutton and Walker, 24, 41)

Wellington became embroiled in the Napoleonic Wars in Western Europe in the early 19th century. The British landed to help the Spanish against a French invasion. The Portuguese oxcarts used fixed axles that made horrible noises. Wellington had carts redesigned to reduce the noise, but did his best to transfer the loads to mules and horses to avoid wagons altogether. Unfortunately, supplies were so scarce in the Spanish expedition that hundreds of the horses died. (ibid., 32)

In South Africa during the 1834 Kaffir War, the British designed long 10-oxen wagons for pulling heavy loads. They worked well, but moved very slowly. (ibid., 40)

The history of the United States includes the slow but steady ox as a key figure. Settlers traveling to the unexplored west preferred oxen to horses because of their greater endurance and ability to last longer on simple prairie grasses. The U.S. Army, though preferring mules, always had some oxcarts in tow. Occasionally an officer would propose using beef cattle to carry baggage so that the animals doubled as "meat on the hoof" and cargo carriers, but this never worked. In the Mexican War under Gen. Zachary Taylor in the 1846, the army had 307 wagons, 84 of them pulled by bullocks. When requested reinforcements marched toward the Army of the West, almost three-fourths of the 20,000 animals were oxen. They were marched so hard and relentlessly by inexperienced teamsters, over 900 miles in 50 days, that many died of starvation and exhaustion. (Steiner, 157; Prucha, 33; Essin, 17–18, 28–29)

The U.S. Army usually sent long wagon trains of supplies from east to west without escorts, and thus they were very tempting targets for the Native Americans. Near the Arkansas River, one raid drove off 80 yoke of oxen from the main wagon train and then "wantonly and cruelly slaughtered them for amusement." By the 1850s the army began to show preference for mules over oxen, because the mules were faster, were easier to herd, and needed less water. Oxen could still pull heavier loads, but other factors all favored the mule. Of course, mules were not always available or cheap. As the U.S. 2nd Cavalry moved toward Texas to stop Comanche raids, a harsh winter killed three men and 113 oxen pulling their supplies. (Essin, 35, 55–56; Arnold, 71)

The Union army used oxen during the Civil War, perhaps a couple of thousand, compared to hundreds of thousands of mules. General Buford used heavy wagons drawn by oxen in a spring 1864 offensive through Tennessee. (Essin, 70; Jacobs, 103)

One place where oxen remained an important part of military supply trains was South Africa. Difficult terrain and a troublesome climate for horses meant that bullocks did much of the cargo work. On the Natal frontier, long trains of lumbering oxwagons were the only way to supply British troops. Whenever rains created muddy conditions, the massive 16-ox cart would have another 16 oxen hooked on, so that the 32 beasts could lunge ahead even on slopes. Cargo trains like this could snake across the terrain for many miles. (Snook, 25)

During World War I in East Africa, the British sought to fight the Germans, but the biting, disease-transmitting tsetse fly hindered their supply trains. The flies killed 28,000 oxen and mules in one campaign alone. (Sutton and Walker, 109)

A Stubborn Ox

During a war between Greece and Turkey in the early 1920s, journalist Arnold Toynbee followed a Greek army in retreat, writing this in the *Manchester Guardian* on April 5, 1921: "As I watched, one of two oxen yoked to a cart just below me lay down deliberately in the road, and the whole file of carts, guns, and lorries halted behind him for miles. It was a dramatic act on the part of the ox, for there, far away on the road zigzagging down into the plain from Nazyf Pasha, I could see the dust raised by the Turkish cavalry as they came down at last in pursuit. In some circumstances, an ox may decide the fate of an army, but the driver of this ox was more than a match for him. After kicking and prodding the animal with no result whatever, he stooped down, picked up its tail, and, to my amazement, started carefully parting the hairs. Then, assuming a ferocious expression, he dug his teeth into the tail flesh. Perhaps this was an *ultima ratio* for dealing with oxen which has been handed down in the man's family for generations. Anyhow it worked. The ox got up with alacrity and walked on, the whole column followed." (Toynbee, 99)

In 1935, as the German Army began its rapid buildup, so many horses were purchased for cavalry and supply trains that peasants in Germany and Italy could no longer afford or find horses. They were forced to go back to oxen as farm workers and draft animals. (Dinardo, 10)

The World War II Asian theater provided many opportunities for oxen to work for the armies of Japan, Britain, and the United States. Oxen were not an official part of the quartermaster's lists of provisions; the soldiers simply appropriated local bullocks and carts and put them to use. One instance is the small guerrilla movement in the Philippines against the Japanese Army, led by U.S. colonel Ed Ramsey. Carabao, similar to oxen, were used by many of the rebels to pull carts and carry wounded men through the dense jungles. U.S. marines used oxen to pull heavy loads in Saipan, Marianas Islands. (Ramsey and Rivele, 131; Gardiner, 77)

Bullocks have never received any real recognition for their work among humans, either civilian or military. The "dumb ox" does a lot of work without much glory.

10

Llamas

Four types of camelids, relatives of the Bactrian and dromedary camels of Asia, dwell in the Andes Mountains of South America. The guanaca and vicuna are thought to be the ancestors of the domesticated llama and alpaca. No one knows the exact time period when llamas first became domesticated, though 1000 BC is the most common guess. Of the four types of camelids, only the llama worked for the military. Though the llama is much smaller than the camel and has no hump, the invading Spaniards immediately dubbed the animals "the little camels of the Andes." The llama has a head like a camel's, a two-toed foot (not cloven), large eyes, a split nose, and a harelip. (Conklin, 13, 27; Hyams, 131, 136; Von Hagen, 237–38)

The llama stands about four feet tall at the shoulder, and like a camel, can work for days without food and water. The animals can carry no more than a hundred pounds each because of their relatively small size. Despite the small load capacity of the llama, the animal was much used for centuries because there were no other draft animals available. Further, American natives never invented the wheel. Without carts, all loads were carried by human or llama workers. Like the camel, the llama has a temper and attitude. If overloaded, the animal kneels down and refuses to move. If badgered, the llama launches a glob of spittle at the offender. (Bleeker, 36–37; McIntyre, 739; Conklin, 27–32)

One reason the llama excels as a pack animal is because it can walk about 20 miles per day at high elevations, even above 17,000 feet, where the air is thin. They move at a slow, steady, sure-footed pace, in a single line. They rarely make noise, except for a low humming sound when contented. Because llamas bear a thick, matted wool, they need no saddles to protect their backs. The handlers simply tie on a load with soft rope. Since nothing but moss grows at such high altitudes, the handlers must carry some food for the animals, but at lower heights the llamas graze on pretty much anything, including Ichu grass that no other animals will touch. The handler uses hissing sounds to order them: a sharp hiss means "stop"; a different tone of hiss means "come to me." (Kelekna, 382; Bleeker, 37–39; Conklin, 27–34)

When needed, the Peruvians or Incas would hold a province-wide hunt, using thousands of men to drive game to a central point. The wild predators and sickly camelids were killed. Many strong llamas were corralled for army use, while the remaining camelids were shorn for their wool and released. This sort of hunt was held every fourth year, to allow for populations to grow and their wool to become thick again. As for the number of llamas kept, it must have been vast, since one Inca army was said to use 25,000 llamas for its pack train. At times, the pasture lands were inadequate for the large numbers of beasts. Some of the animals were used as "meat on the hoof" to feed troops. Private persons were not allowed to own or hunt llamas; they belonged to the government. Young boys between the ages of 9 and 16 were the official shepherds, called "llama-michec." Small dogs were also used to keep herds from running off. The Incas believed that burying a llama fetus under one's home would bring good luck. Periodically, the Incas would hold a vast religious ceremony where a priest would cut a llama's breast open and remove its beating heart before cutting off its head. (Hyams, 23, 134; Conklin, 28–32; Kelekna, 361; McIntyre, 754, 764)

The Incas kept llamas with an excellent system of organization and a type of veterinary care. Recent historians believe that they found a "llama reconditioning center" at Cahua Marca, something like a camelid rest area, where the animals could rest and fatten after arduous journeys over the Andes. Ceramic arts suggest that the Indian domestication of the llama predates the Incas by at least a thousand years. Mummified llamas, naturally desiccated in desert terrain, still have ancient scarlet fringes that the natives hung over the llamas' eyes. These cloth coverlets helped to keep out the glare of the bright sun. The leading llama in a pack train wore copper bells, and his or her ears were often decorated with brightly colored dangling woolen streamers. (Von Hagen, 237–38; Conklin, 27–34)

Llamas carrying cargo in the high Andes of South
America. (Mary Evans Picture Library.)

Most of our historical knowledge of llamas used in the military comes
from the records of the Spanish conquistadores, because the Incas did not
have a written language. They used "quipu," a system of tying knots in
ropes, understood only by trained accountants who kept records for the
Incas. Spanish priests thought these dangling colorful ropes were some
sort of idols. Most were burned, leaving us with the records of the invaders only, and not the Incas themselves. The Incan Empire controlled Peru,
northern Chile, and parts of Bolivia and Argentina from about AD 1438 to
1533. (Von Hagen, 157; Bleeker, 11)

A civil war between rival Incan rulers left the empire weak at a bad
time, and the first visit of Europeans in 1527 started a plague of smallpox
among the Incan peoples. When Francisco Pizarro landed in 1532 looking
for gold, the Incan ruler Atahuallpa was not ready. Atahuallpa may also
have been overconfident, learning that the Spanish force included only

The llama of South America. (Courtesy John Kistler.)

180 soldiers, 37 "short-necked llamas" (horses), and some strange weapons. The horses, cannons, and crossbows would cause much devastation to the Incan armies. (McIntyre, 767; Bleeker, 130–31; Von Hagen, 276–78)

The Spaniards captured and killed Atahuallpa quickly, though his people brought a ridiculous amount of golden loot for his ransom. By 1536 the Incan armies had the Spanish under siege at Cuzco, but a counterattack sent the Incas fleeing to their stronghold Vilcabamba with llamas loaded with gold. The Spanish pursued, wanting the gold, but their horses, "whose iron shoes [could] find no purchase on the stone steps," were not happy on the treacherous mountain paths. In the end, the Spaniards sent hundreds of "loot-laden llamas" back to the coast, burdened with gold. The Spaniards destroyed the llama rest areas, enslaved the herders for mine work, and the institutional use of llamas in South America was largely forgotten and lost. (Von Hagen, 93, 102–3, 149)

Animals in Experimental and Incidental Roles

11

Bats

Probably the most unlikely animal to work for the military is the bat. Except for the infamous vampire bat, which extracts blood from other mammals, bats are rather harmless creatures. Commonly known as the "flitter mouse," bats are creatures of the night, unnoticed by most people. Most species are rather small, with four fingers spread out "like the ribs of an umbrella" to extend their wings, and the remaining fifth finger used like a hook to hang from a roof to sleep. (Adams, 138–40; Johnson, Isaac, 39)

Bats indirectly helped armies even before the 20th century. During the American Civil War, the Confederate States of America used a dozen caves in Texas to collect saltpeter for their gunpowder, while the Union fleet kept a stranglehold on southern imports. Frio Cave still has the remains of a kiln where bat guano was leached and dried to make the saltpeter. The guano that piles up in caves was used even in World War I to increase ammunition production. (Mohr, 93; Couffer, 92)

On December 7, 1941, Japan launched its surprise attack on Pearl Harbor, Hawaii. Dr. Lytle S. Adams, a surgeon and inventor from Pennsylvania, had been visiting caverns. "Now the thought flashed through my mind—couldn't those millions of bats be fitted with incendiary bombs and dropped from planes?... [T]he bats would seek shelter in inaccessible cracks and crevices above and below the surface of the ground and set off without warning a multitude of explosions and fires." Adams knew important people in Washington, DC, and so the White House and President Roosevelt personally read his proposal on January 12, 1942. His proposal said, in part, "As I vision it the millions of bats that have for ages inhabited our belfries, tunnels and caverns were placed there by God to await this hour to play their part in the scheme of free human existence, and to frustrate any attempt of those who dare desecrate our way of life. This lowly creature, the bat, is capable of carrying in flight a sufficient quantity of incendiary material to ignite a fire." The brass was open to any ideas during these early months of World War II, and leaders encouraged Adams to pursue the project. No one asked, "What about the bats?" Today, animal welfare views would disallow such a project. (Mohr, 89; Couffer, 6–7)

Dr. Adams put together a small team of scientists and specialists to begin the research and determine the logistics to make the project work. The first important questions to be answered included:

1. Where, and how, can millions of bats be captured?
2. How far can a bat fly with a small bomb?
3. Will a bat fly to dark corners where it can start fires?
4. How do you design triggers for the little bombs without endangering the aircraft?
5. How do we disperse the bats from the aircraft? (Couffer, 14)

A few men were sent to search the caves of the American southwest, looking for the best places to capture bats. They would explore 4,000 mines and caves before deciding on the best locations. Although there are large bats, like the 20-inch mastiff bat, that could carry larger bombs, these animals are scarce. It was decided to use vast numbers of tiny bats with tiny bombs rather than a few huge bats capable of carrying a whole stick of dynamite. Smaller bats also require less food, are easier to care for, and hibernate at cool temperatures. (Mohr, 89–91)

Another team including U.S. Army munitions specialists began to design the delivery system. A bomb was designed to carry 1,040 bats with their tiny incendiary explosives inside, stacked in 30-inch round trays, with cups as if to hold eggs, one tray stacked upon another. When the bomb popped open at an altitude of 1,000 feet, a parachute deployed to slow the fall of the connected trays. As air warmed the bats, the animals would awake and fly off the tray, pulling the safety pin on each of their incendiary bombs. The bats, not preferring to be outside in the sunlight, would fly to wooden buildings all over Japan, to hide in corners. Soon, their incendiary devices would ignite and start fires. The hope was that Japanese fire departments would be overwhelmed by the high number of fires and that whole towns might burn. (Mohr, 91; Couffer, 109)

The tiny, one-ounce bomb was a marvel of engineering in itself. It was an oblong nitrocellulose case filled with thickened kerosene (napalm) and a delayed-action timer designed for a four- or six-minute delay. Once ignited, the capsule produced a two-foot-long flame for eight full minutes. Members of the team started to call the creatures "bomber bats." (Brophy et al., 188; Mohr, 92)

Testing the equipment and bats proved to be more difficult than expected. The idea of cooled bats in hibernation, to awaken when the bomb opened at altitude, was easier said than done. Many bats died when they did not awake quickly enough before hitting the ground. Some bats flew quite a bit farther than expected, with a radius of up to 20 miles, jeopardizing the secrecy of the project when members had to go knocking on farmers' doors for permission to search their attics and barns for lost bats. Perhaps the biggest blunder came when the bomber bats actually wore the newly designed bombs, hanging on their chests with a surgical clip and string. Army photographers wanted some good close-up shots of the animals with their bombs. Unfortunately, the bats awakened from slumber more quickly than expected. They immediately flew to the nearby wooden buildings of the abandoned air base used for trials. Within 15 minutes the barracks, offices, hangars, and other structures were burning. Fire department crews could not be called because of the project's secrecy, so the Carlsbad Auxiliary Airfield burned to the ground. One bat took refuge under a general's car. Happily, no one was in the car when it burned and exploded. Though not planned, this incident showed that bomber bats could be an effective weapon. (Brophy et al., 188; Mohr, 92–93; Couffer, 115–20)

Project members found that the abundance of free-tailed bats at two caves in Texas made them the ideal choice for capture. The army backed out of the bat bomb project when the airbase burned, but the navy took over, leasing four caves in 1943 and assigning marines to guard them. Ney Cave was believed to hold some 20 million to 30 million bats, so in

October 1943, fences were installed to trap the bats for easier capture. The navy named its new work "Project X-Ray." (Mohr, 92)

One member of Project X-Ray sent a proposal to increase the scope of the work by including rats. He wrote that by using the same napalm bomb-clip system on the tail of a rat, the animal would scurry into holes all over Japan and start fires that way. Spies could capture local rats (not having to import bats) and wreak havoc. This imaginative proposal was ignored. (Fieser, 1–2)

Project X-Ray seemed well on its way to full-scale trials and neared deployment planning, in late 1944, when the military brass began to sour on the idea. The Pacific war against Japan was beginning to culminate, and since summer 1945 was the soonest the bats could be dropped, it was feared the war might be over by then. Perhaps the White House had more confidence in the atomic bombs of the Manhattan Project, which was entering the final stages of testing. After millions of dollars spent on bomber bats, Project X-Ray shut down in October 1944. (Brophy et al., 199; Mohr, 92)

The entertaining true story of the whole bat project can be found in the book *Bat Bomb* by Jack Couffer.

12

Mascots and Miscellaneous Creatures

Mascots

The idea of a mascot, while it can be a person or inanimate object, has largely come to be seen as the adoption of an animal as a symbol of good luck to a group or institution. Armies have frequently adopted mascots and treated them as community pets during wartime and peacetime. The creatures have included common animals like dogs and cats, and stranger beasts like a scorpion in a jar, and a goldfish in a whiskey bottle. (Kramer, 1; Cooper, 174)

The first known British regimental mascot was a goat of the Royal Welsh Fusiliers who fought at the Battle of Bunker Hill during the American Revolution. The soldiers gilded his horns and put ringlets of flowers over him. Henceforth, a goat became the traditional mascot for the group, and British kings and queens donate a new goat whenever the old one dies. The honored animal wears a silver shield on his head, naming the royal who gave him to the Fusiliers. (Kramer, 5, 13–14)

A British goose, saved from a fox in 1830 by a soldier of the Coldstream Guards, became the mascot of that group. Jacob the Goose once alerted his post to a rebel attack, and so became a hero. Later, Jacob was accidentally run over by a wagon. (Kramer, 11–12)

The American Civil War is replete with stories of mascots and pets that cheered the men of North and South.

The Confederates kept a pelican and a wild cat from Arkansas. J. E. B. Stuart's men chained a raccoon to their cannon. Stonewall Jackson's troops adopted a pig. Robert E. Lee kept a pet hen that would lay an egg under his cot most mornings. When the Battle of Gettysburg was lost, the hen went missing. Lee himself and others searched for the hen and would not leave until it was found. They found her perched on her regular wagon, ready to go. When food was running out, however, Lee's servant cooked her for dinner. (Davis, 67; Seguin, 10–11, 56–57; Williamson)

The 60th Tennessee Regiment kept a mascot rooster named Tennessee. He would keep all other roosters out of the camp and fly to the shoulders of soldiers to crow from a higher perch. At the siege of Vicksburg in 1863 he flapped and crowed whenever Union artillery shells landed in the city. Tennessee was captured when Vicksburg fell, but the rooster was set free and returned to farm life. (Morton, 508–9)

Union soldiers kept gamecocks, badgers, a squirrel, a gander, and even a bear. In 1864, the 2nd Rhode Island Volunteers adopted a pet lamb and named him Dick. The men loved Dick until they had a brief leave in Washington, DC; wanting money for booze, they sold him to a butcher. (Seguin, 10–11, 54–55)

The most famous Civil War mascot was a bald eagle. The bird was probably born in 1861 near the Flambeau River in Wisconsin, where an Indian caught it and traded it for a bag of corn. The 8th Wisconsin Volunteer Infantry adopted the eagle and named him Old Abe. James McGinnis became Abe's appointed caretaker. The men built a T-shaped perch for the bird, five feet tall with small U.S. flags on each side. Old Abe loved music and often carried a small flag in his mouth while the unit marched. Mc-Ginnis carried the perch alongside the standard-bearer with their colors. A 20-foot cord attached to a leather ring on Abe's leg kept him from flying away. (Kramer, 14–15; Catton, 33)

During a parade in St. Louis, Missouri, a crowd became hostile and called Old Abe a buzzard. The eagle broke his cord and flew to a nearby chimney, where it took 30 minutes of coaxing to bring him down. The men said he was not frightened by the mob but offended at being labeled a vulture. In later years, he no longer needed a tether and was free to roam about, though Abe always returned. Abe would fly out to grab and dine upon loose chickens. He learned to drink from a canteen by putting his head straight up and letting a soldier pour the water down his throat. Abe chuckled as if laughing at dinnertime, but he would coo like a dove when his friends came up to pet him. (Catton, 106–7)

During the Vicksburg Campaign when Generals Grant and Sherman rode by to the cheering of the men, Old Abe screamed and flapped his wings, and the generals doffed their hats to him. At Vicksburg, however, an artillery shell wounded the eagle and killed three of his human friends next to the perch. Henceforth whenever the Union soldiers lay down under artillery fire, Abe would hop down and hide too. (Catton, 106–7; Seguin, 90–91)

When the 8th Wisconsin Volunteer Infantry disbanded in the summer of 1864, Old Abe took up residence in the Madison, Wisconsin, capitol building. For dinner one day, a rooster was given to Abe. Instead of eating the bird, Abe adopted him as a friend, and they shared their roost. In 1881 a small fire in the Capitol filled the building with smoke, suffocating Old Abe. He was stuffed and mounted for a museum. (Catton, 106–7; Seguin, 90–91)

As the world descended into war in the 20th century, the French experimented with placing parrots high in the Eiffel Tower. The birds' extra-sensitive sense of hearing could detect aircraft long before any humans could hear them. However, because the parrots could not distinguish between Allied planes and German planes, the trial came to a quick end. (Cooper, 102)

Soldiers in the trenches of World War I often kept dogs and cats as mascots. Such animals could provide companionship, increase morale, and kill rats and mice. Jimmy the anteater, actually a coatimundi, lived in a trench with U.S. marines in France, but he actually had to be rescued from a gang of

Princess Patthe, mascot bear of the Canadian Light Infantry, World War I. (Courtesy John Kistler.)

20 rats. Other creatures, like canaries and mice, hung in cages in the trenches as poison-gas detectors for the troops. (Kramer, 118; Barber, 123–24)

Not all mascots were equally welcomed. The British 19th Division near Ypres acquired a baby lion named Poilu as a mascot. The animal grew quickly, and an aide had to be put in charge of finding food for the animal. Most mornings the aide would telegraph nearby allies asking for dead horses. A new general put in charge of the division did not like the lion, and he sent Poilu back to England to live in a zoo. (Gardiner, 151)

In 1915, the British sank the German cruiser *Dresden*. Once the vessel sank, a pig was found swimming amid the wreckage, and was rescued by the British ship *Glasgow*. The crew named him Tirpitz after the famous Prussian admiral, and he became the ship's mascot. In general, cats have been the best mascots for ships, because they are more attached to locations than to people, it is said. Cats also help to kill off rats and mice aboard ship. (Gardiner, 152; Cooper, 177)

As German U-boats prowled the seas around England, many strange plans arose to find and destroy the submersibles. In 1917 the British hoped to train seagulls to poop on periscopes, thus mucking up the lenses and forcing the vessels to surface for cleaning. A more clever plan was to use the ubiquitous gulls to simply locate submarines, not damage their viewing gear. A British submarine would regularly stalk the coasts; when it surfaced, crew members would toss bread into the air to feed the gulls. Eventually the birds learned to watch for the large submarine shadows and flock above, waiting for their daily bread. Then sentries on the beach would watch for flocks of gulls hovering in an area and call the location in to the British navy. If a British ship was not known to be in the region, destroyers were dispatched to hunt for U-boats. (Wilson; Cooper, 110)

The Royal Society for the Prevention of Cruelty to Animals (RSPCA) helped many military units to bring their mascots home to England after World War I. British quarantine laws required that all imported animals be kept away from other animals for six months, to ensure that foreign diseases would not plague the land. The RSPCA held the mascots for many regiments and soldiers who could not afford to pay for the six-month quarantine facility. (Kramer, 6)

In Thailand, the Japanese kept many British prisoners of war during World War II. The 2nd Gordon Highlanders had a mascot duck named

Donald. When the Japanese said the men could keep no pets, Cpl. William Gray explained that Scots worshipped ducks, so they were allowed to keep the bird. It laid 160 eggs, which supplemented the diet of sick prisoners, and in 1945 the duck returned with William Gray to Scotland. (Roberts, 40)

Aircraft crews sometimes kept a mascot. Skipper, a black Scottish terrier, belonged to a B-17 Flying Fortress crew. He was considered to be lucky. Once when the plane ditched in the sea, the men and dog survived in rubber lifeboats and were rescued for return to Hawaii. Skipper accumulated about 100,000 miles or 600 flying hours. (Dempewolff, 10–12)

The Royal Air Force 27th Squadron used a cumbersome-looking plane, the Martinside Scout. They adopted a baby Asian elephant and called the squadron the Flying Elephants. (Kramer, 120)

The U.S. Navy used its famous mascot pig "King Neptune" to sell almost $20 million in war bonds. (Kramer, 133)

Private Wojtek the Bear

The 22nd Company of the Polish Army Corps adopted a sickly brown bear cub while stationed in the Middle East in 1940. The men tried to release the animal when he was healthy, but the bear refused to leave. They named him Private Wojtek, meaning "happy warrior" in Polish. Soldier Peter Prendys took care of the bear, who entertained the soldiers by getting stuck in palm trees. The 22nd took Private Wojtek along for the invasion of Italy. The bear helped his men carry artillery shells while under fire during the Battle of Monte Cassino. After the war, Private Wojtek moved into the Edinburgh Zoo, where he remained until his death in 1963. In 2010 the city of Edinburgh unveiled a statue of Wojtek and Prendys. (*Telegraph*; Their)

Not all mascot bears were so successful. A British regiment kept a bear as a guard in the baggage train. The animal took his job too seriously, perhaps. One soldier lost an arm when he tried to steal something, and the bear killed a child who tried to steal, so the animal was shot. (Worcester, 67–68)

Miscellaneous Creatures

Clever and creative military commanders have, from time to time, used very unusual animals to aid their armies or plague enemy forces. Results have varied, but the stories can be entertaining.

Some scholars believe that the reindeer may have been the first domesticated pack animal, pulling sledges as early as 7000 BC, though that date is not widely accepted. Early pack reindeer wore saddles similar to Turk or Mongol designs among the peoples of the north, who also used the reindeer's milk. British forces used reindeer for pulling sleds full of supplies in northern Russia in 1918–1919. (Hyams, 120; Sutton and Walker, 115–18)

The Persian king Cambyses attacked Egypt in the 6th century BC. As the Egyptians were known for their worship of sacred animals, Cambyses purportedly countered the Egyptian archers by driving cats, dogs, sheep, ibexes, and other sacred creatures in front of the Persian army. The Egyptians stopped firing their arrows and artillery, leading to a Persian victory. (Mayor, *Greek,* 189–90)

Alexander the Great supposedly used sheep to deceive the enemy. His armies tied tree branches to their sheep's tails, so that when they marched the tree branches dragged on the ground. This created a lot of dust, so that Persian spies would "see" a much larger army marching than the Greeks actually possessed. Ptolemy of Egypt may have used a similar ruse against the Greek general Perdiccas. Ancient Greek myths have characters like Odysseus using poisonous stingray barbs as spear tips. Although the Greeks did use snake poisons to envenomate arrowheads, no evidence shows the actual use of stingray barbs. The Suya Indians of Brazil did fashion arrowheads from stingray barbs, in the 20th century. (Mayor, *Greek,* 75, 96–97, 189)

In 386 BC while invaders from Gaul laid siege to Rome, the attackers found a way to climb the rock mount to enter the city. Livy says the spies were so quiet that even the dogs did not hear them coming. However, the sacred geese at the temple of Juno cackled and flapped, awaking the guards, who repelled the invaders. (Lubow, 26–27)

The famous Hannibal of Carthage worked with more than just elephants in his attacks. Late in life, circa 188 BC, he led a navy in the eastern Mediterranean. His men gathered snakes from their territories, put them in jars, and then catapulted the jugs of reptiles onto the larger fleet of King

Eumenes of Pergamum. Hannibal's navy won the battle. Mahmud would imitate this strategy some 1,500 years later by using catapults to heave sacks of snakes into an enemy fortress. (Mayor, *Greek,* 169, 184–89)

One story of Genghis Khan claims that during his invasion of China in 1211, his troops caught a thousand local cats and 10,000 local swallows. They attached flammables to the animals' tails and feathers, then ignited the material and released them. Purportedly the creatures ran and flew to their homes in terror, setting fires throughout the region. Regarding the cats, the idea is quite similar to the tale of Samson lighting foxes' tails aflame and sending them through Philistine fields in the Bible book of Judges. As for the swallows tale, true or not, it is strangely like the true World War II bats plan, to be found in the previous chapter. (ibid, 203–4)

A Chinese account from 1610 claims that General Tseh-ki-kwang trained hundreds of monkeys to shoot firearms. Japanese raiders were terrified by the monkey soldiers and were ambushed by Chinese troops. (ibid, 204)

Emperor Napoleon of France asked friends to prepare a field for him where he could hunt rabbits for a vacation day. Colleagues found a small

Mikhail the Mouse

Armies found uses for even the smallest of creatures. A professor from the University of Smolensk says that in April 1942, Soviet aircraft dropped live mice on German panzer divisions. The Soviets claimed that these mice were chewing through the electrical wires found throughout tank chassis, disabling the armored vehicles. One mouse's body was later found in a disabled German tank. The Soviets named the mouse Mikhail and honored it with the Hero of the Soviet Union medal. To counter this media hero, the Nazis said they were sending in cats to eat the mice before any tanks could be damaged. The Soviets then assured the populace that dogs had entered the fray to kill the cats that might harm the hero mice. Whether the tank-killing-mice story is true or not, German tanks quickly adopted new plastic coated wires that rodents could not chomp. (Gardiner, 111) field and put 1,000 rabbits there, and sent a man to feed them every morning so there would be plenty of targets for the emperor. When Napoleon arrived one morning with shotgun in hand, the 1,000 bunnies mistook him for the breakfast lettuce man, and they jumped all over him until he fled to his carriage to escape. (Cotterell, 241)

Various animals have been used in mine-clearing roles. Usually this was a suicide mission. Many armies have used animals in this way, at various times. As the Nazis advanced on Egypt in 1942, they sent riderless camels, cows, and pigs through minefields to clear the way as they pursued the retreating British army. Some claim that the U.S. Army sent sheep back and forth across minefields since they had no mine-clearing equipment available. Some animals with sensitive noses can detect the smell of explosives even when the devices are buried deep underground, and so can be trained to point out the munitions. The use of trained dogs for mine-clearing is detailed in chapter 1 of this book, and the more recent experimental trials of bees and moths as mine detectors appear in chapter 4. Other creatures have been used for detecting explosives. The French used miniature pigs along the Maginot and Siegfried Lines even before World War II to locate mines. In the 21st century, Israel uses miniature pigs for mine-detection, and Morocco trains small monkeys for the same purpose. A Dutch company has trained giant African pouched rats to find and mark mines in heavily mined areas of Africa, with great success. Parts of Africa are filled with mines from wars ended long ago, causing at least 74,000 casualties between 1999 and 2009. Because of their small size, the animals do not set off the explosives; rats are cheaper to buy and train; and they are native to Africa and do not require special kennels. In 2008–2009, 30 trained rats checked a million square meters of Mozambique and located 400 live mines. The U.S. Army Research Office recently began funding research into the use of the African giant pouched rat for locating IEDs (Improvised Explosive Devices) and other mines. (Dempewolff, 56; Cooper, 91; Gardiner, 115; Mayor, *Greek,* 204; McLaughlin; Weinberger)

Recently, the U.S. Navy found that a non-indigenous and poisonous brown snake species had infested the island of Guam. Without natural predators there, the snakes were killing off many true native creatures. In September and October 2010, the navy bombed Guam with unusual payloads: dead, poisoned mice, fitted with cardboard wings and green streamers. The brown snakes live in the trees, and so the streamers and wings helped to land the dead rodents in the high foliage. Brown snakes die when they eat the generally harmless acetaminophen, known also as Tylenol. (Tritten)

Works Cited

Abbott, Jacob. *Alexander the Great*. Makers of History Series, vol. 6. New York: A. L. Fowle, 1906.

Ackerman, Spencer. "$19 Billion Later, Pentagon's Best Bomb Detector is a Dog." ABCNews.com, Oct. 23, 2010.

Adams, John. *Kingless Folk and Other Addresses of Bible Animals*. Edinburgh: Oliphant, Anderson & Ferrier, 1897.

"Afghan Police Stop Bombing Attack from Explosives-Laden Donkey." Associated Press, June 8, 2006. http://www.foxnews.com/story/0,2933,198637,00.html.

Anderson, Edward L. *Curb, Snaffle, and Spur: A Method of Training Young Horses for the Cavalry Service and For General Use under the Saddle*. Boston: Little, Brown, 1894.

"Animals in Polish Army." *Army and Navy Register*, May 1, 1937.

Aristotle. *Historia Animalium*. Vol. 4, bk. 9, of *The Works of Aristotle*, edited by J. A. Smith and W. D. Ross. New York: Oxford University Press, 1910.

Army Times editors. *Great American Cavalrymen*. New York: Dodd, Mead, 1964.

Arnold, James R. *Jeff Davis's Own: Cavalry, Comanches, and the Battle for the Texas Frontier*. Edison, NJ: Castle Books, 2000.

Arrian. *Anabasis Alexandri Books V-VII and Indica*. Translated by P. A. Brunt. Cambridge, MA: Harvard University Press, 1983.

Arts, David Jay. "Loyalty Betrayed: Comparing the Fates of the American Military Working Dogs that Served in World War II and the Vietnam War." Master's thesis, William Paterson University of New Jersey, June 2006.

Ascoli, David. *A Day of Battle: Mars-La-Tour 16 August 1870*. London: Birlinn, 2001.

Axell, Albert. *Russia's Heroes 1941–45*. New York: Carroll & Graf, 2001.

Baker, Alan. *The Knight*. New York: John Wiley & Sons, 2003.

"Balaclava 1854: The Charge of the Light Brigade." *The History of Warfare*. DVD, Allegro Corporation, 2007. Narrated by Brian Blessed.

Bandopadhyay, A. "Reappraisal of an Ancient Text on Elephants." *Current Science* 77, no. 1 (1999).

Barber, Carolyn. *Animals at War*. New York: Harper & Row, 1971.

Bar-Kochva, Bezalel. *The Seleucid Army*. New York: Cambridge University Press, 1976.

Basham, A. L. *The Wonder That Was India*. 3rd revised ed. Vol. 1. New York: Taplinger, 1968.

Baur, John E. *Dogs on the Frontier*. Fairfax, VA: Denlinger, 1982.

BBC News. "Iran Buys Kamikaze Dolphins." March 8, 2000.

Beckett, Ian F. W. *Encyclopedia of Guerilla Warfare*. Santa Barbara, CA: ABC-CLIO, 1999.

Benitez, M. "Japanese Cavalry in the War with China." Condensed from an article in *Krasnaya Konitza*, No. 2, 1939.

Benyus, Janine M. *The Secret Language and Remarkable Behavior of Animals*. New York: Black Dog & Leventhal, 1998.

Bevan, Edwyn Robert. *The House of Seleucus*. Two volumes in one, reprint of 1902 edition. Chicago: Ares, 1985.

Billows, Richard A. *Antigonus the One-Eyed and the Creation of the Hellenistic State*. Berkeley: University of California Press, 1990.

"Black Lab Receives Top British Military Honor." Fox News.com, Feb. 24, 2010.

Blechman, Andrew D. *Pigeons: the Fascinating Saga of the World's Most Revered and Reviled Bird*. New York: Grove Press, 2006.

Bleeker, Sonia. *The Inca: Indians of the Andes*. New York: William Morrow, 1960.

Blum, Jonathan. "Armor to Guard $50,000 Dogs." *Fortune Small Business*, Nov. 30, 2009.

Bonner, Mary Graham. *Couriers of the Sky: The Story of Pigeons*. New York: Alfred A. Knopf, 1945.

Bosworth, C. E. *The Ghaznavids*. New Delhi: Munshiram Manoharlal, 1992.

Bottero, Jean. *Everyday Life in Ancient Mesopotamia*. Edinburgh University Press, 2001.

Braider, Donald. *The Life, History and Magic of the Horse*. New York: Grosset & Dunlap, 1978.

Brophy, Leo P., Wyndham D. Miles, and Rexmond C. Cochrane. *United States Army in World War II. The Technical Services. The Chemical Warfare Service: From Laboratory to Field*. Washington, D.C.: Office of the Chief of Military History, Dept. of the Army, 1959.

Brown, Dee, with Martin F. Schmitt. *Fighting Indians of the West*. New York: Ballantine Books, 1974.

Burnam, John C. *Dog Tags of Courage: The Turmoil of War and the Rewards of Companionship*. Fort Bragg, CA: Lost Coast, 2000.

Caesar, Julius. *Alexandrian, African and Spanish Wars*. Translated by A. G. Way. Cambridge, MA: Harvard University Press, 1955.

Carroll, Charles M. *The Government's Importation of Camels: A Historical Sketch*. 1904. Reprinted from the 20th annual report of the Bureau of Animal Industry co 53, 1903. Washington, D.C.: Government Printing Office, pp. 391–409. http://www.nal.usda.gov/awic/pubs/camel import.htm.

Carter, Samuel III. *The Last Cavaliers: Confederate and Union Cavalry in the Civil War*. New York: St. Martin's Press, 1979.

Catton, Bruce. "'Old Abe' The Battle Eagle." *American Heritage*, Oct. 1963: 32–33, 106–7.

Clough, Patricia. *The Flight across the Ice: the Escape of the East Prussian Horses*. London: Haus Books, 2009.

Conklin, Gladys. *The Llamas of South America*. New York: Holiday House, 1975.

Cooper, Jilly. *Animals in War: Valiant Horses, Courageous Dogs, and Other Unsung Animal Heroes*. Guilford, CT: Lyons Press, 2002.

Coren, Stanley. *The Pawprints of History: Dogs and the Course of Human Events*. New York: Free Press, 2002.

Cotterell, Arthur. *Chariot: The Astounding Rise and Fall of the World's First War Machine*. Woodstock, NY: Overlook Press, 2004.

Couffer, Jack. *Bat Bomb: World War II's Other Secret Weapon*. Austin: University of Texas Press, 1992.

Coultas, Harland. *Zoology of the Bible*. London: Wesleyan Conference Office, 1876.

Crawford, J. Marshall. *Mosby and His Men*. 2007, audiobook on Audible. com. Original from 1867.

Creel, Herrlee Glessner. *The Birth of China*. New York: Frederick Ungar, 1964.

Cummings, Lewis V. *Alexander the Great*. Boston: Houghton Mifflin, 1940.

Darwin, Charles. *The Expression of the Emotions in Man and Animals*. Chicago: University of Chicago Press, 1965.

Davis, Burke. *Jeb Stuart: The Last Cavalier*. New York: Rinehart, 1957.

Dean, Charles L. *Soldiers & Sled Dogs: A History of Military Dog Mushing*. Lincoln, NE: University of Nebraska Press, 2005.

Delbruck, Hans. *Warfare in Antiquity*. History of the Art of War, vol. 1. Translated by Walter J. Renfroe Jr. Lincoln: University of Nebraska, 1990.

Del Castillo, Ivan, and Benitez De Lugo. "About the Arrival of Camels in the Canary Islands." 2003. http://www.camellosafari.com/camels/camels.html.

DeMares, Ryan. *Dolphins, Myths & Transformation*. Boulder, CO: The Dolphin Institute Press, 2002.

Dempewolff, Richard. *Animal Reveille*. Garden City, NY: Doubleday, 1946.

Denega, Danielle. *The Cold War Pigeon Patrols and Other Animal Spies*. New York: Franklin Watts, 2008.

De Segur, Count Philippe-Paul. *Napoleon's Russian Campaign*. Translated by J. David Townsend. New York: Time Inc., 1965.

Diaz, Bernal. *The Conquest of New Spain*. Translated by J. M. Cohen. London: Folio Society, 1974.

DiMarco, Louis A. *War Horse: A History of the Military Horse and Rider*. Yardley, PA: Westholme, 2008.

Dinardo, R. L. *Mechanized Juggernaut or Military Anachronism? Horses and the German Army of WWII*. Stackpole Military History Series. Mechanicsburg, PA: Stackpole Books, 2008.

Dio [Cassius Dio Cocceianus]. *Dio's Roman History*. Translated by Earnest Cary. 9 vols. Cambridge, MA: Harvard University Press, 1954.

Diodorus. "The Armies of Eumenes and Antigonus at the Battle of Paraetacene." In *The Hellenistic World from Alexander to the Roman Conquest*. New York: Cambridge University Press, 1994.

Diodorus. *Diodorus of Sicily in Twelve Volumes*. Vol. 9. Cambridge, MA: Harvard University Press, 1969.

Dionysius of Halicarnassus. *The Roman Antiquities*. Translated by Earnest Cary. 7 vols. Cambridge, MA: Harvard University Press, 1950.

Dolenc, Milan. *Lipizzaner: The Story of the Horses of Lipica*. St. Paul, MN: Control Data Arts, 1981.

"Dolphins Find Mine-Clearing Role." Reuters, March 30, 2001. http://archives.cnn.com/2001/WORLD/europe/scandinavia/03/30/usnavy.dolphins/.

Downey, Fairfax. *Clash of Cavalry: The Battle of Brandy Station*. Gaithersburg, MD: Butternut Press, 1985, reprint of 1959 original.

Duffy, Christopher. *Prussia's Glory: Rossbach and Leuthen 1757*. Chicago: Emperor's Press, 2003.

Durant, Will. *The Life of Greece*. The Story of Civilization, part 2. New York: Simon and Schuster, 1966.

Edwards, Elwyn Hartley. *Horses: Their Role in the History of Man*. London: Willow Books, 1987.

Eisenschiml, Otto, and Ralph Newman. *The American Iliad: the Epic Story of the Civil War*. Indianapolis: Bobbs-Merrill, 1947.

Elvin, Mark. *The Retreat of the Elephants*. New Haven, CT: Yale University Press, 2004.

Encyclopedia Judaica. Edited by Cecil Roth. New York: Macmillan, 1971.

Essin, Emmett M. *Shavetails & Bell Sharps: The History of the U.S. Army Mule*. Lincoln: University of Nebraska Press, 2000.

Everson, Tim. *Warfare in Ancient Greece: Arms and Armour from the Heroes of Homer to Alexander the Great*. Gloucestershire, UK: Sutton Publishing, 2004.

Feiser, Louis D. April 23, 1943 letter to Dr Warren C Lothrop from Harvard Univ. Dept. of Chemistry, declassified letter copied at National Archives. 2 typewritten pages.

Felber, Bill. *The Horse in War*. Philadelphia: Chelsea House, 2002.

Ford, Sewell. *Horses Nine*. Scribners, 1903, reprinted 2009 by Dashers of Nashville, GA.

Forster, E. S. "Dogs in Ancient Warfare." *Greece & Rome* 10, no. 30 (1941): 114–117.

Fraser, Antonia. *The Warrior Queens*. New York: Alfred A. Knopf, 1989.

Froman, Robert. "The Red Ghost." *American Heritage: The Magazine of History*, April 1961: 35–37, 94–98.

Gabriel, Richard A., and Donald W. Boose Jr. *The Great Battles of Antiquity*. Westport, CT: Greenwood Press, 1994.

Gaebel, Robert E. *Cavalry Operations in the Ancient Greek World*. Norman, OK: University of Oklahoma Press, 2002.

Gardiner, Juliet. *The Animals' War: Animals in Wartime from the First World War to the Present Day*. London: Portrait, 2006.

Gasperini, W. "Uncle Sam's Dolphins." *Smithsonian*, Sept. 2003: 28–29.

Geer, Andrew. *Reckless: Pride of the Marines, an abridgement*. In "Books Abridged, Inc." 1955, pp. 235–308.

Gies, Frances. *The Knight in History*. New York: Harper & Row, 1984.

Going, Clayton G. *Dogs at War*. New York: Macmillan, 1944.

Goodrich, Thomas. *Scalp Dance: Indian Warfare on the High Plains, 1865–1879*. Mechanicsburg, PA: Stackpole Books, 1997.

Grandin, Temple. *Animals in Translation: Using the Mysteries of Autism to Decode Animal Behavior*. Orlando: Harvest, 2006.

Grant, Robert M. *Early Christians & Animals*. London: Routledge, 1999.

"The Great Indian Wars: 1540-1890." 5 DVD documentary set. Mill Creek Entertainment, 2009.

Griffith, Paddy. "Civil War Cavalry: Missed Opportunities." *MHQ* 1, no. 3 (1989): 61–71.

Gutierrez, Jason. "'Dogs of War' Saving Lives in Afghanistan." Yahoo! News, Jan. 28, 2010.

Hamer, Blythe. *Dogs at War: True Stories of Canine Courage under Fire*. London, UK: Andre Deutsch, 2006.

Hamid, S. Shahid. *So They Rode and Fought*. New York: Midas Books, 1983.

Hammerstrom, Michael L. "Ground Dog Day: Lessons Don't Have to be Relearned in the Use of Dogs in Combat." Master's thesis, 2005, Naval Postgraduate School, Monterey, CA. http://www.dtic.mil/cgi-bin/Get TRDoc?Location=U2&doc=GetTRDoc.pdf&AD=ADA442891

Hammerton, J. A. ed. *Wonders of Animal Life by Famous Writers on Natural History*. London: Waverley Book Company, circa 1930.

Haran, Peter. *Trackers: the Untold Story of the Australian Dogs of War*. Sydney: New Holland, 2004.

Harfield, Alan. *Pigeon to Packhorse: The Illustrated Story of Animals in Army Communications*. Chippenham, UK: Picton Publishing, 1989.

Harmer, Mabel. *Famous Mascots and K-9's*. Self published, n.d., circa 1950.

Harris, Sheldon H. *Factories of Death: Japanese Biological Warfare, 1932–45, and the American Cover-Up*. London: Routledge, 1994.

Harter, Walter. *Feathered Heroes: Pigeons from Ancient Times to Now*. New York: Criterion Books, 1968.

Helvarg, David. "Whales, Sea Lions, Dolphins Used as 'Spies' by U.S. Navy." *Ottawa Citizen*, May 30, 1985.

Herzog, Chaim, and Mordechai Gichon. *Battles of the Bible*. Mechanicsburg, PA: Stackpole Books, 1997.

Higham, Robin. "The International Commission for Military History, Meeting, Tehran, 6–16 July 1976." *Military Affairs* 40, no. 4 (1976).

Hildinger, Erik. *Warriors of the Steppe: A Military History of Central Asia, 500 BC to 1700 AD*. New York: Sarpedon, 1997.

Hindus, Maurice. *The Cossacks: the Story of a Warrior People*. Garden City, NY: Doubleday, Doran, 1945.

Hodges, Henry. *Technology in the Ancient World*. New York: Alfred A. Knopf, 1970.

Hodges, Richard. "Charlemagne's Elephant." *History Today*, Dec. 2000.

Hoff, Brent. "Free the Advanced Biological Weapons System: An Interview with Richard O'Barry." April 2003. http://www.dolphinproject. org/dolphins-of-war.html.

Hoig, Stan. *Perilous Pursuit: The U.S. Cavalry and the Northern Cheyennes*. Boulder, CO: University Press of Colorado, 2002.

Holder, Charles Frederick. *The Ivory King: A Popular History of the Elephant and Its Allies*. New York: Charles Scribner's Sons, 1886.

"Horses of Gettysburg." *Civil War Minutes IV*. DVD. Narrated by Ronald F. Maxwell. Inecom, 2006.

Huxley-Blythe, Peter J. *The East Came West*. Idaho: Caxton Printers, 1968.

Hyams, Edward. *Animals in the Service of Man*. Philadelphia: J.B. Lippincott, 1972.

Jacobs, Lee, comp. *The Gray Riders: Stories from the Confederate Cavalry*. Shippensburg, PA: Burd Street Press, 1998.

Jager, Theodore F. *Scout, Red Cross and Army Dogs: Historical Sketch of Dogs in the Great War and a Training Guide for the Rank and File of the United States Army*. New York: Arrow Printing, circa 1916, Kessinger Publishing Legacy Reprint 2010.

James, Miller. "Marvelous Carrier Pigeons, with Heroic War Records, Gaining Prestige in Peace." *The Evening Star*, Washington, D.C., May 24, 1936.

Johnson, David. *Napoleon's Cavalry and its Leaders*. Staplehurst, UK: Spellmount, 1999.

Johnson, Isaac Thorne, ed. *Young People's Natural History*. Chicago: Hemlandet Premium, 1908.

Johnson, William M. *The Rose-Tinted Menagerie: A History of Animals in Entertainment*. Online at http://www.iridescent-publishing.com/rtm/ch5p9.htm.

Kaplan, Robert D. *Soldiers of God*. New York: Vintage Books, 2001.

Karunanithy, David. *Dogs of War: Canine Use in Warfare from Ancient Egypt to the 19th Century*. London: Yarak Publishing, 2008.

Kelekna, Pita. *The Horse in Human History*. New York: Cambridge University Press, 2009.

Kidd, J. H. *A Cavalryman with Custer: Custer's Michigan Cavalry Brigade in the Civil War*. New York: Bantam Books, 1991.

Kincaid, C. A. *Successors of Alexander the Great*. Chicago: Ares Publishers, 1980.

Kistler, John M. *War Elephants*. Westport, CT: Praeger, 2006.

Koenig, Robert. *The Fourth Horseman: One Man's Mission to Wage the Great War in America*. New York: Public Affairs, 2006.

Kohut, John J., and Roland Sweet. *Strange Tails: All-Too-True News from the Animal Kingdom*. New York: Plume, 1999.

Kramer, J. J. *Animal Heroes: Military Mascots and Pets*. Novato, CA: Presidio Press, 1981.

Lajos, Kassai. *Horseback Archery*. Budapest, Hungary: Puski Kiado kft., 2002.

Lankester, E. *The Uses of Animals in Relation to Industry of Man*. London: Hardwicke & Bogue, 1876.

LaPuzza, Tom. *A Brief History of the U.S. Navy Marine Mammal Program*. n.d., SSC Pacific Public Affairs Office, pp. 1–5.

Lawford, James, ed. *The Cavalry*. Indianapolis: Bobbs Merrill, 1976.

Lawrence, T. E. *Revolt in the Desert*. Garden City, NY: Doubleday, Doran, 1927.

Le Cheyne, Evelyn. *Silent Heroes: the Bravery & Devotion of Animals in War*. London: Souvenir Press, 1994.

Leinwand, Donna. "Sea Lions Called to Duty in Persian Gulf." *USA Today*, Feb. 13, 2003.

Leckie, William H. *The Buffalo Soldiers: a Narrative of the Negro Cavalry in the West*. Norman: University of Oklahoma, 1970.

Lemish, Michael G. *War Dogs: A History of Loyalty and Heroism*. Washington, D.C.: Brassey's, 1996.

Lengel, Edward G. *George Washington: A Military Life*. New York: Random House, 2007. Audiobook version on audible.com.

Leong, Jeffrey Say Seck. "Storming the Last Hindu Fortress." *Military History*, Feb. 1999.

Lesley, Lewis Burt, ed. *Uncle Sam's Camels: The Journal of May Humphreys Stacey supplemented by the Report of Edward Fitzgerald Beale (1857–1858)*. Berkeley, CA: Huntington Library Press, 2006. Original published 1929.

Lewinsohn, Richard. *Animals, Men and Myths: An Informative and Entertaining History of Man and the Animals Around Him*. New York: Harper & Brothers, 1954.

Linden, Eugene. *The Parrot's Lament and Other True Tales of Animal Intrigue, Intelligence, and Ingenuity*. New York: Dutton, 1999.

Livingston, Phil, and Ed Roberts. *War Horse: Mounting the Cavalry with America's Finest Horses*. Albany, TX: Bright Sky Press, 2003.

Lockwood, Jeffrey A. *Six-Legged Soldiers: Using Insects as Weapons of War*. New York: Oxford University Press, 2009.

Lockwood, Samuel. *Animal Memoirs, Part I: Mammals*. Readings in Natural History Series. Ivison, Blackman, circa 1888.

Longacre, Edward G. *Mounted Raids of the Civil War*. New York: A. S. Barnes, 1975.

"The Long Knives: True Stories of the U. S. Cavalry's Fight to Win the Old West." DVD. Simitar Entertainment, 1997.

Lubow, Robert E. *The War Animals*. Garden City, NY: Doubleday, 1977.

MacMunn, George. *The Martial Races of India*. Quetta, Pakistan: Gosha-e-Adab, 1977.

Maenchen-Helfen, Otto J. *The World of the Huns*. Berkeley, CA: University of California Press, 1973.

Maitland, Francis Hereward. *Hussar of the Line*. London: Hurst & Blackett Ltd., 1951.

Malaparte, Curzio. *Kaputt*. Translated by Cesare Foligno. New York: EP Dutton, 1946.

Malaparte, Curzio. *The Volga Rises in Europe*. Edinburgh: Birlinn Ltd. Reprint of 1951 original.

Maloney, Katie. "The Dogs of War Get Their Due in New Jersey." *Newsweek*, Sept. 18, 2010. http://www.newsweek.com/2010/09/18/an-unofficial-medal-for-war-dogs.html.

Man, John. *Attila the Hun*. London: Bantam Books, 2006.

Manual of Horsemastership, Equitation and Animal Transport. Manuals 26–1712. London: His Majesty's Stationery Office, 1937.

Mayor, Adrienne. *Greek Fire, Poison Arrows & Scorpion Bombs: Biological and Chemical Warfare in the Ancient World*. New York: Overlook Duckworth, 2003.

Mayor, Adrienne. *The First Fossil Hunters: Paleontology in Greek and Roman Times*. Princeton, NJ: Princeton University Press, 2000.

McClure, Thomas, and Burgess Meredith. Radio Interview in August 1941 about military pigeons. Transcript copied from the National Archives.

McIntyre, Loren. "Lost Empire of the Incas." *National Geographic*, Dec. 1973: 729–786.

McLaughlin, Eliott C. "Giant Rats Put Noses to Work on Africa's Land Mine Epidemic." CNN.com, Sept. 8, 2010.

Meistrich, Ira. "En Avant!" *MHQ* 1, no. 3 (1989): 46–49.

Milloy, Steven. "PETA: No Porpoise in War." April 3, 2003. www.foxnews.com/story/0,2933,83116,00.html.

Mohr, Charles E. "Texas Bat Caves Served in Three Wars." National Speleological Society Bulletin Number 10, April 1948.

Montgomery, Viscount (Field Marshal). *A History of Warfare*. Cleveland: World Publishing, 1968.

Morgan, Morris H. *The Art of Horsemanship by Xenophon*. Boston: Little, Brown, 1893.

Morris, Desmond. *Horse Watching*. New York: Crown Publishers, 1988.

Morris, Jim. *Fighting Men*. New York: Dell, 1993.

Morton, Joseph W., Jr., ed. *Sparks from the Campfire: Tales of the Old Veterans*. Philadelphia: Keystone Publishing, 1890.

Mott, Maryann. "Dogs of War: Inside the U.S. Military's Canine Corps." *National Geographic News*, April 9, 2003.

Murphy, Edwin. *The Antiquities of Asia: A Translation with Notes of Book II of the Library of History of Diodorus Siculus*. New Brunswick, NJ: Transaction Publishers, 1989.

Nazim, Muhammed. *The Life and Times of Sultan Mahmud of Ghazna*. New Delhi: Munshiram Manoharlal, 1971.

Newark, Peter. *Sabre & Lance: An Illustrated History of Cavalry*. Dorset, UK: Blandford Press, 1987.

Oakeshott, Ewart. *The Knight and His Horse*. 2nd ed. Chester Springs, PA: Dofour Editions, 1998.

O'Ferrall, Charles T. *Confederate Cavalryman*. Audiobook on Audible. com, originally named *Forty Years of Active Service*, circa 1904.

Olive-Drab. Website. http://www.olive-drab.com (accessed Sept. 13, 2010).

Ottevaere, James A. *American Military Horsemanship*. Bloomington, IN: Authorhouse, 2005.

Overy, Richard. *Why the Allies Won*. New York: W. W. Norton, 1996.

Palagruto, Anne. *Civil War Dogs and the Men Who Loved Them*. Create-Space, 2008.

Pant, G. N. *Horse & Elephant Armour*. Delhi, India: Agam Kala Prakashan, 1997.

Paradine-Palmer, Greta. *Jhools in the Dust*. York, UK: Wilton 65, 2002.

Peduto, Gregory. "War Takes Wing." *WWII History*, March 2010: 26–29.

Perry, John. *Lee: A Life of Virtue*. Nashville, TN: Thomas Nelson, 2010. Audiobook on audible.com.

Philbrick, Nathaniel. *The Last Stand: Custer, Sitting Bull, and the Battle of the Little Bighorn*. New York: Viking, 2010.

Pickrell, John. "Dolphins Deployed as Undersea Agents in Iraq." *National Geographic News*, March 28, 2003.

Piekalkiewicz, Janusz. *The Cavalry of World War II*. Lanham, MD: Stein and Day, 1980.

"Pigeons Save Life in RAF." *New York Times*, July 11, 1943.

Piper, Elizabeth. "Careers Bloom Anew for Former Soviet Navy Dolphins." Reuters News Agency, July 4, 2002.

Pliny. *Natural History*. 12 vols. Vol. 3, Libri 8–11. Edited by H. Rackham. 2nd edition. Cambridge, MA: Harvard University Press, 1983.

Plutarch. *Plutarch's Lives of Illustrious Men*. Translated by John Dryden. 3 vols. New York: John W. Lowell, circa 1880.

Podhajsky, Alois. *The Complete Training of Horse and Rider in the Principles of Classical Horsemanship*. Translated by Eva Podhajsky and Col. V. D. S. Williams. Garden City, NY: Doubleday, 1967.

Polybius. *The Rise of the Roman Empire*. Translated by Ian Scott-Kilvert. New York: Penguin, 1979.

"Post World War II Dog Program." http://community-2.webtv.net/Hahn-50thAP-K9/K9History5/ (accessed Sept. 2010).

Prados, John. *The Blood Road*. New York: John Wiley & Sons, 1999.

Presnell, Judith Janda. *Navy Dolphins*. Animals with Jobs Series. Farmington Hills, MI: KidHaven Press, 2002.

Prucha, Francis Paul. *The Sword of the Republic: The United States Army on the Frontier 1783–1846*. Toronto: Macmillan, 1969.

Puck (pseudonym). "Advanced Biological Weapons Systems: The Plight of Animals in the Military." http://www.earthfirstjournal.org/article.php?id=174.

Putney, Capt. William W. *Always Faithful: A Memoir of the Marine Dogs of WWII*. New York: The Free Press, 2001.

Quammen, David. "The Ineffable Union of Man and Horse." *MHQ* 1, no. 3 (1989): 36–44.

Ramsey, Edwin Price, and Stephen J. Rivele. *Lieutenant Ramsey's War: From Horse Soldier to Guerrilla Commander*. Washington, D.C.: Brassey's, 1996.

Ranking, John. *Historical Researches on the Wars and Sports of the Mongols and Romans*. London: Longman, Rees, Orme, Brown, and Green, 1826.

Rattenbury, R. M. "An Ancient Armoured Force." *The Classical Review* 56, no. 3 (1942).

Rawlinson, George. *The Five Great Monarchies of the Ancient Eastern World.* 3 vols. 2nd ed. New York: Scribner, Welford, 1871.

Rawlinson, George. *The Sixth Great Oriental Monarchy.* New York: Scribner, Welford and Armstrong, 1873.

Rawlinson, George. *The Seventh Great Oriental Monarchy.* New York: Dodd, Mead, circa 1875.

Regan, Geoffrey. "The Battle of San Pasqual." On the California State Military Museum website at http://www.militarymuseum.org/San Pasqual.html (accessed 2010).

Reid, Frank. *The Fighting Cameliers: The Exploits of the Imperial Camel Corps in the Desert and Palestine Campaigns of the First World War.* Leonaur, original 1934, reprint 2005.

Rennie, James. *The Elephant Principally Viewed in Relation to Man.* New rev. ed. London: Charles Knight, 1844.

Reston, James, Jr. *Warriors of God: Richard the Lionheart and Saladin in the Third Crusade.* New York: Doubleday, 2001.

Richardson, E. H. *British War Dogs: Their Training and Psychology.* London: Skeffington & Son, n.d., circa 1920.

Riley, Harvey. *The Mule.* 1867 original, reprinted 2005 by the Dashers of Nashville, GA.

Roberts, Yvonne. *Animal Heroes.* London: Pelham Books, 1990.

Robinson, Charles Alexander. *Ancient History.* New York: Macmillan, 1961.

Rogers, Katharine M. *First Friend: A History of Dogs and Humans.* New York: St. Martin's Press, 2005.

Romanes, George J. *Animal Intelligence.* International Scientific Series, vol. 41. London: Kegan Paul, Trench, 1882.

Roth, Jonathan P. *The Logistics of the Roman Army at War (264 BC–AD 235).* Boston: Brill, 1999.

Salisbury, Harrison E. *The 900 Days: The Siege of Leningrad.* London: Pan Books, 1969.

Sanderson, Jeannette. *War Dog Heroes: True Stories of Dog Courage in Wartime*. New York: Scholastic Inc., 1997.

Scigliano, Eric. *Love, War, and Circuses*. Boston: Houghton Mifflin, 2002.

Scullard, H. H. *The Elephant in the Greek and Roman World*. Cambridge: Thames and Hudson, 1974.

Seguin, Marilyn W. *Dogs of War and Stories of Other Beasts of Battle in the Civil War*. Brookline Village, MA: Branden Publishing, 1998.

Sekunda, Nick. *Seleucid and Ptolemaic Reformed Armies 168–145 BC*. 2 vols. Stockport, UK: Montvert Publications, 1994.

Silvers, Kate. "Dolphins Help Navy Steer Clear in Gulf." *Stars and Stripes*, Sept. 14, 2003.

Sinclair, Andrew. *Man and Horse: Four Thousand Years of the Mounted Warrior*. Gloucestershire, UK: The History Press, 2008.

Smith, Gene. *Mounted Warriors*. Hoboken, NJ: John Wiley & Sons, 2009.

Snook, Lt. Col. Mike. *How Can Man Die Better: The Secrets of Isandlwana Revealed*. Mechanicsburg, PA: Stackpole Books, 2005.

Stall, Sam. *100 Dogs Who Changed Civilization: History's Most Influential Canines*. Philadelphia: Quirk Books, 2007.

Steidle, Brian, and Gretchen Steidle Wallace. *The Devil Came on Horseback: Bearing Witness to the Genocide in Darfur*. New York: Public Affairs, 2007.

Steiner, Stan. *Dark and Dashing Horsemen*. New York: Harper & Row, 1981.

Sullivan, Rohan. "Sea Lions Used as Gulf Guardians." Associated Press, Feb. 18, 2003.

Sutton, John, and John Walker. *From Horse to Helicopter*. London: Leo Cooper, 1990.

Swank, Walbrook Davis. *Battle of Trevilian Station: The Civil War's Greatest and Bloodiest All Cavalry Battle with Eyewitness Memoirs*. Civil War Heritage Series, vol. 4. Shippensburg, PA: Burd Street Press, 1994.

Sykes, Percy. *A History of Persia*. 2 vols. 3rd ed. London: Macmillan, 1951.

Talmadge, Eric. "Dog Surge Along with Troop Surge in Afghan War." Associated Press, Jan. 23, 2010.

Tarn, W. W. "Greece: 335 to 321 B.C." In *The Cambridge Ancient History*, vol. 6: *Macedon, 401–301 BC*, edited by J. B. Bury et al. New York: Macmillan, 1933.

Tarn, W. W. "The Heritage of Alexander." In *The Cambridge Ancient History*, vol. 6: *Macedon, 401–301 BC*, edited by J. B. Bury et al. New York: Macmillan, 1933.

Telegraph. "Polish Bear 'That Fought Nazis' to Be Commemorated." Oct. 13, 2010. http://www.telegraph.co.uk.

Their, Dave. "Scotland Honors Nazi-Fighting Polish Army Bear." AOL News Surge Desk (accessed Oct. 15, 2010).

Thomas, Hugh. *Conquest: Montezuma, Cortes, and the Fall of Old Mexico*. New York: Simon and Schuster, 1993.

Toperoff, Shlomo Pesach. *The Animal Kingdom in Jewish Thought*. Northvale, NJ: Jason Aronson, 1995.

Toynbee, Arnold. "A Ridge Too Far." *MHQ* 1, no. 3 (1989): 98–99. An excerpt from The Manchester Guardian in 1921 about the Anatolia Campaign.

Tremain, Ruthven. *The Animals' Who's Who*. New York: Charles Scribner's Sons, 1982.

Tritten, Travis J. "Mice Join Fight against Invasive Snakes in Guam." *Stars and Stripes*, Sept. 2, 2010. http://www.stripes.com/news/mice-join-fight-against-invasive-snakes-on-guam-1.116810.

Turnbull, Stephen. *The Book of the Medieval Knight*. New York: Crown, 1984.

"UK Army Dog May Have Died from a Broken Heart." Associated Press, March 10, 2011.

Urwin, Gregory J. W. "A Mad-Brained Trick: The Charge of the Light Brigade." *Combat Illustrated*, Dec. 1980: 32–37, 66–74.

Urwin, Gregory J. W. *The United States Cavalry: An Illustrated History*. Dorset, UK: Blandford Press, 1985.

U.S. Marine Corps. Dog Record Book of Prince, enlisted 21 December 1943 serial no. 217. Filed at the National Archives.

Utley, Robert M., and Wilcomb E. Washburn. *The American Heritage History of the Indian Wars*. New York: American Heritage Publishing, 1977.

Von Hagen, Victor W. *Highway of the Sun*. New York: Duell, Sloan and Pearce, 1955.

Walsh, George. *Those Damn Horse Soldiers: True Tales of the Civil War Cavalry*. New York: Forge, 2006.

Webb, John A. "Summary of Information upon Pigeons as Couriers in the Military Service and upon the Work of the Pigeon Service." For the 828th Signal Pigeon Replacement Company, US Signal Corps. Copied at the National Archives.

Weinberger, Sharon. "Army Eyes African Giant Rat as Bomb Detector." AOL News, March 15, 2011.

Welsby, Derek A. *The Kingdom of Kush*. London: British Museum Press, 1996.

Wendt, Lloyd M. *Dogs: A Historical Journey*. New York: Howell Book House, 1996.

Williams, A. R. "Animals Everlasting." *National Geographic*, Nov. 2009: 30–51.

Williams, Peter, and David Wallace. *Unit 731: Japan's Secret Biological Warfare in World War II*. New York: Free Press, 1989.

Williamson, Mary L. *The Life of General Robert E. Lee in Easy Words for Children*. Richmond, VA: B. F. Johnson, 1895. Online at http://rich mondthenandnow.com/Life-of-Robert-E-Lee-Chapter-4.html.

Wilson, David A. H. "Avian Anti-Submarine Warfare Proposals in Britain, 1915–1918: The Admiralty and Thomas Mills." *International Journal of Naval History* 5, no. 1 (2006). http://ijnhonline.org/volume5_num ber1_apr06/article_avian_wilson_apr06.htm.

Wilson, David A. H. "Sea Lions, Greasepaint and the U-Boat Threat." *Notes and Records of the Royal Society* 55, no. 3 (2001): 425–55. http://rsnr.royalsocietypublishing.org/content/55/3/425.full.pdf+ html

Wood, Forrest G. *Marine Mammals and Man: The Navy's Porpoises and Sea Lions*. Washington, D.C.: Robert B. Luce Inc., 1973.

Woodward, W. E. *Meet General Grant*. New York: Sun Dial Press, 1939.

Worcester, John. *The Animals of the Bible and Their Correspondences*. London: James Speirs, 1884.

Wyman, Walker D. *The Wild Horse of the West*. Lincoln, NE: University of Nebraska Press, 1966.

Yeide, Harry. *Steeds of Steel: A History of American Mechanized Cavalry in World War II*. Minneapolis: Zenith Press, 2008.

Index

About the Author

John M. Kistler, MLS, M.Div., is a freelance writer, amateur historian, and small business owner. He has written several books, including *War Elephants*.